HANDBOOK OF CONVEYANCING PRACTICE IN SCOTLAND

For Sandra

HANDBOOK OF CONVEYANCING PRACTICE IN SCOTLAND

John Henderson Sinclair BA (QUB), LLB (Glas)
Solicitor in Scotland
Professor of Conveyancing Practice
and Director of Legal Practice
in the University of Strathclyde
Formerly (1983–1993) Clerk, Treasurer and Fiscal
of the Royal Faculty of Procurators in Glasgow

3rd Edition

Butterworths
Law Society of Scotland

Edinburgh   1995

United Kingdom	Butterworths a Division of Reed Elsevier (UK) Ltd, Halsbury House, 35 Chancery Lane, LONDON WC2A 1EL and 4 Hill Street, EDINBURGH EH2 3JZ
Australia	Butterworths, SYDNEY, MELBOURNE, BRISBANE, ADELAIDE, PERTH, CANBERRA and HOBART
Canada	Butterworths Canada Ltd, TORONTO and VANCOUVER
Ireland	Butterworth (Ireland) Ltd, DUBLIN
Malaysia	Malayan Law Journal Sdn Bhd, KUALA LUMPUR
New Zealand	Butterworths of New Zealand Ltd, WELLINGTON and AUCKLAND
Puerto Rico	Butterworth of Puerto Rico Inc, SAN JUAN
Singapore	Butterworths Asia, SINGAPORE
South Africa	Butterworths Publishers (Pty) Ltd, DURBAN
USA	Butterworths Legal Publishers, CARLSBAD, California and SALEM, New Hampshire

Law Society of Scotland
26 Drumsheugh Gardens, Edinburgh EH3 7YR

A CIP Catalogue record for this book is available from the British Library.

ISBN 0 406 04494 5

Typeset by Phoenix Photosetting, Chatham, Kent
Printed in Great Britain by Mackays of Chatham plc

PREFACE

It is, as I found out many times, generally supposed that the writing of a third edition is a relatively easy task – just a few updates here, and a few corrections there, and then off to the printers, no problem.

In fact this is not what I found, and this book is virtually a new species. So many things have happened, some great, others small, that the practice of conveyancing has changed vastly in the past five years. I hope that this edition reflects these changes – whether brought about by statute, case law, European law, environmental law, delegated legislation, custom, practice or otherwise. In particular, a number of events have happened, or may happen, which I have so far as possible tried to predict in the text, but I would like to sum these up.

1. The Requirements of Writing (Scotland) Act 1995 became law on 1 May 1995, and will come into force on 1 August 1995. While this is a revolutionary Act, it does not greatly affect the nature of professional conveyancing, except that signatures to deeds need only be witnessed by one person, instead of two, and there are particular rules for execution by partnerships, limited companies and incorporations, which are quite self-explanatory, but will require study.

The use of the device 'adopted as holograph' is brought to an end, and I think most conveyancers will have their signatures to offers and letters of obligation witnessed by one person, to give these documents self-proving status – but it will not be fatal if they are not witnessed, because the signature can be proved before the court.

Because writings need no longer be self-proving to form part of the contract, care should be taken not to make any representations or concessions on an informal basis, without ensuring that they cannot be construed as part of the contract. This could quite easily happen, especially in letters between clients, which should be discouraged.

New and more coherent testing clauses will be introduced by regulation over the summer.

Obviously this Act requires careful scrutiny, and I would recommend a reading of the book on the Act by Professors Robert Rennie and Douglas Cusine (*The Requirements of Writing*, Butterworths, 1995).

2. The Land Registers (Scotland) Bill may become law in June 1995. If so, recording dues will have to be paid when the deeds are submitted, and not when they are returned. Any deeds sent without payment will simply be returned, unprocessed.

3. The appeal in *Sharp v Thomson* was duly heard in the Inner House (1995 GWD 19-1054) and was disallowed unanimously. This poses considerable problems when a title is being taken from a limited company, as most limited companies will have granted at least one floating charge, and the search in the Register of Charges should now be taken down to 36 days (ie 22 + 14) after settlement to be entirely safe.

The case also spells the possible end (subject to the House of Lords appeal decision) to the concept of delivery being all important, as the Inner House decided that *Thomas v Lord Advocate* 1953 SC 151, and subsequent cases, had been wrongly decided, and thus delivery of the disposition is not necessarily effective against a trustee in bankruptcy. This may or may not be so – it is not however for conveyancers to worry about such matters, but instead to protect their clients, and indeed themselves.

The missives should contain a provision requiring that there be inserted into every disposition a clause along the lines stated below. This clause creates a trust after delivery (which the courts assure us is no longer relevant) until registration has taken place, and the real right has been created (which the courts assure us is all important):

> 'Notwithstanding that we (the sellers) have sold the subjects to (the buyer) and have received payment of the price in exchange for delivery of the disposition, we hereby confirm and declare that in so far as we remain infeft in the said subjects prior to the registration of these presents in the (Register as appropriate) we shall hold the same as trustees in an irrevocable and binding trust for the (purchaser) until these presents have been registered.'

Needless to say, it now becomes of paramount importance for the deed to be registered as swiftly as possible, especially in light of the wording of the classic letter of obligation which only allows 14 days for registration, before it becomes inoperative.

4. On 2 June every solicitor in Scotland received a letter from the Law Society stating that coal mining searches should be obtained from the Coal Authority. This provided information on past, present and future underground coal mines; shafts and adits; surface geology; past, present and future opencast coal mines; subsidence; withdrawal of support; working facilities orders. A form is available from The Coal Authority, DX 29281 BRETBY or at Ashby Road, Stanhope Bretby, Burton-upon-Trent, DE15 0QD.

This applies to properties lying in the regions of Borders, Lothian, Central, Dumfries and Galloway, Fife, Tayside, Highland, Strathclyde and Western Isles (would it be easier perhaps to say the whole of Scotland excepting Grampian, Orkney and Shetland?). Particular areas within these regions are listed in a directory available from the Coal Authority. It doesn't leave out much, so offers should be amended to be conditional upon receiving these searches. See article 'Coal Mining Enquiries' in June 1995 JLSS 238.

Now do you understand what I mean about the speed of change! Let us hope there is not much more for a short time at least.

My thanks are due to a wide variety of people who have helped me with this book, whether wittingly or otherwise. Among the former category, particular thanks are due to Alex Falconer and Alistair Rennie of the Registers of Scotland for many interesting insights into the workings of land registration, to George Clark of the ESPC, to Norma McLeod of the Bradford & Bingley for advice on mortgages, to Douglas Mill of Strathclyde University for advice on practice management, and to other university colleagues for various insights from their various fields, to David Semple of Semple Fraser and Co for mediation advice, to Roy Stirrat of SPH for valuable information on property enquiry certificates, to David Brunton of Hutcheson's Grammar School for artwork, and to many, many others. I am also grateful to Anne Ferguson and Karen Sandison for the many hours they spent typing up the book.

The contents of the book are, however, my sole responsibility.

John H Sinclair
Glasgow
June 1995

CONTENTS

Contents

Contents

Contents

TABLE OF STATUTES

References are to paragraph numbers; numbers in square brackets refer to material in the appendices.

TABLE OF ORDERS, RULES
AND REGULATIONS

References are to paragraph numbers; numbers in square brackets refer to material in the appendices.

Table of Orders, Rules and Regulations

TABLE OF CASES

References are to paragraph numbers; numbers in square brackets refer to material in the appendices.

Table of Cases

PROCEDURAL TABLES

Procedural Table I

CHRONOLOGICAL STEPS IN A TRANSACTION INVOLVING REGISTRATION OF DOMESTIC PROPERTY IN THE GENERAL REGISTER OF SASINES

Note: This example includes repayment of the sellers' loan and the constitution of the purchasers' loan.

SELLERS	PURCHASERS
1 Ideally the sellers inform their solicitor of intention to sell. Solicitor then:— (a) informs lenders of clients' intention and asks for the title deeds; (b) obtains the writs referred to for burdens (or quick copies) if these are likely to be required and are not with the title deeds, and requests Local Authority Certificate *re* roads and planning, required permissions for any work done on the building and any guarantees for work done.	
2 The solicitor may or may not act in the marketing of the property. If so instructed, advertisements are placed, the property is registered with the property centre, a schedule is drawn up, enquiries answered and arrangements made to show potential buyers around the property. If solicitors do not act at this stage, they may not be instructed until the purchaser has been found, in which case steps 1(a) and 1(b) are taken at the earliest opportunity.	
	3 Purchasers inspect property and consult their solicitors, who intimate purchasers' interest to selling agents. Further details of the property are obtained at this stage, and preferably a copy of the particulars of the property for particular reference to moveables included. Purchasers' solicitors enquire if there is a closing date for offers.

3

Procedural Table I

SELLERS	PURCHASERS
	4 Purchasers are advised to contact lenders *re* loan. If lenders are satisfied as to purchasers' income and credit rating, they will arrange to have the property valued. If the valuation covers the amount of the loan, the lenders will make a verbal offer of loan.
	5 Once the purchasers' finances are seen to be in order, solicitors submit offer on behalf of the purchasers.
6 (a) Offers are considered and sellers' instructions taken. Best offer is accepted conditionally or unconditionally, and others are informed. Advertisements are cancelled and boards removed. Property is deregistered with property centre. Fire insurance is maintained, unless in special circumstances. (b) Lenders are informed of sale and date of entry, and are asked to state how much is to be repaid at the date of entry. (c) Diary entries as to various steps in transaction are made.	
	7 Purchasers' solicitors accept sellers' qualifications and generally ensure that parties are completely in consensus and there are no loose ends in Agreement. Due consideration should be given to any time limits in the acceptance, within which the purchasers' solicitors must satisfy themselves as to conditions of title. Temporary insurance cover is arranged, unless sellers accept responsibility in terms of missives which is the usual case. Diary entries are made.

GOLDEN RULE:– Fire insurance is cheap, and double insurance is always better than no insurance!

8 Sellers' solicitors send purchasers' solicitors (a) title deeds; (b) draft discharge of security; (c) draft letter of obligation; (d) search; (e) draft memorandum for continuation of search; (f) draft state for settlement and all other relative receipts; (g) all certificates of permission and guarantee available; (h) property enquiry certificates and (i) any other information that may be useful. If a non-supersession letter is requested, a draft of this can also be sent.

SELLERS	PURCHASERS
	9 Purchasers' solicitors:– (a) examine title, approve sellers' drafts and draft disposition in favour of purchasers; (b) carefully peruse lenders' loan instructions, and accordingly draft standard security and assignation of any policy; (c) If loan is taken in one name only, or in the names of two persons who are engaged, or who have the potential of being married, the appropriate affidavit(s) under MH(FP)(S) Act is prepared to protect lenders' interest; (d) If the loan is an `endowment loan', assignation of policy is prepared; (e) The draft disposition with the title deeds and all other papers are now returned to sellers' solicitors, and (f) purchasers' solicitors also make observation on title at this stage.
	10 Purchasers' solicitors make any enquiries that the sellers' solicitors have not undertaken in missives (eg Roads certificates et cetera).
	11 Solicitors report to clients on any important feuing conditions or other important matters of title.
12 Sellers' solicitors serve notice of redemption of feuduty if this has not already been attended to, and inform council tax office of the region to intimate change of ownership; also remind the sellers to contact gas, electric and telephone companies to arrange final meter readings.	
13 (a) Sellers' solicitors revise disposition and return this to purchasers' solicitors, answering observations on title at the same time. (b) Discharge of loan is typed and sent to lenders asking them to execute this and return it on understanding by sellers' solicitors to hold it as undelivered pending repayment of loan. (c) Interim report on search is obtained and sent to purchasers' solicitors.	

SELLERS	PURCHASERS
	14 (a) Disposition is engrossed, compared with draft and returned to sellers' solicitors for signature, with the draft for comparison. (b) Standard security, assignation of policy, and appropriate affidavit are signed in good time for settlement. (c) Report on title and request of cheque is sent to lenders, allowing at least five days for return. Purchasers are requested to provide balance of price in order to have cleared funds ready at settlement. (Another GOLDEN RULE: see Chapters 10–11.)
15 Sellers' solicitors either get keys or arrange for their transfer on date of entry. The engrossed disposition is compared with draft, and signed by sellers together with any affidavit. Draft disposition is returned to purchasers' agents. Solicitors ensure discharge of security and retrocession of any policy are available and put in testing clauses. Letter of obligation is typed.	
16 Once everything is ready, sellers' solicitors arrange settlement. Have letter of obligation signed.	**16** Purchasers' solicitors having ensured there are sufficient funds in clients' account to settle, and that no points are outstanding, arrange settlement.
17 *Settlement*	*Settlement*
Sellers' solicitors hand over: 1. keys (or have arranged for their collection by purchasers); 2. signed disposition and draft (if not already returned); 3. deliverable title deeds and writs referred to for burdens; 4. letter of obligation and draft. 5. Feu duty redemption receipt. 6. Receipted sale for settlement and draft. 7. Any matrimonial affidavit and draft. 8. Discharge of standard security and draft. 9. Signed letter to keeper requesting registration of discharge. 10. Non-supersession letter, if required. 11. Permissions and guarantees.	Purchasers' solicitors hand over cheque. Check all items handed over, with drafts where appropriate, and return drafts to sellers' solicitors.

SELLERS	PURCHASERS
	18 (a) Testing clause is added to disposition, and disposition is stamped (if appropriate) and sent to register of sasines with standard security and discharge with Keeper's letter signed by sellers' solicitors. All deeds are checked before dispatch to ensure that they are sufficiently stamped, testing clauses are correct, all signatures of granters and witnesses are furnished, and that the warrant of registration is signed. (b) Purchasers' solicitors ensure that fire insurance arrangements have been made. (c) If appropriate, notice of assignation of life policy in duplicate is sent to life assurance company who are requested to receipt and return the duplicate. (d) Notify lenders of completion of transaction and encashment of cheque.
19 (a) Loan is repaid. (b) Having deducted the loan, all fees and outlays, sellers' solicitors send cheque for proceeds to sellers with statement of accounts. Alternatively payment may be made to sellers' bank (designating sellers' account on the cheque) or as otherwise instructed, or proceeds applied to purchase of new house. (c) Fire insurance is cancelled and all standing orders for premiums, rates et cetera.	**19** Purchasers' solicitors should send statement of account showing receipts and payments, fees and outlays to clients with explanatory letter. Fee note should include registration dues for disposition and standard security which however are not paid until **25** and are kept in **clients'** account meantime.

20 BOTH PARTIES SHOULD NOW CHECK FILE AGAIN FOR ANY LOOSE ENDS.

SELLERS	PURCHASERS
	21 The recorded disposition and standard security are received. After a reasonable interval, sellers' solicitors are asked for search.
22 When completed search is received, this is sent to purchasers' solicitors.	
	23 On receipt of search, the letter of obligation is returned to sellers' agents marked as 'implemented'.

7

SELLERS	PURCHASERS
	24 Disposition, standard security, title deeds and other certificates (eg NHBC, roads and planning, woodworm treatment et cetera) are sent to lenders with life policy, assignation and receipted intimation of assignation.
	25 Pay registration dues from funds retained in clients' account for the purpose.

26 BOTH FILES ARE CLOSED AND PUT AWAY.

Notes: 1. If the Land Registers (Scotland) Bill of 1995 becomes law, registration fees will be payable at the time of presentation of the deeds to the Register.
2. From 1 August 1995 it will only be necessary to provide one witness to each signature. Furthermore it will not be necessary to sign offers and acceptances 'adopted as holograph' (Requirements of Writing (Scotland) Act 1995). Limited companies will execute deeds by the signature of a director, secretary, or other authorised official, which will require witnessing.

Procedural Table II

CHRONOLOGICAL STEPS IN A TRANSACTION INVOLVING THE FIRST REGISTRATION OF DOMESTIC PROPERTY IN THE LAND REGISTER

Note: This example includes repayment of the sellers' loan and the constitution of the purchasers' loan.

SELLERS	PURCHASERS
R1 Ideally the sellers inform their solicitors of intention to sell. Solicitors then: (a) inform lenders of clients' intention and asks for the title deeds; and (b) obtain the writs referred to for burdens (or quick copies) if these are likely to be required and are not with the title deeds, and request Local Authority Certificates *re* roads and planning; (c) send Form 10 in DUPLICATE and Form P16 to Keeper of Land Register or searchers requesting reports. (**Note**: P16 Report is not provided for flats.)	
R2 The solicitors may or may not act in the marketing of the property. If instructed to act, advertisements are placed, property is registered with the property centre, enquiries answered, and arrangements made to show potential buyers round the property. If the solicitors do not act at this stage, they may not be instructed until the purchaser has been found, in which case steps R1(a), R1(b) and R1(c) are taken now or at the earliest opportunity.	

SELLERS	PURCHASERS
	R3 Purchasers inspect property and consult their solicitors, who intimate purchasers' interest to selling agents. Purchasers' solicitors enquire if there is a closing date for offers. Further details of the property are obtained at this stage, and preferably a copy of the particulars of the property, for particular reference to moveables included in the sale. Solicitors enquire if property is already registered – if in doubt an enquiry to the Keeper can be made on a Form 10 or 14.
	R4 Purchasers are advised to contact lenders *re* loan. If lenders are satisfied as to purchasers' income and credit rating, they will arrange to have property valued. If the valuation covers the amount of the loan, the lenders will make a verbal offer of loan.
	R5 Once the purchasers' finances are seen to be in order, solicitors submit offer on behalf of purchasers.
R6 (a) Offers are considered and sellers' instructions taken. Best offer is accepted conditionally or unconditionally, and others are informed. Advertisements are cancelled, property centre informed and boards removed. Fire insurance is maintained, unless in special circumstances. (b) Lenders are informed of sale and date of entry, and are asked to state how much is to be repaid at the date of entry. (c) Diary entries as to various steps in transaction are made.	
	R7 Purchasers' solicitors accept sellers' qualifications and generally ensure that parties are completely in consensus and there are no loose ends in agreement. Due consideration should be given to any time limits in the acceptance, within which the purchasers' solicitors must satisfy themselves as to conditions of title. Temporary insurance cover is arranged, unless sellers accept responsibility in terms of missives. Diary entries are made.

SELLERS	PURCHASERS

GOLDEN RULE: Fire insurance is cheap, and double insurance is always better than no insurance!

R8 Sellers' solicitors send purchasers' solicitors (a) title deeds; (b) Form 10A and P16 Reports; (c) draft Form 11; (d) draft discharge of security; (e) draft letter of obligation; (f) the search but without a draft memorandum for its continuation; (g) draft state for settlement and all relative receipts; (h) permissions and guarantees; (i) property enquiry certificates and (j) any other information that may be useful. If a non-supersession letter is required, a draft of this may also be sent.

R9 (a) Purchasers' solicitors examine title, approve sellers' drafts, and draft disposition in favour of purchasers and Forms 1 (Pink) and 4.

(b) Carefully peruse lenders' loan instructions, and accordingly draft standard security and Form 2 (Blue) in respect of the standard security which is treated as being the first dealing in registered land. (**Note**: Where the same solicitors act for purchasers and lenders, it is only necessary to prepare one Form 4 – to include the standard security – in duplicate.) If loan is taken in one name only, or in the names of two persons who are engaged, or who have the potential of being married, the appropriate affidavit(s) under MH(FP)(S) Act, is prepared to protect lenders' interest.

(c) If the loan is an 'endowment loan', assignation of policy is prepared.

(d) The draft disposition and draft Forms 1 and 4, the title deeds, and all other papers are returned to the sellers' solicitors.

Purchasers' solicitors also make observation on title at this stage.

R10 Purchasers' solicitors make any enquiries that the sellers' solicitors have not undertaken in missives (eg roads certificates et cetera).

R11 Solicitors report to clients on any important feuing conditions or other important matters of title.

SELLERS	PURCHASERS
R12 Sellers' solicitors serve notice of redemption of feuduty if this has not already been attended to and contact council tax office of the Region to intimate change of ownership; also remind the sellers to contact gas, electricity and telephone companies to arrange final readings.	
R13 (a) Sellers' solicitors revise disposition and Forms 1 and 4 and send these to purchasers' solicitors, answering observations on title at the same time. (b) Discharge of loan is typed and sent to lenders with letter asking them to execute this and return it on the undertaking by sellers' solicitors to hold it as undelivered pending repayment of loan.	
	R14 (a) Disposition is engrossed, compared with draft and returned to sellers' solicitors for signature, with the draft for comparison. (b) Forms 1 and 4 are typed, the latter in DUPLICATE. (c) Standard security, assignation of policy and appropriate affidavit are signed in good time for settlement. (d) Report on title and request of cheque is sent to lenders, allowing at least five days for return. Purchasers are requested to provide balance of price in order to have cleared funds ready at settlement. (Another GOLDEN RULE: see Chapters 10–11.)
R15 Sellers' solicitors either get keys or arrange for their transfer on date of entry. The engrossed disposition is compared with draft, and signed by sellers together with any affidavit. Draft disposition is returned to purchasers' agents. Solicitors ensure discharge of security is available, put in a testing clause and prepare Form 2 for discharge. Letter of obligation is typed.	

SELLERS	PURCHASERS

R16 Once everything is ready, sellers' solicitors arrange settlement. Have letter of obligation signed (see Appendix 11.18(b)).
The sellers should also arrange for a Form 11A Report to be sent by the Keeper just prior to settlement (allow five working days). If short of time, a verbal report may be obtained, at an additional fee.

R16 Purchasers' solicitors having ensured there are sufficient funds in clients' account to settle, and that no points are outstanding, requisition cheque, have this signed and arrange settlement.

R17 *Settlement*
Sellers' solicitors hand over:
1. Keys (or have arranged for their collection by purchasers);
2. signed disposition and draft and particulars of signing (if not already returned);
3. deliverable title deeds and writs referred to for burdens;
4. letter of obligation and draft;
5. feu duty redemption receipt;
6. receipted state for settlement and draft;
7. any matrimonial affidavit and draft;
8. discharge of standard security and draft and Form 2 for discharge (signed by sellers' solicitor);
9. Form 11A Report;
10. Non-supersession letter if required.
(**Note**: The discharge is registered in the Land Register and no warrant of registration is put on discharge.)

R17 *Settlement*
Purchasers' solicitors hand over cheque. Check all items handed over, with drafts where appropriate, and return drafts to sellers' solicitors.

R18 (a) Testing clause is added to disposition, and disposition is stamped (if appropriate).
(b) Form 1 is *signed* and *dated* and sent to Land Register with Form 4 (IN DUPLICATE) and all documents mentioned in Form 4 (which includes discharge of sellers' loan and relative Form 2). Check all deeds and forms to ensure that they are sufficiently stamped, testing clauses are correct, all signatures of granters and witnesses are furnished, and that the Form 1 is signed.

13

SELLERS	PURCHASERS
	R18 (continued)
	(c) Form 2 is sent to Land Register with standard security. Sellers' solicitors' Form 2 is sent to Register with discharge.
	(d) Purchasers' solicitors ensure that fire insurance arrangements have been made.
	(e) If appropriate, notice of assignation of life policy in duplicate is sent to life assurance company who are requested to receipt and return the duplicate.
	(f) Notify lenders of completion of transaction and encashment of cheque.
R19 (a) Loan is repaid.	**R19** Purchasers' solicitors should send statement of account showing receipts and payments, fees and outlays to client with explanatory letter. Fee note should include land registration dues for disposition and standard security which are not however paid until **R22**. Meantime the recording dues are retained in **clients'** account.
(b) Having deducted the loan, all fees and outlays, sellers' solicitors send cheque for proceeds to sellers with statement of account. Alternatively payment may be made to sellers' bank or as otherwise instructed (ensuring that cheque is designated with sellers' names), or proceeds applied to purchase of a new house.	
(c) Fire insurance is cancelled and all standing orders for premiums and rates et cetera.	

R20 BOTH PARTIES SHOULD NOW CHECK FILE AGAIN FOR ANY LOOSE ENDS.

R21 Purchasers' solicitors await any observations from Land Register. If any are received these are dealt with if possible or referred to sellers' solicitors for clarification under terms of letter of obligation.

R22 Eventually the land certificate and charge certificate are received together with documents submitted to Land Register. Both are checked for any exclusion of indemnity or other irregularity. Upon satisfaction, the letter of obligation is returned to sellers' solicitors. Land certificate and charge certificate and any other certificates (eg NHBC, roads, planning, woodworm treatment et cetera) are sent to lenders with life policy, assignation and receipted intimation of assignation. Any writs referred to for

SELLERS	PURCHASERS
	R22 (continued) burdens which were borrowed from a third party are returned to the sellers' solicitors. Pay Land Register fees from funds retained in clients' account for this purpose.

R23 BOTH FILES ARE CLOSED AND PUT AWAY.

Notes: 1. If the Land Registers (Scotland) Bill of 1995 becomes law, registration fees will be payable at the time of presentation of the deeds to the Register.
2. From 1 August 1995 it will only be necessary to provide one witness to each signature. Furthermore it will not be necessary to sign offers and acceptances 'adopted as holograph' (Requirements of Writing (Scotland) Act 1995). Limited companies will execute deeds by the signature of a director, secretary, or other authorised official, which will require witnessing.

Procedural Table III

CHRONOLOGICAL STEPS IN A TRANSACTION INVOLVING A SECOND OR SUBSEQUENT REGISTRATION OF DOMESTIC PROPERTY

Note: This transaction closely resembles the First Registration in Procedural Table II, and many steps are given only by reference to Procedural Table II to avoid repetition.

SELLERS	PURCHASERS
SR1 Ideally the sellers inform their solicitors of intention to sell. Solicitors then: (a) inform lenders of clients' intentions and ask for the Land Certificate, and any other papers that were sent (see **R22**); (b) obtain local authority planning certificate to date, and (c) send Form 12 in duplicate requesting report. (**Note:** Form 12 replaces Form 10 and a Form P16 is not now sent as the boundaries are plotted on the ordnance survey map in the land certificate.)	
SR2 as in **R2**	
	SR3 as in **R3**.
	SR4 as in **R4**.
	SR5 as in **R5**.
SR6 as in **R6**.	
	SR7 as in **R7**.
SR8 Sellers' solicitors send purchasers' solicitors (a) land certificate and charge certificate; (b) Form 12A report; (c) draft Form 13; (d) draft discharge of security;	

SELLERS	PURCHASERS

SR8 (continued)
(e) draft letter of obligation; (f) draft state for settlement and all relative receipts; (g) permission and guarantees and (h) any other information that may be useful.

SR9 (a) Purchasers' solicitors examine the land certificate and charge certificate and draft disposition and Form 2 (Blue) if the whole of the registered holding is being transferred or Form 3 (Yellow) if only part of a registered holding (eg a new house on a building estate) and Form 4.

(b) Carefully peruse lenders' loan instructions and accordingly draft standard security, Form 2 (blue) in respect of the standard security. (**Note:** Where same solicitors act for purchasers and lenders it is only necessary to prepare one Form 4, incorporating the standard security, in duplicate. If purchase is taken in one name only, or in the names of two persons who are engaged, or who have the potential of being married, the appropriate affidavit(s) under MH(FP)(S) Act is prepared to protect lenders' interest.)

(c) If the loan is an 'endowment loan' assignation of policy is prepared.

(d) The draft disposition and draft Form 2 or 3 and Form 4, the land and charge certificates and all other papers are returned to the sellers' solicitors. Purchasers' solicitors also make observations on title at this stage.

SR10 as in **R10**.

SR11 as in **R11**.

SR12 **R12** (redemption of feu duty) is no longer appropriate as this will have been done, unless the feu duty is unallocated in which case it will remain in force until voluntarily redeemed. Sellers' solicitors contact council tax office of the Region to intimate change of ownership.

SELLERS	PURCHASERS
SR13 (a) Sellers' solicitors revise disposition and Form 2/3 and 4 and send these to purchasers' solicitors, answering obligations on title at the same time; (b) as in **R13**(b).	
	SR14 (a) Disposition is engrossed, compared with draft and returned to sellers' solicitors for signature, with the draft for comparison. (b) Forms 2/3 and 4 are typed, the latter IN DUPLICATE. (c) and (d) as in **R14**(c) and (d).
SR15 as in **R15**.	
SR16 as in **R16** (except read Form 13A Report for Form 11A, which is only competent on first registration).	**SR16** as in **R16**.
SR17 Sellers' solicitors hand over: 1. keys (or have arranged for their collection); 2. signed disposition and draft (if not already returned); 3. land certificate and change certificate; 4. letter of obligation and draft; 5. receipted state of settlement and draft; 6. any matrimonial affidavit and draft; 7. discharge of standard security and draft and Form 2 for discharge; 8. Form 13; 9. Non-supersession letter, if required.	
	SR18 (a) Testing clause is added to disposition and disposition is stamped (if appropriate). (b) Form 2/3 is signed and dated and sent to the Land Register with Form 4 IN DUPLICATE and all documents mentioned in Form 4 (which includes discharge of sellers' loan). (c) Form 2 for standard security and Form 4 (latter in duplicate) are sent to Land Register with standard security. All deeds are checked before dispatch to ensure that they are sufficiently stamped, testing clauses are correct, all signatures of granters and witnesses are furnished, and that the form 2/3 is signed.

SELLERS	PURCHASERS
	SR18 (continued)
	(d) Purchasers' solicitors ensure that fire insurance arrangements have been made.
	(e) If appropriate notice of assignation of life policy in duplicate is sent to life assurance company who are requested to receipt and return the duplicate.
	(f) Notify lenders of completion of transaction and encashment of cheque.
SR19 as in **R19**.	**SR19** as in **R19**.

SR20 BOTH PARTIES SHOULD NOW CHECK FILE AGAIN FOR ANY LOOSE ENDS.

SR21 as in **R21**.

SR22 as in **R22**.

SR23 BOTH FILES ARE CLOSED AND PUT AWAY.

Notes: 1. If the Land Registers (Scotland) Bill of 1995 becomes law, registration fees will be payable at the time of presentation of the deeds to the Register.

2. From 1 August 1995 it will only be necessary to provide one witness to each signature. Furthermore it will not be necessary to sign offers and acceptances 'adopted as holograph' (Requirements of Writing (Scotland) Act 1995). Limited companies will execute deeds by the signature of a director, secretary, or other authorised official, which will require witnessing.

Part one

A TYPICAL TRANSACTION INVOLVING REGISTRATION IN THE GENERAL REGISTER OF SASINES

Chapter one

WELCOME TO THE PROFESSION (?)

'Having seen the cost to his father of having no qualification to fall back on, Sir Denys determined to finish his law training at Aberdeen University and at a lawyer's office, despite finding it "singularly dull".'
(*Daily Mail*, on Sir Denys Henderson, Chairman of ICI and Zeneca PLC)

'For the love of Money is the root of all evil.'
(2 Timothy 6, 10)

'This story goes far in explaining why The Law Society (of England and Wales) is faced with a £31 million payment to client victims this year (report April 19). When I took articles in 1956 it was necessary to be vetted thoroughly, but now anyone can enter the profession who passes the exams and the result is painfully obvious. As soon as there is £1 million in the client account, off they go!'
(Letter to *The Times* April 1994)

'Scottish solicitors have been issued with a helpful little booklet entitled *Money Laundering – Guidance Notes for Wholesale, Institutional and Private Client Investment Business*. It did not take long before a legal wit (yes, of course it was Austin J Lafferty) was heard to inquire: "Is the purpose of this booklet to discourage money laundering or to teach you how to do it better?"

To confuse matters further, an application form for a Law Society of Scotland seminar on the above topic refers to "Monday laundering" which had at least one Hamilton practice wondering if they were now required to take in washing.'
(Tom Shields in *The Herald* March 1994)

'Money Laudering Seminar'
(Edinburgh University advertisement)
Roamin' in the Gloamin'?

1.1 A conveyancer is, at present, a solicitor who deals in practice mainly with the purchase and sale of heritable property. A solicitor in Scotland is a person who is qualified to practise as such by having obtained a law degree from one of the five Scottish universities offering this degree (or passing equivalent examinations assessed by the Law Society of Scotland), Diploma in Legal Practice, and then having served a two-year traineeship in a solicitors' office. This rigorous basic training occupies at the very least six years, which is the equivalent of the basic medical training. The aspiring Scottish solicitor must also be shown to be a fit and proper person to be a solicitor.

Admission to the profession is regulated by the Law Society of Scotland, in terms of the Admission as Solicitor (Scotland) Regulations 1986 and 1991.

The solicitor is governed by the Solicitors (Scotland) Acts 1980 and 1988, which supercede the Solicitors (Scotland) Act 1949, the foundation Act which set up the Law Society of Scotland as the governing body for the profession. Section 5 of the 1980 Act empowers the Council of the Law Society to make regulations, with the concurrence of the Lord President of the Court of Session. Many of these regulations will be referred to throughout this chapter, and are printed in full in the Parliament House Book, or in the off-print known as the Solicitors' Compendium (W Green & Son Limited).

A practising solicitor must be a member of the Law Society of Scotland under the Solicitors (Scotland) Act 1980, s 4, (unlike English solicitors who need not belong to their Law Society) and must hold a practising certificate in terms of the Solicitors (Scotland) Practising Certificate Rules 1988.

1.2 The reasons for entering the profession are perceived to be: (a) it should ensure a comfortable lifestyle, and a safe job for life, although it is doubtful if any such thing now exists; (b) despite the comments of the media, it is still a profession that inspires a certain amount of respect in the general public, especially in smaller communities; (c) there is a genuine sense of satisfaction in helping out people in the worst times of crisis in their lives, although it should be noted that even the nicest clients can turn into monsters in a crisis, and a good job well done does not necessarily imply that your fee will be unquestioningly paid; (d) law can become a totally absorbing discipline, and a great deal of intellectual stimulation can be obtained from solving its complexities; and (e) if it all gets too much, the lawyer is fairly qualified to turn to another career in, for example, commerce, industry or politics (see Sir Denys Henderson above).

Well, er, that's it, as *Private Eye* would say. What of the disadvantages?

You have probably chosen the most tightly regulated of occupations. The main problem is that while the legal profession handles huge amounts of clients' money – even a small practice can have an annual turnover of several million pounds in its clients' account – many solicitors take a perverse pride in being innumerate. This breeds problems, which in turn breed regulations.

Where there is money, there is temptation for the dishonest, the weak, and the badly organised. The Journal of the Law Society of Scotland regularly carries a dismal little column detailing the offences of solicitors who have come to grief through misuse of their clients' account, as does the Annual Report of the Disciplinary Tribunal. While some offences are hair-raising in their dishonesty, the remainder are committed by people who have simply got out of their depth.

What is even more alarming is where solicitors have entrusted the running of the cash room to a cashier, who has then done the embezzling. Not only do the solicitors have to refund the money from their own pockets (failing which the profession does through the Guarantee Fund), but the solicitors are guilty of an offence under the Accounts Rules of the Law Society, as the liability is strict, and the firm must designate a cashroom partner, who is responsible for the actings of the staff.

In one such case in 1993, the Tribunal ruled that 'even although an established shortfall may be attributable to dishonesty among members of a solicitor's staff, such circumstances do not necessarily provide an answer to a charge of professional misconduct on the basis that it always remains the solicitor's duty to take all reasonable steps to ensure that clients' funds are safeguarded'.

1.3 The Law Society of Scotland (hereinafter referred to – following the practice of good conveyancers – as 'the Law Society' or as 'the Society' although this name, without territorial designation, officially belongs to the English counterpart) governs the actions of Scottish solicitors from its offices at 26 Drumsheugh Gardens, Edinburgh EH3 7YR (Telephone 0131–226 7411; FAX 0131–225 2934). The Society also has a Brussels office (Telephone 00 832 502 2020; FAX 00 322 502 2292).

In terms of s 1(2) of the Solicitors (Scotland) Act 1980, the objects of the Law Society shall include the promotion of (a) the interests of the solicitors' profession in Scotland and (b) the interests of the public in relation to that profession. It might be said that these two objects are contradictory, but this proposition demands rather closer examination.

The Law Society has to walk a very thin line between representing the interests of its members, and representing the interests of members of the public who think – rightly or wrongly – that they may have been ill-treated by their solicitor. Thus while many lay persons might think of the Law Society as being 'a lawyers' trade union', many solicitors would equally think of the Society as a body which exists to wrap the solicitor in a web of petty regulations, and to punish the solicitor for any minor transgression of these.

1.4   The Law Society, as part of the first object of the Act, is responsible – among other things – for the training and admission of solicitors, compulsory Continuing Professional Development, legal education, practice development, maintaining links with other Societies, publications, giving advice on numerous professional topics through a network of specialist committees and the secretariat, scrutinising proposed legislation and making representations as necessary, ensuring that accounting rules and the regulations under the Financial Services Act 1986 are observed, liaising with the Scottish Law Commission, corporate public relations and advertising, arranging mediation proceedings through an organisation called 'Accord' and negotiating professional indemnity insurance.

1.5   The Law Society, as part of the second object of the Act, maintains a Complaints Supervisory Committee and secretariat, which has three Committees (A, B and C) considering complaints received from members of the public against solicitors. According to the Annual Report of the Society for 1993, 1,294 complaints were lodged in that year by members of the public, compared to 875 in 1988. The increase is apparently accounted for by the introduction in the Solicitors (Scotland) Act 1988 of the concept of inadequate professional service (IPS), which led to a sharp and sustained increase in complaints.

Where the Society concludes that there has been IPS, which means very much what it says, it may modify a solicitor's fee, order a solicitor to correct the fault, or to pay for having the fault corrected. An aggrieved solicitor may appeal the decision to the Disciplinary Tribunal within 21 days, and it may 'quash, confirm or vary the determination or direction being appealed against'. It may not, however, refer the determination back to the Society. The procedure is fully set out in the Tribunal's Report for 1993.

The Law Reform (Miscellaneous Provisions) (Scotland) Act 1990 places a statutory duty on the Society to investigate complaints, which means that all mail received has to be analysed and categorised. The complaints are duly categorised in the Society's 1993 Report – conduct unbecoming a solicitor

(89); failure to communicate (217); failure to follow instructions (157); breach of Practice Rules (69); failure to advise adequately (99); delay (474); dishonesty (15); failure to prepare adequately (71); and Breach of Code of Conduct (103). Total 1,294.

The Society employs a Complaints Investigator, who in the year 1993 investigated 413 complaints, and dealt with 3,500 telephone calls. Many complaints can, however, be simply resolved by conciliation procedures involving the secretariat.

If, however, a complaint cannot be resolved in this way, it is then referred to one of three Complaints Committees, made up mainly of lawyers, but with two lay members on each committee. The Solicitors (Scotland) Act 1988 widened the powers of the Society in this respect – formerly the Society might deal only with complaints about the professional conduct of solicitors; now it may act where the solicitor has provided an inadequate professional service. In these circumstances, the solicitor concerned may be required to reduce or waive the fee charged, rectify the defect, or pay for someone else to rectify it.

Of course not all complaints are justified, and 278 were abandoned without reference to a Complaints Committee, 382 had no action taken, 197 were referred to dispute resolution, and 43 were referred to conciliation. Of complaints that went to a committee, 107 were dismissed, and in 43 complaints the solicitor was censured, but in 220 cases there was a finding of misconduct with varying consequences.

1.6 In serious cases of professional misconduct arising from complaints received – or from the investigations of the Society, principally under the Solicitors (Scotland) Accounts Rules 1992 – the Society may make a complaint to the Disciplinary Tribunal. This body operates under the Scottish Solicitors Discipline Tribunal Procedures Rules 1989, and its members are appointed by the Lord President of the Court of Session. The members of this Tribunal are predominantly, but not exclusively, lawyers, but it must be stressed that the Tribunal operates wholly independently of the Society. The Society is not, as some may suspect, therefore judge and prosecutor.

The Tribunal has power to order a solicitor's name to be struck from the roll of practising solicitors (eight in the year to 31 October 1993) or to suspend or restrict their practising certificates (two in the same year). An appeal against the Tribunal's decision lies to the Court of Session, but there were none in 1993.

1.7 Disgruntled members of the public who cannot be appeased by any of these means, may additionally make a complaint to the Scottish Legal Services Ombudsman. The Ombudsman replaced the Lay Observer as a result of the Law Reform (Miscellaneous Provisions) (Scotland) Act 1990, s 34 (1), which gave the Ombudsman wider powers than the former Lay Observer had, including a power to raise a matter in the Disciplinary Tribunal, and a jurisdiction over advocates.

In the year to October 1993 the Ombudsman received 295 new cases and enquiries, of which he investigated 78, and was satisfied with the Law Society's handling of the complaint in 52 cases, and critical in 26. The reasons for criticism were – inadequate investigation (9); inadequate consideration

(16); inadequate action (3); inadequate explanation (6); delay (2); other reasons (0).

But, writing in September 1994, there is clearly a move gaining strength to impose independent regulation on the profession. Nigel Griffiths MP is quoted (*Sunday Times* 28 August 1994) as saying:

'There is need for a truly independent body to regulate this industry (*sic*) in Scotland. The time has come to set up such a body and I would expect the legal profession to fund it.'

1.8 While there is no room for complacency, it will be seen that a remarkably small proportion of the many transactions that must be carried out by solicitors every year in Scotland, actually come to grief. It should be a matter of pride that this is so, and the standard should be maintained and improved in the interest of the profession. It will also be seen that the Society is fairly vigilant in rooting out its bad apples. While this does necessitate a high degree of regulation of its members, it should be appreciated that the disciplinary functions of the Society are a vital part of the Society's broad duty to represent the interests of the profession, by maintaining public confidence. The two objects of the Solicitors (Scotland) Act 1980 (**1.2**) are not therefore self-contradictory after all.

1.9 Despite this many solicitors – especially those in smaller firms – still feel that, in the event of their getting into trouble with the Society or otherwise, they are left with no professional body to assist them. For this reason, there was established the Legal Defence Union, which is analogous to the well-established Medical Defence Union. Membership of the Union (17 Ainslie Place, Edinburgh EH3 6AU – Telephone 0131–226 2053: FAX 0131–226 2479) offers members insurance cover for legal expenses incurred in respect of complaints and disciplinary proceedings, criminal and certain civil proceedings, and employment disputes for employed solicitors, and industrial tribunal proceedings for partnerships. In addition a solicitor with a professional problem should be able to obtain advice through the local Faculty of Solicitors.

1.10 The solicitors' profession was the last of the non-specialising professions, and a solicitor is qualified to advise on a great number of matters, although inevitably specialisation is becoming increasingly prevalent. The solicitor, like other agents, is bound by duties of agent to client imposed by the law of agency which may be summarised as follows:

(a) The agent must carry out the principal's instructions.

(b) The agent is in a personal relationship with the principal, and may not therefore – in general – delegate, without the principal's instructions.

(c) The agent must keep the money and property of the principal separate from the agent's own money and property, and keep accounts of dealings with it.

(d) The agent must give the principal the full benefit of contracts made with third parties. Any secret commission must not be gained without the principal's consent.

In return, the agent is entitled to receive a reasonable remuneration, reimbursement of expenses, to be relieved of all liabilities incurred in the performance of the agency, and to the agent's lien over the property of the principal in the agent's hands in the course of the agency, until remuneration has been received.

1.11   To the law of agency there must now be added statutory controls, most importantly under the Financial Services Act 1986. This Act was introduced with the stated intention of offering an investor protection from incompetent and unscrupulous advisers and dealers, of whom there was apparently no shortage.

While the Act is framed on the basis that investors must accept personal repsonsibility for the risk involved in every investment to be made, and are thus not protected from the consequence of their own folly, they are nevertheless entitled to sound and impartial advice. This is known technically as 'best advice' and is similar in concept to the obligations laid down in the law of agency.

Best advice is therefore precisely what every competent solicitor would, or should, have offered anyway. The Act is aimed at rather more colourful figures on the financial spectrum. Nevertheless solicitors who give financial advice, as do most, are inevitably brought into the regulatory net. Again this involves the Law Society.

1.12   Solicitors who give any form of financial advice must now be registered under the Financial Services Act 1986. The giving of financial advice, without registration, is a criminal offence, punishable by up to two years in prison. The communication of a stockbroker's report, for example, on investments to a client, without comment, is not however covered by the Act. Sales of heritable property are not covered by the Act, but often the solicitor will be asked to give financial advice to clients as part of sale or purchase.

Investor protection is under the overall control of the Department of Trade and Industry (DTI). The DTI delegates regulatory powers to the Securities and Investment Board (SIB). SIB, in turn, has recognised a number of self-regulating organisations (SROs) and recognised professional bodies (RPBs) which, subject to the supervision of the SIB, are empowered to monitor the conduct of investment business by their members.

The Law Society of Scotland is an RPB, and thus is the regulatory body under the Financial Services Act 1986 of the solicitors' profession in Scotland. The Society has enacted the Solicitors (Scotland) (Conduct of Investment Business) Practice Rules 1994, which replace similarly named rules of 1989. Thus the solicitor who wishes to give investment advice is at the end of this chain of acronyms, and must comply with the Practice Rules, and submit to regular inspection to ensure that this is so.

While the whole question of the Financial Services Act 1986 and the Law Society Rules requires a separate and detailed study, the main requirements of the Act and Rules, so far as concerning solicitors, may be summarised thus:

(a) There is a polarisation choice open to financial advisers (see below) but this is *not* open to solicitors in private practice. The polarisation choices require agents who sell financial services to decide whether they are either 'independent intermediaries' *or* 'authorised representatives'.

The former approximates to the older concept of an 'insurance broker', who had access to the products of a number of companies – the larger the brokerage, the more products available – and advised which product was currently the best available in the circumstances. The latter approximates to the older concept of the 'insurance agent' (eg 'the man from the Pru'), who sold the products of only one company, and did not make any pretence to the contrary.

Unfortunately the two concepts had become hopelessly mixed, and agents might have represented themselves as 'brokers' but in reality were selling the products of one company, and stating that the product was the best available in the market. The truth was usually that it was not, only that it paid the best commission to the agent. That is the reason why the agent must decide which status to adopt (the polarisation option), and must advertise this clearly, and maintain that status.

No one person can be both independent intermediary and authorised representative, although large bodies like banks and building societies may be authorised representatives at branch level and independent intermediaries at head office level. Of the top ten building societies in size, only the Bradford and Bingley Society is an independent intermediary, while the others (excepting the Cheltenham & Gloucester which has now stopped selling life policies) are tied to a particular Life Office. This does not seem to be entirely within the spirit of the Act, which was intended to make good and impartial financial advice available to everybody, at local level, and not just in gilded banking halls.

(b) The solicitor in private practice is not allowed to be an authorised representative (rule 3.5) nor have an exclusive arrangement with another intermediary. This does not, however, apply to solicitors employed in public service or commerce, whose employers may maintain an exclusive arrangement with an insurance or other financial company.

(c) A solicitor may not give or receive any gifts, services or inducements which might be regarded as likely to influence, improperly, a recommendation for a particular service (rule 3.7). There have been instances where inducements have been given, to get around the requirement on an agent to give the benefit of financial commission to the client (see the Law of Agency).

(d) A solicitor is required to know the client's personal and financial circumstances, and the investments available on the market. The solicitor must have an adequate and reasonable basis for any recommendation of an investment, and where the investment is a life policy or unit trust the solicitor must be sure that there are no other investments which would be more advantageous to the client. Further the solicitor must be satisfied that the investment is suitable for the client's purposes (best advice rule – rule 4.1). The solicitor must also take reasonable steps to ensure that the investment is effected on the best terms available at the time (best execution rule – rule 4.2).

(e) The solicitor must maintain records to demonstrate compliance with the best advice and best execution rules. The required records are fully detailed in the Conduct of Investment Business Rules 1994 and obviously must be complied with. The Law Society makes frequent periodical inspections of solicitors' books to ensure compliance with the Practice Rules.

(f) The solicitor must now disclose the commission to be received in respect of a packaged product, which includes commission. If the solicitor is to be paid a commission by a third party to whom business is passed, the amount of the commission must be disclosed to the client, and not be hidden as a fee paid to the solicitor.

The Practice Rules do not, however, particularly affect conveyancing as such, as purchase and sale of heritable property are not counted as a financial service. When, however, the conveyancing solicitor offers advice as to financial services in connection with the purchase of heritage, that is financial advice and is dealt with in greater detail in Chapter 12.

Financial regulation is much more strictly applied than previously, and these rules are ignored at your own peril, as several 'household name' insurance companies have found out to their cost.

1.13 Other duties incumbent on the solicitor are:

(a) to effect through the Law Society's brokers, professional indemnity insurance, covering the solicitor's clients against any loss through the solicitor's negligence (Solicitors' (Scotland) Professional Indemnity Insurance Rules 1988); as a guideline only, the premium for a solicitor with no loading, and a clear claims record, in 1994/95 is approximately £1,500.

(b) to subscribe to the solicitors' Guarantee Fund, which reimburses persons who have been defrauded by their solicitor (Scottish Solicitors' Guarantee Fund Rules 1985); again as a guideline the amount payable in 1994/95 is approximately £300. Speaking at the 1994 AGM of the Law Society, the Convenor of the Guarantee Fund stated that there was a team of 12 inspecting accountants who had carried out 488 Guarantee Fund inspections, and 60 re-inspections, in the year 1993/94.

(c) to observe the Solicitors' (Scotland) (Advertising & Promotion) Practice Rules 1991. These Rules have been substantially liberalised, but solicitors must follow rule 8 which does not allow solicitors to claim superiority over other solicitors, nor make any reference in advertisements to volume of business or fee income, the identity of their clients or item of business without the prior written consent of the client, any item of business entrusted to them, or the outcome of any such business. Solicitors may not compare their fees with those of any other solicitor, make any inaccurate or misleading statements, nor bring the profession into disrepute. These Rules differ quite markedly from those of other professions, particularly accountants. In summary therefore the solicitor is still restricted very much to advertising a corporate image.

(d) to observe the Solicitors' (Scotland) Accounts Rules 1992, Solicitors (Scotland) Accountants Certificate Rules 1992 and the Solicitors (Scotland) Compliance Certificate Rules 1994. In as much as these concern conveyancing in particular, they are discussed at **10.16**. The general reminder is merely given that 'each partner of a firm of solicitors shall be responsible for securing compliance by the firm with the provisions of these Rules' (rule 13). The operation of this rule is slightly mitigated for junior partners who were given no responsiblity in accounting matters (*Sharp v The Council of the Law Society of Scotland* 1984 SLT 313 at 316), but basically lawyers cannot stand by and ignore accountancy matters, muttering how they are 'men of letters' and therefore, apparently, quite innumerate.

The Accounts Rules are a separate and very important study. The Disciplinary Tribunal Report for 1993 devotes a whole chapter to cases concerning a failure to comply with the Rules. Reliance on staff, reliance on computer programmes, without understanding them, and the 'particularly distressing' case of a solicitor who committed his client account to a withdrawal of almost three million US dollars, without ensuring that there were cleared funds to meet the transaction.

Some larger practices now employ chartered accountants as their partnership accountants or secretaries, and they may also employ other professional people, such as chartered surveyors and social workers, for specialist functions within the firm. The names of such persons may be printed on the firm's letterhead, provided that the public are in no way misled as to the status of the individual within the firm (Solicitors (Scotland) (Associates, Consultants and Employees) Practice Rules 1989). A smaller practice could not probably justify having a chartered accountant in the practice, but there should certainly be access to the services of a competent bookkeeper, who is preferably trained in the excellent courses run by the Society of Law Accountants (SOLAS).

(e) to accept unlimited liability for the debts of the partnership, and even, in extreme cases, of the other partners. The financial obligations of this requirement are, however, to some extent mitigated by compulsory Professional Indemnity Insurance (see Appendix VII).

In a case of major embezzlement in a firm, the Law Society will appoint a trustee to run the business, and will settle immediate claims from the Guarantee Fund. The Society will look first to the partners of the firm for recompense, to the limit of their assets. The indemnity policy will cover the partners for the first £100,000, but that may not be enough to protect their assets. Any balance will then be met by the Guarantee Fund.

(f) not to act in the same matter for two parties who might have a conflicting interest (Solicitors (Scotland) Practice Rules 1986). It must be said that formerly a solicitor might have acted, and often did, for both seller and purchaser. In most cases, where there was no substantial conflict of interest, the result was entirely satisfactory to all. It should be stressed, however, that where one person is selling, and another buying, however amicably, there is always a latent conflict of interest, and it was the cases where a dispute arose in the course of the transaction that gave tremendous difficulty. A solicitor cannot obviously act for both parties in a court case. By logical extension, the same applies in house purchase.

Having said that, there is considerable difficulty in country areas, where there are few solicitors, and certain exemptions are therefore made, to cover transactions between parties who are related, where both parties are established clients of the solicitor, or where there is no other solicitor in the area whom the client could reasonably be expected to consult.

Probably the most major exemption is that a solicitor may act for an institution, such as a building society or bank, which is lending money to the client in connection with a purchase, provided that the terms of the loan have been agreed before the solicitor is instructed to act. This last exemption is dealt with at r 5(f) of the 1986 Rules. However this is moderated by a change in banking practice set out in the terms of a circular from the Law Society in March 1994, which states that the banks now intend to instruct separate solicitors to represent their interest in commercial transactions. A further discussion of this topic follows in Chapter 12.

Further, the building societies are known to be unhappy with the conveyancing services they are getting in English cases where the solicitors are acting for both borrower and the Society, and at the time of writing (November 1994) there is an appeal pending in the House of Lords in a case where a solicitor was held to be in breach of trust to a building society. A spokesperson for the Woolwich Building Society is quoted in *The Times* as saying:

> 'The problems are not going away. We never find out about the negligence or sloppy conveyancing until the time comes to sell the house. With so many trapped in negative equity, many of the problems of 1988–89 have yet to see the light. We have found that the solicitors' compensation and indemnity funds are taking longer and longer to make up their minds, and writs do serve the purpose of concentrating the mind.'

Sloppy solicitors therefore beware!

(g) to observe the code of conduct contained in Schedule 1 to the Code of Conduct (Scotland) Rules 1992 which relate to general conduct, and particularly in court by solicitors and solicitor-advocates.

(h) to observe the Money Laundering Regulations 1993. Briefly these Regulations are intended to cover the placing of 'dirty' money (eg profits from drug-dealing or terrorism) into a 'clean' investment, such as a house or bonds. The investment can be subsequently sold, and the resulting proceeds are 'clean'. A person may commit five money laundering offences – assistance, concealment, acquisition, failure to disclose or tipping off. Basically, if a client approaches you, whom you have not known for at least two years, with a lot of unexplained cash, you are expected to 'verify' that the money has been legally obtained, and if you are still not certain you would be well-advised to discuss the matter, on a confidential basis, with the National Crime Intelligence Service (Telephone 0171–238 8271). It is appreciated that this is against the whole concept of client confidentiality, but desperate problems require desperate measures.

(i) the solicitor will also, like other mortals, be subjected to visits from VAT and tax inspectors.

1.14 Having outlined how difficult it is to become a solicitor, and how carefully regulated one's conduct is after that, and perhaps having indicated how expensive all of this is going to be for the solicitor, it is now appropriate to consider the benefits of being a solicitor, before too many people take fright and run.

Quite apart from the intangible benefits of the profession, which are many and which depend in their intensity upon the individual, the most important privilege is the so-called 'solicitors' monopoly' of conveyancing matters. This is contained in the Solicitors (Scotland) Act 1980, s 32 which states:

> 'a person including body corporate, not being qualified as a solicitor or advocate who draws or prepares a writ relating to heritable or moveable estate shall be guilty of an offence.'

Section 32(3) then continues to exclude from the definition (a) a will or other testamentary writing; (b) a document *in re mercatoria*, missive or mandate; (c) a letter or power of attorney; and (d) a transfer of stock containing no trust or limitation thereof.

Thus, of the four major steps of a property transaction – marketing, completing missives, completing title and drafting the deed, and settling up, it is only the third that is protected by the conveyancing monopoly. A person who is not legally qualified may market heritable property, and even complete a missive on behalf of purchaser or seller. When, however, it comes to drawing up formal deeds (ie those deeds not excepted by sub-s 3) this work must then be done by the solicitor.

Nothing said above, however, limits the ability of non-qualified parties selling or buying houses, to act entirely or partially on their own behalf in the matter. Thus if the Smiths buy a house, there is no reason why they should not complete their own missives and disposition, and present the disposition for recording. A solicitor need not be employed, but a non-solicitor may not be employed, at a fee, to draw up a writ covered by the solicitors' monopoly. If that person will perform the service gratuitously, that is permitted.

Further it should be noted that advocates are covered by the conveyancing monopoly as well, but as a matter of tradition they do not handle conveyancing.

1.15 Monopolies are, however, currently not at all in favour, and are gradually being dismantled, the ultimate authority being The Treaty of Rome, articles 88 and 89, which set out prohibitions on restriction of trade. These articles are being enthusiastically implemented throughout the European Community, not least in the United Kingdom.

For example, opticians have lost their monopoly on providing spectacle frames, and newspapers now advertise that you can buy reading spectacles for a few pounds at a variety of places, which include service stations and tobacconists. The person who had predicted this a few years ago would have been labelled as unquestionably insane. I recall hearing a prosecution, a few years ago, of an optician who had dared to advertise his services in the telephone directory IN BLOCK CAPITALS, thus presumably unfairly attracting business! He was duly prosecuted for this heinous crime, but was admonished, the defence agent having poured scorn on the prosecution case, and having very logically suggested that those who needed the service most would perhaps have been more at ease with block capitals!

It tends to be the case that other peoples' monopolies are seen to be monopolistic and oligarchic, whereas one's own monopoly is 'in the public interest'. Bearing this in mind, one turns to the Law Reform (Miscellaneous Provisions) (Scotland) Act 1990, which unleashed two new legal animals – the licensed conveyancer or licensed executry practitioner, and the solicitor-advocate. A licensed conveyancer would be a person not qualified in law, but in the particular discipline of conveyancing or executry practice. Licensed conveyancers practise happily in England, although mainly as part of a solicitor's business, but not yet in Scotland. For a definition of the limit of services that should be offered by licensed conveyancers see *Hall v Eade* reported in *The Times* of 18 January 1989.

The government set up a Licensed Conveyancer's Board to draw up rules, but the whole project was suspended in 1992 when it became apparent that, because of the recession, there was not enough work to go around, even to keep solicitors busy. Had the project materialised, licensed conveyancers would have been under similar constraints as to financial probity and conduct as solicitors.

1.16   Solicitors have traditionally been known as 'men of business' who were willing and able to advise on the whole spectrum of business affairs.

Formerly solicitors performed a wide variety of tasks, including accountancy, being bank agents in smaller communities, and being part-time clerks to smaller local authorities, clerks of court in smaller jurisdictions, as well as running their own practices. In the present century, however, there has been a drive towards specialisation, and inevitably the man of business is yielding to the specialist – both inside the legal profession and outside it.

1.17   This removing of items of general practice into specialist niches can, and does, produce friction. By and large the legal profession enjoys fairly amicable links with other professional bodies.

Frankly, however, a fair amount of animosity exists between some solicitors and some estate agents, whom solicitors see as removing a very important part of their livelihood. It is not only the mere fact that estate agents will market their clients' houses that troubles solicitors; it is that estate agents, who are predominantly now owned by banks, building societies and life assurance companies, will sell them life policies of their own tied company, suggest that they surrender other policies, and direct the client to a 'tame' solicitor, who offers a low fee. It really all boils down to a single question – who has control of the transaction, the solicitor or the estate agent?

Of course, the only answer to competition is to go out there and compete; if you think that an estate agent is taking your business, there is nothing to stop you practising as an estate agent.

Solicitors may, however, justly feel that they are entitled to compete on 'a level playing field', with a referee who is not wearing reading spectacles he bought at the filling station that morning. Solicitors with their complex training, and intricate web of self-regulation should not be asked to contend with someone who was selling groceries last week, and who has no real professional regulations as to conduct.

1.18 Estate agents were virtually unknown in Scotland until about 1960, except in the sale of specialised properties. Landed estates, very grand houses, farms and industrial properties might have been marketed by specialised agents, but solicitors handled the bulk of routine property sales as part of the whole selling process. Quite frankly, they had become extremely complacent about this, and the fact that nearly all property throughout the English-speaking world was marketed by estate agents, did not seem to ring any warning bells.

In 1963, however, the first commercial or 'high street' estate agency came to Scotland, in the shape of the Villa Estate Agency in Glasgow. The proprietor of this venture, one James Davidson, a chartered surveyor (it should perhaps be mentioned that two solicitors were also initially involved) attracted customers to the agency by his cheerful advertising. This was quite different from anything house buyers in Scotland had seen before, although the great Roy Brooks had been using this technique in England for many years. (See his two books of advertisements *A Brothel in Pimlico* and *Mud, Straw and Insults*, both available from Roy Brooks, 395 Kings Road, London.)

As an example of James Davidson's advertising:

'POLLOKSHIELDS (Ayton Road) Well – what a bargain for anyone who wants to make a home out of a decrepit mausoleum. The electricity bills in this 6/7 apartment SEMI greystone VILLA are nil, simply because there is no electricity. Yes, dignified Victorian gas lighting sets the Dickensian scene where the grotty dull ancient decoration somehow seems in place. Massive two tractor and car garage (there presently are two tractors and what once passed for a car in it now!). Regardless of your fears of "strange houses" surely £1,850 must tempt a lot of viewers.'

You will incidentally note the price, merely 32 years ago. Such a house might now attract around a six-figure offer, but that is another matter.

1.19 These advertisements were allied with considerable marketing flair, attractive shops, attentive receptionists, block advertising, informative details. Further, lists of potential sellers and buyers were maintained, and these were constantly updated and cross-referenced, so that a seller who went to an estate agent would be impressed when the agent could produce a list of potential buyers. The seller would be even more impressed if a sale resulted, without the property being advertised.

These techniques are standard nowadays, but were not then, and one winces at the thought of the amateurism of the legal profession at that time. House sales were usually deputed to the newest apprentice, who had probably never seen the house, didn't even know where it was, and had no idea of the asking price. As a result, estate agents were able to secure a fairly firm beachhead on the market very quickly, and have since then made very substantial inroads into this business.

To the chagrin of the legal profession, many estate agents have subsequently sold their businesses to banks, building societies and life assurance companies at very large sums. This has often resulted in tears, and large institutions have learnt the hard way that a small personal business like estate agency cannot be easily institutionalised, and that the cobbler should stick to the last. In October 1994 the Nationwide Building Society was reported as selling its estate agency chain of 305 branches for the sum of £1. They had made a loss of £200m in seven years. In 1993 Abbey National sold its 347-branch chain for one-tenth of the price paid for each outlet. The Prudential lost £340m on its 500-branch chain. (Financial figures – *Daily Telegraph* 12 October 1994.)

This whole process hopefully taught the legal profession a never-to-be-forgotten lesson in the joys of competition. What was perhaps even worse, in many cases the legal profession surrendered the opportunity of first contact with the client.

1.20   It should be pointed out that, nationally, solicitors still market around 70 per cent of residential property. In most areas, solicitors fought the fire of competition with fire, and in most areas solicitors have been able to maintain a healthy share of a greatly increased market. In most cities and towns, solicitors' property centres exist where the individual solicitor can enjoy the benefits of a main street shop window, corporate advertising, Solicitor Referral Schemes, property matching, financial advice, and a permanent staff to answer enquiries. These solicitors' property centres have proved highly successful throughout Scotland; until 1993 everywhere except Glasgow and its environs. Further details are given in Chapter 2.

The property centre concept was not initially successful in Glasgow, and when the original centre collapsed it was replaced by the Solicitors Estate Agency Limited (SEAL), a limited company owned by participating solicitors, but run by professional estate agents. In addition, several solicitors ran their own agencies, either under their own names or under an independent company. In 1993 the property centre idea was revived in Glasgow, and appears to be doing well. It is claimed that the centre accounts for (in May 1994) 20 per cent of residential sales in Glasgow and the west of Scotland. The Glasgow centre is centrally sited – 145/147 Queen Street, Glasgow (Telephone 0141–248 9044). For details of other centres, consult the legal directories.

1.21   Formerly, solicitors might not refer to themselves as 'estate agents' but have been permitted to do so for some years now. Solicitors may also refer to themselves by some of the more traditional designations, such as Writers to the Signet, Writers, or Advocates (member of the Society of Advocates in Aberdeen as opposed to a member of the Faculty of Advocates). This often causes confusion, as where the first edition of Yellow Pages in Glasgow listed all firms describing themselves as 'writers' under the generic heading of 'authors'.

A further designation widely used by solicitors is that of 'notary public'. A notary public is a person who can administer solemn oaths to persons signing deeds, the most common being inheritance tax forms being signed by executors, and affidavits prepared in terms of the Matrimonial Homes (Family Protection) (Scotland) Act 1981, as amended. (See Appendix III.) A notarial instrument had originally to be signed by a notary public, but the Conveyancing (Scotland) Act 1924 provided for a new notice of title, with the same feudalising function of the notarial instrument, which could be signed by any solicitor, whether a notary or not.

A notary public may also perform, in Scotland, the function of the roughly similar English functionary, known as the commissioner of oaths, and vice versa. When signing an English document, the Scottish notary signs as 'Notary Public, and as such a Commissioner of Oaths.'

The office of the notary public is an ancient one – said to date from the Holy Roman Empire – and the admission and conduct of notaries is now regulated by the Solicitors (Scotland) Act 1980, Part V.

1.22 Writing in 1990, I then quoted an article entitled 'Big Bang for the City's Law Firms' (*The Economist* 9–15 September 1989) which prophesied:

> 'By the end of the next decade there will probably be ten giant commercial law firms in the City of London, some of which will be American. They will each have a gross fee income of around £500 million. Alongside them will be niche firms, specialising in insolvency, tax, intellectual property, and entertainment etc. Partnerships will be a thing of the past. Most firms will have incorporated and are likely to belong to multi-disciplinary practices (ie part of a holding company of accountants, architects and surveyors), with Chinese walls and all.'

If we accept this as being a prophesy for London, it would probably apply equally in Scotland, but on a smaller scale, and a bit later in time.

'Chinese walls' are, incidentally, an informal arrangement devised under the re-structuring of the City (which allowed stockbrokers to be owned by banks). The concept purports to prevent one part of these huge businesses (eg stockbrokers dealing in shares) from benefiting from confidential information imparted to another part of the business (eg merchant banks who are selling a company, whose shares are being traded by the stockbrokers). The efficacy of this arrangement remains questionable, and there are still many allegations of persons with inside knowledge trading in the Stock Market, although this is now a criminal offence.

Writing in 1994, these prophesies still seem on course for fulfilment, although most legal firms have had to trim their size to cope with the recession. An article, again in *The Economist*, on 9–15 July 1994, predicts the end of partnership as a business organisation, and the end of unlimited liability for negligence. Because of the recession, however, it reports that fee income levels for corporate lawyers have little changed since 1989.

The law partnership was devised for the horse and carriage age (compare the firm of Spenlow & Jorkins in Charles Dickens' *David Copperfield*), and this was recognised by the Companies Act 1967, s 22, which abolished the rule preventing most partnerships having more than 20 partners. There are a considerable number of Scottish firms with more than 20 partners, and many London firms have around 50–100 partners.

Maintaining a balance between so many partners must be extremely difficult under the law of partnership as it stands, as must be the terms on which a new partner is admitted.

Many in the legal profession would argue that a company structure would be more suitable for the larger firms that now exist (the international accountancy firm KPMG has 6,000 partners and a fee income of $6 billion worldwide).

The Law Society has already enacted rules to allow solicitors to incorporate (Solicitors (Scotland) (Incorporated Practices) Practice Rules 1987). These allow (rule 4(8)) the companies to have limited liability, provided that the solicitors have a joint and several personal liability for any money misappropriated.

The Law Society has set its face against multi-discipline partnerships (MDPs). While it argued trenchantly, the white paper of October 1989 nevertheless recommends (at Chapter 3) the introduction of MDPs.

The legal profession will have to compete, but is surely strong enough to do so, and where the skill is deficient, it should be brought in (eg bookkeeping). Firms will probably become larger, and lawyers will spend less time on routine clerical work, which they should never have been doing in the first place. Lawyers will work more in teams, with each member of the team contributing specialist knowledge. There should, however, still be room for good general practitioners, who can handle the wide scope of day-to-day business. There will almost definitely no longer be any room for the practitioner who does not do anything particularly well.

1.23   As to the question in the title of this chapter, by all means you are welcome to the profession. These have not been easy years since the optimism of the late 1980s – for anyone, not just the legal profession. The recession bit very deeply, and there is argument as to whether it is really over. Writing in November 1994, no one seems certain whether the house market is going up or down. Firms have come and gone, other firms and their profits have shrunk, there have been redundancies, even at partner level. Training places in firms have proved increasingly difficult to obtain, although the problem is rather worse in England.

In the late 1980s, prices of houses rose at an unsustainable level, particularly in the south east of England. The joke was that houses made more per week than their owners did, except that it was not all that funny, because of the tremendous damage that it did to the economy. The government seems determined that this will not happen again, and appears to have inflation under control at last. The process has left many burned fingers, and the once unthinkable concept of 'negative equity' (when the amount borrowed to buy the house is now less than the sale price) has become a reality for many.

The disappearance of property inflation is not, I suppose, particularly good news for property lawyers, but the adjustment to a genuinely inflation-free economy could prove to be a pleasant one for us all.

Let us hope so!

Chapter two

Marketing the Property

'We were very concerned, bearing in mind the Property Misdescriptions Act, that we would be misleading by not telling about a ghost, but also misleading if we did come clean about it and then it didn't appear. We felt that if we knew of a ghost which eventually appeared it would only seem fair to tell the purchasers in case they freaked out later when they saw it.'
(Christopher Calcutt, estate agent in Kent, discussing the problems of haunted houses – *The Sunday Times*)

2.1 Most sale and purchase transactions start with houseowners deciding to move, and putting their property up for sale, although it is not unknown for the purchaser to initiate the process. It has been suggested that the entire contracting process could be speeded up if the seller issued an offer of sale, rather than the other way around. This idea has yet to be tested thoroughly.

As discussed above (**1.14**) the marketing process is not part of the solicitors' monopoly, and may be done by anyone. The choice between solicitor and estate agent is the houseowners', and to a large extent the answer to this question will depend on the services respectively offered, and the part of the country in which the house is situated.

2.2 For present purposes we shall assume that the houseowners choose to employ a solicitor to market the property, and that the solicitor is a member of a solicitors' property centre. It should be made quite clear, however, that property marketing has become a separate skill, and if a solicitor is to market property it must be done professionally and properly.

2.3 Some solicitors, particularly in Glasgow, may prefer to pass the marketing of houses to estate agents, and indeed many are members of SEAL (see **1.20**), and this is usually done on a reciprocal basis of instruction. In the case of a reciprocal arrangement being reached it should be remembered:

(a) That a solicitor may not share with any unqualified person any profits or fees derived from any business transacted by solicitors in Scotland in the course of or in connection with their practice. Certain exemptions, particularly relating to retired solicitors and their dependants, are made by the Solicitors (Scotland) Practice Rules 1991.

(b) Formerly under Practice Rules, a solicitor might not share an office in conjunction with a person who was not legally qualified. This rule has now been relaxed, provided that there is no question of breach of confidentiality in the sharing of staff, and provided that the accommodation is self-contained, and provided there is no suggestion of business being channelled unfairly to the solicitor by the other party involved. If you contemplate such an arrangement, it would be best to obtain a waiver from the Law Society. Among waivers granted are for small offices in supermarkets, and a solicitor and accountant in a remote area using the same premises on alternate days.

(c) That the basic philosophy of the Law Society is that the only acceptable form of channelling clients to a solicitor is on the personal recommendation of a satisfied client, although the Society admits that it is not always possible to prevent 'less desirable' forms of enticement (Law Society Annual Report 1981, p 14).

(d) Any suggestion of unfair enticement of clients should be most scrupulously avoided.

In essence the question of whether or not to use an estate agent is one of circumstances, and the only important criterion is the interest of the clients, which in the long run is also the interest of the solicitor.

2.4 If your clients are going to employ an estate agent, it is as well that the wording of the contract is carefully considered. A contract is only likely to diminish the rights of the client. The estate agents will seek sole selling rights, that is they are entitled to commission if the property is sold during the agreed period, whoever finds the buyer – even if it is the clients themselves. Some agents will try to make the agreed period a long one – six weeks should be sufficient, and not any longer. As to commission, the law is quite clear on the subject – if the estate agent is instrumental in the sale of the house, the agent is entitled to claim commission at the standard rate (*Walker Fraser & Steele* 1910 SC 222). If the agent is unsuccessful, the agent is then entitled to a reasonable remuneration for work done (*quantum meruit*) and for refunding of outlays incurred.

In particular, the clients should not be panicked into employing two agencies. The dangers of this arrangement were highlighted in an unreported case in Paisley Sheriff Court.

Mr & Mrs A decided to sell their house, and asked estate agents F to handle the sale. F duly advertised the sale, and several parties, including a Mr Q, inspected the property. No sale resulted. Mr & Mrs A then saw a property advertised by estate agents Z, and while negotiating with Z, they decided to entrust the sale of their own house to Z. They signed Z's standard sale contract, which required a commission to be paid on sale, whether they were instrumental in effecting a sale or not.

In the meantime, Mr Q returned from abroad, looked again at Mr & Mrs A's house, and bought it. Agents F claimed a commission as they had introduced Mr Q to the sellers. Agents Z also claimed a commission in terms of their contract. It was held that Mr & Mrs A had to pay both agents. (See also *Lordsgate Properties v Balcombe* [1985] 1 EGLR 20, (1985) 274 EG 493, and an article 'Double Jeopardy' in the Scottish Law Gazette December 1985.)

2.5 At whatever stage the solicitor is instructed (and we are assuming here that it is at the outset, although sometimes it is not so simple – the first thing you know about your client's intention to sell is when an offer drops onto your desk) the first thing is to obtain the title deeds of the property. This is important in order that you can ascertain whether or not the title is a registered one, and if there are any unusual conditions of title, such as rights of pre-emption or unusual servitude rights.

If the titles are missing, extracts or quick copies may be obtained from the Register, or in the case of a registered title, a new land and charge certificate can be obtained from the Register. It is also helpful at this stage to obtain a planning certificate from the district council (**3.20**), a roads certificate from the regional council (**3.23**), planning certificates, building warrants, completion certificates and superior's consent certificate authorising any development of the property which requires these permissions, or some of them (**3.24**), and guarantees of timber treatment, and double glazing (**3.25**). In the case of a first registration, it is also important to receive a Form 10A report, which is equivalent to a search, and P16 Report (**14.3**) lest there be any major discrepancy in the boundaries.

These papers should all be scrutinised carefully to ensure that there is nothing in them which would make a sale difficult, such as a clause of pre-emption (**7.28**) or in land registration cases, an exclusion of indemnity (**14.15(b)**) on the land certificate. Bearing in mind the complexity of offers, and the number of warranties that they now require (Chapter 3) it is as well to know your title before entering into missives, and if there is a weakness in your title, to compromise it with the purchasers' agents before missives are concluded. Better that than to reveal the weakness after conclusion of missives, when the purchasers may be happy to accept a breach of warranty, given blindly, as an excuse to resile from the transaction.

2.6 Armed with as much knowledge as possible, the solicitor who is marketing the property, can then prepare property details and instruct advertising.

It is therefore suggested that the solicitor who engages in selling houses should adopt a procedure broadly similar to that outlined here (although practice will obviously vary from office to office).

(a) **Register the house with the local solicitors' property centre,** if that is the chosen method of sale, which will help with the marketing by providing a 'high street' display facility for all properties, and will publish an advertisement in its weekly property list. The centres charge a one-off fee, and will hold the property until it is sold.

(b) **Obtain as much information as you can, as soon as you can.** The sellers' solicitor should at this stage obtain letters from the regional council (as to the roads etc) and district council (as to planning etc) and any necessary affidavits required in terms of the Matrimonial Homes (Family Protection) (Scotland) Act 1981 (see Appendix III). The reason for this is to avoid unfortunate delays by others at a future date, when the pressure is on you.

(c) **Visit the house in question, and take measurements and details.** Take a photograph for publicity purposes. Commercial processors will be able to provide you with 'sticky-backed' prints for annexing to particulars. Arrange the viewing – the easiest arrangement is to have the owners show the property, at times that suit them. If the house is empty, you can arrange to show it, but you may wish to agree extra remuneration for this. It is advisable that, wherever possible, two people conduct the viewings, and a representative of your firm should not be alone in an empty house, especially at night. If the house is empty, make sure that you have the key, and at least one spare in the office. NEVER let the key out of your control.

(d) **If the clients ask you to advise them on how to make the property more attractive to buyers, there are a few basic rules** – make the house and garden appear attractive from the street; attend to essential repairs; don't spend money on expensive redecoration which may not be to potential buyers' tastes, and is thus a waste of money; keep the house clean and tidy and well lit; avoid cooking and other smells; make sure that there is a parking space for buyers' cars; be ready to show the house at short notice. While furnishing, decor and personal items are usually insignificant compared to structure and location, it is nevertheless important to make a good impression on potential buyers.

(e) **Form a reasoned evaluation and advise the client.** If in doubt, consult a chartered surveyor for a valuation. The question of the surveyor's fee should, however, be discussed with the client before the surveyor is instructed.

(f) **Prepare an attractive, concise and truthful advertisement, giving rough details and a telephone number for further details and viewing.** If the house is not constantly occupied, do not indicate this by saying, for example 'viewing after 6pm'. You might as well put a notice in the *Crooks Gazette* intimating that the house will be unoccupied all day. Do not waste your clients' money on wasteful and over-elaborate advertisements. Eschew the temptation to advertise your firm more than the property. Outline your advertising proposals to your client, and provide a rough guide to the cost. When writing the advertisement, stick to the facts – try to avoid 'estate agentese'; some actual examples:

'Situated at a desirable crossroads';
'Designed by the celebrated Scottish architect, Ronnie Mackintosh';
'set in a child-safe cul-de-sac within this sought-after developing area';
'… with a field for the possible horse';
'suitable for the disearning (*sic*) purchaser';
'with an Adam TV den';
'positively oozing with olde worlde charm';
'with a 9ft high widow, overlooking the garden';
'with a glazed door in vestibule leading to hell'.

Such language is a casualty of the Property Misdescriptions Act 1991. Travel agents have had this problem for years and have evolved a new form of language which cannot be held as untruthful. Thus 'rapidly developing resort' means tower cranes and 'ideal for sun worshippers' means there's nothing else to do.

(g) **Similarly, prepare a schedule of particulars to be handed out to reasonably interested enquirers, giving truthful and accurate particulars of the house, preferably with a photograph and plan (if available)**

attached. Moveable items included in the sale should be clearly specified (see Appendix II. 12(3)). Bear in mind the Property Misdescriptions Act 1991 which makes it a criminal offence for an agent to misdescribe a property, or to 'touch up' a photograph to give a false impression. The Property Misdescriptions (Specified Matters) Order 1992 gives a list of specified matters that must be correctly stated in particulars of the property.

Oddly enough the Act ignores a misdescription by a person who sells the house personally.

(h) **Keep main details (eg price, entry, moveables included, rateable value, etc) preferably on computer or a card index.** Keep a list of all serious enquiries for future reference. Note in particular all formal notifications of interest, preferably on the back of the card.

(i) **Fix a closing date and advise all parties who have notified interest when it becomes clear that there is going to be competition (rough rule: when two surveyors have been to the property).** Collect all offers, and arrange to discuss these with the sellers, giving them your advice. Accept the offer most attractive to your clients (see **4.1**) and advise all unsuccessful offerors.

(j) **When missives are concluded, inform the property centre, cancel all advertisements and remove all boards, etc.** Nothing so much infuriates the general public as applying for details of an advertised house and being informed that 'it's sold'.

Chapter three

THE PURCHASERS MAKE OVERTURES

'How can we have a standardised offer for property when offers differ not only from town to town, but from firm to firm, and in our case from husband to wife?' (Letter from a married solicitor whose husband worked in a different firm)

'The reporter took the view that an estate agent's office, although classified as an office, was by nature a quasi-retail function involved in the buying and selling of property. The frequently changing window display was compulsive viewing for many people, necessary for others, and had a drawing power that could benefit other enterprises.'
(Scottish Planning Appeals, no 6, 117)

3.1 Really the first thing the purchasers should do is tell their solicitor that they are 'house-hunting'. This can hardly be done soon enough, as it gives the solicitors an opportunity to make available to the purchasers their expertise in the property market. The solicitors may even know of a suitable house on the market, and can give general advice on areas, neighbourhood schools and shops, price ranges and so on. The solicitors should at this stage also be able to give a good indication of the costs involved as these may make a substantial difference to the purchasers' target.

In particular, purchasers tend to forget that they may be liable to pay stamp duty on their purchase, and it really hurts them when they find that they have (say) an extra £700 to pay on a house costing £70,000.

The solicitors should warn the clients about this and other charges that may be overlooked. In terms of the Solicitors (Scotland) Act 1980, s 61A(a) where the solicitor and the client shall have reached a written agreement as to fees, it shall not be competent, in any litigation as to those fees, for the court to remit the solicitor's account for taxation. In terms of the Solicitors (Scotland) (Written Fee Charging Agreements) Practice Rules 1993 a written fee charging agreement shall not contain a consent to registration for preservation and execution, which would permit summary diligence to be done against the client. A quotation of fees and outlays may now be prepared (see examples in Appendix II.2).

Persons who buy a house at £75,000 may seem very rich to you but remember that they may be selling their old house at say £50,000 and finding the rest of the price by an increased loan. They are therefore paying by transfer of paper, and never really have this money: this is vulgarly referred to as 'buying with monopoly money'. If the purchasers do their sums wrongly, they have to make up the difference in 'real money', and usually at fairly short notice. It is only correct to advise them as to the costs involved, even if this has the effect of changing their mind about moving at all! Particular care should be taken to state whether or not a fee includes the VAT content – it can make a very significant difference (see **11.13**).

3.2   At the first meeting with the intending purchasers, the solicitors should take down the purchasers' instructions clearly and in detail, so that they are in a position to make an offer. Obviously the price and date of entry are the most crucial matters, but instructions should also be taken on every point that may arise in the missives.

The solicitors will also want to satisfy themselves that the clients can afford the property that they are bidding for. While the solicitors are only agents, and not financially responsible, if the clients default, the solicitor is nevertheless left in a very embarrassing position.

Anyone can make a mistake, but solicitors who get the reputation of acting for a series of defaulting clients can hardly expect their offers to be taken seriously in future. Like so many financial institutions the house market depends on a measure of mutual trust, which should not be breached lightly.

Solicitors should have a good idea of the financial worthiness of their existing clients and of persons recommended by existing clients. When, however, they do not know the clients, solicitors now have extra responsibilities under the Money Laundering Regulations (see **1.13(h)**) to verify the means of clients whom they have not known for two years. They are recommended, in these circumstances, to seek proof of identity by seeing full (not visitors') passports, full driving licences or signed company identity cards, with a photo forming an integral part of the card. Addresses can be verified by inclusion on the voters' roll, invoices for utilities payments, and a full driving licence.

Many lenders will now issue mortgage certificates which state exactly how much they will lend on the borrowers' income. This involves verifying income details in advance of the purchasers choosing a house, and puts the clients on the starting block while the rest are still in their tracksuits.

3.3   The solicitors should then notify the selling agents of their clients' interest in the house concerned. To respectable agents, this means that a sale will not be concluded without notifying all those who have notified an interest (see **2.6(i)**) and giving them a chance to offer, even on a short time limit. You should also note carefully the terms of the Law Society Guidelines on Closing Dates 1991, which, in summary, do not permit a solicitor, who has been instructed by a client to enter into negotiations with a party to complete a bargain, to accept subsequent instructions to enter into negotiations with, or accept an offer from, another party. At this stage the solicitors should also ask for full details of the property, if they have not already received these.

3.4   The next point to be considered is that of survey, probably the single most controversial topic in the whole process of house purchase. The difficulty is the apparently very high cost of surveys. Having said that, like any other good professional advice, a good survey can save thousands of pounds and much heartache. The difficulty arises when a survey is not properly done, and the purchasers find themselves without recourse against the surveyors who were negligent.

Surveys are broadly of four types:

(a) The 'walkthrough' valuation. This means exactly what it says; the surveyor walks through the property, and gives what all understand to be a rough valuation for whatever purpose it is required. This valuation confers no rights on the persons instructing it.

(b) A mortgage valuation survey, which is instructed usually by a lending institution, and is rather more thorough than (a), but less thorough than (c). The institution requires to know what value could be realised in the event of the property having to be sold on default by the borrowers before it lends money (**3.6**). No liability to the prospective purchaser is accepted by the surveyors, as to the condition or value of the property.

(c) A full structural survey, which is a very thorough survey, and which gives the persons instructing the survey a right to reparation in the event of there being negligence on the part of the surveyor. This survey obviously is very much more expensive than the others, but should be seriously considered in every case, but especially where an older house is being bought.

(d) House buyer's report and valuation, which is a halfway house between (a) and (b). Building societies will arrange for the surveyor making a valuation for them to prepare a short, written report for the purchaser. This will cost more than (b) and less than (c), and will give much less detail than (c). The surveyor will generally not move fitted carpets or heavy furniture, climb onto sloping roofs, or test drains, electrical, gas, heating and water services. This report is also heavily hedged with disclaimers against any form of negligence claims.

The exact value of such disclaimers has recently been the topic of much litigation, which disclosed a worrying discrepancy between Scottish and English practice. In *Harris v Wyre Forest District Council, Smith v Bush* [1989] 2 All ER 514, HL (both decisions of the House of Lords in English appeals) it was held that the disclaimers contained in a survey report fell foul of the provisions of Part I of the Unfair Contract Terms Act 1977. The particular sections referred to are s 2 (2) where it is provided that a person cannot exclude or restrict liability for negligence except in so far as the terms or notice satisfy the requirement of reasonableness; and s 11(3) which provides that in relation to a notice (not being a notice having contractual effect) the requirement of reasonableness is that it should be fair and reasonable to allow reliance on it, having regard to all the circumstances obtaining when the liability arose or (but for the notice) would have arisen.

A similar case was that heard in the Court of Session in June 1989, which considered the recent House of Lords judgment in *Harris* – the Scottish case being *Robbie v Graham & Sibbald* 1989 SLT 870, 1989 SCLR 578. In this case the pursuers' building society instructed a survey and the buyers accepted the option of a report and mortgage valuation. The pursuers signed the loan application, requesting the report, wherein it was stated:

'(a) the survey is limited and may not reveal defects that a more detailed survey would discover;

(b) neither the society nor the surveyor gives any warranty regarding the report's accuracy;

(c) the surveyor does not accept responsibility to applicants or to any other person.'

Subsequently dry rot was found in the house and the pursuers had to take remedial steps, and sued the defenders for the losses incurred.

These disclaimers are precisely the kind of disclaimers that were blown aside in *Harris*, yet it was held by the court in *Robbie* (albeit rather reluctantly) that if the disclaimer was in clear and unambiguous terms – as in this case – then it must be upheld in the Scottish courts. The reason for this is that Part I of the Act did not apply in Scotland, but Part II does, and by s 15(1) that the provisions preventing a party relying on an exclusion or restriction of liability clause apply only to contracts, and it is further provided by s 25(3)(d) that any reference to excluding or restricting any liability includes notices 'having contractual effect'.

The court held that the disclaimer by the defenders in this case was not a notice having contractual effect, that there was not contractual relationship between the pursuers and the defenders, and accordingly effect must be given to the disclaimers.

Fortunately the Law Reform (Miscellaneous Provisions) Act 1990 was going through its Bill stage at this time, and the law was amended to apply Part I of the Act to Scotland, and thus to bring Scottish law in line with English law on the point of disclaimers, which do not therefore now protect the negligent surveyor. Surveyors, however, now combat the danger of litigation by suggesting that the report of a specialist contractor be taken if there is any sign of a defect in a house, such as dry rot, wet rot or woodworm.

3.5   When purchasers are buying solely from their own resources, and the house is old or unusual, the advice of the solicitors to their clients clearly must be to have a structural survey done. If, despite this advice, the purchasers say they do not want a survey, that is their privilege. The solicitors should, however, (as a matter of self-preservation) obtain a letter from the purchasers stating that they were advised by the solicitors to have the property surveyed, but decided against this on their own volition, or at least the solicitors should write to the purchasers advising a survey, and keep a copy of the letter on file.

3.6   The real trouble arises, however, where a building society is involved. The building society will require (Building Societies Act 1986, s 13) its own valuation survey to be prepared. While the fee is payable to the surveyor by the society, and then refundable by the purchasers, and the purchasers have no rights under this contract, they are not parties to the contract and cannot therefore take advantage of it (*Gloag on Contract*, 2nd Edn, chapter XIII).

Complaints are, therefore, frequently made by purchasers: (a) that the house they have bought is in some way defective, and why did the surveyor instructed by the society not tell them? (b) what did they pay a surveyor for? (c) further, have they a claim for damages against the surveyor?

The answer to these questions is (a) the surveyor is not in contractual relationship with the purchasers, and need not tell them anything; (b) the surveyor is paid by the society technically; and (c) for the same reason, no! The surveyor may, however, be liable in delict. (See **3.4**.) In any event the survey is a valuation survey which costs less than a structural survey but is also much less rigorous than a structural survey and it usually means that the surveyor has not checked under the floor, the roof space, or the plumbing and electrical systems, and followed the trail of any rot.

All the surveyor is doing is telling the building society that the property is sufficient security for the loan requested, although as a matter of practice, if the surveyor sees a defect he will point it out to the society, who will tell the borrowers.

3.7 While this is impeccable law, it is poor common sense, and purchasers having (in their minds) paid for a surveyor, will obviously be aggrieved to find that they have no recourse against that surveyor. Really the only safe course open to the purchasers is to instruct a structural survey for themselves (the halfway house) as well as paying for the society's valuation survey. These can be done simultaneously, with an appropriate reduction in fees. It is nevertheless an expensive business, but particularly to be recommended, especially with older property.

3.8 One might ask why, in a perfect world, the sellers should not instruct a survey, which would be available to all interested parties? There are, however, tremendous problems of privity of contract, and liability in negligence, to say nothing of fairly strenuous opposition from building societies and surveyors. This item surfaces from time to time but nothing much seems ever to be done about it.

3.9 Having looked at the property, obtained full details, satisfied themselves that the clients can afford the property and that the house has had some sort of survey, the purchasers' solicitors are now in a position to lodge their clients' offer.

3.10 The offer should be made by the purchasers' solicitors, on behalf of and to the instructions of their clients, to the sellers or the selling agents. Only in the most unusual circumstances should the principals' name not be disclosed, bearing in mind the liabilities upon agents for undisclosed principals.

If solicitors or estate agents are selling the house, do not send an offer directly to the clients and, conversely, if you have been dealing exclusively with the owners ask them to whom the offer should be sent. Do not in the latter case send an offer to someone who claims to be the selling agent. Not only is it discourteous to do so, but you may land the purchasers as witnesses in the middle of a squabble between the sellers and their agents.

Only in the most unusual circumstances should the principals' names not be disclosed, bearing in mind that solicitors who do not disclose the fact that the offer is on behalf of named clients may be personally liable to fulfil the contract, and definitely liable if the fact is not disclosed at all that the offer is made on behalf of clients.

3.11 The offer is made (generally) in the form of a letter on the solicitors' notepaper, and 'adopted as holograph' (see below, however) and signed by a partner of the firm, indicating an intention to make the offer binding upon their clients. Do not fall into the trap of letting a person who is not a partner of the firm sign the letter. In the case of *Littlejohn* 1974 SLT (Sh Ct) 82 the manager of the branch of an estate agency, who had a mandate from his firm to run the branch, but who was not a partner of the firm, signed the firm's name on an offer on behalf of a client. This was held not to be binding on their client in terms of the Partnership Act 1893, s 6 and the 'agreement' completed was annulled by the court. It is not necessary to sign every page (Conveyancing and Feudal Reform (Scotland) Act 1970, s 44) but a cautious practitioner will normally do so. The Scottish Law Commission issued a report entitled Report on Requirement of Writing (Scot Law Com no 112) suggesting widescale changes in the practice of formal writings, including the replacement of the 'adopted as holograph' device, and this has (from 1 August 1995) been implemented by s 11(3)(b) of the Requirements of Writing (Scotland) Act 1995.

3.12   If the solicitors do not wish their name to be involved in the contract, for whatever reason, the offer may be drawn up in the offerors' name and be signed by the offerors themselves.

Every firm has its own style of missive, but a reasonably typical exchange of letters is printed in Appendices I and II and explanations are made in **3.13** of their different forms.

Please do not forget that every house has its own different features, and each offer must be very carefully drawn up on its merits, and not merely copied from your last offer without thought.

3.13   As mentioned, every firm has its own letter of offer, and there is no style that I can hold before you as 'totally typical'. The letter of offer should be simply a letter containing the full offer, but it is probably more common today for the letter to be quite short and to contain only essential details (address, price, date of entry, and specification of moveables contained in the sale) and for there to be a Schedule annexed containing compendious and all-embracing clauses.

In England there is a National Conveyancing Protocol (Third Edition 1994) which very much standardises the documentation of conveyancing, but not so in Scotland. The Law Society introduced a standard offer for property, but this met with derision from the profession, for a variety of reasons, some bad, some good. Suffice it to say that the standardised offer has not caught on in Scotland.

While the production by firms of their own conditions of offer (as opposed to the proposed standard Law Society conditions) is attractive for the sake of speed and uniformity, it has these drawbacks:

(a)   as every firm has its own, sometimes very lengthy, conditions, each of these long offers must be carefully evaluated against a variety of equally long offers from other firms. This can be a very complex business.

(b)   From the point of view of the offeror, the temptation exists to use these Schedules uncritically, thereby leaving in conditions that have become out of date or are inappropriate, and omitting new conditions framed to suit changed circumstances. Stories abound of solicitors receiving offers for a farm, and finding in it a clause relating to common parts of a tenement, or of solicitors selling a chip shop receiving an offer which demanded a matrimonial affidavit to be produced. The reply to the latter demand was that this particular shop was not a matrimonial chip shop. This, however, is careless conveyancing, and surely with the aid of modern technology, the profession can do better.

(c) A less scrupulous firm may be tempted to insert a 'poison pill' – that is a provision prejudicial to the seller hidden in a long formal clause that the eye is tempted to skip.

(d) Solicitors who use standard forms uncritically and repetitively may remember the arguments that it doesn't require a lawyer to press the start button on a word processor or photocopier. (Compare **1.18**.)

3.14 Having said that, I have printed in Appendix II.11 a long letter of offer which is really a set of standard conditions that are disguised to look like a letter. I would like to examine this letter in detail, and explain its purpose, because it does include a lot of points that should be remembered.

The preamble

3.15 The client's name and address should be stated quite clearly so that the principal is fully 'disclosed' in the legal sense. A selling solicitor should think very carefully before accepting an offer that does not disclose the principal, lest the missives have to be enforced. The question then is 'against whom?' and why not the solicitor? The subjects are then clearly described, but a postal address, rather than a full conveyancing description will suffice. A postcode, wherever possible, should be used, to help avoid ambiguity. People tend to be vague about postcodes, but try and get this information. It can always be obtained from the Postcode Directory at the Post Office.

The date of entry

3.16 This is the date when the price is paid and possession is given and titles handed over. The date is a matter for negotiation between the parties but it should allow time for both parties comfortably to meet their obligations.

A small point to be considered by both parties is the availability of removal firms. For example, the last Friday of any month is a popular date for flitting and it may be very difficult to make suitable arrangements.

It was decided in *Gordon District Council* 1988 SLT 481 that a stated date of entry is not essential to the validity and enforceability of missives.

Specification of moveables

3.17 The more carefully these are specified the better, especially in cases where there may be genuine doubt as to whether an object is heritable or moveable. While it may appear to be a bit fussy to include bulbs and flexes, please bear in mind that these indispensable objects are fully moveable. They may be removed by the seller if not specified to be included in the sale – and often are! By and large the law of fixtures applies, except as modified by agreement, but nothing should be left to the mercy of this vague law. Consider, for instance, the telephone. Formerly this instrument was hired from British Telecom and was not removable except by one of their engineers. Now you can buy a plug-in telephone, which is moveable, and remove it on leaving. A price for moveables only may be stated in the offer, for only heritage bears stamp duty. Stamp duty currently starts at £60,001 and is at a rate of one per cent of the total price. Thus, if you buy a house at £61,000, you will pay stamp duty of £610. But if the seller can fairly certify that the moveable property is valued at £1,000, then the value of the heritage is £60,000 and no stamp duty is payable. It must be stressed, however, that the valuation of moveables must justify the certificate given by the seller, who does not enjoy the benefit anyway.

Consideration should be given to the case of *Saunders* ([1987] 1 WLR 116, CA) where it was stated that if the valuation of moveables is artificially inflated, the court may not enforce other parts of the contract, and that a solicitor indulging in this practice may be guilty of professional misconduct. Such a practice may also be classed as tax evasion, with the consequent penalties.

Title conditions

3.18   This is a reasonable clause, but these are technically matters for the purchasers to satisfy themselves on, when examining titles. In particular, the term 'unusual' conditions is a vague one, and this term invites an answer from the sellers' solicitors, sending the title deeds and inviting the purchasers' solicitors to satisfy themselves on the point within so many days. The case of *Morris v Ritchie* 1992 GWD 33–1950 commented on in the *Scottish Law Gazette* in March 1993, makes it clear that all unusual conditions, including servitudes, should be disclosed before missives are concluded.

Maintenance of property

3.19   The common law rule, enshrined in this clause, is that the person who orders the repairs shall pay for them, unless the contract provides otherwise. The prudent purchasers' solicitors may want confirmation that no such repairs have been ordered and not yet done, or have been done but not yet paid for. This may be verified by a certificate from the appropriate district council.

Planning et cetera, certificates and environmental matters

3.20   The entire question of local authority notices is dealt with at **18.7** in connection with flats. Such notices are more likely to be a problem in flatted property, but the notices can basically be served on any property. It is considered generally to be a primary responsibility of the sellers to obtain the certificate, in the view of the Law Society, and sellers' solicitors should not be allowed to contract out of this, unless in exceptional circumstances. It is obviously a matter of some importance to ensure (for example) that the regional or district council is not about to acquire the house, or knock it down for any one of a multiplicity of purposes.

The existence of any such notices may be ascertained by writing to the planning department of the district council, who will issue a letter stating either that there are no such notices, or alternatively that there are. The correct addresses of various councils are detailed in the Scottish Law Directory and The Blue Book. You can obtain a note of the fee payable by telephoning the authority in question.

In purchases of development property particularly, it will now be important to obtain a clear environmental audit, for in many cases houses are built on land that has been used for contaminative uses. In its very useful booklet 'Buyer Beware', Friends of the Earth tells of land near Chatham on which it was intended to build 2,000 houses. Although the land was thought to be virgin agricultural land, it turned out to be heavily contaminated with heavy metals and blue asbestos, and had been part of the naval dockyard. The developers were forced to spend £30 million on cleaning up the site before building work commenced. There are many such examples in Scotland as well, and obviously a builder would not want to purchase such land, and such a liability.

Further, owning a building listed as of special architectural or historical interest, or a piece of land listed as a SSI (special scientific interest – the rural equivalent of a listed building) may be very pleasant, but there are many restrictions on development, which a purchaser may not wish to undertake.

The sellers' obligations

3.21 This is an extremely long clause because it contains the sellers' obligations in (a) a register of sasines sale, (b) a first land registration sale and (c) a second or subsequent land registration sale.

The obligation in (a) is to produce a disposition, marketable title and a clear search. In the other two cases the sellers have to produce a disposition but then the obligations vary widely. They are further discussed at **7.4, 14.2** and **15.2**. The most significant difference between the sasine obligation and the land register obligation is that in the former the sellers more or less disappear at settlement, it being a case of *caveat emptor*, while in land registration the sellers are kept 'on the hook' until a land certificate is issued, which is clear of any restrictions of indemnity.

Rates and feuduty

3.22 (See Chapter 11.) The absence of this clause would not prejudice the offer. A reasonable rateable value and feu duty are presumed by law and the redemption provisions for feu duties and other pecuniary burdens are statutory. A slight misstatement of either of these figures (or of the council rate band) would be ignored under the rule *de minimis non curat lex*, but a serious misstatement might lead to the purchaser resiling. Thus in *Bremner* 1911 SC 887 the contract stated that the feu duty was £2.25 but in fact this was an unallocated portion of a feu duty of £4.40. The purchaser was entitled to resile. While under the C & FR (S) Act 1970, ss 3 to 6, this could not happen today, for the feuduty could be allocated, the general principle probably still remains.

Settlements are dealt with in Chapter 11. This clause sets out the division of rates between the parties at that time.

Rates do not now apply to domestic properties (see Chapter 10) and any reference to rates is only applicable to commercial properties.

Roads, footpaths, and sewers

3.23 Generally the region will maintain these artefacts, but if they do not, the purchasers will want to be assured that there is no liability for formation or maintenance. This is most crucial in the purchase of a newly-built house and in rural areas. This topic is discussed in detail in **6.6 ff.**

Most houses in cities, towns and even villages in Scotland have public road, mains water and mains drainage. This may not be the case in the country. In which case please consider:

(a) has the house got sufficient access for the needs of the purchasers, and what are the rights of other parties over the road? Who pays for maintenance?

(b) is there a sufficient water supply (*tantum et tale*) – as to amount and quality and adequate rights to pipe this water into the house (vice versa drainage)?

Extensions and alterations

3.24 If these are material the sellers should obtain planning consent, building warrant and if required, superior's consent. When the work is done a completion certificate from the building sub-committee should be obtained, vouching that the work has been properly done. The purchasers should require to see all of these documents. In *Winston* (see infra **3.28**) the work was not properly done and all sorts of trouble was caused by this, because the house had been accepted without this point being verified.

Treatment certificates

3.25 These should be produced by the sellers as stated, and may be simply assigned to the purchasers if desired.

NHBC certificates

3.26 These certificates guarantee the owner against loss through faulty workmanship not being corrected by the builder (see **7.33**) in various degrees for a period of ten years. These should be handed over on sale. This request should not be made for an older house which is obviously more than ten years old. In the case of a small builder who is not a member of NHBC, the purchasers should see an architect's certificate of inspection, which certifies that, in the architect's opinion, work is complete (see **7.33**).

Insurance risk

3.27 The rule is *res perit suo domino*: the thing perishes to (the risk of) its owner. In the case of *Sloans Dairies* 1979 SLT 17 it was clearly re-affirmed that once missives have been concluded the risk of damage or destruction of the subject passed to the purchasers (even where, as in this case, a date of entry had not yet been agreed). Technically the *emptio* becomes *perfecta* on completion of missives. (See the comments on this case by Professor Robert Black in JLSS, October 1982, p 405.) It may not seem entirely logical that risk should pass without possession, which is the reason for inserting this clause which returns the risk to the sellers. The sellers, of course, sensibly maintain their fire insurance until the date of entry.

Where this clause is not inserted, risk passes to the purchasers, who must insure this interest forthwith by taking out fire cover. Their insurable interest is 'as purchaser, price unpaid', a clearly defined category of insurance.

It is of course up to the solicitors to make sure that this is done, because a layman could not be expected to understand this quirk of property law. If the solicitors are worried about forgetting this, they can buy a lot of contentment for a small price by having their own 'longstop' fire insurance policy – which gives block cover against damage over all houses the firm is handling in the event of their being uninsured elsewhere. The Scottish Law Commission has prepared a discussion paper on this topic entitled 'Passing of Risk in Contracts for the Sale of Land' (1989 Scot Law Com no 81).

Survival of provisions in missives

3.28 This clause is incorporated because of the decision in *Winston v Patrick* 1981 SLT 41.

In *Winston*, the pursuers were the purchasers of a detached bungalow which had an extension at the rear, which extension had been constructed by the removal of part of the original wall.

The defenders had obtained a building warrant for this extension and had undertaken to construct it in accordance with the approved plans.

Clause 9 of the missives provided:

'The seller warrants that all statutory and local authority requirements in connection with the erection of the subjects and any additions, extensions and alterations thereto have been fulfilled.'

The pursuers accordingly contended that the defenders were in breach of contract and thus liable in damage. The defenders argued successfully that the disposition had been delivered to the pursuers and accepted by them, and that the missives were accordingly superseded.

The basic rules of Scots law in the sale of heritage is that:

(a) formal missives supersede all prior communings (eg property circulars et cetera), unless there is a misrepresentation when reference may be made to these prior communings; and

(b) that the disposition on delivery supersedes missives unless:

   (i) the point at issue is not one that would normally arise in a contract for the sale of heritage – for example, furniture included in the sale; see *Jamieson v Welsh* (1900) 3 F 176.

   (ii) where there is essential error in the description of the heritage in the disposition, but the description is correct in the missives, then the missives may be referred to – *Anderson v Lambie* 1954 SC (HL) 43.

   (iii) where the disposition is ambiguous but the missives are not, the missives may be referred to – *Duke of Fife v Great North of Scotland Railway Company* (1901) 3 F (HL) 2.

   (iv) where the disposition is delivered, but there turns out to be a conflicting interest under previous missives, the disposition will be reduced – *Rodger (Builders) Ltd* 1950 SC 483.

   (v) where the parties agree to leave the missives or any part of them applicable.

Winston v Patrick does not displace this provision of law, rather it confirms it (see 1981 SLT 41 at 49). Where it does create difficulties is for the practical conveyancer who wishes to keep a personal or collateral obligation in force despite the delivery of the disposition, owing to the confusing and contradictory litigation and comment that has followed *Winston* (for a full account of this see 6 *Stair Memorial Encyclopaedia* para 566 and its updating service).

It is now perfectly obvious, however, that the only safe advice a book of this nature can give is (i) to put a clause into missives, keeping the missives alive for a two-year period (Appendix II.11); (ii) to insert a non-supersession clause in the disposition which has the same effect (**9.73 (g)**); and (iii) to deliver a letter after delivery of the deed at settlement, stating more or less the same thing (Appendix II.11 (Schedule 2)). This procedure is cumbersome and repetitive, but above all it is safe.

Matrimonial affidavits

3.29   This clause reflects the provisions of the Matrimonial Homes (Family Protection) (Scotland) Act 1981, as amended by the Law Reform (Miscellaneous Provisions) (Scotland) Act 1985. This first Act was one of impeccable social purpose, but which neglected to allow for the problems it might create in numerous cases where there was no particular social purpose to fulfil. It is a matter of great pleasure to record that the second Act considerably simplified the operation of this first Act, without diminishing the social usefulness of the first.

A matrimonial home is a house, caravan, houseboat et cetera, provided by one spouse for the use of his or her spouse and their family (MH(FP)(S) Act 1981, s 22). The scope of the legislation also includes persons who co-habit without being married to the extent mentioned in the Act.

If the title stands in the name of one spouse only ('the entitled spouse') and a sale is to be made of the matrimonial home, or if the matrimonial home is to be burdened with a security in favour of a third party, it is required that the other spouse ('the non-entitled spouse') should either be a consenter to the sale document, or should sign a renunciation of his or her right to remain in occupation of the property, or (if not in occupation) his or her right to re-enter the home and re-occupy it.

Styles of the forms of consent and renunciation are given at Appendix III with detailed notes as to their preparation. The form of renunciation requires to be signed before a notary public or any other person outwith Scotland who is authorised by law to administer oaths or receive affirmations in the country of signature. In England, this would be a commissioner of oaths (**1.21**). As this all requires a great deal of additional work, it is usually simpler to include the consent in the deed, and to have the non-entitled spouse sign the deed as a consenter. (Appendix III.)

If the title to a matrimonial home is in joint names of the two spouses, as is increasingly the case these days, both will sign the deed transferring or burdening the property, and nothing further is required under the legislation.

Where the property being sold is not a matrimonial home (eg an investment property, or a holiday house), or the proprietor is not married, the proprietor is required to sign an affidavit to the effect that the property is not a matrimonial home. (Appendix III.)

The necessary consent, renunciation or affidavit formerly had to be delivered at or before delivery of the disposition or standard security in favour of the third party, but now may be retrospective (Law Reform (Miscellaneous Provisions) (Scotland) Act 1985, s 13(5)(b)(iii). In registration of title cases the Keeper must be satisfied by a statement from the solicitor presenting the deed for registration that this is the case. (Forms 1, 2, and 3, and question 8 in Form 1, reproduced in Appendix II.21(h).)

Where the seller has signed a power of attorney authorising another person to conclude the documentation on their behalf, please note that an attorney cannot sign a matrimonial document, and that alternative measures should be taken in this respect.

Failure to observe these rules can have disastrous consequences. The worst things that could happen are as follows:

You act for clients purchasing a house from a person who produces a title in his or her own name. You forget to ask for a consent, renunciation or affidavit from the non-entitled spouse. Your clients settle into their new home. The non-entitled spouse of the previous owner then asserts his or her right to re-occupy the house.

Alternatively, although the occupancy right is not claimed, your clients try to sell the house within the five-year period, in which the non-entitled spouse could have asserted the right. Your clients will have considerable difficulties in selling, because the title is simply not marketable, owing to the risk of re-occupancy.

The second possibility is stronger than the first, but neither is fanciful. The only way out of the dilemma is for an insurance indemnity to be obtained against the possibility of the non-entitled spouse re-appearing (**7.44(f)**). Clearly you, not having done your job properly, should pay the single premium involved. It is actually not very expensive, when compared to the possible embarrassment that might result otherwise.

Family Law (Scotland) Act 1985

3.30   The Family Law (Scotland) Act 1985, s 8(1)(aa) enables either party in an action of divorce to apply to the court for an order transferring property to him or her by the other party to the marriage. Such a decree will of course be registered in the General Register or Land Register, but purchasing solicitors should be careful in case such an order has been granted, but not yet registered. The sellers' warranty that there are no such orders is an additional protection.

This provision has given many difficulties, principally with valuation of the property, but difficulties can also arise where the divorcing couple owns the property on a survivorship destination. See John H Sinclair 'Conveyancing Aspects of Property Transfer Orders' January 1993 *Greens Family Law Bulletin* 3.

Time limit

3.31   A time limit may be put in the offer to put pressure on the sellers. If this device is used, it should be a realistic time limit and should allow time for the letter to arrive and for the sellers' agents to take instructions according to circumstances (ie a solicitor in Glasgow should not put a 24-hour time limit on an offer to a solicitor in, say, Inverness, unless special arrangements are made). If the sellers' solicitors do not wish to be put under pressure, or if they have another buyer 'up their sleeve', they should inform the purchasers' solicitors accordingly, and delete this clause if they do accept the offer. (Condition 17 of your offer is deleted.) Please also note that the time limit contained in the offer in question states that the offer must be received 'here' by such and such a time, which cuts out ambiguity. The entire negotiation process can be telescoped by intelligent use of FAX. (See **4.6**.)

The minerals clause

3.32   'The minerals are included in the sale only in so far as belonging to the seller.'

This clause is really a nonsense, but it has to go in, unless you are sure that you are in a position to sell the minerals, which is very seldom the case – certainly in urban areas.

The reason for this is a logical one – although the practical result is ridiculous. When you buy land, you buy the slice of earth's crust from the centre of the earth to the heaven (*a coelo usque ad centrum*). If someone else owns the minerals, you cannot give this layer, and the missives must therefore be qualified to that effect. The case of *Campbell* 1963 SLT 290 quite clearly sets out this doctrine, and in this case missives not containing the clause were declared to be non-binding because the sellers could not give what they have contracted to sell. What is more, the sellers were not allowed time to acquire these mineral rights. The Halliday Committee (Cmnd 3118, 1966) suggested that the requirement for this clause be made unnecessary, but nothing was done about this apparently quite uncontroversial recommendation, presumably an oversight, which could easily be remedied.

If the minerals do not belong to the sellers, the purchasers' solicitors may want to provide that the minerals cannot be exploited by a third party without adequate compensation being paid to the house owner.

The *actio quanti minoris*

3.33   This phrase can be very literally translated as 'the action of how much less'. (Literal translations of Roman maxims usually produce such clumsy results, which is why we tend to retain the original Latin.) It is an action of Roman law that was imported into Scots law for moveable property, but not for heritable property. (For a fuller discussion of the law on this topic, see 6 *Stair Memorial Encyclopaedia* para 566.)

This action allows the purchasers of property that is subject to a fault, which was not apparent at the time of purchase, to recover part of the purchase price, while retaining the property. Strangely enough this equitable solution is not available in Scots law for heritable property, unless it is specifically included in the contract. (See *Fortune v Fraser* 1993 SLT (Sh Ct) 68, where the Sheriff Principal held that the contract contained no provision for the *actio*, and as it did not exist in Scots law, the pursuer had no remedy.) If it is not included, the purchasers who discover a fault in the property have no remedy other than *restitutio in integrum* (total restitution of the property to the sellers and the price to the purchasers) which is usually impossible by the time the fault is discovered. It seems rather odd that Scots law, which so enthusiastically welcomed other Roman law equitable remedies, does not accept this one, and leaves people to include it by contract.

In the case of *Campbell* (**3.32**) if the *actio* had been available, a reduction in the purchase price might simply have been ordered, and the sale might have proceeded as agreed.

While there is no recent case law specifically on the matter, the inclusion of this clause appears to be a sensible precaution.

3.34   These are the most standard of conditions contained in missives, but there may of course be many others. The only 'right' offer is the one your firm uses.

Acceptance of this offer constitutes a binding contract which the courts will enforce (see *Rodger (Builders) Ltd* 1950 SC 483; *Johnstone* 1978 SLT (N) 81 and many others). The sellers should not therefore accept any of the conditions of the purchasers' offer unless they are sure they can fulfil these.

It is, however, permissible in certain circumstances to insert a suspensive condition; eg you buy a house intending to turn it into a hotel; you offer £50,000 instead of the market value of £30,000 but only if you get planning permission for use of the house as a hotel. You therefore 'suspend' the deal until this permission is obtained; if it is not granted, the deal falls. A prudent seller will put a time limit on the suspension. In such circumstances see *Imry Property Holdings Ltd* 1979 SLT 261. On this topic see also the article by RB Wood in JLSS June 1980 Workshop, p 129.

If purchasers insert a suspensive clause which permits them to withdraw if planning permission is not 'to their satisfaction', the courts will construe this clause as excluding capriciousness and arbitrary actings, and will imply a condition of reasonableness. (*Gordon District Council v Wimpey Homes Holdings Ltd* 1989 SLT 141.)

If the date of entry is left unascertainable, the courts will have little power to fix a date of entry which is indeterminate. Thus, while the Conveyancing (Scotland) Act 1924, s 28, allows a date of entry to be fixed in conveyances, this does not include missives (see *Gordon District Council v Wimpey Homes Holdings Ltd* above).

Chapter four

THE SELLERS ACCEPT

'When acting for an elderly lady, I was instructed to accept a far lower offer for her house than had been made by someone else. In enquiring the reason for this, the lady explained that the higher offeror owned an alsatian, and the cat next door would not like that.'
(Clydebank conveyancer, as told to the author)

4.1 The sellers' agents receive all offers and submit them to the sellers for instruction together with such advice as they may feel necessary.

Thus a slightly lower offer may actually be preferable to a higher offer, if there is a significant difference in the dates of entry and the lower offeror is prepared to name a date of entry suitable to the sellers, while the higher offeror is not. If the sellers want to sell in a month's time a slightly lower offer with this date of entry may well be preferable to a higher offer with a date of entry in two months. Think of the interest the sellers may lose by accepting the second offer.

That apart, the highest offer should in normal circumstances be preferred although in law the sellers are not bound to accept the highest offer, or indeed any offer.

However, there have doubtless been many occasions on which a lower offer has been accepted for extraneous reasons, eg 'they were such a nice young couple' is a very common syndrome. Sellers can also take a violent dislike to viewers who criticise the house too volubly.

This pleasure of accepting a poorer offer from someone you like is not, however, open to persons acting in a fiduciary capacity, such as trustees, heritable creditors, et cetera. Please note also the possibly contrary effects of the Race Relations Act 1976, ss 21, 22, 43 and 57.

4.2 What is important is that there must be fair dealing by the sellers' agents, and that everyone should get a fair chance. Our selling system of closed bidding is a fertile breeding ground if not for malpractices, then for suspicion and accusation of malpractice.

The rule is that the terms of no one's offer should ever, under any circumstances, be made known to another offeror. This is an ethical rule, not enforceable at law, but solicitors break it at the peril of their good reputation. You may, by bending the rule, have some cheap triumph at the start, but sooner or later your reputation will overtake you. If you are tempted, as with all ethical considerations, think 'would I like someone to do that to me?'.

4.3 The following practices are extremely dubious.

(a) The Dutch auction. Anybody who has been at a flower auction in Holland will tell you that a 'Dutch auction' is simply a sale in which the auctioneer offers the goods at gradually decreasing prices, the first bidder to accept being the purchaser. This is just as legitimate as a system of starting with a low bid and moving progressively higher.

The words 'Dutch auction' have, however, acquired a slightly sinister meaning (compare the British habit of blaming the Dutch and the French for everything as in Dutch courage, Dutch treat, Dutch talent, et cetera) of an underhand sale, where the sellers take advantage of our system of closed bidding by revealing genuine offers to other bidders in an attempt to force up the price. You should not get involved in this, especially as a seller, but also as a lawyer. If the purchasers are suspicious that a Dutch auction may develop, they should put an offer in with a very short time limit. Quite apart from moral considerations, if someone says to you 'We have an offer of £x, can you beat it' you have not the slightest idea whether they are telling the truth or not, and if you accept their word then you may be the laughing stock.

(b) The referential bid. Similarly any such arrangement as an offer of '£5 more than the highest offer received by you' should be avoided, because it makes reference to another offer and it is unfair to put the highest offeror to expense and trouble of survey and putting in an offer without giving his offer a fair chance. Further, if two or more such offers are received the whole thing is a nonsense. (On this topic generally see 1967 JLSS 2, and see the case of *Harvela Investments Ltd* [1985] 1 All ER 261, [1985] 2 All ER 966, where a referential bid was briefly approved by the court, but the decision was reversed by the House of Lords.)

(c) The progressive bid. Here a bidder frames a number of offers that are identical except that the price in each is progressively higher than the last. They are then put in numbered envelopes, and the sellers are told to open them in sequence, until a satisfactory price is reached. The snag from the bidders' point of view is that the sellers must be tempted to open only the envelope last in the sequence!

4.4 Other perfectly legitimate ways around the problem have been tried, and may commend themselves:

(a) Raffle. There seems to be nothing to prevent you from copying Mr Barney Curley of Dublin, who raffled his country house and made a profit of £1 million in the process, except that a public raffle on this scale in Scotland is probably illegal in terms of the Betting, Gaming and Lotteries Act 1963, s 45, in that 9,000 tickets were sold at £175 each, which exceeds the permitted ticket price and the value of the offerable prize. What you can do, however, is have a 'test of skill', requiring entrants to answer questions and complete a tie breaker.

This form of enterprise was last heard of in use in the sale of the Royal Hotel in Anstruther.

(b) The 'fixed price offer'. This is basically an acceptable idea, in that the first offer of the price fixed by the seller is accepted. It is abused, however, when the price fixed is too high. Sellers who adopt this method really should inform their solicitors, otherwise embarrassing situations may arise. Two examples:

(i) Prospective purchasers saw a house being sold on a fixed price basis, and informed their solicitors, who intimated the clients' interest and instructed a building society valuation. When the valuation was received, the solicitors were instructed to lodge an offer which was posted by first class mail. The following day, having received no reply, the solicitors telephoned the sellers' solicitors and were told that the house had been sold to an offer received earlier on the previous day. The solicitors concerned were, to say the least, extremely unhappy. (Letter, 1985 JLSS 346.)

(ii) A house was advertised personally by the sellers at a fixed price of £x. Offerors had a valuation made and instructed their solicitors to offer for the property at the fixed price. The solicitors hand-delivered the offer because there was word of another party being interested. The sellers' solicitors informed the offerors' solicitors that although their offer was the first received, it would not be accepted and that a closing date had been fixed. The selling solicitors had not apparently been informed of the method of sale. In due course the offerors' solicitors received a letter stating that a higher offer had been accepted. Furious exchanges followed, but the offeror had no grounds for action. (Reason: see *Pharmaceutical Society of Great Britain* [1983] 1 QB 401 – the advertisement is only an offer to treat, and the bargain must be concluded by written offer and acceptance, as is the rule with heritable property generally.)

(c) Auction. There is no reason why the property should not be sold by auction, or to use the old Scots word, 'roup'. This was the method by which many sales were formerly made, and sales under bonds had to be made in this manner. The modern law of securities now, however, allows sales under securities to be made by private bargain, provided that the best price is obtained. There is a fairly brisk market in auctions of unusual properties, such as railway and Telecom property, and a firm in Edinburgh specialises in such auctions. Auction sales of heritable property generally are making a modest revival. There is a body of opinion that says that sale by auction, being open and fair, and producing a fair market price, should be used universally.

When there is a sellers' market, as there was – with occasional slips – from 1950 to 1990, the sellers of property can choose the method of sale, and will usually prefer a sale by closed offer. The reason for this is that this method will probably produce not so much a fair market price, as a much higher 'shutout' bid, that will easily top all the other offers. For that reason a return to full-scale sale by roup is not foreseeable.

The process of a sale by roup is (1) the sellers prepare Articles of Roup, which is effectively an open offer to sell; (2) the auction takes place, and when the hammer falls, the highest bidder is preferred; (3) the successful bidder and the auctioneer then sign a Minute of Enactment and Preference, which has the effect of an acceptance of the offer, yielding a binding contract, similar in effect to missives.

4.5 When one offer has been identified as being better than the rest, the offeror should be told, and the disappointed bidders should also be told. They will want to know how much they missed out by, and a vague indication may be given. Do not, under any circumstances, tell people that they missed by only a few pounds, for the immediate reaction will be to up the bid, and under the Law Society Guidelines on Closing Dates 1993, you are not allowed to negotiate with anyone other than the chosen offeror.

There may be allegations of shady dealings made, and allegations of Dutch auctions. You only have your own clear conscience to defend you against these allegations. The practice followed in Aberdeen is worth noting – all parties who have bid are invited to the opening of the offers, and can thus see that there is no shady dealing. The prices are not, however, revealed.

4.6 When a successful purchaser has been selected by any method other than roup, the sellers' agents then send a formal acceptance, which again is in the form of a letter (Appendix II.15).

Technically it should be sufficient to simply say 'On behalf of A, I hereby accept your offer of yesterday's date for the property at ...'

Unfortunately, life is not so simple, and more complex offers produce more complex acceptances. An example of such, and more detailed remarks as to acceptance of offers are contained in Appendices I and II.

What must always be uppermost in your mind is that there must be a complete agreement as to details (*consensus in idem*) before a binding contract exists.

4.7 If a complex offer is followed by a complex acceptance, there is still no *consensus in idem*, and the purchasers' agents will have to write again formally, accepting the qualifications made by the seller before a binding contract can exist.

Theoretically this process can go on indefinitely. It should not be allowed to do so. A 'three letter contract' is ample. The more letters that are exchanged, the more complex the contract becomes, and the longer the missives remain unconcluded, thereby yielding uncertainty and the possibility of the whole deal collapsing.

It is suggested that, rather than exchanging letters like tennis lobs, you have a meeting with the other solicitors, thrash out the differences, and then the purchasers should produce a new offer, reflecting the agreement, to be accepted *de plano* (ie unconditionally) by the sellers. The dire consequences of having too many letters can be seen in the case of *Rutterford* 1990 SLT 325.

If the other solicitors are far away, the same result can be achieved by the sensible use of FAX, which can greatly speed up a transaction. Thus you can have points clarified by return, and have an offer in another solicitors' hands immediately, thus enabling them to take instructions right away. It should however be remembered that faxes are not probative or privileged, as they are not signed, and it is therefore recommended that the original of the fax be sent to the addressee forthwith.

It should also be remembered that we have a very good document exchange post service (DX) guaranteeing next day delivery, unless the weather is very bad, and also an excellent postal service. Non-urgent mail should be sent by these methods, and not FAX. Writing in the *Journal of the*

Law Society (June 1994, p 197) Mr Graeme Pagan from Oban says: 'In an uncomplicated non-urgent conveyancing transaction, I received by fax, twenty minutes before the office closed, a seventeen page draft feu charter, the principal of which reached me at 7.45 the following morning.'

This is a wasteful practice which should be avoided. The recipients of such junk mail can feel aggrieved, because it is their paper that is used for printing the document, and their machine is tied up for a few minutes, when somebody might be trying to send an important document – known in the jargon as 'opportunity costs'.

4.8   A typical acceptance of offer is printed at Appendix II.15. The contents of the acceptance are, of course, dictated by the contents of the offer. Typically, however, the acceptance should contain the following matters:

(a) Interest clause.   This clause rectifies by agreement (*ex pacto*) the complex situation outlined in **10.9**. It makes the date of entry and the price material conditions, and provides that interest shall be payable at overdraft rate (base rate + 4% or 5%) if the price is not paid on the date of entry. It reserves the right to the sellers to resile if settlement is not made by a certain date; and to claim damages from the defaulting purchasers, which are assessed in terms stated in 6 *Stair Memorial Encyclopaedia* para 575.

This clause will normally be accepted substantially by the purchasers, but care should be taken, from the purchasers' point of view, that these fairly drastic remedies apply only if the purchasers are at fault. They will not apply if the delay is the sellers' fault, when the rule is that contained in *Bowie v Semple's Executors* 1978 SLT (Sh Ct) 9 – the purchasers need not take entry, and if they do the agreement has to be re-made to this extent, usually to favour the purchasers.

It should also be noted that following the case of *Lloyd's Bank v Bamberger* 1994 SLT 424 it has been necessary to recast this clause completely to allow the sellers to claim interest on the price when the price is not paid through the sellers breaking the contract. The use of the word 'resile' in the context of such a clause is inappropriate, and the word 'rescind' should be used in preference. The remedies should also be specified. Two tentative clauses are given, one by Professor Robert Rennie and one by Professor Douglas Cusine, in November 1993 JLSS, and there is a very clear discussion of the topic by Richard Leggett in the June 1994 *Scottish Law Gazette*.

(b) Detailed alterations to furnishings et cetera included.   If the purchasers have included an item or items of furniture in the offer, which the sellers would rather keep, now is the time to say, and to put the matter beyond doubt.

(c) Deletion of time limit offer.   It is as well to delete any time limit, to stop any future argument as to whether the time limit was in fact met. At the same time, the sellers may want to place a time limit for acceptance of the qualifications imposed by this letter, and for conclusion of the contract.

(d) Deletion of provision of certain certificates.   The purchasers may provide for roads and superior's certificates, which the sellers are disinclined to provide, because they feel that they are not really required. The provision can therefore be altered, to exclude the provision of these. If the purchasers really want these, they can apply themselves. The Law Society has ruled, however, that the provision of a planning certificate is a duty which the sellers should not attempt to avoid, as it is so fundamental to the nature of the transaction.

(e) Clearing away redundant clauses.   If for example the offer stipulates that the sellers should provide a Charges Register Search, and the sellers are not a limited company, you can delete the clause. On the other hand you might equally take the attitude that it is clearly inapplicable, and just leave it. It is a matter of personal choice.

(f) Deletion of anything else that is clearly wrong.   This helps to achieve the great goal of *consensus in idem*.

Chapter five

THE PURCHASERS CONCLUDE

'A verbal contract isn't worth the paper it's written on.'
(Samuel Goldwyn)

5.1 The bargaining process has already been discussed in Chapter 4. As contract lawyers say 'these remarks are held to be herein repeated *brevitatis causa*' (for the sake of brevity).

5.2 Similarly, the topic of risk was covered at **3.27**. It is important, however, to underline that the risk passes to the purchasers on completion of the missives *unless* that risk is shifted back to the sellers in missives (see Appendix II.11, condition 11). It is unusual for the sellers not to accept the insurance risk until entry.

If the risk is not so shifted back, it should be insured again immediately on completing missives by instructing cover in the name of the purchasers 'as purchaser, price unpaid'.

At this stage, as always, the insurance cover should be for full re-instatement value, and not for market value. In a modern house there may not be much difference between the two values but in an older house, built of traditional materials, the cost of repairing the house to the same standard may well be considerably in excess of what the house cost to buy.

5.3 The solicitors then tell the purchasers of their good fortune and advise them to get their finances and the removal van ready.

5.4 The purchasers might also be reminded that they have entered into a formal binding contract, and the consequences of failing to meet the commitment are severe. They should have been kept informed at all stages of formation of the contract.

Chapter six

THE SELLERS SHOW THEIR HAND

Before the Town and Country Planning Acts,

'When I was young, train tracks criss-crossed the area, with no means of keeping people and trains apart, and there was a whisky bond that discharged effluent directly into a burn where the children played. We used to wonder why no fish were to be caught there.

On the other side we had a chemical factory and a gas plant that had no filters, so at especially busy times when more gas was needed, before lunch or dinner for example, the by-products were discharged directly into the air. The local people knew the times, and if the gas works was due to "come out", would rush home, take in any washing and close all windows. If you were caught outside, the sulphur fumes caused choking and streaming eyes.

We also had a canal, a delight for the children and a constant source of terror for our parents. We loved to play in and around it and our parents feared we would be drowned, a fairly common occurrence.'
(Meg Henderson on her 'bittersweet' childhood in Blackhill, in the Fifties, before the Planning Acts took effect)

And after,

'Meanwhile I pursued the question of planning permission. It seemed that it would be unlikely to be granted. The site (at Robroyston) was in a green belt and the mooted office, retail, and hotel developments breached Strathclyde Region's structure plan and other planning structures. I phoned Glasgow's Director of Planning to get an informed view. He told me quite bluntly that the chances of any such scheme gaining consent were remote. He would recommend the housing for approval because the Secretary of State perceived there was a shortage of housing land in Glasgow and would not necessarily object to the green belt being breached. He might also approve the planned stadium – but he would not approve both the housing and the stadium together, because he regarded them as incompatible uses.'
(Michael Kelly, discussing the possible relocation of Celtic FC to Robroyston, in his book 'Paradise Lost' Canongate Press 1994)

6.1 As mentioned previously, the sellers' agents should ideally have obtained the title deeds as soon as they were instructed. They should have had these to hand when missives were completed, lest any title problems or discrepancy arose. If they did not have the title deeds then they should most certainly get them now, and hope that they have not made a mistake in the missives. They should also have obtained from the local authority letters at that time, but if they did not do so then better late than never.

6.2 The sellers' agents should then send the various items mentioned in **6.3** to the purchasers' agents. These matters will be referred to further in

Chapter 7, which deals with what happens when these reach the purchasers' agents.

6.3 With the title deeds, there should be sent an inventory in duplicate (see Appendix I.20). The purpose of this is to allow the purchasers' agents to check the deeds they have received. Assuming that the inventory is correct, they should receipt the copy and return it to the sellers' agents. If it is not correct, they should raise the matter with the sellers' agents immediately.

6.4 The list of items to be sent is indicative only and not claimed to be exhaustive. Basically, careful solicitors are going to send out everything that their opposite number will need, and not much more, such as old security writs, and dispositions outwith the prescriptive period. The minimal requirements of deeds required to be submitted for land registration should also be borne in mind. It is also wise to answer questions before they are asked, especially difficult ones, thereby avoiding a last minute rush.

6.5 When the Local Government (Scotland) Act 1973 divided the functions of local government between regional and district councils (excepting of course the three all-purpose authorities in Orkney, Shetland and the Western Islands. In 1996 the responsibility will pass to the unitary authorities: see Appendix V) the regions were given the responsibility for roads, footpaths and sewers and the districts were made responsible for domestic planning matters.

As both of these matters are of great importance, you should therefore ask the regional council to confirm condition 7(d) of the offer and must ask the district council to confirm condition 8 of the offer in Appendix II.11.

6.6 The point of confirming that the region maintains roads, footpaths and sewers is to ensure that the purchasers do not take over a liability either for the formation or the maintenance of these. In cities and towns it is generally the responsibility of the region, but you can never be certain. In semi-urban and suburban areas there can be private roads, but they are usually perfectly obvious.

Before putting in an offer for a house, the purchasers' solicitors should, if possible, inspect the property, at least from the outside. This should readily reveal a private road or footpath, most of which look like dried-up river beds, but there are always exceptions, and how does one inspect a sewer?

6.7 If the road is private the responsibility of the owners generally extends *ex adverso* the property, that is to say to the extent that their property fronts the road, and to the centre of the road (*medium filum*). This, however, varies and the situation must be verified from the title deeds.

6.8 The problem is at its most critical when the house has been recently built. Builders will usually bind themselves under their contract of sale to form the roads, footpaths and sewers to standards required by the regional council, and will then request the region to adopt the roads, footpaths and sewers. It is for the solicitors acting for the purchasers, and any subsequent purchasers, to ensure that this process has been properly done, otherwise their clients may incur a substantial liability for putting the matter right.

Some years ago a number of builders became insolvent, leaving unmade roads, to the detriment of the purchasers in the estate. Nowadays, therefore, builders must grant a 'road bond' in favour of the local authority, which is simply a form of credit insurance (Roads (Scotland) Act 1984, s 17). If the builder becomes insolvent the insurers will pay for the completion of the roads. In rural areas, the questions posed in **3.23** require to be considered.

In towns, a roads certificate may be kept with the title deeds, and as it is fairly unusual for a road to revert to private ownership, no further enquiry is necessary. Further it is probably a waste of money to obtain a certificate saying that (say) Sauchiehall Street is public, and many sellers will perhaps delete the appropriate clause from the offer.

6.9   The property enquiry certificate from the district is, however, a necessity, and it is the sellers' obligation to produce one. The sellers may not contract out of this obligation. A list of the appropriate authorities to ask for a property enquiry or roads certificate is given in the Scottish Law Directory or The Blue Book, and if you are unfamiliar with a particular area, it is wise to check the charges by a quick telephone call to the authority concerned. You should send a cheque with your enquiry. Do not write without a cheque, asking for the charge – this is a complete waste of time, as nothing will be done until your cheque is received.

6.10   Solicitors very frequently send enquiries to the wrong local authority, usually because of strange boundaries. (See for example Thornliebank which is partly in South Glasgow and partly in Eastwood District; and nearby Busby which is partly in Eastwood and partly in East Kilbride. The boundaries are not in any way apparent.) This can be best clarified by checking the council tax or rates notice, which the solicitors will require to have anyway. This is of course conclusive evidence of the district in which the property is situated.

6.11   The planning questions that the purchasers' solicitors will ask are covered at **7.22**, and a copy of a certificate is printed at **18.16**.

The certificate, as well as covering notices and applications under the Town and Country Planning Acts, additionally discloses a variety of other searches under the Public Health, Clean Air, Building, Civic Government, and Housing Acts.

6.12   For properties that lie in the urban part of Strathclyde Region, a property enquiry certificate in either region or district or both, may be obtained from a firm called SPH Property Search, DX GW 352, telephone 0141–353 26800. This service is claimed to be both quicker and slightly cheaper (in Glasgow in 1994 a combined search in regional and district registers would be charged at £117.50, against a local authority charge of £142.80) than for sellers obtaining their own searches, one from the region, and one from the district.

This service was not introduced without acrimony, as in the case of *SPH v Dumbarton District Council* 1994 SCLR 631. In this case SPH successfully challenged the imposition of a charge by the council for making available the information required for property enquiry certificates. It was held that the imposition of a charge would create a serious obstacle to public access to planning information.

Another advantage of this form of search is that it is in a standardised form.

It is usually sufficient to instruct an SPH search three days before settlement, for those who like to live dangerously. Should the search prove inaccurate, and loss be suffered, there is an insurance indemnity of £1 million.

Searches for evidence of past contaminative uses of land can also be obtained from this source (see **3.20**).

Chapter seven

THE STUFF OF CONVEYANCING

'This registration of title is all very well, but it's not the stuff of conveyancing.'
(A Glasgow solicitor)

'Thurrock District Council in Essex, has threatened to drag Teresa Gorman, the MP for Billericay, through the courts for 33 alleged breaches of planning law. It claims that she and her husband began alterations on her Grade II–Listed, 15th Century farmhouse, without permission and have caused irreparable damage in the process. The offences each carry a maximum penalty of a £20,000 fine or six months imprisonment.'
(*The Sunday Times*)

7.1 Missives having been concluded, it is now for the sellers' solicitors to show that the sellers have a valid marketable title, and for the purchasers' solicitors to be satisfied that this is so. This is truly the stuff of traditional conveyancing.

In their book *Conveyancing*, page 91, Professors Reid and Gretton define a marketable title as one:

(a) which makes the buyer the owner of the property;

(b) contains no heritable securities adverse to the new owner's interest;

(c) contains no unusual conditions of title; and

(d) contains no leases adverse to the new owner's interest.

To this might be added that, in land registration areas, a marketable title is one that can be sent to the Keeper immediately after purchase, and on the basis of which the Keeper will, without making further enquiries or requisitions, issue a land certificate without restriction of indemnity.

7.2 Modern conveyancing practice has placed much more emphasis on the preparation of missives than previously, and many of the matters formerly dealt with at the examination of title stage are now dealt with before missives are completed.

Thus, for instance, it is a usual stipulation of missives that the title shall contain 'no unduly onerous conditions or restrictions' (see **7.1 (c)**). It is very hard to know exactly what is meant by this statement, and its meaning depends very much on the circumstances of each case. This is not satisfactory at all, as the word 'unusual' is subjective. If the sellers give this warranty in missives, purchasers can claim at a later date that there is, in their opinion, an onerous condition or restriction in the title, and the matter will have to be argued and compromised, although – at worst – the purchasers may resile.

The question of what is an 'unusual condition' is considered in *Whyte* (1879) 6 R 699, 701, and Lord Young commented on the phrase as follows:

> 'If a man simply buys a house he must be taken to buy it as the seller has it, on a good title of course, but subject to such restrictions as may exist if of an ordinary character, and such as the buyer may reasonably be supposed to have contemplated as at least not improbable.'

The leading modern case is *Armia* 1979 SC (HL) 56, where a property in Kirkcaldy High Street, which had been bought for redevelopment, was found to be subject to a servitude right of access, which included a ten foot frontage with the street. It was held that this was a sufficiently unusual condition to allow the purchaser to resile.

In the case of *Morris* 1992 GWD 33–1950 a piece of ground being sold turned out to be burdened by a servitude right of access, which would have reduced the number of car parking spaces by seven out of eighteen, and would therefore have a bad effect on turnover and thus market value of the property. This only became known to the pursuer after missives had been concluded, and a deposit had been paid. The pursuer was allowed to withdraw from the purchase because of the diminution in value of the ground. On a practical note, sellers who know of restrictions of this nature should disclose them to the purchasers before missives are concluded.

The chief ambition of the conveyancer must be never to let any matter near the court, as – at best – a reference to court entails expense and delay, and – at worst – an adverse decision, whether right or (even worse still) wrong.

For that reason it has been suggested (**6.1**) that the sellers' agents should obtain the titles, and as many other relevant certificates et cetera as possible, before exposing the property for sale. When an offer is received, containing the stipulation as to unusual or unduly onerous conditions, the sellers' agents should then send the title deeds, and other relevant papers, with the acceptance, and require the purchasers' agents to satisfy themselves prior to completion of the contract. This is good practice and will save arguments at a later date, probably arising shortly before the date for settlement. (See Appendix II.21(a) and following letter.)

7.3 For the purposes of this chapter, we shall assume that such matters have not been dealt with before missives are completed, and that the full examination of title takes place after completion of missives. It is not always possible to assemble title deeds and other papers, and as indicated previously (**2.5**) the first intimation the solicitor may receive of a sale is when an offer drops through the letter box, requiring urgent attention. In that case, the missives must proceed on the basis of warranties given and proved to be correct when the title is available.

7.4 The obligations of the sellers for (a) a Sasine transaction, (b) a first registration in the Land Register and (c) a subsequent dealing in registered land, are set out in clause 12 of the offer in Appendix I.11. In the disposition the sellers grant absolute warrandice, that is to say, they undertake to compensate the purchasers for any title defect.

Why then should the purchasers' agents have to examine the title in such detail? The reasons are (a) professional pride dictates that the purchasers shall get a title that can be passed on without question when the purchasers eventually sell, be that next month or next century; (b) the person who prepared the sellers' title may not have had the same standards, or perhaps there has been an innocent mistake perpetuating itself over the years; (c) the obligation in the missives is superseded and falls when the disposition is delivered (Lord Watson in *Orr* (1893) 20 R (HL) 27), unless there is a valid non-supersession clause (see **9.7**); (d) warrandice is not in practice a particularly effective remedy, as it depends on 'eviction' having taken place, and the victim has to go through the process of losing his case before he can claim warrandice. (See *Welsh* (1894) 21 R 769.) It should be noted that 'eviction' in this case means any interference with the property right, rather than being put out of the property. Even if there is a valid remedy under warrandice, you may not be able to trace the granters of warrandice, or if appropriate, their predecessors in title; (f) lawyers are not paid to get their clients into dispute, quite the opposite; and (g) the *caveat emptor* rule applies, in Sasine transactions at least.

7.5 On the assumption that your clients have purchased the house at 3 Barrie Drive, Glasgow in terms of the missives contained in Appendix I.11, you will receive the title deeds of the house, as set out in the inventory of titles in Appendix I.20(a). You will also receive a draft memorandum for continuation of search, draft letter of obligation and draft state for settlement.

7.6 If the house had been situated in the counties of Renfrew, Dumbarton, Lanark, the Barony and Regality of Glasgow, Clackmannan, Stirling or West Lothian, and from April 1995 in Fife, the procedures for registration of title would apply where a sale of the property is made. You would therefore require now to turn to Chapters 13 to 16, and Appendix II and follow the procedure outlined there.

In a first registration, the procedure of examining title is very much the same, but in a subsequent dealing, the title deeds are replaced by a land certificate. This contains all the essential parts of the title, and none of the non-essential, and should therefore be read very thoroughly. The fact that all inessential details are stripped out, and the remainder is clearly printed, should make this a very much easier business than reading through a lot of old titles written in spidery handwriting on disintegrating paper.

7.7 For ease of treatment, we are assuming that your clients are not obtaining a loan. The additional procedure to be adopted when they are getting a loan is contained in Chapter 12 and Appendix I.

7.8 The first thing that you must do is to check the title deeds against the inventory and (assuming they are in order) return the inventory marked 'Borrowed the above title deeds; to be returned on demand' and signed. Then put all the title deeds into order and check them against the search, making sure that all the deeds mentioned in the search have been sent to you. Form in your mind a rough history of the property, and in particular spot any split-offs or acquisitions and the writs referred to for burdens.

7.9 Next, put to one side the writs that do not concern you, bearing in mind the following provisions of statute that are designed to make life easier for you (**7.10** to **7.13**).

Prescription and Limitation (Scotland) Act 1973, section 1

7.10   Section 1 provides (in paraphrase) that where a person has possessed land openly, peacefully and without interruption for ten years, on the basis of a sufficient title, then after ten years the title shall not be challengeable on the ground that it was not valid *ex facie* (on its face), the only exception being if it turns out to have been forged. This process is known as positive prescription.

It is not thought that many pieces of land are acquired in this way, yet this is, for another reason, a vital provision for the conveyancer. What it means, in effect, is that if you take the first transfer of the land that you are buying, which is more than ten years old, and find that it is free from an intrinsic objection (that is an objection showing on the face of the title, and not requiring proof from outside sources) then that is a valid foundation for a prescriptive title, and you need look back no further.

Therefore you may set aside all older transfers of the land, unless these contain valid land obligations to which you must refer. You must, however, check this foundation writ for any intrinsic objection, and check everything after it to make sure that it correctly flows down to the present seller. An intrinsic objection is one which can be observed from the terms of the deed itself.

An example of what might have been called an intrinsic objection is given in *Cooper Scott* 1925 SC 309, where a destination detailed in the narrative clause did not correspond with a further narration of the same destination in the dispositive clause. A majority of the seven judges, however, held that this deed was not intrinsically null and was therefore a good foundation for prescription. (See also *Simpson* (1900) 2 F 447.)

An extrinsic objection, that is to say an objection which can only be proved from outside evidence, or an intrinsic objection that can be proved only by extrinsic evidence, does not affect the use of the disposition as a foundation of title.

As an example of the power of prescription, consider the disposition *a non domino* (a disposition granted by someone who is not the owner). If a piece of land lies vacant, and the owner cannot be traced, it is possible for someone who does not own that land to obtain a disposition, granted by anyone in favour of a grantee. Only simple warrandice is given, for the granter has no claim to the land at all. The disposition is then recorded to make it public and the disponee occupies the land 'openly and peaceably', as if it was owned, so that anyone who has a better title may see the occupation and object. If no objection is made by anyone having a better title, within ten years, the disponee then becomes the owner of the land.

If prescription can cure a disposition that is so obviously bad, it will be seen that it can also cure any minor defect in a deed.

Prescription and Limitation (Scotland) Act 1973, section 8

7.11   Section 8 provides (again in paraphrase) that where a right has not been enforced or exercised for a continuous period of 20 years, then that right shall be extinguished. This is known as negative prescription.

Again, this does not clearly state the benefit to the conveyancer, who only need look back for securities over a 20-year period. Thus (writing in November 1994) if a bond was recorded before November 1974, and no interest has been paid on it in that time, and it has not been enforced, it can be said to have prescribed. The snag is to know whether or not interest has been paid, and this will be dealt with under searches in Chapter 8. All kinds of out-of-date obligations can be cleared in this way.

The Succession (Scotland) Act 1964, section 17

7.12   This section provides that where a person for good faith and for value (ie the average house purchaser) acquires title to land from an executor, or from somebody who has derived title directly from an executor, the title shall not be challengeable on the ground that the confirmation of the executor was reducible, or had in fact been reduced, or even that the title should not have been transferred by the executor to the person who is offering the title.

Thus, for example, you may be offered a title by X and Y, who produce (a) a confirmation in the estate of their uncle (V), whereby Z is appointed executor and (b) a docket in terms of the Succession (Scotland) Act 1964, s 15 transferring that property to X and Y, as, say, the persons entitled to take the property under V's will.

Provided your client is buying in good faith and for value (ie the average house purchaser), it need not concern you (a) if someone produces a later dated will appointing A as executor and B the legatee, or (b) someone alleges that the will is a forgery.

In summary, you need look no further than the confirmation itself.

An analogous provision is made in the Trusts (Scotland) Act 1961, s 2 which provides that titles acquired from trustees or executors are also protected from challenge on the ground that the transaction was at variance with the terms or purpose of the trust.

Conveyancing and Feudal Reform (Scotland) Act 1970, section 41

7.13   This section provides that where a discharge of a security bears to be granted by a person entitled to do so (eg the creditor) subsequent acquirers of land bona fide and for value, shall not have their title to the land challenged after the expiration of a five-year period from the recording of the discharge, merely by reason of the discharge being reduced.

Thus, if a discharge is more than five years old, and appears to have been granted by the creditor of the security that is discharged, you need not examine the origins of that discharge any further.

7.14   The first step in examining title is to identify your foundation writ, and examine it for intrinsic defects.

Then examine the writs that follow the foundation writ, ensuring that one follows on from another smoothly. If the grantee of one deed is not the grantee of the next deed, examine the deduction of title, and ensure that the link in title is in order. (Example: if a writ is in favour of Brown, and the next deed is granted by Black, check exactly why Black is selling a house that appears to be owned by Brown. Generally there will be a good reason, and if Brown has died and Black is his executor, or if Brown is bankrupt and Black is the trustee, ensure that title is properly deduced in the second writ using confirmation to vouch this.)

Recall two reminders contained in the Halliday Report (Chapter IV):

(a)   That only certain deeds in terms of the Conveyancing (Scotland) Act 1924, s 3 (dispositions of land, or assignations, discharges or restrictions of heritable security) may be granted by uninfeft proprietors, and, for instance, feu grants and deeds of conditions may not. A surprising number of these deeds are granted by uninfeft proprietors, and are invalid until a recorded title is obtained, usually by means of a notice of title which is recorded, and which cures the defect by accretion. Formerly, heritable securities could not be granted by persons without a recorded title, but standard securities and their transmissions may now be granted by uninfeft proprietors in terms generally of the C & FR (S) Act 1970, Part II.

(b)   That the style of deduction of title in the C (S) Act 1924, Schedule A, Form 1, requires a designation of the person last infeft, and is ineffective otherwise. Thus, the designation of the granter, which appeared in the narrative clause, must be repeated. While this may seem harsh and inconsistent with the liberal terms of Schedule D, Note 1 of the same Act, that is nevertheless the law, and it must be followed.

7.15   Check carefully the first description of the land, either with your own observations or with a survey plan of the property and make sure that the first full description has been validly referred to throughout the progress in titles in conformity with the Conveyancing (Scotland) Acts 1874 and 1924. Note all additions to the land and disposals of any part of the land.

7.16   Examine the burdens contained in all writs referred to for burdens in the title, and assess their possible impact on your client. Properly created burdens do not, of course, ever prescribe, and thus you must still examine writs outwith the prescriptive periods that are referred to as burdens. Have all feuing conditions been implemented? If they have not (eg if walls and fences around the plot are not in conformity with the feuing conditions) the purchaser may be called upon to remedy the defect and this may prove expensive. If in doubt ask the sellers' agents to obtain a superior's certificate stating that feuing conditions have been implemented. If they will not obtain this (and they are probably under no compulsion to do so, unless the missives state that they shall or if the title is not marketable because of this) write to the superior's agent in terms similar to this:

Messrs Morrison & Goodfellow
Solicitors
23 Hamill Street
GLASGOW

Dear Sirs,

Mr James Meikle, Strathclyde Estates Limited, 3 Barrie Drive, Glasgow

Please confirm that all feuing conditions, other than those of a continuing nature, have been implemented to the satisfaction of the superiors, Strathclyde Estates Limited.

When sending this confirmation, please let us have a note of your fee in this matter.

Yours faithfully,

DAVIDSON & CARSWELL (signed)

7.17   Superiors roughly fall into three categories: (a) caring superiors, who genuinely care about the appearance of the estate, and who coincidentally own some of the finest residential property in Scotland, such as the New Town in Edinburgh, the terraces in the West End of Glasgow, the fine shipbuilders' houses in Helensburgh and so on; (b) the commercial superiors, who are in it for the money (see Chapter 17) ((a) and (b) are not mutually incompatible categories); and (c) the uncaring superior, who has lost interest, or has disappeared. In many ways, this is the most dangerous superior, because while no permissions are necessary from uncaring superiors, they may sell on to commercial superiors, who will start to delve into the estate and make life difficult.

It should be noted that if an uncaring superior was a limited company which has probably been dissolved, the superiority, if not transferred (see the search) will belong to the Crown, and a waiver may be received from the Queen's and Lord Treasurer's Remembrancer who is at the Crown Office (Telephone 0131 226 2626).

A bit of commonsense is required about this condition. If the house is over ten years old, say, to ask for this information is probably to waste everyone's time, and it may be expensive. If the superiors have not objected in this time, they are highly unlikely to do so now, and if they do, they will possibly have lost their right through acquiescence. It may be more useful in the case of a new house, where it is not immediately obvious that all feuing conditions have or have not been complied with. Do not ask for this information as a matter of course without considering what other ways you might obtain it.

7.18   Check that all parties granting deeds had the capacity to do so, that the form of all deeds is correct, that they are properly executed and that the testing clause is correctly completed, that all deletions, interlineations, additions and erasures have been properly stamped and recorded in the General Register of Sasines. This will require a knowledge of the law both before and after the Requirements of Writing (Scotland) Act 1995.

Planning permission and building warrants are obtained from separate committees of the district council, and both must be obtained separately. The grant of one does not necessarily imply that the other will be given. Planning permission is given where (broadly) you are building the right kind of building for the zoning laid down. (Thus where an area is zoned for residential purposes, you should have little difficulty obtaining permission to build a house; if, however, you wish to build even a small factory or shop you will have difficulty.) Building warrant is given (again broadly) where a planned building complies with the building regulations, as to materials used, space available, hygiene arrangements, fire precautions, ventilators, et cetera.

Failure to obtain or comply with either of these provisions may eventually lead to the owner having to reinstate the property to its original condition.

Incidentally, even district councils are not exempt from this provision of law: Dundee District Council was ordered by the Scottish Development Department to reinstate Camperdown House (built in 1824) to its original state after modernisation was carried out without planning consent. Retrospective consent had also been refused by the Department (*Sunday Standard* 14 November 1982).

Similarly, all new buildings and extensions to buildings and proposals for such buildings should comply with the feuing conditions. If they do not, the owners will have to deal with the superior. Even worse, they may have to deal with a number of '*tertii*' (that is persons who enjoy an *ius quaesitum tertio*) – groups of property owners are notoriously hard to deal with, as they seldom seem to agree. The superior may irritate the feu, if the condition is breached, or the superior of the *tertii* may seek interdict, or both.

The only way around this problem is to negotiate a waiver of the feuing condition (presumably for a consideration) or, if that fails, to take the matter to the Lands Tribunal under the C & FR (S) Act 1970, s 1. For a case dealing with the interests of both superiors and *tertii* see *Main* 1972 SLT (Lands Tr) 14.

7.19 Check that the house possesses suitable rights of access. This applies particularly to property in the country. Land is obviously useless unless it enjoys proper access, unless, of course, you own a helicopter.

The problem is not so acute in the city and towns where, generally, but not universally, the streets have been taken over and are maintained by the local authority. In that case anyone can use the road, but the downside is that the local authority can paint yellow lines on 'your' road and, even worse, charge you for parking outside your own house.

The local authority maintains the road, and is responsible for any accident that occurs through lack of maintenance.

Where the road remains private, and this can be found even in towns and cities, the frontagers own the road to the centre point, along the length of their frontage. They are responsible for maintenance, and usually don't trouble to do any, because of the near impossibility of getting agreement from all the frontagers to pay for the work. If there is an accident through lack of maintenance, the appropriate frontagers are responsible, but should be covered by the public liability of their household insurance.

If a road is built to a certain standard, the builders can, and will, ask the local authority to take over the maintenance of the road. Owners of existing private roads seldom do this, again usually for lack of agreement to spending money on turning their quiet road into a public highway.

In the country, purchasing solicitors must ensure that purchasers enjoy an unrestricted right to all necessary rights of access, and are not expected to pay a disproportionate amount of maintenance. A servitude right of access is a licence to use someone else's ground for certain purposes, and if the owners of the dominant tenant exceed this use they can be interdicted. The division of large estates, and the sale of redundant estates and farm houses, has led to an increasing number of 'townspeople' now living in the country, often not happily with the country people. There have been an increasing number of cases that have illustrated the trend towards bad relations between the two. (See an article on the subject by Douglas Patience in December 1993 *Scottish Law Gazette* 127.)

In *Caveat* (a monthly article outlining the mistakes, hopefully, of others) December 1993 JLSS 490, there is a cautionary tale of a couple who bought a house in the country, with an adjoining disused water mill. The access to the mill was over the farmer's land. There was nothing in the titles about this right, which had arisen from use, and positive prescription. The farmer objected to the use of the road to the mill, which was intended for use as a holiday cottage. It was held by the court that the access had been created for use of the building as a mill, and not as a cottage. The solicitor who had acted for the pursuers was liable for the costs of forming an alternative access, and loss of income.

In addition, the owners of the dominant tenement cannot increase the burden on the servient tenement, and cannot therefore increase the usage. Professor Halliday in *Conveyancing Law and Practice in Scotland*, volume II, 20, 11, suggests that when a servitude of access is created, words such as the following should be used:

> 'The servitude has been granted with reference to the present state of the property and shall not be extended to apply to any substantially different condition thereof.'

Grants of servitudes should be drawn very carefully, and are construed *contra proferentem*. For example, one frequently sees a servitude right of access for 'pedestrian and vehicular' use. Does that include the right to drive cattle over the road? You might argue that the word pedestrian is derived from the Latin word for feet, and that cattle have feet, however that is not the ordinary meaning of the word. Further, the law of servitudes is drawn from Roman law, and it had three classes of servitude – *via* (the right to use the road for carriages drawn by horses or other beasts of draught); *iter* (allowing a person a right of way to pass over the land of another on horse or on foot); and *actus* (the right of use for carriages drawn by men, and for driving cattle), indicating a more precise distinction between the uses.

Servitudes should be used *civiliter* (ie with civility). The owner of the servient tenement is not under an obligation to maintain the ground, and should not obstruct the way.

Where there is an agreement for the maintenance of a road, liability should be apportioned according to the extent of the respective uses.

7.20 The position with new houses is rather different. The builder will undertake, as part of the price of the house, to form the road to the appropriate council standard and to request the council to take it over, without it, of course, giving any guarantee that it will do so. (Provided the road is built to standard, a refusal to take over is virtually unknown.) Despite this partially incomplete work, the builder will nonetheless require the full price.

The builder should also provide a road bond (see **6.8**). You may wonder why the purchasers should pay the full price before all work is complete. While payment is only made on completion of the house, the completion of roads is an exception, for it is useless to complete someone's road while there is work going on in the estate and the builder may have heavy plant using that road. A builder will normally complete all the houses in an estate, then finish the roads. The road bond covers the purchasers against the builder's insolvency in the intervening period between payment of the price and completion of the roads.

On the basis that good advice cannot be repeated too often, (1) the sellers' agents should obtain a letter as to roads from the appropriate council the minute the sellers instruct the sale (see JLSS Council Notes, October 1982 as corrected in Council Notes, November 1982) and (2) the purchasers and their agents should deal with such matters before completing missives, by personal observation, inquiry and survey.

7.21 Approximately the same position applies with the supply of water, gas, electricity, et cetera and with drainage. Most of us take these services for granted, but lawyers cannot do this, particularly when purchasing a property in a rural or even semi-rural area.

(a) Water. The appropriate authority will not necessarily run water into every house, especially those that are isolated, and the water may be drawn from a stream or well situated in someone else's land (*aquaehaustus*) and be carried from the mains to the house by a private pipe (*aquaduct*). Where this pipe crosses the land of another, make sure that there are clear servitude rights for running the pipe, and a right to gain access to the pipe if it requires maintenance.

In very rural areas the water system will be no concern of the appropriate board, and the conveyancer should ensure that the arrangement is adequate *tantum et tale* (both as to quantity and quality). Where the source is in someone else's land, make sure that the supply cannot be interfered with, and that the necessary servitude rights for pipes exist. Bear in mind the seasonal nature of water supply, even in Scotland.

(b) Gas, electricity and telephone. British Gas, Scottish Power, Scottish Hydro Electric and British Telecom will take care of the servitude rights (or wayleaves) for cables and pipes, under statutory powers, and these will not therefore concern the average conveyancer in the active sense. In the passive sense, however, note should be taken of wayleaves for cable and pipes leading to other properties, which must not be disturbed by digging, or obstructed in any way, eg by building over the wayleave area. Thus, for example, if you have a mains water pipe in your property, or a gas pipe line, you would be well advised to know about these and to leave them well alone. Modern pipelines are sunk to a great depth, but the same cannot be said of Victorian pipelines.

(c) Drainage. The position is as with water supply, but in reverse. In many rural areas drainage is not to a mains, but a private septic tank. It is a matter of survey to ensure that this tank is in order, and capable of treating the volume of waste generated by the household it serves. A properly constructed and maintained tank should do this without giving trouble. The local council should empty it from time to time. Again, if waste is piped through the land of another, the appropriate servitude rights must be seen to exist. There is, according to Professors Reid and Gretton (*Conveyancing*, W Green, 1994, p 199), a servitude of 'sinks' which covers this, although this is not one of the classic servitudes (although it perhaps should be).

In the case of a new house, all services will be (or at least should be) 'laid on'. Each house in a new estate will be transferred subject to a variety of servitude or wayleave rights, which may be expressed as follows:

> 'There is reserved to us and our successors as proprietors of the remaining area or piece of ground of which the feu forms part of a servitude right of wayleave for all necessary water pipes, sewers, drains, electricity cables, Post Office underground and overhead cables, field drains and whole other necessary pipes and cables passing through the feu and the feuars are prohibited from erecting any permanent construction on the lines of said water pipes, sewers, drains, electricity cables, underground and overhead communications cables and field drains if any within the feu and shall not do or permit to be done any act which may cause damage to said water pipes, sewers, drains, electricity cables, underground and overhead communications cables and field drains; and the feuars shall further be bound to allow all parties interested in said water pipes, sewers, drains and whole other pipes and cables right of access to the feu on all necessary occasions for opening up, uncovering, inspecting, maintaining, cleaning, repairing and renewing the same on payment of compensation to the feuars for any surface damaged which may be thereby occasioned; further declaring that there is reserved to us and our foresaids in all time coming a right to lay on, in or over the feu such water pipes, sewers, drains and whole other pipes and cables as we in our sole discretion shall consider necessary for the amenity of the feu and of the remaining area or piece of ground of which the feu forms part but that always on payment of compensation for the feuars for any surface damage which may be thereby occasioned.'

7.22   Every new house, or every new extension or alteration to a house, must carry the following permissions:

(a) planning permission from the district council under the Town and Country Planning (Scotland) Acts 1972 and 1977;

(b) building warrant from the district council under the Building (Scotland) Acts 1959 and 1970 and completion certificate;

(c) superior's consent (if applicable);

(d) the consent of any third parties 'tertii' who may have an *ius quaesitum tertio* (ie a right given to a third party over land which is subject to a contract between the first and second parties only).

Planning permission and building warrants are often confused, perhaps because they cover roughly the same problems of decent building standards, and are obtained from the offices of the same council. They should not, however, be confused. They arise under different Acts and regulations, and are administered by different officials and committees. The existence of one does not in any way guarantee the existence of the other. Separate applications must be made for each.

Planning permission covers, very broadly, the appearance of an area, and the zoning of that area. If an area is zoned as residential, you would be very unlikely to get permission to build a factory there; but you would probably get permission to build a house, assuming all the other requirements of the district, as to density, the suitability of the roads, et cetera, are met.

Building warrant is given (again broadly) where a planned building complies with the building regulations as to materials used, space available, hygiene arrangements, fire precautions, ventilation, lack of dampness, et cetera. A completion certificate is granted when the building is complete to the building department's satisfaction, and only then may it be occupied.

Failure to obtain these certificates can, in the worst cases, lead to an order being made to restore the land or building to its original condition.

Particular care should be taken with buildings of special historical or architectural significance, or which form part of a special townscape, and which are accordingly 'listed'. All alterations require listed building consent (Mrs Gorman, supra, please note), and many owners may find the local councils and bodies such as Scottish Historic Buildings a bit pernickety. It is very pleasant to live in a listed building, until you come to alter it, when it can prove extremely expensive.

There is a dispensation contained in the Town and Country Planning (Scotland) Act 1972, s 84 to the effect that an enforcement action for breach of planning law is not enforceable after four years. It should be noted that this dispensation does not apply to a breach of building regulations. If obtaining permission or a completion certificate has been overlooked or forgotten, a retrospective warrant or certificate has to be obtained in cases of a serious breach. This can be extremely expensive, as the building work has to comply with current building regulations. Thus, even if a building was built in 1985, say, to comply with the regulations then, there is no guarantee that it would comply with 1995 regulations.

Alternatively, in less serious cases, the council may be prepared to issue a 'letter of comfort' covering the breach. An example of this might read:

'With reference to the above mentioned subjects I confirm that no action will be instigated by this Council in respect of these subjects not having a Completion Certificate under the Building (Scotland) Acts 1959 and 1970 due the time elapsed since they were first occupied.

I would also confirm that as far as can be ascertained the subjects would appear to have complied with the Building Standards in force at the time the property was constructed.'

This letter is pretty qualified in its terms, and does not bind the council at all, but it may provide some comfort which should be acceptable to a purchaser. In truth, a completion certificate does not offer a great deal more protection, as it can be changed anytime.

Similarly, all building work should have the consent of superiors and third parties, if this is written in the titles. Great care should be taken with these rights, especially where you have a vigilant superior. Unless appeased, the superior may interdict the work or irritate the feu. Third parties can also give trouble, as groups of people are very difficult to deal with.

Care must be taken with replacement windows, to ensure that (1) in a listed building they are compatible with the building and have council approval; (2) that they can be cleaned from the inside, unless they are at ground level; and (3) that they permit escape in case of fire. Practice varies from district to district, and if you are in doubt the matter should be discussed with the local council.

7.23 Where a sale is made by a person or persons on behalf of someone else, or in default of someone else, care must be taken to ensure that the power of sale is competent, and that it was properly exercised.

(a) Trustees. Trustees have wide powers to sell, lease and grant securities over heritage under the Trusts (Scotland) Act 1921, s 4. The term 'trustee' includes (s 2) – trustee *ex officiis* (namely trustees who are appointed by virtue of an office they hold, say a president and secretary of a bowling club, and who cease to be trustees when they demit office, giving way to the next incumbents automatically), executors-nominate, tutors, curators and judicial factors. This power of sale has now been extended to executors-dative by the Succession (Scotland) Act 1964, s 20. Further reference is made to the immunities at **7.12**.

(b) Creditors selling under a standard security. The power of sale may be exercised among other remedies (see Appendix VI) when the debtor is in default. Appendix VI also shows how such default arises, and the remedies that are available on default.

The C & FR (S) Act 1970, s 25 imposes a duty on the selling creditor to advertise the sale in a medium that is seen in the locality of the property being sold. Reference may be made to the more defined rules of advertising of a sale under a bond, referred to in paragraph (c) below; further, the seller shall take all reasonable steps to ensure that the price at which the sale is made is the best that can be reasonably obtained. The sale may either be made by private bargain (ie a sale normally concluded as outlined in previous chapters) or by public auction followed by articles of roup and a minute of preference stating the name of the successful purchaser and the offer made. The articles of roup and minute of preference have a similar effect to missives.

(c) Sellers under a bond and disposition in security. Prior to the C & FR (S) Act 1970 the rules of sale under a bond and disposition in security were strict, in that the sale had to be by public auction, and certain rules of advertisement had to be implicitly followed. (See Halliday Report, paragraphs 107–118 for a critique of these rules.)

These rules were relaxed by the C & FR (S) Act 1970, s 33 et seq, but only to some extent. Thus, in terms of s 35(1), the sale may now be alternatively made by private bargain, for 'the best price that can be reasonably obtained'. A calling-up notice may take place two months after the date of service of notice, or such shorter period as may be agreed with the debtor and postponed creditors.

The C & FR (S) Act 1970, s 35 provides that a creditor in a standard security may sell either by private bargain or by auction, provided that the sale is advertised and all reasonable steps taken to ensure that the property is sold at the best price.

Section 36 of the 1970 Act imposes certain rules of advertisement which may be briefly summarised (under the *caveat* that a perusal of the Act is essential if you are involved in a sale) as follows:

Advertisements must be placed (1) if the property is in Midlothian in a daily paper published in Edinburgh; (2) if the property is in Lanarkshire in a daily paper published in Glasgow; (3) if the property is elsewhere in Scotland in a daily newspaper circulating in the district where the property is situated and in one newspaper (ie a local paper that may be weekly or twice weekly) circulating in the district and published in the county where the property is situated. (Note that the county system prior to local government reorganisation in 1973 still pertains – see Appendix IV.)

When the sale is by public roup, one advertisement a week for three consecutive weeks must be made.

When the sale is by private bargain, one advertisement a week for two consecutive weeks must be made.

These stipulations are the minimum requirements of law. The purchasers' agents must see copies of the advertisement certified as to date of publication by the newspaper publisher.

The final rule (C & FR (S) Act 1970, s 26), and one that can easily be forgotten, is that where a sale is by private bargain, the sale must be concluded within 28 days of the date of the second advertisement. This is taken to mean that missives must be concluded within the 28 days. If they are not concluded, the sale and every subsequent deed is invalid, so obviously this must be checked.

(d) Trustees in bankruptcy. Trustees in bankruptcy should, in terms of the Insolvency Act 1986, s 338, be qualified insolvency practitioners, as should liquidators, receivers and administrators of limited companies.

Sequestrations commenced after 1 April 1986 are governed by a completely new code introduced by the Bankruptcy (Scotland) Act 1985. This provides, in summary, that an interim trustee in bankruptcy shall be appointed by the sheriff to preserve the estate, and he will be replaced by a permanent trustee who is elected by the creditors. The property vests in the permanent trustee on behalf of the creditors. The Accountant in Bankruptcy issues Notes for Guidance (printed as an appendix to Professor William McBryde's Commentary on the Act) which should be closely read by anyone practising in this field.

The interim trustee has no power to sell property. The decree in bankruptcy is registered in the Personal Register by the clerk of the relevant court (s 14). The trustee cannot sell without the consent of the heritable creditors unless there are sufficient funds realised to pay off the heritable creditors, and the trustee cannot sell if a heritable creditor has intimated an intention to sell (s 39). In the case of a sale of a family home (s 40), the consent of the bankrupt's spouse (s 40), or of the court if this is not forthcoming, is required. Inhibitions against the bankrupt need not be discharged (s 31(2)).

There is no requirement for any further sequestration orders to be lodged in the Personal Register.

Title to sell is deduced through the decree in bankruptcy from the last infeft proprietor to the purchaser, as with confirmation of a deceased person (see **9.8**).

(e) A trustee under a trust deed. A trust deed is a document signed 'voluntarily' by the bankrupt, without the necessity of a court order. The trustee grants the disposition, deducing title through the trust deed, which will have been registered in the Books of Council and Session.

(f) Liquidators of limited companies. The deed to be granted here is in the name of the company and the liquidator, who signs on behalf of the company which now has no directors or secretary. As the conditions of the Companies Act 1985, s 36(3) (formerly CA 1948, s 32(4)) are not met, the signature must be witnessed. Title is deduced through the interlocutor ordering the winding up, if the liquidation is compulsory, and through the special resolution of the company, if it is voluntary. These documents should have been registered in the Companies Register as should the appointment of the liquidator.

Where the sale is by private bargain, as is usual, the consent of the creditors and of the Accountant of Court are not required (*Phillips, Liquidator of Style & Mantle Ltd* 1934 SC 548) in the disposition. The powers of a liquidator are detailed in the Companies Act 1985, s 539 (formerly CA 1948, s 245) and include the power to sell, feu or otherwise dispose of property by public sale or private bargain.

In practice, the liquidation of a company is a matter of public knowledge, and is intimated widely in the *Edinburgh Gazette* and in newspapers which should be read by legal practitioners as part of their 'common knowledge', although in all cases of dealing with a limited company the searchers should be asked if there has been any liquidator, receiver or administrator appointed, or if the company has been struck off for failure to lodge documents.

The question of the 'gap' between the appointment of a liquidator or receiver, and the printing of the advertisement is dealt with at **7.35**.

(g) Receivers. In this case the floating charge should be carefully inspected to see that it has been properly executed and registered in the Companies Register within 21 days of its registration in the Land Register or Sasine Register (a requirement of the Companies Act 1985, s 410 and the Companies Act 1989, s 95). It should also be checked to see that it includes the property purported to being sold.

The deed by the receiver runs in the name of the company and the receiver and is signed as with a deed by a liquidator.

(h) Administrators. This order proceeds upon a court interlocutor which is registered in the Companies and Personal Registers. Again, a disposition by an administrator runs in the name of the company and the administrator, and is signed by the latter.

Discharge of securities

7.24 Bearing in mind the valuable protection afforded by the C & FR (S) Act 1970, s 41(1) (see **7.13**) it is important to check discharges which have been recorded within a five-year period.

You should therefore check (1) the details of the discharge – does it fully discharge the obligation that was created?; (2) the form of the discharge; (3) the execution of the discharge; and (4) the recording of the discharge.

As to the form of the discharge, the required forms are:

(a) *Bond and disposition in security*:
 C (S) Act 1924, s 29 and Sch K(3).
 This is a very simple form of discharge, and contains no conveyancing description of the property or reference to burdens.

(b) *Standard security*: the form is provided in the C & FR (S) Act 1970, Sch 4 and Form F. Again this is a simple form.

(c) *Ex facie absolute disposition in security*: This covert security may be discharged in one of two ways:

 (i) the traditional method: a disposition back to the owner of the subjects, which takes the form of an ordinary disposition but which sets out in the narrative that the original disposition to the lenders was truly in security of a loan of £X which has now been repaid, and it is now 'right and proper' that the subjects be reconveyed. The lenders grant warrandice only from their own facts and deeds;

 (ii) the shorter statutory method: s 40 and Sch 9 of the C & FR (S) Act 1970 provide for a short form of discharge, analogous to discharges (a) and (b). This has the effect (on being recorded) of disburdening the land and vesting the land in the person entitled to it.

Generally, it makes little difference which method is used. One school prefers to discharge securities in the manner in which they were created (*unumquodque eodem modo dissolvitur quo colligatur*); the other school prefers the shorter modern method.

In addition to being discharges, a security may also be partially discharged on part payment, or restricted to any part of the land, thereby freeing the remainder for sale. (For the appropriate forms see the C & FR (S) Act 1970, Sch 4, Forms C and D.)

Fences, walls and gables

7.25 As a general rule, fences, walls and gables that lie between the properties of two persons are owned to the centre line by each proprietor, with each proprietor having an interest in the other half. It is possible, however, that the wall is owned jointly, in which case the boundary of each property is the nearest outside face of the wall, and the wall is jointly owned and maintained. Obviously this must be closely checked from the deeds.

When there is no adjoining proprietor, the wall, fence or gable is usually owned and maintained solely by the houseowner. It may be provided, however, that at a future date when someone builds on the adjoining property and uses that fence, wall or gable then that person should refund one half of the cost of building to the person who paid for it and become partly responsible for its maintenance.

When acting for purchasers of a house, particularly a new one, you should ensure:

(1)   that the fences or walls are in conformity with the feuing conditions;

(2)   the exact ownership of the fences or walls; and

(3)   that there are no outstanding charges for formation or maintenance of mutual fences, walls or gables.

Rivers and lochs

7.26   Where a property is bounded by a non-tidal river, and there is no specification of the boundary, this is taken to be the middle line (*medium filum*) of the river. This includes the fishing rights, excepting salmon fishing which must be specifically transferred to the purchasers (*McKendrick* 1970 SLT (Sh Ct) 39). The same applies to non-tidal lochs. Care should be taken when purchasing a riparian property that the landowner has not retained a narrow strip of land between the property purchased and the loch or river. If this is the case, the purchaser is not a riparian proprietor and has no rights in the loch or river.

This should have been checked before missives were concluded but better late than never.

Use

7.27   Many houses carry feuing conditions that prohibit certain uses: trade or business or profession. If your clients wanted the house for any particular business use you should really have cleared this up before completing missives. Even if your clients do not have a business use in mind, still note the restriction and inform your clients of it, in case at some time they want to pursue a business from the house. They will, of course, require to get a waiver from the superiors or (if no such waiver is forthcoming at a reasonable price) from the Lands Tribunal under the C & FR (S) Act 1970, s 1. Older, redundant uses are now omitted from a land certificate in land registration.

Feuduty

7.28   Feuduty may be allocated or unallocated. As a general rule, in Glasgow at least, detached, semi-detached and terraced houses have allocated feuduties, and flats in tenements have a cumulo feuduty (as defined in the C & FR (S) Act 1970, s 3(2)) apportioned informally, without the consent of the superior, over the various flats. (See Chapter 18.)

When the feuduty is allocated it may have been redeemed previously, either voluntarily (LTR (S) Act 1974, s 4) or compulsorily on a previous sale (LTR (S) Act 1974, ss 5 and 6).

If not, it must be redeemed by the sellers now, and a feuduty redemption receipt produced to the purchasers' agents (s 5). When a local authority is compulsorily purchasing the property, the acquiring authority should redeem the feuduty (s 6).

It is a major, and often very dangerous, misconception that the redemption of feuduty extinguishes the feudal relationship. This can only be achieved by purchasing the superiority and consolidating it with the feu (or vice versa). Redemption is purely the extinction of an annual payment; it does not otherwise affect the superior/feuar relationship (see **7.5**). Redemption does not extinguish land obligations, but these may, however, be extinguished *confusione* by consolidation. The two transactions should be distinguished clearly.

An unallocated feuduty need not be redeemed, but it is a prime duty of the purchasers' solicitors to ensure that the feuduty has been fully paid up to date, otherwise purchasers may find themselves responsible for arrears not only of their own unallocated share, but also of the *cumulo* feuduty.

Clause of pre-emption

7.29 This clause gives a person who has sold land or buildings the choice to repurchase the first time they are resold. The duty to offer the land back now affects only the first sale after the commencement of the C & FR (S) Act 1970, and after the offer has been made and refused one time the right lapses. (Conveyancing Amendment (Scotland) Act 1938, s 9, as amended by the C & FR (S) Act 1970, s 46.)

The price at which the property is to be offered back is usually the amount of the highest offer received from other parties, although occasionally the contracting parties may fix another price (for example, a price fixed at the date of agreement) in the contract containing the pre-emption clause.

From the sellers' point of view, a valid clause of pre-emption is particularly irksome, especially if they know that the right is to be exercised (say by a local authority who sold the land, but have now decided that they would like it back). The sellers must nonetheless go through the deception of a bona fide sale to establish the market value. The prospective purchasers are put to the trouble of obtaining a survey and submitting an offer. Yet if the sellers warn the purchasers of the true position, the sellers will not get a good offer for the superior to match.

The sole remedy of persons who have a right of pre-emption, which has not been observed, is to seek a court order to reduce the disposition granted without the right having been observed, and all other deeds flowing from it (*Roebuck v Edmunds* 1992 SLT 1055).

The right of pre-emption is another point that should ideally be cleared up before missives are completed. If it is found that missives have been completed and that a pre-emption clause has been overlooked, the sellers cannot give a valid title without offering the property back to the person entitled to benefit from the clause. If that person then accepts the offer, the sellers will not be able to fulfil their part of the agreement to the purchasers and will be liable in damages.

It should be mentioned that, while the clause of pre-emption is a nuisance, it now only operates between the two contracting parties, and is not a perpetual nuisance as is the case with other land conditions. If people do not like it, they should not have contracted for it.

Clause of redemption

7.30   This clause is similar in effect to the clause of pre-emption, but in this case the original owners may call for the land to be resold to them at anytime they choose, and not just when a resale takes place.

In deeds executed after 1 September 1974 a clause of redemption is exerciseable only within 20 years of its creation (LTR (S) Act 1974, s 12). (The reason for this rather unexpected provision is to prevent owners circumventing the restriction on creation of residential leases for more than 20 years, by selling property subject to a redemption clause and then redeeming it some time after 20 years have expired.) You will not therefore see a redemption clause after 1974, BUT be carefully aware of such clauses granted before 1974!

Limited time for feudalising a personal right

7.31   A deed may provide that it shall only be a valid warrant for registration for a certain time. This is to ensure that feu grants (especially) are recorded quickly and the rights of both parties made real. If this provision is not followed to the letter, and a deed is recorded despite the ever-watchful eye of the Keeper of the Register, then the registration and all that follows it are invalid.

Property bought subject to lease

7.32   Most houses are bought with vacant possession, but occasionally a house may be sold subject to a tenancy (colloquially 'with a sitting tenant'). Indeed a house may be sold to the sitting tenant (particularly local authority housing under the Housing (Scotland) Act 1987). (See Chapter 19.)

Where a house has a sitting tenant under the old Rent Acts the price will be accordingly abated where that tenant enjoys security of tenure. The value is (very roughly) around 50–60% of the value of the same house sold with vacant possession, but it depends on the circumstances (compare Chapter 19).

The intending purchasers of a house with a sitting tenant should realise what they are taking on: rent regulations, security of tenure, et cetera. The purchasers do not of course get 'vacant possession' and the sellers' warrandice must exclude the lease from its scope ('and we grant warrandice subject to the Lease between us and (et cetera)').

Moveable effects contained in missives

7.33   When the purchasers of a house buy furniture and furnishings with that house, the purchasers' solicitors should ask the sellers to confirm that they own these effects, and that there are no outstanding hire purchase, credit sale, leasing or other debts, which would mean that the sellers do not own the moveables they have sold.

NHBC

7.34   Most builders are registered members of the National House Builders Council, and this implies that a certain standard of work may be expected from the registered builder.

When a new house is built by a registered builder, the council will issue an agreement and certificate of registration. Ninety per cent of new houses in Scotland are covered by this scheme.

In the first two years of the certificate the builder (whom failing through insolvency, the council) is bound to make good any defects consequent on a breach of NHBC requirements. This does not, however, include: (i) fair wear and tear; (ii) damage caused by shrinkage to plasterwork, cement, timber et cetera as the house sheds its considerable water content after occupancy and regular heating.

After two years and up to ten years, the builder (again whom failing, the council) is bound to make good any major defects in the structure. In inflationary times, the 'top-up cover' options should always be taken. This means that the cover will increase progressively over the years to meet the cost of any repair that may be required.

The registration certificate transmits automatically from owner to owner but the purchasers should ensure that this certificate is handed over to them at settlement.

Small builders, particularly in country areas, may not be registered with the council. This implies no disrespect to most of them, as a good small builder may not find it worthwhile to join the NHBC scheme. In such a case, however, the purchasers should get a certificate from a qualified architect who is covered by indemnity insurance and who was involved in the building at all stages, that the house is complete.

Dealing with limited companies

7.35   Most limited liability companies are reputable, especially public limited companies (PLCs) which have to submit to very rigorous scrutiny, although they can quite suddenly get into serious financial difficulties.

Unfortunately, however, not all limited companies are reputable, and it should never be forgotten that the forming of a limited company is a method of escaping unlimited personal liability in the event of liquidation. In terms of the Insolvency Act 1986, s 214, personal liability for a company's debts may be placed upon directors of a limited company where, before the commencement of the winding up of that company, they knew or ought to have concluded that there was no reasonable prospect that the company would avoid going into insolvent liquidation. Such personal liability was placed upon directors in *Re Produce Marketing Consortium Ltd (in liquidation)* [1989] 3 All ER, but this may only be cold comfort for a disappointed creditor.

Some extra formalities are therefore required when dealing with companies, unless you are dealing with a company of outstanding quality. Such a company might rather resent being treated like a company, with two £1 shares issued, which was floated yesterday. This is a matter of personal judgment in all the circumstances, but you can never be wrong to ask.

There are a number of questions you should ask when purchasing, or taking security, from a limited company:

(i) Has the company been properly incorporated and constituted? You do not want to buy property from a company that does not yet exist. This information may be received by instructing the searchers to search in the Companies Register.

(ii) Is the company incorporated in this country, and as such subject to the Companies Act 1985, and other company legislation and safeguards? This applies particularly to companies registered in the Isle of Man, the Channel Islands, the Cayman Islands and Gibraltar, which can have very British names, without having the protection of British law.

(iii) Is the company properly registered, and has it been dissolved by the Register of Companies without formal liquidation in terms of the Companies Act 1985, ss 652, 653 (formerly CA 1948, s 353)? If you buy property from a dissolved company the disposition is invalid, and your only remedy is to petition the court for a restoration of the company to the Register. A search can be obtained from the Register of Companies certifying that the company has been continuously registered.

(iv) Has the company power in its Memorandum to do what it proposes to do? This has not been so crucial since the passing of the European Communitites Act 1972, s 9 (now the CA 1985, ss 35 and 36), but it is as well to see the Memorandum and articles of the company and to ensure that the action proposed is *intra vires* (within the power of the company as opposed to *ultra vires*). This is of particular relevance in land registration (see Chapters 13 to 16).

(v) *Floating charges and receiverships.* Floating charges show up in a search in the Charges Register. A receivership is public knowledge which a solicitor should know. There exists the slight difficulty (see *Gibson*, supra) that a deed has been recorded adversely, affecting the company's property, or that the company is no longer solvent, and that these events have occurred so recently that they have not been included in the search or advertised. In practical terms, and it is a practical problem, a personal warranty by the company's directors may be obtained (although there may be some resistance to this from the sellers' agents) in the terms following (adapted from JLSS Workshop 1):

'We, John Smith and Jane Smith both of 173 Cathedral Street, Glasgow, respectively a Director and the Secretary of Smiths Reciprocating Sprockets Limited (hereafter called "the Company"), HEREBY CERTIFY and WARRANT after due and diligent enquiry:

(i) that no deeds of any kind which are capable of being recorded in the Register of Sasines in respect of or affecting the subjects of sale have been granted by the company other than as were disclosed in the Search (including Interim Reports in the Search) in the Companies Register exhibited to the said Messrs Campbell, Kinloch & Co, and

(ii) that the Company is solvent and no steps have been or are about to be taken by us or any third party to commence liquidation proceedings which would prejudice the validity of the Disposition of the subjects of sale now being granted to Steelhenge Property Co Ltd, or to appoint a Receiver or otherwise place the company in a position whereby it cannot execute and deliver to you a valid and unobjectionable title.

We further agree and acknowledge that in the event of Steelhenge Property Co Ltd incurring any loss, damage or expense as a result of any of the matters included in this certificate and warranty being untrue or proving to be unfounded we shall be liable personally and individually, and jointly and severally, to make good all such loss, damage and expense to Steelhenge Property Co Ltd.

Yours faithfully,'

In addition, a letter of non-crystallisation should be obtained from the floating charge holder.

CALEDONIAN BANK
Westport
Edinburgh EH1

The Directors
Smiths Reciprocating Sprockets Limited
173 Cathedral Street
Glasgow G4

Dear Sirs,

173 Cathedral Street, Glasgow

As holders of a Floating Charge over the whole assets of Smiths Reciprocating Sprockets Limited, dated 2nd July and registered 14th July 1986, we hereby confirm that:

(1) As at that date we have taken no steps to crystallise the said Floating Charge, and we shall take no steps to crystallise the said Floating Charge within 21 days from this date, nor take any steps to impede the purchasers from obtaining a valid and marketable recorded title to the property specified in the heading of this letter.

(2) We have no objection to the sale of the above building by Smiths Reciprocating Sprockets Limited.
(3) We shall take no steps to deprive Smiths Reciprocating Sprockets Limited of right validly to convey the said subjects, provided that the Disposition thereof is recorded in the Land Register within 22 days of this date.
Yours faithfully,

Although there is still some uncertainty about this matter, this letter should meet the difficulties raised in the case of *Sharp v Thomson* 1994 GWD 19–1181, discussed in an article by Richard Leggett in September 1994 Scottish Law Gazette 99.

Adjudication titles

7.36   An adjudication may be granted against a person who either (a) does not pay a debt or (b) contracts to sell property under missives and then refuses or delays to transfer the property.

In case (a) the title given is a security title only, and the debtor may redeem within 'the legal', which is a ten-year period from the date of decree. Such a title should not be accepted by a purchaser until the legal has lapsed.

In case (b) the title is absolute and may be accepted by a purchaser or a lender in security.

A decree of adjudication is equivalent to a conveyance of lands, and the creditor (or 'adjudger' to give the proper name) completes title by recording the decree in the Personal Register, and then using the decree as a link in title to expede a Notice of Title which is recorded in the Register of Sasines.

Decrees of irritancy *in absentia*

7.37   A decree of irritancy is granted at the instance of the superior when the feuar either (a) does not implement feuing conditions contained in a contract ('conventional irritancy') or (b) fails to pay feuduty for five years (a 'statutory irritancy' under the Feuduty Act 1597 as amended by the LTR (S) Act 1974, s 15). More rarely, a feuar may irritate the superiority for failure of the superior to implement his or her undertakings in a feu writ (eg not making up roads).

An action of irritancy may be raised either in the Court of Session or in the sheriff court. The Conveyancing Amendment (Scotland) Act 1938, s 6(4) provides that a Court of Session decree shall be final and not subject to challenge in a question with third parties who have acted onerously and bona fide in reliance of the records once an extract has been recorded in the Register of Sasines.

If an action of irritancy is raised in the sheriff court the proceedings are governed by Rule 26, which was introduced to reflect the changes made in the law of irritancy by the LTR (S) Act 1974. The provisions are:

(a) If the decree is awarded *in absentia* and an extract is recorded in the General Register of Sasines or the Land Register, then in a question with third parties who have acted onerously, and in good faith in reliance on the records, the decree is final and not subject to challenge.

(b) If personal service of the decree is effected upon the debtor, the decree becomes final six months after the date of decree or after the date of the charge served upon it.

(c) Notwithstanding any of the foregoing, the decree will become final in any event after the expiry of 20 years.

Extracts

7.38 The original being locked up in Register House, an extract from the Books of Council and Session has always had exactly the same status as the original.

Not so an extract from the Register of Sasines where the original has been returned to the presenter.

Prior to 1970 a sasine extract would only be accepted with great misgivings and an insurance indemnity.

The C & FR (S) Act 1970, s 45 now provides that a sasine extract shall be accepted for all purposes as sufficient evidence of the contents of the original.

One cannot, however, help having slight misgivings about accepting a title entirely made up of extracts!

Contracts of ground annual

7.39 This hybrid document, which perpetrated a legal fiction, was created to get around the restriction against owners of property in Royal Burghs from granting feus, or where there was a restriction in a feu grant on the feuar sub-feuing part of the property. The granting of feus in burgage property became competent by the C (S) Act 1874, s 25. The provisions against sub-infeudation were repealed by the CA (S) Act 1938, s 8, and it is no longer possible to create ground annuals (annual payments similar in form but not in nature to feuduties) by the LTR (S) Act 1974, s 2. The point of granting a contract of ground annual these days is therefore small, although the practice can still occasionally be found to preserve uniformity in selling off flats in a tenement.

Contracts of ground annual, however, contained land obligations and must still be referred to for this purpose. Further, an annual payment in perpetuity was created, which can or must be redeemed in the same way as an annual feuduty (LTR (S) Act 1974, ss 4–6) if it is allocated.

The form of the deed is a disposition by the granter ('creditor') to the grantee ('debtor') in return for certain obligations running with the land and the ground annual. In security of these obligations, the debtor then grants a disposition in security back to the creditor.

The remedies of the creditor are more or less the same as those of a superior, including irritancy, which is the most important.

The contract of a ground annual is therefore both a transfer of land and a security deed – a clumsy deed that we can do well without, but which must still be treated with respect.

Power of attorney

7.40 A power of attorney is granted by a person who, for any reason (be it illness or absence abroad or any other reason), is unable to deal with his or her affairs either temporarily or permanently. This person is known as 'the constituent' and the power is granted in favour of another person or persons known as 'the attorney'. The important point is that the power must contain an exact specification of the act or acts that are permitted to the attorney. Unlike a will, *no* powers are vested in the attorney by law. Thus, if a power does not give the attorney power to sign a disposition of heritable property, for example, then no such power exists, and the power is valueless for that purpose. Obviously, therefore, where a deed is granted by an attorney, the conveyancer must ensure that the terms of this deed were permitted by the power.

A power of attorney may be either in general terms, empowering the attorney to do literally anything, or it may be in particular terms, empowering the attorney to do only one thing, such as to sell a house. An example of such a power is as follows:

'I, (name and designation), CONSIDERING that I am about to be absent from the United Kingdom and temporarily absent abroad and to facilitate the management and sale of subjects at (specify property to be sold), owned by me it is convenient that I should grant a Power of Attorney and having full trust and confidence in the integrity and competence of (name and design Attorney) THEREFORE I appoint the said (name) as my Attorney with full power to enter into any agreement for the sale of the said subjects and to sign all conveyances and other documents related thereto on my behalf and from the proceeds of sale to discharge any standard security or other form of security in connection therewith and to sign any documents related thereto; Thereafter from the net free proceeds of sale, to settle all expenses legally incurred in connection with the sale and generally to do whatever in his discretion my Attorney may think expedient for enforcing, carrying out and settling the said transaction; And I further grant to my said Attorney power to employ the firm of (name and design) to attend to the legal matters arising from the said sale; And I further authorise my Attorney to institute on my behalf, pursue to finality, defend, compromise, all and any suits or actions, disputes or differences arising from the execution of these presents or otherwise affecting me or my property; And I do hereby ratify and confirm and hereby promise to ratify, allow and confirm all and whatsoever my Attorney shall lawfully do or cause to be done in the premises in virtue hereof without prejudice always to my right demand just count and reckoning with me for the whole intromissions of my Attorney in terms hereof; And I declare that this Power of Attorney shall subsist until the same is recalled in writing; And I consent to registration hereof for preservation: IN WITNESS WHEREOF.'

A power of attorney may now be 'continuing', that is to say it continues after the constituent has become incapacitated. This has the tremendous advantage that a *curator bonis* does not have to be appointed, and the administration becomes much easier. On the other hand, it presents a temptation, for there is no real control over the attorney. For that reason the Law Society is very vigilant about solicitors who are appointed attorneys, and it is recommended that if an alternative person is available to act as attorney, then the solicitor should not be involved, except as agent for the attorney.

When a deed is signed under a power of attorney, it is signed by the attorney. The narrative of that deed may either (a) run in the name of the attorney narrating the power, and state in the testing clause that it is signed by the named attorney; or (b) run in the name of the constituent without mentioning the power, and then state in the testing clause that it is signed by the attorney on behalf of the constituent, by virtue of the power, which is then specified.

Either method may be used, but in both cases the power of attorney must be produced with the deed to authorise the signature of the attorney.

Uninfeft granters of deeds

7.41 You do not need to have a recorded title (or 'be infeft') to grant many deeds, in terms of the C (S) Act 1924, s 13, which allows an uninfeft granter to grant certain deeds using a mid-couple or link in title (see **7.14**).

Certain deeds, by virtue of not being mentioned, do not come into this category. Among the most important are feu charters, feu dispositions, feu contracts, and deeds of conditions. If they are not granted by an infeft owner, they are inept, and the important conditions that they contain are not applicable. This is not a difficult mistake to make, but it can be an embarrassing and costly one.

The remedy is for the granter to expede a notice of title, record it, and the defect is cured by accretion. The damage may, however, be done by then.

7.42 These are some of the major points to be kept in view when examining and there are many more that could be mentioned! In a routine house purchase, however, there should not be too many other points which occur regularly. If you know of any that I have missed please do not hesitate to let me know.

Remedies for an unmarketable title

7.43 The purchasers are of course entitled to resile if presented with an unmarketable title, but we will presume that the purchasers and sellers are both keen to complete the purchase. There are many varied ways of reaching settlement, but the following should be considered:

(a) The disposition *per incuriam*. If a disposition has a bad mistake in it, for example you sell the flat 1/right instead of 1/left, which is probably the commonest conveyancing mistake, you can grant this form of disposition. It simply narrates that *per incuriam* you have sold the wrong flat, and then goes on to dispone the correct one. The use of the Latin tag hides the fact that it was done (literally) 'by mistake'!

(b) By skilful use of the Conveyancing (Scotland) Act 1874, ss 38 and 39 (now the Requirements of Writing (Scotland) Act 1995, ss 4 and 5). All manner of defects of execution and mistakes in the deed can be rectified by careful use of the provisions of these sections.

(c) By use of the Law Reform (Miscellaneous Provisions) (Scotland) Act 1985, s 8(1)(a). This useful provision of law allows a disposition to be rectified by the court if it does not reflect the agreement in missives.

(d) Positive and negative prescription. You should bear in mind that prescription cures all blemishes if it is appropriate.

(e) The Keeper's discretion. In Land Registration cases the Keeper has absolute discretion to record what he wants. Thus, for example, he keeps an 'elastic tape measure' for wrong measurements, which are not too wrong.

Similarly he will turn a blind eye to other blemishes of title, which therefore disappear through not being shown on the Land Certificate. The only trouble is he will not tell you what he proposes to do, and turning a blind eye to something once does not mean that he will do it again. There is no doubt that judicious use of this power has made life much easier for conveyancers in operational areas for registration.

(f) The insurance indemnity. An indemnity policy can be taken out to cover a defect in title, which recompenses the purchaser if a claim arises from a third party. One insurance company advertises indemnity policies available against: absence of matrimonial affidavit, giving rise to a claim by a non-entitled spouse; *a non domino* disposition, where there is a claim by the true owner within the prescriptive period; failure to establish a link in title; lack of access rights; burdens imposed on the feu, and a possible claim by the superior when they have been contravened without having been discharged; discrepancies in the description of land and incorrect detailing of plans. A purchaser is not, however, obliged to accept an indemnity, as it does not render a title marketable. It is only an indemnity until prescription extends its healing balm.

(g) The *actio quanti minoris*. This remedy, which can be imported by contract, is available. It involves a reduction of the price where there is something wrong in the title or the subjects.

(h) *De minimis non curat lex*. 'The law does not care about little things'. Try and persuade the purchaser that no court would accept the objection to your defective title!

Chapter eight

NOTES ON TITLE, SEARCHES, CONTINUATIONS, OBLIGATIONS AND DRAFTS

' "Habit and Repute Skilful" was the phrase used by Lord Advocate J B Balfour in 1879 to define those who could be entrusted with the responsibility of carrying out searches. This opinion, prepared on memorial for the firm of Millar and Bryce, was instrumental in shaping our profession, and forms the basis of the current trusts between conveyancers and searchers.'
(Circular 1994)

Notes on title

8.1 We have already been through the main points of observation in a title. A methodical way of noting title is to prepare 'Notes on Title' – which are a summary of the main parts of the deeds you have been given. I have given an example of sample Notes on Title in Appendix I.25.

I fully appreciate that some conveyancers will criticise my Notes for being too short; and others will say that they are over-detailed! In my defence I can only say I choose a middle course, and I do not expect to please everybody.

The main points of Notes are that at any future date, when you do not have the titles before you, you can prepare a disposition or security at short notice, or answer any question which arises in a title.

Good Notes on Title also have an archival interest. The 'good conveyancing firm' where I served my apprenticeship kept all notes in bound volumes. It was surprising how often reference was made to these volumes, both for details of the properties in question and for neighbouring properties.

The search

8.2 The search is an indispensable part of any property title. It is prepared and continued (when necessary) by one of the firms of professional searchers. All are covered against the financial consequences of error in preparing searches, which could be considerable. In practice all are careful and accurate, and mistakes are mercifully rare.

The search has two aspects, or in the case of limited companies selling, three aspects. These are:

(a) The General Register of Sasines (Property Register)

(b) The Register of Inhibitions and Adjudication (Personal Register)

(c) The Register of Charges (for limited companies and unlimited companies under the Companies Act 1985 only).

The principles of the search in the Sasine Register are carried forward to the Land Register, where the search is in the shape of Forms 10, 11, 12 and 13 as appropriate. (See Chapters 14–17.) The forms are answered, however, in much less detail.

The property search

8.3 The search in the Property Register contains a note of the principal details of all feu writs, dispositions, securities, discharges, et cetera which affect the property or any part of it.

This register of property writs is of ancient origin, having been set up as 'ane publick Register of Sasines, reversions, et cetera' by a Scottish Act of 1617, c 16.

The Register has, however, been kept up to date through frequent innovation, the latest being microfilming of record books, computerisation of the Presentment Book and optical scanning of presentation forms.

The Register is now governed by the Land Registers (Scotland) Act 1868, as subsequently amended. This Act incidentally abolished the Particular Register of Sasines (eg Renfrewshire and the Regality of Glasgow) kept locally, and moved the registration of all property writs to Register House in Edinburgh, which has now been replaced by the modern Meadowbank House. Register House in Princes Street (opposite Waverley Station) still serves as the storehouse of older documents, and has no role in the everyday conveyancing transaction.

The search discloses only the matters detailed below. It does not disclose a variety of other matters which are detailed in Appendix 8 to the Reid Committee Report on Registration of Title (1963 Cmnd 2032) the more important of which are:

leases unless recorded under the Registration of Leases (Scotland) Act 1857 as amended by the Land Tenure Reform Act 1974;

old heritable securities kept alive by payments (see **8.9**);

servitudes created informally and not by recorded deed;

planning notices unless recorded;

demolition orders and other notices affecting the structure;

details of company liquidations and receiverships.

8.4 The abridged details of deeds given in the search are the names and designations of parties, short details of the property, dates of signing and registration date.

Although financial details of securities and their transmissions and discharges are given, prices paid for property are not given, and this information must be obtained by consulting the deeds themselves. The searchers can provide this information.

8.5 It is a matter of personal preference, of course, but I recommend that the first document to be looked at when examining title, should be the search. This gives a checklist of the deeds you have been given (or should have been given) and gives you a potted history of the property, which makes things much easier. The Law Society recommend that you look back for 40 years, but there is no reason why you should not look back further, for all the time it takes. You might find something of interest or use.

The personal search

8.6 The Register of Inhibitions and Adjudications was established in its modern form by the Conveyancing (Scotland) Act 1924, although again its origins are much more ancient. By s 44 of that Act it is a register for 'Inhibitions, Interdictions, Adjudications, Reductions, and Notices of Litigiosity'.

That is to say it is a register containing certain notifications, required by statute, that the owners of the property have for some reason become barred from granting future, voluntary, deeds of their property. This is what is called 'a state of litigiosity' and why the notices are called 'Notices of Litigiosity'.

Naturally the existence of such a notice is a matter of great importance to the intending purchaser, or to someone who intends to lend money on the security of the property.

The matters contained in this Register are as follows:

(a) Inhibitions. An inhibition is a personal prohibition at the instance of the creditor, restraining the person inhibited from contracting any debt or granting any deed by which the land, or any part of it, may be alienated to the prejudice of the inhibiting creditor. Please note that it relates to the person only as a property owner and not to the property itself.

It may be obtained either in execution of a decree or following execution of a decree of registration following on consent to registration for execution, or in security when the debtor has a liquid ground of debt, and on the dependence of an action of a pecuniary nature, pending judgment.

The nature of an inhibition is entirely negative. It only stops the debtors from dealing with their property if they are contemplating doing so anyway; if they are not, the remedy is quite ineffective and duly prescribes after five years, unless renewed. It may, however, cause considerable embarrassment to the person inhibited.

If, however, the debtors are about to sell, the inhibition has to be cleared before they can do so. Thus if A owes B £5,000 and B finds that A is about to sell the house, B can raise an action and immediately inhibit A from selling. A thus cannot sell without settling with B. What is less desirable is where B raises a speculative action and inhibition against A, who is thereby forced into a difficult position. B then possibly settles the case disadvantageously to be rid of this nuisance, and to settle the sale.

An inhibition affects only future voluntary deeds, thus if A has completed missives, A is bound to grant a disposition. This is not a future voluntary deed, and is not stopped by the inhibition. It is questionable, however, if a clear search can be delivered in these circumstances, but the matter may be put beyond doubt by exhibiting missives concluded before the inhibition, but this is extrinsic evidence. On this topic generally, see *Newcastle Building Society v White* 1987 SLT (Sh Ct) 81. Further, an inhibition does not affect a sale by a creditor under a security (*McGowan* 1977 SLT (Sh Ct) 41).

A threatened inhibition apparently may not be forestalled by lodging a *caveat* with the court. A *caveat* (literally 'a warning') when properly lodged requires the court to inform the person or firm who lodged the *caveat* of any process in dependence of an action, that is before the action is decided on its merits. The *caveat* is most particularly used in the case of a possible action of interdict, when a decree of interim interdict may be granted on the statement of the person seeking the interdict, without the person being interdicted having to be informed. Another use of the *caveat* is to warn of arrestments on the dependence of an action.

While the aim of the interdict procedure is to allow a wrong to be interdicted quickly, it does encourage some speculative interim interdicts, where the purpose is either blackmail or revenge. These actions can cause considerable, wrongful, harm to the person interdicted. The interdict can be withdrawn – with cause shown – at a reasonably early date on cause shown, and possibly damages be awarded for wrongful interdict. By that time considerable harm may have been done.

For that reason most commercial firms lodge *caveats* in various courts as necessary, to prevent a speculative interim interdict being obtained against them.

The same process is available as a warning against arrestments of sums due on the dependence. Again, considerable harm may be caused by a speculative arrestment in the hands of a firm's bank or major customer, and a *caveat* is a protection against wrongful use of the process. It might be thought that the same argument would apply to inhibitions, but this apparently is not the case. In a judgment (reported without citation in September 1989 JLSS 318) Lord Cullen said:

> 'Having heard counsel I took the view that the *caveat* should not be entertained. I considered that it was of the essence of an effective inhibition, in security that it should be obtained promptly and without warning to the debtor, who might otherwise arrange his affairs so as to avoid its effect. It is not surprising that there is apparently no precedent for a *caveat* against a bill for letters of inhibition, let alone against a warrant contained in a summons. I did not consider that the use of *caveats* in regard to interim interdict in a petition or an action provided a good analogy to the present *caveat*.'

This statement may justify further discussion.

A completed and recorded inhibition can only be discharged:

(a) by a formal discharge granted by the creditor, which is recorded in the Personal Register;

(b) re-call by the court, which is noted in the margin of the Register;

(c) prescription after five years. This prescriptive period applies to all notices of litigiosity.

Letters of inhibition can be obtained only from the Petition Department of the Court of Session. The letters are executed against the debtor, and preliminary notice in terms of Sch PP of the Titles to Land Consolidation (Scotland) Act 1868. The date of this notice is the effective date of the inhibition provided that the inhibition itself is executed and registered within 21 days. If it is not, the effective date of the inhibition is the date of the registration of the inhibition (ie the latter date).

A detailed study of the entire matter of inhibitions and adjudications and their complex relationships with sequestrations and liquidations is contained in *The Law of Inhibition and Adjudication* by G L Gretton (1987).

(b) Adjudications. Unlike the inhibition the adjudication is an active form of diligence. It permits the creditor to attach the heritage of the debtor in satisfaction of a debt. It can also be used where the debtor is under a duty to convey heritage, but does not do so; an adjudication which gives the creditor a judicial title. (Eg A sells property to B in terms of missives, but refuses to complete, B may obtain an adjudication which gives B an absolute title.) Where a decree of adjudication is granted for a debt, the decree is only a security title and may be redeemed within TEN years on payment of the debt. This ten-year period is known as 'the legal'.

A notice of adjudication has to be lodged in the Personal Register in terms this time of TLC (S) Act 1868, Sch RR and this notice has the effect of rendering the property litigious from the date of the notice.

(c) Reductions. Where there are grounds of objection to a deed involving essential error, or fraud, or force and fear, or facility and circumvention, or undue influence, or want of title, or power to grant, or of requisite solemnities, or minority and lesion, or where a deed has been granted in prejudice to lawful creditors, then that deed may be reduced by an action of reduction in the Court of Session.

As with an adjudication (see C (S) Act 1924, s 44) where the deed refers to heritable property, it is necessary to prepare and register a notice in terms of TLC (S) Act 1868, Sch RR.

(d) Sequestrations. The Bankruptcy (Scotland) Act 1985, as amended in 1993, replaces the Bankruptcy (Scotland) Act 1913, which latter Act still regulates bankruptcies arising before 1 April 1986.

Under the 1985 Act, the Accountant in Bankruptcy replaces the Accountant of Court and the Accountant's general function is defined in notes issued by the Accountant as 'the exercise of overall supervision of the administration of all sequestrations and the conduct of those involved in that administrative process'. The notes (printed as an Appendix to *Bankruptcy* by Professor W W McBryde (1989)) should be carefully read by anyone practising in this specialised field.

The 1985 Act requires registration in the Personal Register of certain events affecting the capacity of the bankrupt as follows:

(i) A certified copy of the award of sequestration by the court (B (S) Act 1985, s 14(2)). The date of the order is the date of sequestration, and operates as an inhibition of the bankrupt's heritable property;

(ii) A certified copy order of court refusing an award of sequestration (s 15(5)(a));

(iii) A certified copy order recalling an award of sequestration (s 17(8)(a));

(iv) A certified copy of discharge (Sch 4, para 11);

(v) A certified copy order deferring discharge of the debtor beyond the normal three-year period (s 54(7)).

These notices are registered to provide public notification of the event concerned.

It should be noted that the normal period of bankruptcy is three years, and not five as was suggested by the Scottish Law Commission, to conform with the short prescriptive period.

(e) English bankruptcies. These are governed by the Insolvency Act 1986. Where an English bankrupt has property in Scotland, an order for the adjudication of bankruptcy and appointment of the trustee is certified in the Petition Department of the Court of Session. This is then registered in the Personal Register.

8.7 The Personal Register is computerised. The information contained is virtually up to date. The computer also searches against all names which either look the same, or sound the same, as the one you are enquiring about. Thus if you ask for a search against John Smith it will also search against Smyths and Smythes.

The Register of Charges

8.8 This applies only to limited or unlimited companies which own heritage. The Register was established by the Companies (Floating Charges) (Scotland) Act 1961, s 6 which was re-enacted by the Companies (Floating Charges and Receivers) (Scotland) Act 1972, s 6, which in turn was consolidated into the Companies Act 1985.

Since 27 October 1961, the date of inception of the Register, it has been necessary to register all Charges (as defined in the Companies Act 1985, s 410 (formerly CA 1948, s 106 A(2)) – a fairly mixed bag, of which securities granted over land are the most important to the conveyancer and the crystallisation of charges.

This Register is not kept at Meadowbank House, but at the Companies Office, 37 Castle Terrace, Edinburgh, EH1 2EB (Telephone 0131 535 5800).

Separate instructions for search are not, however, necessary, and the searchers will search in the Charges Registers, and the G fiche and AR fiche, if you ask them in your memorandum. The former will tell you whether the company is in liquidation, receivership, administration or has been struck off for failing to lodge annual returns, which is fairly vital information, especially in the case of a striking off. If a company is struck off the fact is not publicised, and you may find yourself dealing with a non-existent company. The remedy is then to lodge the missing returns, and petition the court to have the company restored to the roll. This is troublesome, time wasting and expensive. The AR fiche tells you who are the company directors and secretary, and who therefore is entitled to sign deeds on the company's behalf.

Searching procedure

8.9

(a) The Property Register. A ruling of the Law Society (*Council News* May/June 1972) states that

> 'despite the reduction in the prescriptive period from twenty years to ten years, no change should be made in the present practice of requiring a search for forty years, and that a purchaser's agent should ordinarily stipulate in missives that he requires such a search to be exhibited or delivered'.

This clear ruling was, however, replaced by the Conveyancing Committee in a Minute of 23 September 1982, which states that

> 'each transaction depended on its circumstances, and that the basic criterion was that there should be clear searches. The minimum period required by law, unless varied contractually in the missives, was from the date of the recording of the founding writ for prescription'. (See **7.14**.)

Why 40 years when the prescriptive period is only 10 years? Prior to the C (S) Act 1924 the prescriptive period was 40 years and by that Act it became 20. But the search period was not cut then, nor after the C & FR (S) Act 1970 which reduced the prescriptive period of 10 years.

The 40-year figure is an arbitrary one, dictated by the conveyancer's nightmare that there exists an old bond over the property which has not been discharged, nor has prescribed, but has been kept alive by payments of interest to the lender, thus defeating any possibility of its prescription.

It is thought that in a 40-year period there must have been some entry in the Register relating to the bond, which would disclose its existence, such as an assignation, a transmission to trustees on the death of the creditor, or a partial discharge.

While the examination of a 40-year search cannot be absolutely guaranteed to show up evidence of any such old bonds (which in any event must be fairly rare) it is certainly preferable to a 20-year or 10-year search which could easily omit such a bond.

It is not reasonable to ask for a search for more than 40 years. If, however, an older search is presented to you, it should be examined from the beginning. The reason for this is largely one of interest, and then you never know what you may find!

(b) The Personal Register. You should search against every party who had a right to the property within the prescriptive period. You want to ensure that there was no notice of litigiosity to prevent them transferring the property. As such notices prescribe after five years, you therefore need only search back against the granter(s) of a deed for five years prior to the date of recording of each deed.

Thus if you have (in 1995) the following deeds;

(i)   Disposition A to B recorded 5 July 1991

(ii) Disposition B to C recorded 6 November 1993

(iii) Confirmation in favour of C's executor dated 7 October 1994

(iv) Disposition by D the executor of C to E recorded 3 February 1995

and you are buying the property from E with entry on 1 April 1995, you should see personal searches as follows:

against A from 5 July 1986 to 5 July 1991
against B from 6 November 1988 to 6 November 1993
against C from 7 October 1989 to 7 October 1994
against D as executor of C from 7 October 1994 to 3 February 1995
against E for five years prior to date of recording of E's disposition in favour of your client.

(c) The Charges Register. You search against each company appearing in the Property Register within the prescriptive period either (a) from the date of the inception of the Register (27 October 1961) or (b) if the company was incorporated after that date, from the date of incorporation.

You are looking to see that there was no impediment to the company's sale by either (a) standard securities granted to other parties or (b) floating charges granted to other parties, which do not in themselves affect a sale, but which may contain a prohibition against sale without the creditor's consent.

The Charges Register does not disclose the appointment of a liquidator or receiver or administrator of the company, nor the removal from the Register, which information must be gained either from public notice or from the Companies Register (G fiche). Nor does it give details of directors and secretary, which can be gained from the Companies Register (AR fiche). The searchers should be asked to provide this information if it is needed.

8.10   A search is brought up to date by an interim report on search, which is prepared by the searchers at the request of the sellers' agents. This is prepared on the basis of a memorandum for search (if there is no search in existence) or a memorandum for continuation of search (if there is). This memorandum is prepared in draft by the sellers' agents, and is approved by the purchasers' agents. The memorandum is then sent to the searchers with the search (if of course there is one) and the interim report is returned within two or three days. Reference should be made to Appendix I.20(b) and I.35 for the practical aspects of this, and to the Procedural Table I at the front for the procedure to be followed by both agents. An interim report should generally be seen within about seven days of settlement.

Letter of obligation

8.11   The Personal Register and the Charges Register are kept almost completely up to date.

This is not the case with the Property Register. Because of the elaborate and necessary examination of writs procedures in Meadowbank House, the property search is always about two or three months behind time. Computerisation of the Presentment Book should greatly cut down this delay, but the information contained is not warranted. A prudent conveyancer will, however, obtain a search in the Presentment Book before granting a letter of obligation, to minimise the risk.

Thus if purchasers' agents are settling a transaction, they may not be able to get a report on a search which is up to date. This is the problem that the computerised Presentment Book is intended to minimise.

In that blank period, the sellers could quite easily have effected another sale or granted another security over the property. They could have done this by going to a solicitor, other than the one acting already in the transaction, and stated that they wanted to sell the property or take a loan, but had 'lost the title deeds'.

A sale could then innocently be affected by this third solicitor on the basis of extract deeds obtained from the General Register. (See **7.38**.) A more real danger is that the sellers might be persuaded to sign a document for a finance house, which turns out to be a standard security, and which is duly registered after the date of the interim report.

This, fortunately, seldom happens, but it could easily happen where a dishonest person is involved. This difficulty is circumvented (from the purchasers' point of view) by the sellers' solicitors granting an obligation to produce a clear search brought down to the date of sale, within a certain time, usually six or nine months, of that date. (See Appendix I.20 (C).)

Please note that if a fraud occurs the solicitors granting the letter of obligation become personally responsible for the loss jointly and severally with the clients (*McGillivray v Davidson* 1993 SLT 693). As the clients will be unlikely to have the money, and as the solicitors should be protected by insurance, the solicitors will be inevitably chosen, as in the case of *Warners v Beveridge & Kellas* (1993 GWD 34–2187, 1993 GWD 38–2509 and 1994 Scottish Law Gazette 14 and 127).

In *Warners* the letter of obligation read:

'With reference to the settlement of the above transaction today we hereby undertake (1) to deliver to you within 12 months from this date search for encumbrances brought down in terms of the memorandum adjusted between us and showing the records to be clear in the Sasine and Personal Register in so far as affecting our clients' title, which search will disclose your clients' title provided your clients' title is recorded within 21 days from this date.'

The purchasers did not however record their title for some six months, and when the search was produced it was found that there was an extraneous standard security in favour of a third party. A dispute arose concerning the time limit underlined above (by me). The Sheriff took the view in the circumstances that the letter of obligation was granted to protect the purchaser in the delay between settlement and production of the search, and that there is no reason why this obligation should be the subject of a three-week time limit, and that the time limit related only to disclosure of the disposition and that the main obligation to deliver a clear search up to the date of settlement remained intact. An appeal was unsuccessful.

Accordingly the Law Society in a circular of 30 January 1994 recommends a style of letter of obligation, prepared by Professor Robert Rennie with the approval of the Society which should be used and which reads as follows:

> 'With reference to the settlement of the above transaction today we hereby (One) undertake to exhibit/deliver to you within twelve months following the date hereof Searches in the Property and personal Registers brought down to the date fourteen days after the date hereof in terms of the Memorandum adjusted between us, which Searches shall (a) be clear of any entry deed or diligence which is either prejudicial to the validity of or is an encumbrance upon the title of our client and (b) will disclose the Disposition or other deed in favour of your client provided it is recorded in the Register of Sasines within fourteen days of the date hereof and (Two) undertake to deliver to you within six months following the date hereof a duly recorded discharge of (short details of relevant heritable security).'

This is what is known as a classic obligation, and broadly the insurers will pay out if a claim is made under this letter, for the solicitors have taken all reasonable steps to protect themselves from claims. A non-classic obligation on the other hand is one that contains obligations that are not within the solicitors' control, such as delivery of planning permissions, building warrants or completion certificates. For many examples of non-classic obligations, see an article by Professor Rennie in November 1993 JLSS 431.

The sellers' solicitors should therefore be pretty sure of the honesty of their clients before undertaking this obligation upon themselves. If they do not trust their clients, they should not grant the obligation. In fact, if at this stage or any other stage of the transaction they find that they do not trust their clients they should immediately cease to act and direct the clients elsewhere. The solicitor/client relationship must be based on mutual trust.

Moreover it is stressed that solicitors should not grant a letter of obligation covering any matter over which they have no control. Thus it is in order to grant an obligation to produce a search, or a discharge that has not yet been signed and returned by the building society at the time of settlement. It is **not** in order to grant an obligation to produce a clear planning certificate or roads certificate, because there is no way in which its contents can be predicted before it eventually arrives. What is more, the solicitors' indemnity policy will not cover losses arising from such folly.

8.12 The purchasers' solicitors should be satisfied that the draft memorandum for (or continuation of) search and draft letter of obligation to be offered by the sellers' solicitors are sufficient for their purposes. They should then mark the drafts as approved, initial and date these, and return them to the sellers' solicitors. With this they should also send their draft disposition and observations on title. (See Appendix I.34.)

Chapter nine

THE DRAFT DISPOSITION

'Staff in a Glasgow hospital were puzzled to read in a patient's notes that her inability to lose weight was due to her "love of Taggart on telly". A very interesting and specific case of couch potato-ism, they thought. Further enquiries of the doctor involved revealed that there had been a slip twixt dictaphone and typewriter. It should have read that her weight problem was due to "love of tagliatelle".'

(Tom Shields' Diary – *The Herald*)

9.1 There should not, in theory at least, be much difficulty in drafting the disposition of an established house. Unlike the drafting of a feudal grant of a piece of land cut out of a larger area, you should not have to worry about describing the land or creating lengthy and complex land obligations. This work should already have been done, and you simply have to refer to past deeds for these details.

The main attributes of a good draftsman are: (1) a fluency in written English; (2) a complete knowledge of the form of the deed and what should be found in the deed, and in what order; (3) in light of the quotation printed above, if dictating machines are used, clear diction.

No one can help you with the first attribute at this stage of your career, but I can remind you of the contents of a disposition. On the first point, incidentally, I have never understood why the disposition is such a travesty of English: full of obsolete terms, redundant words, and containing the grammatical solecism of being one long sentence, divided by semi-colons. I have expressed my views on this point already in 1975 JLSS 126 and 364 and over the years have not departed one iota from these. Fortunately there are signs that dispositions are becoming more 'user-friendly', but all I can say to the young lawyer at this stage is follow the conventional form now, and hope wiser ways will eventually prevail. A person with a sound knowledge of English should be able to write bad English as well as good! On this whole matter see 'Drafting – Plain English for Lawyers' 1984 JLSS 371 and 411.

If a draft deed is dictated or handwritten, please remember that the typist is not superhuman, and make your intentions crystal clear. Then carefully check the draft. The most dangerous examples are when a typist guesses, and *nearly* gets it right. Thus, a deed that said 'I grant drainage rise'; and another which contained a restrictive covenant, not permitting a seller of a business to trade within one mile of a certain point – unfortunately the typist had not been able to read the writing, and had guessed at a distance of one metre!

Typing errors should not occur so frequently with word processors, and I would advise drafters of deeds to correct the drafts on the screen. Typists, however, do get tired and distracted, and that's when mistakes happen. The most common mistake is when a typist's eye jumps from a word on one line to the same word on a line below, and thus a chunk of the deed is missed out.

9.2 As with all deeds, there are four main parts:

1 narrative clause

2 dispositive clause

3 ancillary clauses

4 testing clause

In the case of a disposition, a fifth part (the warrant of registration) is added, except for deeds to be registered in the Land Register. In the Land Register it is not necessary to insert a warrant of registration, because the Forms 1, 2 and 3 all contain a request to the Keeper to register the deed in the Land Register.
   In a disposition the parts are made up as follows:

1 Narrative: (See 9.3 and 9.4.)
(a) granter's name and designation
(b) grantee's name and designation
(c) any consenter's name and designation
(d) the consideration

2 Dispositive: (See 9.5 and 9.6.)
(a) Words of conveyance
(b) Any special destination required by the purchaser
(c) Description of the land
(d) Conveyance of the parts and pertinents
(e) Any excepted parts of the land, sold separately
(f) The land obligations affecting the land

3 Ancillary: (See 9.7 and 9.8.)
(a) Date of entry
(b) Deduction of title, if appropriate
(c) (Assignation of Writs) (not now necessary)
(d) (Assignation of Rents) (not now necessary)
(e) (Obligation of Relief) (not now necessary)
(f) Warrandice
(g) Non-supersession clause
(h) Stamp Duty Certificate

4 Testing clause. (See 9.9 and 9.10.)

5 Warrant of registration. (See 9.11 and 9.12.)

The narrative

9.3 This clause should set out the reason for granting the deed and the names of the parties and the consideration. All the facts and circumstances affecting the liability of the instrument to stamp duty, or the amount of duty, shall be 'fully and truly set forth'. (Stamp Act 1891, s 5.)

(a) The name and designation he or she or it had in a previous deed, for example: I, John Smith, Architect, residing formerly at 3 Talavera Street, Glasgow and now at 5 Salamanca Drive, Glasgow (where the grantee of the last deed has changed address) *or* I, Mrs Jane Brown or Smith, Computer Programmer, residing at 6 Torres Vedras Road, Glasgow (formerly Jane Brown, University Student, residing at 8 Victoria Crescent, Glasgow) (where the grantee of the last deed was an unmarried female, who has now become married, adopted her husband's name and changed address).

or

We, Smith Limited, incorporated under the Companies Act and having our Registered Office at 100 Leipzig Road, Glasgow (formerly Brown Limited conform to Certificate of Change of Name granted by the Register of Companies on Fifth November Nineteen hundred and seventy three). (Where a limited company has simply changed its name it remains exactly the same company, but with a different name – just like a person who changes his or her name.)

(b/c) The consent would be taken of any person who has a contingent interest in the property, eg a liferenter, a person with a right under missives who has re-sold et cetera or most importantly these days, a non-entitled spouse under the MH(FP) (S) Act 1981 (see Appendix IV. 4). They and the grantees should be designated in the same manner as the granter.

(d) The consideration is either a sum of money in a normal sale; or 'for certain good and onerous causes' where it is a commercial transaction, but no price as such is paid (eg an old *ex facie* absolute disposition to a building society); or 'for the love, favour and affection that I bear for him/her' (eg in the case of a gift to a member of the granter's family).

Example of narrative clause

9.4

'I, John Smith, Solicitor of Twenty three Wilhelmina Street, Ayr, Executor Nominate of William McWilliam, late of Twenty two Juliana Street, Ayr, conform to Confirmation in my favour issued from the Commissariat of South Strathclyde, Dumfries and Galloway at Ayr on Tenth November Nineteen hundred and eighty five, and as such executor uninfeft proprietor of the subjects hereafter disponed IN CONSIDERATION of the price of THIRTY FIVE THOUSAND POUNDS (£35,000) paid to me as Executor aforesaid by JAMES LESLIE and LESLEY LESLIE, spouses, both of Twenty three Utopia Street, Glasgow, of which I acknowledge the receipt and discharge them. ...'

Notes: The granter is an executor and does not have a recorded title. The last name in the title was not his, and we must therefore explain why he is granting this deed, and deduce his title under the Conveyancing (Scotland) Act 1924, s 3. The grantees of the deed are a married couple, and we shall therefore have to consider the special destination in the dispositive clause. We shall assume that in this case there is no consenter. The receipt and discharge is unnecessary, and may be omitted as delivery of the deed amounts to receipt of the price.

The dispositive clause

9.5   (a) The words of conveyance. You do not require to use these exact words, as long as you use words indicating the intention to transfer, but it is customary to say 'HAVE SOLD AND DO HEREBY DISPONE'.

(b) Special destinations. Up till quite recently, it was quite common for the husband in a married couple to take the title to the family home in his (usually) name alone. This has been rendered more and more pointless by changed attitudes and consequent modern legislation, culminating in the Matrimonial Homes (Family Protection) (Scotland) Act 1981 (as amended).

It is suggested therefore that nowadays the family home should be taken in joint names in all but the most exceptional cases.

There are however, two variants of this destination:

(i)   The house may be taken in the names of both spouses and the survivor. Thus, if one spouse dies, his or her share passes automatically to the other spouse without any further formality, as at the time of death. If the survivor sells the house, he or she simply grants the deed as survivor, and title need not be deduced through confirmation, although an affidavit would need to be granted certifying that the property is not a matrimonial home in relation to which a spouse of the seller has occupancy rights (see Appendix III.1) and exhibited with a death certificate. It is also necessary to prove that the destination has been evacuated, and this is usually done by producing a death certificate of the spouse who has died.

(ii)   Alternatively, the house may be taken in the name of both spouses, and their respective executors and representatives. Thus if one spouse dies, his or her share goes not automatically to the other spouse, but to the person entitled under the will or the laws of intestacy.

In the normal case alternative (i) is probably preferable, as it presents a quick and convenient method of giving the surviving spouse a title to the whole house. There may be, however, some convincing reason for not wanting this to happen – eg for inheritance tax purposes the estate of the surviving spouse perhaps should not be increased because he or she is already over the dutiable limit, and property should therefore be passed on to eg children.

In the case of two unrelated persons buying property jointly, they will possibly wish destination (ii) but the alternatives should be explained to them, and careful instructions taken, preferably in writing.

Where an engaged couple is purchasing, a survivorship destination is possibly not appropriate in case one party should die before the wedding takes place, and the whole house therefore becomes the property of the survivor.

That might not be the wish of the deceased person. Again, explain and get instructions.

In all cases of special destinations to two or more persons, remember that effectively you are making a will for them of a substantial asset, and furthermore a will that they do not sign.

(c) Description of the land. The words 'heritably and irredeemably' are surplusage, but are customarily inserted. The description starts with the words 'ALL and WHOLE'.

Your description should be a valid reference to a prior full description, all in terms of the Conveyancing (Scotland) Act 1924, s 8 and Sch D. The Notes in this Schedule should be particularly studied by the conveyancer.

It is absolutely essential for a valid description to name the county in which the property is situated. The parish may also be mentioned, but this is not at all necessary. Please do not forget that conveyancing still operates on the old county system and not on regions and districts. (See Appendices IV and V.) The more modern-minded may want to put in the name of the district and/or region as well as the county, or indeed the new unitary authorities (see Appendix V), but this is not required.

(d) Conveyance of the parts and pertinents.

'A grant of the lands of A is as extensive as a grant of the lands of A with the parts and pertinents.' (*Gordon* (1850) 13 D 1.)

It is customary to insert here (a) the postal address of the house (b) the heritable fittings and fixtures (c) the pertinents, rights, privileges and all common rights and (d) whole right, title and interest. None of these is necessary, except exact postal address, which may clarify or supplement a faulty description, and supply a good common law description, of the statutory description as faulty.

(e) Exceptions. If since the last deed was recorded, part of the garden has been sold for, say, road widening to the regional council, this area of ground should be excepted from the description.

(f) The land obligations. Again it is customary to mention in the title deeds such words as 'BUT ALWAYS WITH and UNDER so far as valid, still subsisting and applicable, the real burdens, declarations, conditions, restrictions, obligations, servitudes and other affecting the plot of ground hereby disponed.' This practice overlooks the tidy definition of land obligations in section 1 of the C & FR (S) Act 1970 which includes all of these older words.

The reference to the earlier deed or deeds containing the land obligations affecting the plot of ground is governed by the terms of the Conveyancing (Scotland) Act 1874, s 32 and Sch H and the Conveyancing (Scotland) Act 1924, s 9 and Sch E. The rules of reference to the earlier deed are similar to those relating to deeds referred to for a description ((c)) and again the notes in the Schedules should be studied carefully.

Example of dispositive clause

9.6

'HAVE SOLD AND DO HEREBY DISPONE to and in favour of the said James Leslie and Lesley Leslie equally between them and to the survivor of them and to the Executor of the survivor (alternatively the ordinary destination – "equally between them and to their respective executors and assignees whomsoever"). ALL and WHOLE that plot of ground lying in the County of Ayr containing Eighty four decimal or one thousandth part of an acre or thereby Imperial Measure, being the plot of ground described in delineated and marked Plot III on the plan annexed and signed as relative to Feu Charter by Millhaugh Development Company Limited in favour of Gregor McGregor dated Third and recorded in the Division of the General Register of Sasines applicable to the County of Ayr on Tenth both days of July Nineteen hundred and fifty three, together with (One) the dwellinghouse known as Twenty two Juliana Street, Ayr and other buildings and erections built on the ground; (Two) the fixtures and fittings therein and thereon; (Three) the pertinents, rights and privileges including common rights (if any) pertaining to the said plot of ground; and (Four) my whole right, title and interest present and future in and to the said plot of ground as Executor foresaid; BUT ALWAYS WITH and UNDER so far as still valid, subsisting and applicable the real burdens, declarations, conditions, restrictions, obligations, servitudes and others specified in (First) Feu Contract between Alpin McAlpine and another of the one part and Hugh McHugh of the other part dated First and subsequent dates of January and recorded in the said Division of the General Register of Sasines on Third February Eighteen hundred and eighty four; and (Two) Disposition by Jon Evans and another the Trustees of Evan Evans in favour of Millhaugh Development Company Limited dated Third and subsequent dates and recorded Twenty fourth all days of June Nineteen hundred and fifty two; and (Three) the said Feu Charter by Millhaugh Development Company Limited on favour of Gregor McGregor dated and recorded as aforesaid; ...'

Note: I have drafted this clause in the traditional manner. It should not be taken as being to my liking, but the great thing for a young lawyer is to plagiarise slavishly at the start of his or her career, and to innovate later!

Ancillary clauses

9.7   3(a) The date of entry. This is simply the date on which the control of the house changes hands. If a date of entry is not inserted in a formal deed of this nature, the court will supply one – generally the next term date of Whitsunday or Martinmas.

3(b) Deduction of title. If this is appropriate (as it is in this case because the granter is an executor and not the person who appears in the search as the last recorded owner) the deduction is made after the entry clause in terms of C(S) Act 1924, ss 3 and 5 and Sch A. This relates back to **9.3(a)**.

The deduction of title is made through a link in title as defined by s 5. In this case it is a confirmation. Other examples of links in title are defined in this section as being 'any statute, conveyance, deed, instrument, decree or other writing whereby a right to land ... is vested in or transmitted to any person'.

(a) English probate or letters of administration which have similar effect respectively to our confirmation nominative and dative.

(b) A will was used prior to the Succession (Scotland) Act 1964 rather than confirmation which then related only to moveable items. A will may still be used as a link but this is not in any way recommended (see Opinion of the Professors of Conveyancing – 1965 JLSS 153 and notes issued by the Law Society 1966 JLSS 84).

(c) A signed but unrecorded disposition which is not correct in form may be used by grantee as a link in title when he conveys the property (eg A sells to B and gives him a disposition which cannot be recorded because there is a mistake in form. B then re-sells to C and grants the disposition as uninfeft proprietor deriving right through the unrecorded disposition which is a link in title).

(d) The decree in bankruptcy granted by the court in favour of a trustee in bankruptcy.

(e) An Act of Parliament may be used as a link. Thus when property was vested in the pre-1973 Corporation of the City of Glasgow, the property either passed to the City of Glasgow District Council or to Strathclyde Region, for their separate functions, in terms of the Local Government (Scotland) Act 1973. If either of these bodies wish to sell that property, they do so as uninfeft proprietors and deduce title through the 1973 Act. Presumably with the passing of the Local Government (Scotland) Act 1994, which will introduce new units of local government, these provisions will also apply.

3(c)(d)(e) Assignation of writs (assignation of rents/obligations of relief). A great deal of substantive law lies under these three headings, but the practical conveyancer can hide behind the Land Registration (Scotland) Act 1979, s 16, which makes it no longer necessary to insert these clauses. Statutory meanings are provided in s 16 which are imported into the deed instead and these are quite sufficient, unless something different from the statutory meaning is required. As this is unlikely, in an average house sale, I shall not deal further with these clauses.

3(f) Warrandice. This is the undertaking by the granters to recompense the grantees for any loss they may suffer through the granters' want of title or their actings, past and future.

In the case of executors or trustees, who act in a purely fiduciary capacity and without personal interest in the property a lesser degree of warrandice is competent – warrandice from their own facts and deeds only. This means that the trustees or executors have not done, nor will do, anything to prejudice the grantees' enjoyment of the land. The executors or trustees do not, however, personally guarantee the title, and that guarantee is carried instead by the beneficiaries under the trust estate, expressed in the words 'and we bind the executry/trust estate under our charge in absolute warrandice.'

Please note therefore the warrandice to be granted by executors. If executors mistakenly grant absolute warrandice, they will be held to this. (*Horsbrugh's Trustees* (1886) 14 R 67.)

The competent warrandice for an individual proprietor granting warrandice in his own right is 'I grant (absolute) warrandice'. In the case of a trustee or executor: 'I grant warrandice from my own fact and deed only and bind the trust estate under my charge in absolute warrandice'. In the case of a gift the competent warrandice is 'I grant simple warrandice', which means that the grantee takes the title as it stands, but the granter will not grant any future deeds which might prejudice the right given to the grantee.

3(g) The non-supersession clause. To avoid any danger of the complicated missives that you have negotiated lapsing through the operation of the doctrine in *Lee v Alexander* (1883) 10 R (HL) 91, it is recommended that a non-supersession clause be inserted. This has the effect of keeping the missives alive for a period of two years (or for such a period as is agreed), or for as long as it may take to determine any court action that arises from the operation of missives. (**3.28.**) This clause should cover all eventualities. Some conveyancers also insist on the exchange of letters of Schedule II of the offer document (Appendix II.11). This is a matter for the individual.

3(h) Stamp duty certificate. Stamp duty, at the time of writing, is 1% of the whole price, if it is £60,001 or over. If the purchasers do not need to pay stamp duty of 1% on the whole consideration, there must be a certificate in the disposition stating that the consideration does not exceed £60,000. The deed is then stamped accordingly.

It is also necessary to certify that the deed is not one of a series of deeds, designed to escape or mitigate liability for duty. Thus, for example, if a house was worth £61,000, the stamp duty on the deed is £610. One might consider then selling the property in two halves, each of £30,500, and thus escaping duty. But this is part of a larger transaction or of a series of transactions, and as such not permissible. The certificate reads:

'And I certify that the transaction hereby effected does not form part of a larger transaction, or of a series of transactions, in respect of which the amount or value or the aggregate amount or value of the consideration exceeds Thirty Thousand pounds.'

Moveable property included in the sale is not subject to stamp duty, so the sensible thing in the above case is to find £1,000 of moveables in the sale, and to reduce the price to £60,000, and to certify the price accordingly. This produces a saving of £610. A stamp duty mitigation certificate should, however, be truthful and not used to achieve a tax evasion. (Consider *Saunders v Edwards* [1987] All ER 651, 1 WLR 1116, CA.) Tax evasion, which is a criminal offence, should be distinguished from tax avoidance, which is perfectly all right, as each person has the right to arrange their affairs so as to pay the legal minimum of tax.

3(i) The consent to registration (for publication and preservation). This clause need not be inserted in a disposition as this registration is administrative and not in any way prejudicial to the granter.

Registration for execution is however prejudicial to the granter, and must be specifically consented to by the granter. (See Appendix I.27.) This is not normally required in a simple deed of transfer such as a disposition, with no continuing obligation, although it may occur in a bilateral deed with continuing obligations such as a feu contract or lease. The consent to registration clause can therefore be safely left out in this case.

Example of ancillary clauses

9.8

'With entry as at the Fifteenth day of January, Nineteen hundred and ninety three; which subjects were last vested in the said William McWilliam, late of Twenty two Juliana Street, Ayr, whose title thereto was recorded in the said Division of the General Register of Sasines on the Third day of March Nineteen hundred and Seventy-nine and from whom I acquired right by the Confirmation hereinbefore mentioned; and I grant warrandice as Executor foresaid from my own facts and deeds only and I bind the Executry Estate under my charge in absolute warrandice; the missives of sale which we, as Executors aforesaid, have concluded with the said James Leslie and Lesley Leslie and which are constituted by letters dated...will form a continuing and enforceable contract notwithstanding the delivery of these presents, except in so far as fully implemented thereby, but the said missives shall cease to be enforceable after a period of two years from the date of entry, except in so far as they are founded on in any court proceedings which have commenced within the said period; and I certify that the transaction hereby effected does not form part of a larger transaction or of a series of transactions in respect of which the aggregate amount or value of the consideration exceeds Sixty Thousand pounds: IN WITNESS WHEREOF.'

Testing clause

9.9 A space is left for the testing clause which is of course inserted after the deed has been signed. The testing clause is a record of the date of execution, and the names and designations of the witnesses. The testing clause should also be used to correct any mistakes that may have occurred. Such mistakes should be initialled and referred to in the deed. The substantive law in this matter is voluminous and should be studied.

Apart from these uses the testing clause should not be used as a means of varying the terms of the deed. (*Chamber's Trs* 1878 5 R (HL) 151.) While the testing clause appears above the subscription it is well known that in point of time it is inserted after a signature and is merely a record of this. Any further provision to the deed is not therefore authenticated by signature.

Example of testing clause

9.10

'IN WITNESS WHEREOF these presents typewritten on this page are
signed by me as Executor foresaid at Glasgow on the Third day of
January Nineteen hundred and ninety in presence of these witnesses
June Jade and Pearl King both Secretaries in the employment of
Messrs Wylde, Lyfe, Solicitors of One hundred and seventy Tiree
Street, Ayr.'

The warrant of registration

9.11   The warrant of registration is a direction to the Keeper of the Register
of Sasines authorising him to register the deed in the appropriate register.

Before a real right can be acquired by registration, it is essential that the
person acquiring the right shall be named and identified in the writ and/or
the warrant of registration.

In the normal case, the disponee will be identified in the writ, and need
only be named, but not designed, in the warrant. If there has been a change
in designation this should be narrated in the warrant.

The warrant is signed by the solicitors for the purchasers, or by the parties
acting on their own behalf. NO ONE ELSE may sign this. (Solicitors
(Scotland) Act 1980, s 32.) This is the crux of the solicitors' monopoly.

Example of warrant of registration

9.12

REGISTER on behalf of the within-named JAMES LESIE and LESLEY LESLIE in
the REGISTER for the COUNTY of AYR.

Solicitors, Ayr, Agents.

9.13   In accordance with the General Regulations of the Law Society Table of
Fees, para 7(1) it is the duty of the solicitors for the grantee or obligee to the
deed to draw up that deed. Special cases of exception are contained in **7(2)**, or
the Tables, the most important of these being the feu writs which are drawn
by the granter.

Chapter ten

THE FINAL STEPS BEFORE SETTLEMENT

'I knew my days were numbered when I was warming up behind the goal at Parkhead and one of our fans shouted "Kinnaird, we like the poll tax more than we like you!" '
(Paul Kinnaird of St Mirren)

10.1 The purchasers' agents have now

(a) examined title;

(b) approved, or revised the draft memorandum for (or continuation of) search; and

(c) drafted the disposition.

In addition the purchasers' solicitors may exercise the option in missives to obtain a letter to be handed over at settlement, after delivery of the disposition, stating that missives will not be superseded by delivery of the disposition. This is ultra-safe (see **3.28**).
Such a letter might read:

> DEAR SIRS,
>
> Nothwithstanding delivery of the disposition relative to the above subjects, which has already taken place, we on behalf of our clients AB hereby agree that the missives relative to the sale of the said subjects dated .... will remain in force as provided therein.
>
> Yours faithfully,

The purchasers' solicitors therefore return the title deeds to the sellers' agents, with these drafts. When doing so, they ask any questions that may arise from examination of title and request the sellers' agents to explain or rectify any defect.

10.2 On receipt of these papers, the sellers' agents:

(a) Send the search and memorandum for continuation of search to the searchers and ask for an interim report which brings the search down to date. Alternatively if there is no search they send a memorandum for search to Edinburgh, and again obtain an interim report.

(b) They obtain any further writs or papers that the purchasers' agents may reasonably require. If the writs required are not in their possession, they obtain these either by borrowing them from the firm who hold them (eg the agents for the builder of the estate). The fee payable to the firm holding the writ is given in the Table of Fees, Chapter 1, paragraph 5(4). Alternatively it may be easier, quicker and cheaper to obtain an extract from the General Register of Sasines, or the cheaper and quicker 'quick copy'. A quick copy is a photocopy made in the Register, but, unlike an extract, uncertified as correct by the Keeper's staff.

(c) Answer the queries made as best they can.

(d) Revise the draft disposition and return it to the purchasers' agents with the interim report and answers to questions.

10.3   The purchasers' agents then have the draft disposition 'engrossed' (or typed) and return the engrossment with the draft to the sellers' agents. The sellers' agents compare the draft with the engrossment, and if it is in order they send the disposition to the sellers for signature. If the property is in the name of one spouse only, the non-entitled spouse should consent to the disposition to renounce the right, or the right should otherwise be renounced. (See Appendix II.20.14 and Appendix III, Forms 2 and 4 for the appropriate style.)

10.4   The purchasers' agents consider whether or not they are satisfied with the title position and with the answers given to their queries. They write to their clients setting out the salient features of the title and may warn the purchasers about any obtrusive conditions (particularly about any prohibition against trade, keeping animals, cutting down trees, et cetera). They further appraise the purchasers of any financial commitment that may arise in the future. The clients should not, however, be swamped with inessential and confusing information. What is inessential or confusing obviously varies from case to case; broadly speaking a minimum of useful information will usually satisfy a residential purchaser, but a commercial purchaser may want a detailed report.

If anything is amiss in the title, and for present purposes we shall assume that it is not, the clients' instructions must be taken as to dealing with this, both at this stage and indeed at all stages of the transaction. If the purchasers' solicitors and their clients are not reasonably satisfied as to any important point, it must be cleared up before settlement takes place.

10.5   We must consider the financial arrangements to be made at settlement. The sellers prepare a state for settlement which is the sellers' account to the purchasers, and this is approved by the purchasers' agents. It should reflect the following items (see Appendix II.20.1):

(a) The price of the house and the price of any moveables included.

(b) In non-domestic properties the apportionment of local rates. First of all, a short explanation of local government financing is required. The bulk of local government spending is funded by central government, but the remainder has to be raised locally. This was formerly done entirely from local rates, which were collected by regional councils, both on their own behalf, and of their constituent districts. In the case of the Western Isles, Orkney, and Shetland areas, these councils are single purpose authorities, because the areas are too remote to belong to one of the larger mainland councils, and too small to be divided into region and district. The new local government structure from 1996 is shown in Appendix V.

Every five years (the quinquennium) a valuation is made of every item of heritable property, except agricultural land which is exempt. There is a revaluation in 1995. The official Government Valuer ('the District Valuer') analyses rental evidence of all commercial property, which is only one element in the calculation of individual rates bills.

Much dissatisfaction was expressed at the fact that rates in the south of England are invariably much lower than those fixed for similar properties in Scotland. Scottish and English rates are now being equalised, but this is a lengthy and complex process.

Rating tends to be a rather specialised subject confined to valuation lawyers and surveyors.

The rates of the property are apportioned on a daily basis as at settlement. The rating year runs from 1 April in each year until 31 March in the next year. Thus if the purchase date is, say 15 November 1994, the sellers pay the rates for 229 days, and the purchasers pay for the balance of the year to March 1995, ie 136 days.

10.6 Meantime in domestic properties rates had been replaced by community charge, otherwise known as poll tax. This was not a charge on properties but on persons who lived in properties, on the basis that if a person used a council service, then they should pay for it, and that the whole burden should not fall on property owners. While the reasoning behind this proposition was quite sound, you could not have called the charge controversial – at the end of the day, everyone hated it.

It was therefore replaced on 1 April 1993 by the council tax, which remains in effect, and while it is unloved, as is any tax, it is seen as being reasonably fair.

Houses are valued as at their market value on 1 April 1991, and are placed in bands A to H according to value, band A being the value up to £27,000 and band H being the value over £212,000.

There are various exemptions – students, student nurses, YT trainees, apprentices, and persons under 18. This gets the tax away from socially divisive 'can't pay, won't pay' argument.

As at the date of settlement a notice of the change of ownership should be sent to the appropriate regional council, who will apportion the tax between the sellers and the purchasers.

Feuduty

10.7 Where an allocated feuduty is still payable in respect of the house, the sellers are under a duty to redeem the feuduty as at the date of sale (see Land Tenure Reform (Scotland) Act 1974, s 5).

Where, however, the feuduty is not allocated, there is no compulsion upon the sellers to redeem the portion of the *cumulo* feuduty, and the payment must therefore be apportioned between the parties as at the date of settlement.

As a quite general rule, apportioned feuduties are most commonly found in tenements, and the factor normally collects this sum along with the other outgoings, and will undertake the apportionment of the feuduty between purchasers and sellers.

Occasionally, however, this may not be the case and the solicitors for the sellers and the purchasers will be required to agree the apportionment.

Feuduty is in almost all cases paid at Whitsunday (15 May) and Martinmas (11 November) in each year. Unlike most payments, it is payable in arrears, ie the payment from 11 November to 15 May is payable on 15 May.

Thus, for example, if a house subject to an unallocated feuduty of £10 is sold at 16 December 1994, the position is:

Sum due by sellers from 11 November 1994 to 16 December 1994 (35 days) $= (35/365 \times £10) = 96p$.

The purchasers therefore get 96p from the sellers at settlement, being the amount the sellers owe, and the purchasers pay the feuduty at 15 May 1995 and thereafter.

The purchasers should see a current receipt for the *cumulo* feuduty payable to the superior, as the liability for payment of arrears could fall on the purchasers if they have not been paid.

Common charges

10.8   Where a flat in a tenement building is sold, the factor should be asked by the sellers' agents to apportion the common charges for maintenance of the building between the parties. (See Form issued by the Property Managers Association, Scotland, Limited at **18.11**.)

This can be done when the factor is informed of the change of ownership by the sellers' solicitors.

In modern practice it is usual for the factor to ask an incoming owner for a deposit to meet future charges. This deposit is set against these charges. (See **18.5**.)

Factors are very wary about instructing repairs, let alone paying tradesmen without having received money from the owners well in advance. The reason for this is that they have incurred huge debts, paying tradesmen in the past, and which have not been repaid. The case of *David Watson Property Management v Woolwich Equitable Building Society* 1992 SLT 430, which held that a heritable creditor who has taken possession of a house on the default of the borrower, is not responsible for common charges which the borrower had failed to pay, amply illustrates this point.

Although the *David Watson* case possibly excuses purchasers from having to pay the sellers' common charges debts, it is the invariable practice for the purchasing solicitors to see a recent common charges receipt.

Interest

10.9   When settlement takes place properly on the agreed date of entry, the question of interest does not arise – that is to say when the full purchase price is paid by the purchaser and the property is made available with the disposition, the titles and the keys. Where, however, one party or the other cannot meet their obligation, the question of interest arises.

Example. Mr and Mrs A contract to sell their house to Mr and Mrs B for £50,000 as at 16 December 1994. For some reason personal to them Mr and Mrs B cannot pay this sum at 16 December. Their building society loan may have been held up, or the proceeds of the sale of their own house may not yet have come through. What do the Bs do?

The position at law is that the purchasers are obliged to pay the price at the date of entry, failing which they are in default, and the obligation can be enforced by the sellers. Thus at law (*ex lege*) the sellers may raise an action of implement, including a crave for interest at the legal rate, which is currently 8% or well below what the sellers would have to pay their bank if they take an overdraft to cover the lack of money received from the purchasers.

Additionally, interest runs only from the date of warranting the action, and not from the date of entry, unless the parties have entered, or enter into an agreement to the contrary. But the parties may agree (*ex pacto*) that a different provision shall apply – see Appendix II.15, clause A and *Lloyds Bank v Bamberger* 1993 SCLR 727 and that interest at a stated rate shall apply if there is a delay or default by the purchasers. If no such agreement is made, there must be doubts as to whether overdraft interest can be demanded by the sellers without entry being given in return, on the basis of a statement in *Erskine* III, 3, 79 to the effect that the sellers cannot gain interest as well as enjoy the 'fruits of the property' – whatever these may be. (See *Thomson v Vernon* 1983 SLT (Sh Ct) 17 discussed by Professor D J Cusine in 1983 JLSS 273.)

If the sellers are unable to settle on the date of entry, there is no obligation upon the purchasers either to take entry or pay interest. See *Bowie v Semple's Executors* 1978 SLT (Sh Ct) 9. If, however, the purchasers wish to take entry they may do so on consigning the price on deposit receipt with a bank. This is in terms of *Prestwick Cinema Co v Gardiner* 1951 SC 98. When the money is on deposit receipt neither party has control over it without the consent of the other. While this may seem to be a very convenient arrangement, it is spoiled as a practical remedy by the extremely poor rate of interest offered by banks on deposit receipt.

The most practical solution to this quite common problem is for the purchasers to ask their bank for a 'bridging loan', that is to say, a short-term loan, usually given on the basis of the probability of the borrower receiving funds on a certain future date. Thus the purchasers can say to their bank: 'Our building society loan is coming through next week and we'll repay you then'. It should be emphasised that bridging loans are expensive and should only be taken on a short-term basis; further the bank may ask for an 'arrangement fee' for arranging the loan – sums of £1,000 being not uncommon, which makes these loans very unattractive, save in an emergency.

Banks are not, however, so keen on lending against a payment on an uncertain future date; for example, if the purchasers are still selling their own house and have not found a buyer yet, their bank may not be willing to provide 'the bridge'. Banks like their loans to be short-term and repayment to be certain, unless they make a specified arrangement as in a 'personal loan'. This provides for regular payments to account, and the banks charge more handsomely for a personal loan.

If the purchasers cannot therefore get a bridging loan, or if the parties decide it is unnecessary, a possible arrangement is for the purchasers to pay the sellers what money they have in return for possession, and for interest to run on the balance at an agreed rate until settlement. This rate of interest might be the rate that would have been payable by the purchasers to their building society. This of course is not necessarily recommended, as it is fraught with danger, but in many circumstances it would be unreasonable for the sellers not to co-operate with such a request, and to insist on implement of the contract strictly.

When both parties agree to this, the sellers get a good rate of interest on their money and the purchasers get possession of the house although they have technically been in breach of contract. What has happened is that the contract has been partially reconstructed by agreement.

This agreement can, however, run deeper. (See 'A Question of Interest' by Professor A J McDonald, 1980 JLSS 103; 'Delay in Settlement' by Professor J M Halliday, 1981 Scottish Law Gazette 68; and 'Delays in Settlement' by Professor Noble in 1984 JLSS 116, which contain a comprehensive review of the law.)

The legal arguments on this matter are so complex that there is every reason for the conveyancer to seek to avoid such a dispute by:

(a) inserting a suitable '*ex pacto*' clause in missives to cover delays; (see **4.8 (a)**)

(b) to ensure that the buyers have made satisfactory financial arrangements;

(c) to choose a sensible and realistic date of entry; and

(d) to keep the transaction running on schedule until settlement.

10.10   The sellers who receive an interest payment without deduction of tax should account for this in their next tax return. They should, in turn, issue a tax receipt for the payment to the purchasers, who should use this to claim tax relief on the payment. Similarly when a bridging loan from a bank is taken, the bank should issue a certificate of interest paid for tax purposes. Interest payments made to persons resident overseas should be made after deduction of tax by the person paying interest, and that person should account to the Inland Revenue for the tax deducted, because the Inland Revenue has no power of collection once the money has left the country.

10.11   When the state of settlement has been agreed and entry is near, both solicitors should ensure that they are ready to settle, and that there are no loose ends which could cause settlement to be postponed.

In particular the purchasers' solicitors should ensure that they have received sufficient money from the purchasers to enable them to settle. They should at this stage also render their fee and get this settled while the clients still depend on the solicitors. This may sound cynical but the lawyers have by this time earned and deserve their fee, and any lawyers will tell you sad stories of highly grateful clients who have become quite the opposite when faced with a bill. I shall however deal with the question of fees in the next chapter.

The purchasers' cheque should therefore be given to the solicitors in *plenty of time for it to be cleared through the purchasers' bank*. This cannot be stressed sufficiently. A solicitors' cheque from clients' account is treated like cash, because of the strict rules (Solicitors' Account Rules 1989, r 4) that solicitors shall ensure that at all times they have enough in their clients' bank account to meet the total amount that the firm is due to clients (irrespective of any money owed to the solicitors by clients). If, therefore, solicitors issue a cheque, and then are informed that the clients' cheque paid to the firm has not been met by the clients' bank, the solicitors may not order the firm's own bank to refuse payment of the firm's cheque.

The loss in other words is the solicitors' and any attempt to shift that misfortune to the sellers may amount to professional misconduct. This point is brought home in a statement contained in 1981 JLSS 357 which is worth repeating verbatim in view of the importance of the matter.

> 'A solicitor acting for a purchaser in a conveyancing transaction has a duty to ensure either that he has cleared funds in his clients' account for the settlement of such a conveyancing transaction or that any cheque which he has received for his client will be met by the paying bank. There is a principle that a cheque drawn by the solicitor acting for a purchaser on his client bank account and handed over in settlement in a conveyancing transaction to the solicitor acting for the seller should not be stopped except in exceptional circumstances.

> Such exceptional circumstances would arise in the event of circumstances amounting to breach of contract on the part of the seller, as for example when the purchasers are unable to receive vacant possession or if the subjects have been destroyed (and these circumstances are contrary to the terms of the missives) or in the event of a postal settlement where the disposition which is delivered contains a defect in execution.'

In this unfortunate event the purchasers' solicitors would be well advised to inform the Law Society before they stop their cheque.

GOLDEN RULE: Always make sure you have cleared funds in your bank on settlement date, and before you write a cheque on the clients' account.

Chapter eleven

THE SETTLEMENT, FEEING-UP AND TIDYING-UP

'The labourer is worthy of his hire' (Modern Version – 'The workman deserves his wage')
(St Luke 10.7)

'As regards solicitors' fees, we think that the elimination of the need to re-examine the validity of the title for each transaction would bring about a material saving in time. The time spent in examining a title for burdens and conditions and ascertaining heritable securities would also be reduced as these would be readily ascertainable from the certificate of title or the deeds referred to in the certificate of title. The solicitor would, of course, have to check the effect of these burdens, conditions and securities as at present. In subsequent transactions also, the solicitor would be able to use fairly simple forms and we are satisfied that such forms could be made adaptable so as to enable all provisions which currently appear in deeds to be incorporated in them. We find it rather difficult to offer an estimate of the amount of time which would be saved by the solicitor as this will vary with each transaction, but in general our view is that there will be an average saving of about one-third of the time which a solicitor spends on a similar transaction under the present system. But this is not the only element which enters into the assessment of solicitors' fees and on the whole we think a reduction of 25 per cent on the present scale of fees should be achieved in transactions in land the title of which has been registered.'
(Reid Report on Registration of Title – July 1963 Cmnd 2032, para 149)

'Although gas prices will be going up from January 1st, you can actually save money by paying your gas bill using British Gas Direct Pay. This is a new tariff whereby anyone who arranges to pay their gas bill by monthly direct debit will be entitled to a discount of up to 0.0% off their gas bill.'
(British Gas advertisement 1994)

11.1 The sellers' and purchasers' solicitors should arrange a time and place for the settlement. Except in unusual circumstances the rule is 'the cheque goes to the disposition' – that is settlement takes place at the sellers' solicitors' office. Both parties should make a check list of what they require for the settlement:

Sellers	Purchasers
Keys	Cheque (As with the letter of obligation opposite, make sure that this is signed by a partner of the firm in good time – the inexperienced lawyer leaves this till the last moment, and then finds everyone is out for lunch.)
Signed disposition	
Detail of signatures	
Title deeds	
Signed letter of obligation and draft for comparison	
Feu duty redemption receipt	
Any other papers to be delivered	
State for settlement and draft for comparison	
Non-supersession letter (if required)	

If it is not convenient for the sellers to hand the keys into the solicitors as is often the case, these may be left with a third party. Then when the sellers' solicitors have the cheque, they telephone the third party and ask them to release the keys to the purchasers.

11.2 The cheque is exchanged for the disposition, letter of obligation, title deeds, keys, the receipted state for settlement and any other papers. Please note that this ceremony amounts to delivery of the disposition, in its technical sense, that is to say the transaction is complete when the disposition is handed over. As to the status of delivery generally, please note carefully the recent case of *Sharp v Thomson*. Reference is made to the comments by Professor Robert Rennie in 1994 SLT 183 and by Mr Richard Leggat in September 1994 Scottish Law Gazette 99.

Ideally settlements should be done face to face, so that the cheque and the disposition are exchanged at the same time. This was the traditional manner of settlement, but many settlements nowadays are carried out by post or courier, owing to constraints of time. To get round the difficulty of the cheque or the deed reaching the other solicitor before the other part is returned, and being misused, the sender of the cheque or disposition writes a short letter to the other solicitor saying: 'We enclose the cheque/disposition and settlement papers, which please hold as undelivered until you dispatch the disposition and settlement papers/cheque to us.' This is a request that mirrors the obligation in missives and must be adhered to, as delivery is postponed until the event happens.

11.3 The sellers' solicitors then bank the cheque and pay any outlays (such as estate agents, advertising accounts and their own fees). They then send the balance to the sellers with a statement of their outlays.

11.4 Other loose ends may remain.

Redemption of feuduty. Ideally this should be redeemed, where necessary, under LTR (S) Act 1974, s 5, before the transaction is settled, and the receipt handed over at settlement. The sellers may not however be in funds to do this, so the letter of obligation may contain an obligation to redeem and produce the receipt within (say) fourteen days. This is an acceptable obligation to give, for fulfilment of the obligation is totally within the solicitors' control.

The redemption is then made by the solicitors from the proceeds of the sale. The basis of redemption is the feu duty factor one month before the date of redemption, plus payment of all arrears. The price paid is therefore:

(Annual feu duty x feu duty factor) + arrears = redemption price

The feuduty factor is worked out on the basis of the price of 2½% Consolidated Stock as its middle price on the appropriate date.

On 22 November the price of 2½% Consols was £29.50 per £100 of stock. If therefore you wanted to redeem a feuduty as at that date, you would notionally give the superior enough money to buy Consols to provide an income of £10 (ignoring all purchase costs). This would be £400 of stock costing (4 x £29.50) = £118. The feuduty factor is therefore 118 divided by 10 = 11.8.

For the unmathematical, feuduty factors are printed monthly in the Journal of the Law Society, and from time to time in stockbrokers' circulars. For this service, much thanks.

Common charges. These are charges levied upon proprietors in respect of maintenance of common property, mainly in flats. It was decided in the House of Lords case of *David Watson Property Management v Woolwich Equitable Building Society* 1992 SLT (HL) 430 that the liability for common charges, that were unpaid by a former owner, did not pass to a creditor who had taken possession. From the reasoning in the case it would also seem likely that the liability for unpaid common charges also does not pass to a purchaser, but in practice a prudent solicitor will require to see an up-to-date receipt for payment of common charges, to be fully satisfied, and to curtail further argument. This should be requested when the factors are asked to apportion the common charges between purchasers and sellers.

11.5   The C(S) Act 1874, s 4(2) and Sch A provides a 'Form of Notice to be given to the Superior of Change of Ownership'. The effect of this notice is to relieve the seller of liability to the superior for (a) payment of feuduty and (b) implement and observation of feuing conditions.

This provision applies only to allocated feu duties, which by LTR (S) Act 1974, s 5, have to be redeemed anyway. Using this provision as their justification, many solicitors no longer send this notice. While the service of this notice, and payment of the ridiculous fee of 25p (C(S) Act 1874, s 4(2)) to the superior, are a nuisance, it can be that it is correct to send a notice of change of ownership, as the sellers can in theory still be held liable if there is a breach of feuing conditions as they are the persons who appear as owners in the superior's list.

It is therefore respectfully suggested that a redemption of the feuduty, at least the notice of redemption, be combined with a notice of change of ownership. This could read as follows:

Drumsheugh Estates Limited
per Messrs Jarvie, Brown & Walker,
Solicitors,
173 Cathedral Street,
GLASGOW

DEAR SIRS,

Notice of Redemption
(Under Land Tenure Reform (Scotland) Act 1974, section 5)

TAKE NOTICE that in terms of Section 5 of the Land Tenure
Reform (Scotland) Act 1974 the feuduty of £10.00 per annum
exigible in respect of 23 Dundee Street, Glasgow as at 16th
December, 1994 will be deemed to be redeemed at that date by
reason of entry having been taken to the said subjects under an
obligation contained in Missives dated 12th and 13th November
1994.

Notice of Change of Ownership
(Under Conveyancing (Scotland) Act 1874, section 4(2))

WE HEREBY INTIMATE to you that as at 16th December, 1994
Mr & Mrs James Leslie will have right to ALL and WHOLE the
subjects 23 Dundee Street, Glasgow, which subjects presently
belong to the late William McWilliam.

MORRISON & GOODFELLOW (signed)
Agent for the Executor of the late William McWilliam

11.6   The sellers' agents make sure that the sellers' home insurances are cancelled.

11.7   The final act in the transaction by the sellers' solicitors is the receipt of
the search from the searchers about three to six months after settlement. They
then send this to the purchasers' solicitors and ask for the return of the letter
of obligation 'duly discharged'. When this is received, the file is checked for
loose ends, useful papers to be retained, and is then put away.

11.8   After settlement the purchasers' solicitors complete the testing clause,
have the deed stamped (for rates see **3.17**) and then send the deed to be
recorded. Before the deeds are sent to the Keeper, these should be carefully
checked to avoid a deed being refused by the Keeper. When sending the deed
for recording, use the form provided by the Keeper, and make sure that the
warrant of registration and form have been signed by a partner of the firm.
(Appendix I.47 and I.48.)
    The deed then goes through the recording process at Meadowbank House
and is fairly carefully checked. If there is anything wrong – and for things
that do go wrong, see the Annual Report by the Keeper – Register House will
either send the deed straight back to you in serious cases (eg forgetting to

sign warrant of registration or not recording within a time limit – see **7. 31**, or a defective form of deed) or telephone you in less serious cases to see what you want done (eg a small mistake in the testing clause or an unauthenticated erasure of a minor nature).

11.9 The deed is duly returned having been recorded. The purchasers' solicitors pay the recording dues which they have (or should have) allowed for in their account to the clients. Shortly afterwards they will get the search from the sellers' solicitors. They check that there are no adverse deeds recorded, that the search is in accordance with the letter of obligation (**8.11**), and that the disposition in favour of their clients has been properly recorded. Having satisfied themselves, the purchasers' solicitors discharge the letter of obligation (usually by writing the word 'implemented' on it and dating and initialling it) and return it to the sellers' solicitors. The file is then checked for loose ends, for useful papers to be retained, and is put away.

11.10 All the title deeds are now in the hands of the purchasers' solicitors. They should report this to the purchasers and ask for instructions as to safe-keeping of the deeds, which are the property of the clients. Should the solicitors keep them, or the purchasers' bank, or the purchasers themselves? The first two courses are preferable. 'In the tin box under the bed' is not to be encouraged, but it is the clients' choice. If there is a lender involved, that lender should be sent the deeds. (See Appendix I. 58.) In the case of deeds that are apparently unwanted by anyone, these may be discarded, but it is useful to ask the local archivist first, to see if the deeds are of any value to the archivist.

Finally do not forget that if the fees have not been paid, the solicitors have a lien over the title deeds until payment. It is recommended (1984 JLSS 198) that conveyancing files be kept for ten years, or at least until the property is successfully re-sold.

Feeing-up

11.11 You've done the work and you are worthy of your fee, but the question is how much?

Fees were fixed by Law Society scales until 1985, when under intense pressure from free traders, the Law Society was forced to abandon these fixed charges based on the value of the property. The weakness in scale fees was that they encouraged 'price fixing', placed low fees on small property transactions, which were often the most work-intensive, and high fees on large property transactions, which were often the least work-intensive. It should be noted, however, that estate agents, architects, surveyors and indeed the government can still charge fees based on the value of the property.

In place of scale fees the Law Society in 1985 issued a set of guidelines which should be followed:

(1) The fee shall be fair and reasonable to both the solicitor and the client.

(2) The fixing of every fee is a balanced judgment rather than an arithmetical calculation.

(3) The solicitor should keep detailed records in respect of work carried out (i) to ascertain total time (ii) to justify the fee fixed if need be.

(4) The fee may consist of charges for detailed items charged at the current unit rate (unit rate for 1995 – £8.10) recommended by the General Table of Fees.

(5) Alternatively the solicitor may charge according to circumstances, taking into account the seven factors following:

    (a) the importance of the matter to the client;

    (b) the amount or value of any money or property involved;

    (c) the complexity or difficulty or novelty of the question raised;

    (d) the skill, labour, specialised knowledge and responsibility involved;

    (e) the time expended;

    (f) the length, number and importance of any documents prepared or perused; and

    (g) the place where and the circumstances in which the services are rendered, including the degree of expendition required.

(6) It is important to establish an hourly charge rate for each fee earner in the firm.

(7) Once hourly charge rates have been set, the first step is to determine the product of the rate charges and the time expended. The result should then be appraised to see if it is reasonable to the client.

(8) The fee may contain an element which reflects all other relevant factors as set out in General Regulation 4 of the Table of Fees.

(9) There may be factors producing a negative weighting eg property of small value or very routine work.

(10) The practioner should then 'step back' and take an overall view to check if the fee thus fixed is fair and reasonable.

(11) Where a solicitor does business which is fairly standard, the solicitor may prepare his or her own table of fees for such work, but it must be prepared in conformity with these guidelines.

(12) Where a first registration of land is induced, some additional weighting is normally appropriate, but negative weighting is appropriate in dealings in a registered interest.

(13) Before embarking on business involving sale or purchase of property, the enquirer is entitled to know the approximate cost in fees and outlays.

Fees should therefore be charged at a rate to enable your firm to reflect the work done, to reflect the resources used (your time at university and training, office rental, stationery, equipment, cost of indemnity insurance, responsibility, continuing legal education, and so on) and to make a decent profit, to make the whole exercise worthwhile.

The unit rate (£8.10 for six minutes) may seem very high, but reflect on the following – I go to the hairdresser who has me out of the door in about six minutes, because it is an increasingly small job. For this he charges me £6, which is not significantly below the unit rate, and the hairdresser doesn't have to keep detailed accounts, files, records of haircuts made, title deeds, and computers, and is not subject to the attentions of various regulatory bodies.

As a rule of thumb, you can perhaps look at the old scale of fees, and see what would have been allowed, although these fees are probably on the high side for modern conditions, bearing in mind the remarks of the Reid report, in 1963, quoted above. Also bear in mind that to open a file and a cash card and to vet the client for money laundering and general financial reliability will probably cost a minumum of £100, before you do very much.

The effect of competition should always be borne in mind – many firms, who had what they considered 'dripping roasts' are now having to quote competitively for the provision of these legal services, which they formerly considered as a job for life. This is of course, in general, a good thing, although it may seem a fairly mixed blessing to those firms.

Estimates should be pretty accurate, although one cannot prepare for the unexpected, and a loophole should be left here. VAT is not, however, unexpected, and should be fully reflected in the quotation. The Ombudsman in his report for 1993 has some fairly tart comments about certain estimates of fees that have been scrutinised by him, and to which reference is made.

The best distilled wisdom in this feeing-up process is contained in guideline number 1 – the fee shall be reasonable to both the client and the solicitor. A fair fee to the solicitor covers the overheads of the practice, and a reasonable profit margin. (For a further discussion on this topic, please see an excellent article by Brian Allingham – 'Conveyancing – the Profit Motive' printed in 1992 JLSS 439.)

11.12 Unless otherwise stated in the missives, each of the parties pay their own fees to their own solicitors. It used to be the case that builders insisted on buyers of new houses paying both the builders' and their own fees. This was not, however, popular, and the practice was scrapped. The builders' legal fees are now, therefore, presumably included in the price of the house!

11.13 VAT at 17½% is currently payable on all legal fees. VAT is not however chargeable on recording dues in the Register of Sasines or Land Register (although if you order an extract deed from the Keeper, VAT is payable on that charge) or stamp duty. VAT is also payable on Land Register reports. For the position of VAT on land prices (if applicable) see *Jaymarke Development Ltd* 1992 SLT 1193.

11.14 In addition a loan fee is payable, which is based on the principles enumerated in **11.11**. Where the same lawyers act for the borrowers and the lenders, less work would be involved, and the fee would presumably be smaller than if completely different solicitors acted for the lenders, and had to go through the title of new. Under the old Table of Fees the reduction in fees was from Scale Fee based on the amount of the loan to 40% of that fee. VAT is payable on these fees, but there is no stamp duty on security documents.

Recording dues or Land Registry dues are payable for the recording of the security. If, however, the security is presented at the same time as the conveyance to the purchaser, only a nominal charge of £22 is payable.

11.15

Some specimen costs of house sale or purchase

Price	Stamp duty (Purchasers only)	Registration Fees Land or Sasine Registers
Up to £10,000	Nil	£22.00
Up to £20,000	Nil	44.00
Up to £30,000	Nil	66.00
Up to £40,000	Nil	88.00
Up to £50,000	Nil	110.00
Up to £60,000	Nil	132.00
Up to £70,000	£700	154,00
Up to £80,000	£800	176.00
Up to £90,000	£900	198.00
Up to £100,000	£1000	220.00
Up to £200,000	£2000	440.00
Up to £300,000	£3000	500.00
Up to £400,000	£4000	550.00
Up to £500,000	£5000	600.00
Up to £1,000,000	£10,000	900.00
Exceeding £1,000,000	1%	1,000.00

Notes:
1 A separate charge may be made for completion of missives, arranging loan, redemption of feuduties et cetera. (See Regulation 21.)
2 A charge may also be made for posts and incidents which is normally about 10%. (See Regulation 14.)
3 The seller will also incur dues of search and Land Register Reports. The cost of a Sasine Search is fixed according to the number of years searched, but the Land Register fees are fixed.
4 The table above is for illustration only and the current Law Society Table of Fees should be consulted, also the Fees in the Department of the Registers of Scotland (Amendment) Order 1990.
5 Land and Sasine Register fees are now identical at all levels and are contained in Table 'A' of Registration Fees.
6. The Land Registers (Scotland) Bill is at the time of going to press making its leisurely way through the Parliamentary processes. If and when it is passed, registration fees will be payable at the time of presentation of the deeds. Otherwise, registration will not be effected.

11.16

Loan fees

Loan of £	Registration Fees Land and Sasine Registers £
20,000	22.00
30,000	33.00
40,000	44.00
50,000	55.00
60,000	66.00
100,000	110.00
200,000	220.00
300,000	250.00
400,000	275.00
500,000	300.00
1,000,000	450.00
in excess of £1,000,000	500.00

Notes:
1   Loan fees are quoted in Table 'B' of Registration Fees. There is no stamp duty on loan documents.
2   In the case of endowments loans the fee may be increased as extra work is involved.
3   Where a security is recorded together with a disposition in favour of the borrower, the dues of recording the standard security are £22.
4   All data is believed to be correct at date of publication but as these figures are liable to frequent change they should be treated as illustrative only. Recording dues are not generally subject to annual upward revision. The apparently automatic rise in house prices, which existed until 1990, has had the effect of increasing the level of dues.

11.17

Land Register report fees (as at January 1995)

Form 10	£ 16.50 + VAT
Form 11	10.00 + VAT
Form 12	16.50 + VAT
Form 13	10.00 + VAT
Form 14 (to ascertain if subjects are registered or not)	16.50 + VAT
Verbal Fax Report	5.00 + VAT
P16 Report	16.50 + VAT

11.18

Register of Inhibitions and Adjudications

A flat fee of £7.00 has been introduced for entries in this Register.

Chapter twelve

BORROWING ON HERITABLE PROPERTY

'Most bankers dwell in marble halls
Which they do to encourage deposits
And discourage withdrawals'
(Ogden Nash)

'I spent a lot of money on booze, birds, and fast cars. The rest I just squandered.'
(George Best)

12.1 We have assumed to date that the sellers are not repaying a loan, and that the purchasers are not taking a loan on the new house. In fact, the main bulk of the work has already been done, and a discharge or a new security do not present any great difficulty, provided you have followed the scheme of things so far.

12.2 Most loans are made by building societies, but banks also lend money for the purchase of houses, as do local authorities if they have the money available. Broadly, however, the procedure is the same whoever the lender may be. Generally, a lending institution will permit the solicitors acting for the purchasers to act also on their behalf in domestic transactions providing that the solicitors are on their approved 'panel'. This means a substantial saving in work, and thus in fees to be paid by the purchasers.

If the institution insists on using solicitors chosen by them, and some will, especially in commercial transactions, then two solicitors become involved in doing the same work and in examining the same title. This fee to the lenders' solicitors is payable by the borrowers, as well as their own solicitors' fee, all in terms of the C & FR (S) Act 1970, Sch 3, condition 12. If the purchasers' solicitors also act for the lender, they are entitled to charge (a) a fee for the purchase and (b) a fee for the loan, based on the principles stated in **11.14**.

12.3 When a lending institution instructs the purchasers' solicitors to act for it as well, the solicitors may do so, provided there is no conflict of interest. If a conflict arises, the solicitors must then decide which party to represent. In all probability they will represent the purchasers, who are their clients and will return the papers to the lenders. The lenders will then instruct another solicitor.

12.4 Where solicitors are acting for more than one borrower, and the security is being given by the borrowers, jointly and severally, it is the responsibility of the solicitors to ensure that all persons signing the security understand the extent of the security, and where appropriate the solicitors should recommend that the individuals take separate legal advice. In particular, where husband and wife are concerned, it is advisable to ensure that both parties obtain separate advice as to the extent of the obligation, from at least another partner in the firm.

12.5   Assuming that the same solicitors act for the purchasers and for the lenders, the following steps should be taken by the solicitors.

(a)   The purchasers' solicitors receive and carefully peruse the lenders' instructions. After examining title, they draft a standard security and assignation of life policy (if it is an endowment mortgage).

(b)   They have the standard security (and assignation) signed by the borrowers. In the event of the title standing in the name of one entitled spouse only, a form of consent of the loan has to be signed by the non-entitled spouse (see MH (FP) (S) Act 1981 as amended). They send the report on title, and certificate that it is in order, to the lenders and request the loan cheque. This should be done in good time for settlement (allow three to five days, shorter if the lenders will telegraph the money).

(c)   The standard security should be sent to the Keeper at the same time as the disposition. A notice of assignation of the life policy to the lenders should be sent in duplicate to the assurance company who issued the policy, to create a real right in the lenders. ('The assignation itself is not a complete valid right until it be orderly intimated to the debtor' – *Stair* III, 1, 6.) One copy of this should be receipted by the assurance company ('the debtor' in Stair's words) and put with the assignation in the title deeds. The lending institution will in virtually every case insure the property in its own name 'as heritable creditors' and in the purchasers' name 'as proprietor in reversion', from the time it receives the report on title. (See standard condition 5 of Sch 3 to the C & FR(S) Act 1970.)

   The purchasers' solicitors need not worry further about this. This insurance cover will be for re-instatement value, and should also be index-linked to increase annually with building costs. It is possible for the borrowers to obtain alternative quotations from other insurance companies, provided they are not on a fixed interest contract, and considerable savings may be made in this way.

(d)   When the titles are all in the hands of the solicitors they should then send these to the lending institution and receive their receipt. Some building societies, however, like to receive the other titles before the disposition and the standard security are returned from the record. It is a matter of reading the instructions.

Golden rule: read the instructions carefully.

12.6   When property is sold and there is an existing security created by the sellers, the sellers' solicitors will (as above) probably be asked to act for the lenders in its discharge. In that case, the solicitors should do the following:

(a) The sellers' solicitors inform the sellers' lenders of the sale, and obtain the title deeds on loan.

(b) The sellers' solicitors inform the lenders of the sale, and the date of entry and repayment. They ask what is the amount required to redeem the loan on that date. They draft the discharge and send it to the purchasers' solicitors for revisal.

(c) They have the principal discharge engrossed and signed by the lenders, who return it to be held as 'undelivered pending repayment of the loan'.

(d) The sellers' solicitors hand the discharge over at settlement, with the testing clause complete and the warrant of registration signed by the sellers' solicitors. They also give the purchasers' agents a form which is sent to the Keeper asking that the discharge be recorded. The letter of obligation is enlarged to include delivery of the duly recorded discharge within (say) fourteen days of the recording date. The purchasers' agents send these documents to the Keeper with the disposition and standard security and all are recorded at the same time in the order: (1) discharge, (2) disposition and (3) standard security.

(e) When the discharge is returned by the Keeper, this is sent to the purchasers' solicitors, who are asked to discharge the letter of obligation to that extent.

12.7 If the lenders insist on their own solicitors acting, a rather cumbersome 'three-cornered' settlement has to be arranged. This involves the lenders' solicitors handing over the cheque in return for the disposition, standard security, title deeds and letter of obligation from the purchasers' solicitors, which the purchasers' solicitors obtain from the sellers' solicitors, by presenting a cheque for the purchase price. This is of course dependent on the lenders' solicitors' cheque being produced. Alternatively this whole process can be conducted by post. The exact ramifications of this complex process depend on the circumstances of each transaction and are, unfortunately, only learnt by experience.

12.8 The interest rate on money borrowed for house purchase generally fluctuates with the level of interest rates on the money market. These rates are all geared around the Bank of England base rate, and rise and fall in conformity with it. The base rate is fixed largely for fiscal reasons, which have little to do with supply and demand, and everything to do with world markets, and the fluctuations are quite unpredictable.

The only borrowers who are not affected are those who took out a 'fixed rate' mortgage in the past. If such a fixed rate contract can be obtained, it has seldom proved a mistake to take advantage of it, but it must be appreciated that if interest rates were to drop, the advantage would be lost.

When taking out any loan, whether over heritable property or otherwise, the borrower should clearly differentiate between 'flat rate' and 'annual percentage' (APR). The APR is the true yardstick of the cost, and must be prominently displayed in all promotional material.

The Independent of 7 October 1989 told the story of a building society which had (quite inadvertently) breached the advertising rules on this topic. The society had offered loans at an interest rate of 12.75%, which was the annual flat rate, and the advertisement also stated that the APR was 13.7%. The latter being the true rate of interest, the amount of interest payable in a year would be amount borrowed × 13.7% rather than amount borrowed × the flat rate (12.75%).

The Consumer Credit Act 1974 requires that the flat rate not be given greater prominence than the APR, for the flat rate, while being mathematically correct, is misleading. The reason for this is that the flat rate is applied at times which distort the amount payable. In some cases this distortion is quite dramatic, and before the coming into force of the Act it was formerly the practice of less reputable lenders to quote a low flat rate to attract investors. This rate was then applied in such a way as to provide a huge APR, which was not of course revealed.

12.9   Against the cost of a home loan must be set the considerable subsidy offered by the Treasury in tax allowances. Thus interest on the first £30,000 of a genuine home loan can be offset against the top slice of a person's income, and there is no capital gains tax on the sale of one's principal residence. The figure of £30,000 (restricted in 1994/95 to 20% and in 1995/96 to 15%) has applied for many years. We must therefore assume that the Treasury is content to leave this well alone, if not to reduce it further.

Capital gains tax is, however, payable on the sale of a second home or on investment properties. If you own two or more houses you must nominate which is to be your 'main private residence' and the exemption can only be obtained on the sale of that house. You can change your election, if your circumstances change (eg you retire to live in the country), but generally speaking you are not otherwise allowed to change your election, and certainly not in such a way as merely to avoid paying tax.

Even when capital gains tax is payable it is relatively light in comparison to income tax. The tax is payable on 'a chargeable gain' on disposal of an asset, which is defined to include land and buildings.

To compute the gain on which tax is payable, you deduct from the disposal consideration (a) any incidental expenses in connection with the original acquisition, (b) any incidental expenses in connection with the disposal and (c) any 'enhancement' expenditure, that is the cost of capital improvements (eg building costs) as opposed to expenditure of a 'revenue nature' (eg decoration and maintenance).

Further, an annual exemption of £5,800 (in 1994/95 rising to £6,000 in 1995/96) may be deducted from the amount of the gain, provided this has not been applied to other gains. Any gains made before 31 March 1982 may be ignored, as only gains made after that date are taxable.

Finally, an indexation allowance is applied to the amount of the gain, to strip out part of the gain that is due to the effect of inflation on the price, as opposed to the pure profit made on the sale. The indexation indices are based on the retail price index, which reflects the rate of inflation monthly.

Example Mr & Mrs Smith bought a holiday house in January 1983, at a price of £20,000. Their total expenses on purchase amounted to £1,000, including surveyor's and lawyer's fees and outlays. They immediately spent £10,000 on building a kitchen extension. In August 1988 they sold the property for £50,000. They spent £250 on advertising the sale, and £1,000 on legal and other sale expenses.

What is their taxation liability on this sale? (The retail price index in January 1983 was 82.61, and in August 1988 it was 107.90.)

Cost of house	£20,000
Add	
Enhancement Expenditure	10,000
Legal and Survey Costs	1,000
Total cost	£31,000
Add	
Indexation £31,000 × (107.9 − 82.61)	
82.61	9,490
TOTAL COST	£40,490
Proceeds of sale	£50,000

Less		
Cost as above	£40,490	
Advertising	250	
Legal and other fees	1,000	
Annual exemption 1988/89	5,000	
		£46,740
CHARGEABLE GAIN		£ 3,260

(Tax is payable on the chargeable gain at income tax rates on Mr & Mrs Smith's top slice of income.)

12.10 An average lending by a bank or building society will be 3 × the borrower's annual income, or, if there are two incomes, 3 × the first income plus 1 × the second income *or* 2.5 × the joint incomes.

There are basically six methods by which borrowers may repay a loan. The repayment figures, which are given for illustrative purposes only, are based on a male, non-smoking, aged 30 next birthday, borrowing £40,000 over a 25-year term. The interest rate as at November 1994 is 8.1%:

(a) The repayment of capital and interest method. By this method a sum is paid monthly to the lenders throughout the life of the loan. This may either be calculated on a varying payment or a level payment basis. Where the former is chosen, the payments start as relatively small and increase annually, presumably in line with the borrowers' ability to repay. When the latter method is chosen, the payment remains fixed throughout the life of the loan. In either event, part of the payment is interest and part is capital. The ratios of income to capital fluctuate throughout the term of loan – at the start of the loan, the interest is high, but steadily falls: about two-thirds through the life of the loan the ratio of interest payment to capital repayment is roughly equal; then the capital repayment content of the monthly sum becomes progressively greater than the interest content. At the end of the loan, the payments are almost entirely composed of capital being repaid.

As a tax allowance can be obtained on the amount of interest paid the tax allowance therefore also becomes smaller every year, which may not be the best idea for someone whose income is increasing every year.

At time of writing, income tax allowance can only be claimed on the amount of interest paid on the loan up to £30,000. You can, therefore, borrow a larger sum if you want, but you get no tax relief on the interest paid to the extent that the loan exceeds £30,000.

A mortgage protection policy should be effected to cover the risk of the borrower dying before the loan is repaid. This is considerably cheaper than an endowment policy.

The monthly cost of this loan on the above assumptions, after deduction of MIRAS tax allowance, would be £278.60. A mortgage protection policy is quoted at anything from £5.20 a month to £12.10 a month, showing the value of good independent advice.

(b) The endowment repayment method. The borrowers take out an endowment policy for the amount of the loan to mature on the date that the loan comes to an end and this policy is assigned to the lenders (although not all lenders insist on this now), who repay their loan from the proceeds on repayment and hand over any balance to the borrowers. Thus if the borrowers borrow £40,000 over 25 years, the policy is on their joint lives for £40,000 and matures in 25 years. The maturity value (see below) is paid to the lenders to repay the loan. Throughout the life of the loan the borrowers pay only interest and repay no capital.

If one of the borrowers does not live to the end of the loan term, the proceeds of the policy are then used to repay the loan, and the survivor gets the house free of heritable debt.

On the above assumptions the net payment of interest is £229.50, and the life assurance premium is £56.70 (best quoted). If the future rate of return is 5% the maturity value will be £27,800, that is not enough to repay the loan; but if it is 10% the maturity value will be £58,100. The loan would be repaid, and no more, at a return of 7.5%. A good insurance company or pension fund should be able to maintain this rate of growth, certainly on historic rates, but one wonders if there is to be genuinely little or no inflation, will it then be so easy?

(c) The pension mortgage. This method was only available to the self-employed, or to those employees who have, say, personal consultancy fees on which they pay Schedule D income tax, or to employees who are not members of an occupational pension scheme. The government has, however, widened the qualifications for personal pensions, not always with happy results.

By this method the borrowers take out a personal pension plan, and the loan is repaid from the fund accumulated at date of retiral, the balance being used to purchase an annuity which will provide a pension for the borrowers. There are enormous tax advantages here; the premiums paid come off the top slice of the borrowers' income; investment income is paid tax free to the pension scheme; and when the pension is claimed, any lump sum payable is tax free. The only difficulty is that a pension plan cannot be assigned in security, as can an endowment policy. A low cost life policy is therefore taken out, providing only basic life cover, and is assigned to the lender. Life policies no longer attract tax relief since 14 March 1984, but this policy is written under the Income and Corporation Taxes Act 1970, s 226A (repealed) which is an exception and does still attract tax relief.

On the above assumptions, and assuming that the borrower is to retire at age 55, when the loan is complete, the net payment of interest is £229.50 and the net payment to the pension fund is £126.62, making a total outlay of £356.12. Assuming growth of 9% the pension fund will pay cash of £40,000 at the end of 25 years, and this will be used to repay the loan. An annual pension will also be available: assuming 6% growth – £5,660, and assuming 12% growth – £20,900. The cost of the pension term assurance would be an average quotation of £10 per month.

(d) Personal equity plan (PEP) method. This method is a relative newcomer to the market, and is not widely canvassed by tied agents. A PEP mortgage is similar in principle to an endowment or pension mortgage, and is repaid on an interest only method, with the capital being repaid at the end of the term. Instead of paying life insurance premiums (other than on a simple protection policy (**12.10 (a)**)) you pay instead into a personal investment plan. The 1990 Budget provided that £6,000 may be invested in a PEP annually, of which £3,000 may be invested in unit or investment trusts. The trust must have 50% of its investment in UK equities, although in the November 1994 Budget, the Chancellor announced plans to widen the scope of investment which are contained in the Finance Act 1995.

On the above assumptions, a payment of £51 per month is recommended to repay this mortgage. If the growth rate is 6% the fund at the end of 25 years is £26,200, that is not enough to repay the loan; assuming 12% growth however, the fund is £63,500. Again life assurance would cost around £10 per month.

(e) Over 60 plan. This is suitable for homeowners aged over 60, who enjoy living where they are, and don't want to move to a smaller house, but would appreciate having extra capital. They may borrow up to 25% of the value of their house, and make no repayments until the house is sold. The interest is accumulated to the capital sum owing, although if the appreciated sum exceeds 75% of the value of the house at any time, a repayment may be called for. The impact, however, on any housing benefit or other state benefit received by a pensioner should be taken into account. There have been some very adverse developments with these loans, and the advice of Help the Aged should be obtained if this is contemplated. Many old people, especially in the south, were tempted into granting mortgages of their properties, which were then invested in bonds, giving, supposedly, a good income. The bonds fell in value, as did the value of the houses, and thus the borrowers lost out twice, often with dire consequences. This, therefore, requires careful consideration.

(f) Interest only schemes. The borrower pays only interest to the society, and is left to work out the best method of repayment. This could be from an inheritance, the lump sum paid from a pension plan, the benefits of a share option scheme, the proceeds of assurance policies, or any combination of these.

(g) Fixed interest loans. A fixed rate is offered for, say, two years, after which the loan reverts to the market rate interest. These should not be confused with the old fixed rate loans, which lasted the whole term of the loan, and gave some lucky people an extraordinary bargain.

(h) Discounted rate loans. First time buyers are given a discount for the first year or two of their loan.

(i) Cap and collar loans. Fixes a maximum and a minimum rate of interest for the loan for a given term.

12.11 MIRAS (Mortgage Interest Relief at Source) was introduced in April 1983. The old method was for the borrowers to make the monthly repayment to the lenders, and then claim tax relief either in their coding under PAYE or in their claim for allowances under Schedule D at the end of the year. Under MIRAS, the borrowers simply make repayments after deduction of the tax relief they would formerly have reclaimed. MIRAS makes no difference to the amount of tax paid, it simply streamlines the organisation a bit.

12.12 Which method should be chosen? This is entirely a matter of circumstances. The following points may be considered.

(a) Expense. While building societies were pretty cagey about the endowment method originally, they now promote it quite widely. Over the years this method soared in popularity, but is now on the wane, as it is thought that the expenses are too high, and there is no tax relief on premiums. The monthly repayment to the borrowers is lower, because no capital is repaid, but the borrowers must pay the assurance policy premiums. The endowment method is therefore slightly more expensive in the average case, but this depends on the amount of the loan and the ages of the borrowers.

(b) Tax relief. Tax relief on the endowment method has the distinct advantage of being on a constant amount of interest paid on the loan through the loan period. The word 'constant' must of course be interpreted in the context of rising and falling relief on interest payments in the first three or four years of the loan, which then begins to fall.

(c) Life cover. The endowment method has the advantage of providing automatic cover on the borrowers' lives; where capital repayment is used the borrowers' lives should be assured separately by the mortgage protection policy. An additional advantage in using the endowment method is that this valuable life cover is provided.

(d) Taxation in the fund's hands. Pension funds pay no income tax and no capital gains tax on disposal of assets. Life assurance schemes receive income on a tax-deducted basis and pay CGT on disposals. PEPs are in between – receiving income on a net basis, but paying no CGT. The effects of these factors on the fund available at the end of the day should be considered.

Thus in summary, the endowment method is possibly better where a person is likely to stay a long time in the house, and the capital repayment method is possibly better for someone who intends to change in three or four years. A young couple may prefer the slightly cheaper capital repayment method at the outset. Self-employed people are probably better with the pension fund method.

While certain conclusions may be drawn from these figures, I should stress that every case should be looked at on its own merits, and no one method is automatically better than the others.

It is essential that the best advice be taken. It is not axiomatic that a bank or a building society which is tied to one life office is giving the best advice, even although the office is a good one. Bear in mind that no one has to take a policy from the same source as they receive a mortgage, although it may well be convenient to do so. Solicitors are not permitted to be tied agents (Chapter 1) and they must seek competitive quotations. Most solicitors will do this through Solicitors Financial Services Limited.

12.13   A house purchase loan may be obtained in a foreign currency, most usually Swiss Francs. The advantage of this is that interest rates can be much lower, say, in Switzerland than in the United Kingdom.

The documentation of such loans should be very much the same as a loan obtained domestically. The disadvantage is that repayments are made in the currency borrowed, and currency fluctuations may negate the savings made. Currency fluctuations can of course be 'hedged', but this process is not recommended for the average house purchaser, although commercial firms with ready access to currency markets may be able to benefit substantially (but see the Baring fiasco in 1995 and be warned). The borrowers should also reserve the right to convert the mortgage back into sterling, in case the fluctuations on the currency markets are too great.

12.14   All loans over heritage must, since 29 November 1970, be constituted by a standard security (C & FR (S) Act 1970, s 9(3)). The law of standard securities is contained in Part II (ss 9 to 32) of the Act.

A standard security may either be in terms of Sch 2, Form A or Form B. Form A is used where the personal obligation and the details of the loan are contained in the standard security, and is widely used by building societies. Form B is used where the personal obligations and the details of the loan are contained in a separate unrecorded document, and is widely used by banks in housing loans, or by 'commercial' lenders eg loans in connection with trade (brewers, garages, et cetera) and large loans over office and factory buildings, where the parties are not anxious to make the details public.

12.15   Form A is made up as follows:

Names of granters
Personal obligation ('Hereby undertake to pay')
Name of lender
Amount of loan
Interest and repayment details
Grant of standard security
Description of property
Incorporation of standard conditions and incorporation of any variations
   (See C & FR (S) Act 1970, ss 11 and 16)
Warrandice
Consent to registration for execution
Testing clause
Warrant of registration (unless land is registered)

12.16 Form B is made up as above, but omitting the personal obligation, the amount of the loan, the interest and repayment details, and the consent to registration for execution. These are contained in a separate unrecorded bond or minute of agreement. In commercial loans this document may also carry heavy variations of the standard conditions, and trading conditions (eg in a brewer's loan). A loan to an individual from a bank will probably also be secured by this method.

12.17 Where a life policy is assigned in security, the age of the policy holder should be proved to the assurance company and 'age admitted', by producing a birth certificate for the policy holder. The solicitors should also ensure that with a new policy, the first premium has been paid and the policy is therefore in operation, and that with an old policy, the premiums are up to date and the policy not invalidated in any way.

12.18 Don't forget to intimate the assignation to the assurance company at its chief office or chief Scottish office, as shown on the policy, if this is required by the lenders. This is done by sending a notice of assignation in duplicate, one copy of which is receipted by the company and returned.

12.19 It is unwise to 'chop and change' with endowment policies. Most of the premiums in the first two years are used in the company's expenses and commission and the surrender value is liable to be very small (if any). Further in a surrender prior to four years of the policy, the Inland Revenue may 'claw back' tax relief given on the premiums. Beware of unscrupulous agents who 'churn' policies, that is when they are arranging a new loan they advise the borrower to surrender existing policies, and take out new ones. This can be a very expensive business.

   If a life policy has to be surrendered, the surrender value offered by the life office can be very disappointing. If a policy is well-established, it can have a substantial surrender value, and it is certainly worth investigating if it can be sold more advantageously at an auction. A firm of auctioneers in London, Foster & Cranfield, run regular specialised auction sales for assurance policies and reversionary interests generally, and there are numerous other companies who buy well-established endowment policies. You are almost guaranteed to get more from them than from the meagre surrender values given by the assurance companies.

12.20 Discharges, partial discharges, and restrictions are discussed at **7.21**. While it is assumed that the borrowers will want to discharge the loan when it has been repaid, the smart thing may be to leave it undischarged with a balance of £1 owing. The advantage of this is that the building society will continue to look after the insurance of the property, and if a loan, say to extend, is required, the expense of creating new security documents is avoided. The society will be quite happy with this arrangement as they will keep the insurance commission.

12.21 It is of course quite permissible for the lenders to assign your loan to someone else, simply by granting an assignation in terms of C & FR (S) Act 1970, Sch 4, Form A. The borrowers' consent is not required, and the assignation is simply intimated to the borrowers. This is a useful way for the lenders to raise money, and was used by Glasgow District Council, for one, when it assigned a large number of loans to the Trustee Savings Bank. The consideration for the assignation was £4, 774, 727, and the deed was recorded in the Register for the County of the Barony and Regality of Glasgow (Book 14657 Folio 54) on 23 May 1985.

12.22 Where a loan is a high proportion of the purchase price, the lenders may insist on the borrowers providing an indemnity policy. Thus, if the sale price does not cover the loan, the policy provides the shortfall. There is generally a single premium payable at the time of making the loan, and as this premium is usually substantial, the purchasers should be clearly advised of the liability. This policy generally confers no benefit on the borrowers, although they paid the premium.

If the borrowers default, the indemnity insurers pay out the sum due to the lenders. The unredeemed portion of the sum owing under the standard security is then assigned to the insurance company, who may in fact pursue the borrowers, using the personal obligation contained in the standard security. The debtor, while paying the premium, generally has no rights at all under an indemnity policy, and it is understood that some lenders will not even make these policies available for inspection by debtors.

12.23 In his Budget proposals of November 1994, the Chancellor proposed restrictions on mortgage payments made on behalf of those on income support. At present (November 1994) the DSS pays half of the mortgage interest for the first 16 weeks and the whole payment thereafter. In future the borrowers will have to pay the first two months' payments, and then qualify for 50% for the next four months. The cost therefore of insuring (mortgage repayment protection insurance) against periods of sickness or unemployment would be approximately £500 for a £100,000 mortgage. It appears that proceeds of such policies are taxable, but the Chancellor has promised to change this, retrospectively, in the 1995 Finance Act.

Part two

LAND REGISTRATION

Chapter thirteen

INTRODUCTION

'Objectives: to extend, as required by statute, the operation of the Land Register throughout Scotland in order to bring the benefits of cheaper conveyancing to the Scottish public and to phase out the General Register of Sasines.'
(Keeper's Annual Report to 31 March 1994)

The land registration scheme

13.1 The applicable law, and the prescribed forms, are contained in the Land Registration (Scotland) Act 1979 ('the 1979 Act') and also in the Land Registration (Scotland) Rules 1980, SI 1980/1413, as amended by the Land Registration (Scotland) (Amendment) Rules, SI 1982/974, SI 1988/1143 and SI 1995/248. Practitioners should also have available the Registration of Title Practice Book (HMSO).

13.2 I have gone into very considerable detail upon the existing system of house transfer, and registration in the Register of Sasines. This is a perfectly sound system, but it has some major defects:

(a) It is time-consuming.

(b) It is repetitive, and potentially involves several people doing exactly the same work in a short space of time. Thus for example, solicitors A may note title for their client X. When everything is complete X sells to Y, whose solicitors B then have to repeat the same process, and so on *ad infinitum*.

(c) Once the sellers' solicitors hand over the title deeds at settlement in a sasine transaction, the sellers' responsibility for the title ceases, unless a successful claim for warrandice is established. This is not the case with Land Register transactions where the sellers' responsibility for the title does not cease until the letter of obligation, which contains the obligation to obtain a land certificate without any exclusion of indemnity, is discharged. (See **13.10** and Appendix II.11–12.)

(d) If there are two solicitors involved in the same transaction, both have to do the same work, and the unfortunate clients have to pay for the repetition. Thus if A buys a public house, A's solicitors have to note the title; if simultaneously a loan is obtained from brewery B, their solicitors will also have to note title. In terms of the standard loan documents (C & FR (S) Act 1970, Sch 3, Standard Condition 12) A has the doubtful pleasure of paying both of them.

(e) Much of the work and the process involved in a sasine transaction is out of date and labour intensive and better suited to more spacious days, when such work could be done cheaply. Because there is a lot of work involved, sasine registration is obviously expensive.

(f) The Sasine Register is a perfectly good register, but it was created in the 17th century. It has been substantially modernised by the introduction of microfilming of Record volumes, and optical reading of presentment forms, leading to a computerised presentment book, thence to a computerised Sasine Register. The staff of Register House are highly efficient and can find any deed you want within minutes even although there are tens of thousands of deeds. It is, however, as a system, susceptible only to limited further modernisation.

(g) Further the Sasine Register is a register of deeds and not of land. The only information it can disclose is that disclosed by the deeds registered. If you do not know exactly what you are looking for, you may have great difficulty in finding what you want.

(h) Many plans presented to the Sasine Register are badly prepared and inaccurate. Further they follow no consistent pattern of scales, or even north points, and matching plans of adjoining lands is difficult.

In his fascinating book *Who Owns Scotland* (Polygon Press, 2nd Edn 1981) John McEwan tells of the difficulties he had drawing up a coherent picture of the ownership of vast acres of land in Scotland, which may only be described in the Sasine Register by a general description, such as 'the Lands of Assynt'.

The principal difficulty is that under our present system huge areas of land, thousands of acres in the country areas, can be transferred by deeds containing only a vague general description, and with no map attached to illustrate the land transferred. Thus no coherent record of land ownership in Scotland exists.

13.3   The idea of registration of title, which seeks to correct these defects, is by no means new. A system of this kind was established in Prussia in 1700, and it was introduced in the whole of united Germany in 1872.

In the English-speaking world, a system of registration known as 'The Torrens System' was introduced into South Australia in 1858 and this system spread widely in the Dominions. It was principally a system for virgin land and not thought to be a suitable system for introduction to Britain, where some land holdings go back to Domesday.

In Scotland, as far back as 1903, Professor Wood wrote in his lectures on conveyancing: 'I am unable to see any real difficulty in the way of introducing registration of title into Scotland'.

In 1959 the Secretary of State set up a Committee under Lord Reid to investigate the introduction of registration into Scotland. This Committee reported favourably (Cmnd 2032) and recommended that another Committee be set up to devise a scheme. This Committee under Professor Henry reported in 1969 (Cmnd 4137) with a workable scheme, which after a trial in Register House, was introduced by the 1979 Act.

13.4   The scheme is based on the Ordnance Survey of Scotland using the scale 1/1250 for urban areas where modern house plots are small, 1/2500 in villages and small towns where plots are rather larger, and 1/10,000 for farms and moorland. Ordnance Survey maps are extremely accurate, and are consistently updated. It should be noted, however, that they reflect boundaries as they actually exist on the ground, and not as they exist in title plans registered in the Sasine Register. This difficulty is met by asking the Keeper, in a form P16 (see **14.3**) to compare the title plan with the Ordnance Survey map.

It should be noted that the Land Register is based, like the General Register of Sasines, on the old Scottish county system, which was phased out for local government purposes in 1974. Thus regions and district have no significance in land registration, nor the unitary authorities that will take over in 1996. The original intention was to make all Scotland operational in 9 years, starting Year 1 on 6th April, 1981 with the County of Renfrew; then in Year 2 – The City of Glasgow; Year 3 – Lanark; Year 4 – Midlothian; Year 5 – Rest of Central Belt; Year 6 – Angus, Kincardine, Aberdeen; Year 7 – Ayr, Dumfries and Galloway; Year 8 – Southern Rural Areas; Year 9 – Northern Rural Areas.

13.5 This scheme (**13.4**), however, proved wildly over-optimistic, and by 1990 only four counties were operational – Renfrew, Dumbarton, Lanark and Glasgow. It appeared at that time that the scheme was irretrievably stalled, for the Register was under-staffed, and could not keep pace with the applications pouring in, let alone the arrears that were building up. Long delays were commonplace, and the Keeper acknowledged this problem in his 1988 report, and explained that the backlogs on his shelves would generate a fee income of £9 million, if only he could process them.

The property boom of the late eighties coupled with the success of the 'Right to Buy' legislation led to a soaring demand for the services of the Department of the Registers at a time when the Department was subject to both staffing and accommodation constraints. The situation was steadily deteriorating and invidious comparisons were being drawn with the English system, which had only covered 50/52 per cent of the country after 63 years. Fortunately the position in both countries has since been rectified.

The Department of the Registers of Scotland was created Scotland's first Executive Agency in 1990 and the consequent removal of constraints enabled the Agency to tackle its problems and meet targets set for it at its creation. These targets included:

(a) to reduce turnround times on registering dealings in the Land Register from 39 to 15 weeks;

(b) to present a phased programme for the extension of the Land Register throughout Scotland, to provide cheaper conveyancing, and to phase out the General Register of Sasines;

(c) to have in operation by April 1993 a branch office of the Land Register in Glasgow;

(d) to eliminate progressively the older casework by the end of 1996–97.

13.6 It is very pleasing to note from the Keeper's report for 1993–94 that these targets have been met, or are well on the way to being met.

In particular the land registration process has picked up momentum, as shown by the extension of land registration to the counties of Clackmannan (1 October 1992); Stirling (1 April 1993) and West of Lothian (1 October 1993). Fife (1 April 1995); Aberdeen and Kincardine on 1 April 1996; Ayr and Dumfries on 1 April 1997; Angus, Perth and Kinross on 1 April 1998; Midlothian on 1 April 2000; Argyll, Berwick, Bute, East Lothian, Kirkcudbright, Peebles, Roxburgh, Selkirk, and Wigtown on 1 April 2002; and Banff, Caithness, Inverness, Moray, Nairn, Orkney & Zetland, Ross & Cromarty, and Sutherland on 1 April 2003.

13.7 When an area becomes operational for land registration, all transfers for value must be registered (ie new securities on existing holdings and gratuitous transfers, as opposed to transfers for value, do not need to be registered). Transfers of tenants' leases must be registered, whether gratuitous or not (1979 Act, s 3(3)).

Thus if Mr and Mrs A had bought a house in the county of Renfrew in 1975, and if they had lived there continuously, the deed in their favour, and the standard security to their building society, would have been registered in the Register of Sasines. The reason for this is that in 1975 the Land Register was not yet established.

If the As then sold their house to the Bs in 1994, the necessary documentation would then be registered in the Land Register.

If, however, the As decided to transfer their house to their children as a gift (there are possible inheritance tax benefits in this action), the documentation would be recorded in the Sasine Register, as the transfer was not for valuable consideration. Rather oddly, if the As gave the house to a child as a gift in contemplation of marriage (this has slightly greater possible inheritance tax benefits), that would then be treated as a transfer for valuable consideration, and the documentation would be registered in the Land Register.

If, however, the As decided that they were staying put, but would get another loan, the documentation would again be recorded in the Sasine Register, as a loan is not treated as being a valuable consideration.

Once the title is registered in the Land Register, all relevant documents are registered in that register, irrespective of whether the consideration is valuable or not.

The Register of Sasines still operates in parallel with the Land Register (see Appendix IV), and will continue to do so until it is finally phased out.

After all areas have become operational, it may be provided that all land shall be registered, whether transferred or not, to give a complete picture of land ownership in Scotland, kept on standard Ordnance Survey maps, and all stored on computer. That date is, however, still a rather long way off.

13.8 In 1994 the Keeper reported that 92,200 titles were registered as opposed to 323,000 writs registered in the Sasine Register. It must also be borne in mind that the land registration process is very elaborate compared to the Sasine Register process, which means that at any time there must be a large number of Land Register applications being processed.

13.9 It should, however, be made plain that there is nothing tricky about land registration. The first registration does, however, require extra work as the sellers' solicitors not only have to satisfy the purchasers' solicitors as to the sellers' title, but the purchasers' solicitors have immediately to satisfy the Keeper of the Land Register that a sufficient title is being registered, and that no restriction of indemnity is called for. If the Keeper is not happy he will notify the purchasers' solicitors who will in turn revert to the sellers' solicitors, demanding answers in terms of the obligation under missives. (See Appendix II.12(7)).

Thus it may be said that while the sasine system is one of *caveat emptor* (buyer beware), the land registration system is one of *caveat vendor* (seller beware), as there is much more of an onus on the sellers' solicitors to prove a good title than there is on the purchasers' solicitors to be satisfied that the title is good.

When the Keeper is satisfied, a comprehensive land certificate is issued, which contains all necessary information on the title (but not the planning or building information) and it is conclusive evidence of ownership, the extent of the property, and the land obligations affecting the land.

13.10   In the case of *Short's Trustee (Laing) v Keeper of the Registers of Scotland* 1993 SCLR 242, the Inner House decided that the Keeper was not obliged to register a decree reducing a transfer of land, as the appropriate course for the holder of the decree is to apply for rectification of the register under s 9 of the Land Registration (Scotland) Act 1979. This section allows the Keeper to rectify the title sheet where an error is brought to his notice, or if ordered to do so by the Lands Tribunal. This provision is, however, restricted by the terms of s 9 (3), which does not allow rectification to the prejudice of the proprietor in possession, except in very limited circumstances:

(a) to note an overriding interest, which does not prejudice the proprietor because an overriding interest is overriding, whether noted or not;

(b) where all concerned consent;

(c) where the error is caused by the fraud or carelessness of the proprietor in possession;

(d) where rectification relates to something for which the Keeper has previously refused to indemnify the proprietor in possession. An example of this would be where the proprietor in possession has only an *a non domino* title, but this has now been perfected by positive prescription, and the proprietor wants the title to be rectified to the extent that the restriction of indemnity is removed.

In this case Lord President Hope said that if a decree of reduction was automatically registrable in the Land Register, that would subvert the whole system of land registration in that any person dealing with the registered proprietor would require to check the previous history of the title, which was what land registration was designed to avoid.

Thus the virtual sanctity of the land certificate, which is an exact record of the title sheet, was established beyond doubt. An appeal to the House of Lords has however been notified, but it is difficult for the author to find any grounds that would suggest the case was wrongly decided by the First Division.

It should be noted that the Keeper asks (Annual Report 1992–93) to be cited in any action for rectification that is raised, although the action is not directed primarily against the Keeper. This is in order that he can enter an appearance if the integrity of the Register appears to be under threat in any way.

13.11 Furthermore if the registered title is successfully challenged in any respect, on the grounds of a matter on which indemnity has not been excluded, the loss is state guaranteed and falls on the Keeper. For that reason the Keeper inspects the title very carefully, and seeks certain information from the presenter of the title (see the questions in Forms 1, 2, and 3) before full indemnity is given.

Due to the care taken by the Keeper and his staff, the claims record has been modest, but ominously has taken an upturn recently. Such claims usually refer to inaccuracies in Agency reports (replies to Forms 10, 11, 12 and 13) but in the last two years rather large sums have been paid (over £100,000 in 1993–94) in respect of lost leasehold casualty rights. These grotesque survivals are discussed at Chapter 21.

13.12 The first registration involves a considerable amount of detailed work for it is effectively a sasine transaction, with the land registration work added. A positive weighting of fees may be justified. The case of any future transfer should be a comparatively simple matter, but there should be a negative weighting in fees for the reduction in work involved. Under the old Scale of Fees, the positive and negative weighting allowed was 25%, but the guidelines for fee charging in **11.11** should be followed in all cases. The government call for cheaper fees is thus met, by greater productivity, and less time-wasting procedures.

13.13 Thus the land registration system is a very good and modern one, with digitised maps, optical reading, computerised Land Certificates either in operation or planned. It seems barely credible that all this sophisticated technology is imposed on a feudal system which derives from mediaeval times and still talks of superiors and vassals, and still accords the superior major powers over land that other people have bought, and would have bought outright in most other parts of the world.

Chapter fourteen

FIRST REGISTRATION

'The Land Register for Scotland is a State guaranteed register of title to interests in land. Registration of a property for the first time in the Land Register results in the creation of a Title Sheet. The Title Sheet defines precisely the property on the Ordnance Map and also gives details of current registered owners as well as charges and burdens upon properties. The accuracy of the Title Sheet is guaranteed by the State and indemnity is payable for loss suffered as a result of an error or inaccuracy in the Register.'
(The Keeper's Report 1993–94)

The first registration

14.1 The basic scheme of a transaction is similar to a transaction in sasine registration, with the addition of certain steps characteristic of land registration. This chapter should be read with reference to the timetable at the start of the book, and to the specimen transaction contained in Appendix II. It should also be read with reference to the following land registration forms:

Form 1   (Pink) and Notes – Application for first registration
Form 4   (White) and Notes – Inventory of writs
Form 6   Land Certificate
Form 10   Application for report prior to registration
Form 10A   Keeper's reply to Form 10 application (similar to a search)
Form 11   Application for update of Form 10A
Form 11A   continuation of the report contained in Form 10A (similar to an Interim Report on Search)
Form 14   Application for report to ascertain whether subjects are registered or not
Form P16   (White) – Application to compare a boundary description with the ordnance map

14.2 The offers in Appendices I and II are basically used in all transactions, and are compendious in that they cover the obligations (1) in a sasine transaction (2) in a first land registration and (3) in a subsequent dealing of registered land. The form of offer for all three should otherwise be basically identical.

'In exchange for the price the seller will deliver a duly executed disposition in favour of the purchaser and will exhibit or deliver a valid marketable title together with a Form 10 Report brought down to a date as near as practicable to the date of settlement and showing no entries adverse to the seller's interest, the cost of said report being the responsibility of the seller. In addition, the seller, at or before the date of entry and at his expense, shall deliver to the purchaser such documents and evidence as the Keeper may require to enable the Keeper to issue a land certificate in the name of the purchaser as the registered proprietor of the whole subjects of offer and containing no exclusion of indemnity in terms of section 12(2) of the Land Registration (Scotland) Act 1979: such documents shall include (unless the whole subjects of offer only comprise part of a tenement or flatted building) a plan or bounding description sufficient to enable the whole subjects of offer to be identified on the Ordnance map and evidence (such as a Form P16 Report) that the description of the whole subjects of offer as contained in the title deed is *habile* to include the whole of the occupied extent. The land certificate to be issued to the purchaser will disclose no entry, deed or diligence prejudicial to the purchaser's interest other than such as are created by or against the purchaser, or have been disclosed to, and accepted by, the purchaser prior to the date of settlement. Notwithstanding the delivery of the disposition above referred to this clause shall remain in full force and effect and may be founded upon.'

You will note that the obligation is similar to a sasine obligation in that a marketable title and a valid disposition are to be produced, and the main differences from a sasine obligation are (1) the search drops out and is replaced by a Form 10 report; (2) there is an extra obligation upon the sellers to provide 'such documents and evidence including a plan' as may be required to satisfy the Keeper and enable him to issue a land certificate with the full state guarantee, without any qualification.

This clause, in the missives, as provided in the last sentence, is not overruled by delivery of the disposition, as is normally the case, and continues in effect (see *Orr* (1893) 20 R (HL) 27; see also *Winston v Patrick* commented on at **3.28**).

This is a clause characteristic of land registration which keeps the sellers' solicitors 'on the hook', and ultimately responsible for the quality of the title presented for registration. (See **13.9**.)

14.3 As soon as instructed the sellers' solicitors should (as well as obtaining roads certificates, planning certificate, matrimonial homes affidavits, planning permissions, building warrants, completion certificates, superiors' permissions (if required), timber treatment guarantees, replacement window guarantees, and any necessary links in title as before), send a copy of any deed plan they have from the titles together with a Form P16 asking the Keeper to compare the plan with the Ordnance Survey map. The title deeds should also be scrutinised to ascertain whether there is any obstacle to a successful sale, such as an obtrusive land obligation or a clause of pre-emption. If the title is registered there will be a land certificate; if not the assumption is that the title is not registered, but there may be some reason for a land certificate not being with the titles. If in doubt the Form 10A report will clarify this (**14.6**). My remarks in the previous chapter as to the quality of plans should be noted (**13.2(h)**).

14.4 The Keeper will reply to the P16 in one of the following ways:

(1) *'The subjects are not identifiable on the Ordnance map'.*
In this case there is a serious problem, and if missives have not been concluded, the seller should be advised to withdraw the subjects from sale while this is cleared up. If this is not clarified before registration the Keeper may restrict his indemnity so as not to cover loss suffered through this defect in title. For this reason the Form P16 report should be ordered before a sale is made, but this is not always possible with an impetuous seller. In practice this reply may not necessarily be difficult to overcome – the plan may be 'floating' – ie it is not related in any way to adjoining geographical features, and the land could be situated anywhere. This can be easily corrected by the insertion of necessary details, such as streets or geographical features.

(2) *'The boundaries of the subjects coincide with those on the ordnance map'.*
This is the answer you hope for, and if you get it, you can proceed without worry.

(3) *'The boundaries do not coincide with those on the ordnance map. Please see print herewith'.*
This indicates a minor, but material, discrepancy, which will have to be cleared up. It does not, however, go to the root of the sale as does Answer 1.

However, failing this discrepancy in the boundaries being clarified, the Keeper would have to give a qualified indemnity, because of the uncertainty of the boundaries. This is contrary to the obligation in the missives. (See **14.2**.) This matter is clarified in the article by the Deputy Keeper in January 1995 JLSS 15 which states:

'If the comparison confirms that the Ordnance map is correct and there is a discrepancy between the legal extent and the occupied extent, what will require to be done will depend on which extent is the greater. If the legal extent is greater than the occupied extent and the latter is contained wholly within the former then, if the purchaser is prepared to accept a title to the occupied extent, the Keeper should be informed of this when the application is made and he will process the application accordingly. The second additional question provides an opportunity to do so. Where, however, the occupied extent exceeds the boundaries of the legal extent, remedial conveyancing will be necessary and should be completed before application for registration is made.'

14.5   If the discrepancy is not major, the Keeper will provide this answer, but will not deal with the matter until the deed is presented for registration. In all likelihood the discrepancy will then be dealt with informally under the Keeper's discretion, or by using the mythical – but indispensable – 'elastic tape measure'. However, where the discrepancy cannot be overlooked, the boundaries may have to be set out in a section 19 agreement, signed by the adjoining proprietors. This agreement reads, in skeletal form, and each such deed will depend on the individual circumstances of the case, as follows:

'WE, Proprietor 1 (name and design and specify title) and Proprietor 2 (name and design and specify title) CONSIDERING that the boundary (state circumstances) of the subjects belonging to me the said (Proprietor 1) shown on the said Plan first referred to does not coincide with the mutual boundary depicted on the current Ordnance

Survey map (specify map) AND FURTHER CONSIDERING that the parties hereto are satisfied that the said mutual boundary is correctly shown on the Ordnance Survey of which a print has been annexed and subscribed as relative hereto; therefore it is agreed between the parties hereto as follows (state agreement); and the parties hereto bind and oblige themselves and take their respective successors and assignees bound and obliged to accept the said mutual boundary as defined in terms hereof: IN WITNESS WHEREOF (Testing Clause).'

A warrant of registration is put on the deed for each proprietor, unless one already has a registered title. As the deed is usually prepared on the occurrence of a first registration on one or other property, the agreement is recorded in the Sasine Register prior to the land registration, and the appropriate correction is carried onto the land certificate.

A P16 report will not be provided by the Keeper for a flat in a tenement, and should not therefore be requested.

14.6 Further before missives are concluded, the sellers' solicitors should send a Form 10 to the Register, which is 'an Application for Report prior to Registration.' The Keeper responds with a Form 10A report which is equivalent to a sasine search. The Form 10A report also contains a definitive statement as to whether the title has been registered or not, if, for some reason, this cannot be deduced from scrutiny of the title deeds (**14.3**).

All requests for reports should be sent to the Keeper (DX ED 300) and requests for reports in the counties of Renfrew, Dumbarton and Glasgow should be sent to the Cowglen office (DX 501750 Cowglen), which now deals with approximately 40% of land registration matters. Small points maybe, but the volume of mail received by the Keeper every day is so huge that this eases the administration, and saves time for the solicitors in receiving the report back.

Alternatively a Form 14 report can be obtained to ascertain whether a title is registered or not ('Application for report to ascertain whether or not subjects have been registered'), but this contains nothing the Form 10A report does not contain. The main purpose of a Form 14 report is where the enquirer has no knowledge of the subjects or the state of the title. The sellers' solicitors should ideally not, of course, be in this position. This is to some extent, it is admitted, a counsel of perfection – but often the first time solicitors know a house is to be sold is when an offer lands at their reception with a twelve-hour time limit for acceptance!

14.7 When missives are complete the sellers' solicitors send to the purchasers' solicitors the following:

(a) The title deeds being sent to the Keeper detailed at **14.15**. It is not necessary to send any other deeds, including the search, although this may be helpful.

(b) Draft letter of obligation for approval.

(c) Any other relevant documents such as roads certificates, property enquiry reports, building warrants and completion certificates, guarantees, links in title, and matrimonial homes consents.

(d) A Form 10A report with a draft Form 11.

(e) P16 report.

14.8   The draft of obligation is in terms similar to:

> With reference to the settlement of the above transaction today, we hereby (1) undertake to clear the records of any deed, decree or diligence (other than such as may be created by or against your clients) which may be recorded in the Property or Personal Registers, or to which effect may be given in the Land Register in the period from*
> .... to† .... inclusive (or to the earlier registration of your clients' interest in the above subjects), which would cause the Keeper to make an entry on, or qualify his indemnity in the Land Certificate to be issued in respect of that interest; and (2) confirm that, to the best of our knowledge and belief, as at this date, the answers to the questions numbered 1 to 14 in draft Form 1 adjusted with you (in so far as the answers relate to our client or to our clients' interest in the above subjects) are still correct.

*Insert date of certificate of Form 10 report.
†Insert date 14 days (or such other period as may be agreed) after settlement.

This letter of obligation is signed and adopted as holograph. This letter keeps the seller 'on the hook' and is the letter of obligation called for in the offer printed at Appendix II.11. It is also a 'classic' letter of obligation (see Appendix II.18(b)).

Due to the Requirements of Writing (Scotland) Act 1995 it is no longer necessary to sign offers and acceptances 'adopted as holograph'.

14.9   The Form 10 asks the Keeper to provide the following details:

(a) A search in the Register of Inhibitions and Adjudication against the party(ies) last infeft for five years to date of certificate, and any other parties interested (eg their building society or other parties who have disposed of the house within the past ten years).

(b) A list of deeds recorded within the prescriptive period (see **7.10**).

(c) A statement of securities within 40 years prior to the date of certificate and for which no final discharge has been recorded (see **7.24**).

(d) A statement of discharge of securities within the five years prior to the date of certificate (see **7.13**).

(e) Deeds other than transfer or deeds creating or affecting securities recorded within the 40 years prior to the date of certificate (any miscellaneous recorded deeds).

14.10   If there is a significant time gap between obtaining the Form 10A report and settlement this report should be brought down to a date nearer settlement by sending a Form 11 to the Keeper for a more current report (11A). This simply continues the Form 10A report.

It may be tempting to delay the ordering of a Form 10A report until a date near settlement, and to save a little money on a Form 11A report, but this is playing with fire, as the Form 10A may disclose something prejudicial that you should have known much earlier.

The Keeper normally will reply to reports within two days, or for a small additional charge will fax the report. An almost instant reply can be obtained by faxing requests for reports, and requesting a faxed reply.

14.11 As previously the purchasers' solicitors note title and the contents of the Form 10A report, which is equivalent to a search, and will prepare their observations on title, revise the draft letter of obligation, draft discharge of the sellers' security, and return these to the sellers' agents. They also send back the draft disposition they will have drafted, which is drawn in exactly the same manner as one for unregistered land but contains no warrant for registration (a much simpler form is used for subsequent transfers) and drafts of Forms 1 and 4. The sellers' solicitors approve these and then return them.

14.12 The Form 1 ('the pink form') is an 'Application (to the Keeper) for First Registration'. A revised Form 1 was introduced in 1989, and a fresh revision will be issued in 1995, which requires the applicant for registration to answer (as at 1994) thirteen questions, which are self-explanatory – except for two. These questions should be answered truthfully. You are asking the Keeper to guarantee a title, and the Form 1 is therefore like an insurance proposal, and is therefore to be completed in the utmost good faith. As with other forms, notes and directions are given for completion. The form itself and the notes are quite self-explanatory, and more or less straightforward, but it might be mentioned that the purchaser has to supply the following information to the Keeper of the Land Register:

(a) A short description only of the subjects to which the deed being registered relates – that is an identifiable postal address, rather than a full conveyancing description.

(b) The full name of the person granting the deed (ie the seller) or the party last infeft if it is not the granter. Thus if John Smith owned the property, but has died, and his executors were granting the deed without having made up a recorded title, the purchasers' solicitors would insert the late John Smith's name here, as the person last infeft.

(c) The name and address of the grantee (ie purchaser) who is applying for registration.

(d) The price.

(e) The purchasers' solicitors sign the application on page one 'I/We certify that the information supplied in this application is correct to the best of my/our knowledge and belief and apply for registration in respect of Deed No   in the Inventory of Writs (Form 4)'.

This certificate and signature are equivalent to the Warrant of Registration placed on sasine dispositions, but not necessary here.

(f) The presenting solicitors' name, address reference and FAS number (for financial accounting purposes).

14.13   Further in Part B a number of questions must be answered, most of which are self-explanatory, but two only require further explanation:

No. 1.   'Is there any person in possession or occupation of the subject or any part of them adversely to the interest of the applicant?'

Here the applicants' solicitors should give details of any tenancy under a lease or any tenant who may have acquired security of tenure.

No. 3.   'Are there any over-riding interests affecting the subjects or any part of them which you wish noted on the title sheet?'

An 'over-riding interest' is defined at s 28(1) of the 1979 Act as including (in summary) a right or interest over land of lessee under a lease which is not a long lease who has acquired a real right by virtue of possession; a crofter or cottar; the proprietor of the dominant tenement in a servitude; the Crown or other authority under an enactment which does not require the recording of a deed in the Register to complete the right; the holder of a floating charge whether crystallised or not; a member of the public in respect of a public right of way or *regalia majora*; any person having a right which has been made real other than by registration.

This definition does not specifically include properly constituted land obligations which are covered in the Schedule of Burdens on page 4 of the form. This section would seem to refer principally to minor public services, rights of way acquired by prescription, et cetera.

The questions asked in the Form 1 are helpful to solicitors and Keeper alike. For solicitors, they present a check list of questions that should be asked of the sellers' solicitors (eg where the deed inducing registration is in implement of the exercise of a power of sale under a heritable security – have the statutory procedures necessary for the proper exercise of such power been complied with? YES/NO). From the Keeper's point of view, it helps him to identify any problem at an early stage.

14.14   On page 4 of Form 1 you are required to state what heritable securities (if any) affect the property. Please note this covers only existing securities transferred with the property, and not any new security created by the purchaser which are dealt with as a dealing in registered land and by use of a Form 2 (blue) for the security.

Similarly you are also required to state the writs concerning the property which state land obligations.

14.15   The other form to be completed by the purchasers at this stage is Form 4 ('Inventory of Writs relevant to Application for Registration'). Again the notes relative to this form require careful study, and most particularly one should note the definition of 'relevant deeds and documents'.

The Keeper does not require all the writs of the property, no matter how old or obsolete, through the acting of prescription.

He does require:

(a)   a sufficient progress of titles including the deed inducing registration and unrecorded links in title;

(b)   all prior writs containing rights or burdens affecting the land;

(c)   a feuduty redemption receipt;

(d)   any existing heritable securities and related deeds;

(e)   a deed outside the prescriptive progress which contains a plan.

(e)   Form P16 (refer back to **14.3**). This Report must now be returned to the Keeper;

(f)   matrimonial affidavits, consents or renunciations, as appropriate;

(g)   any other relevant document.

14.16   On receipt of these documents from the purchasers' solicitors, the sellers' solicitors should then:

(a)   if not already done, send the Form 10 *in duplicate* and Form P16 to the Keeper, and send the resulting reports to the purchasers' solicitors;

(b)   revise and return the purchasers' solicitors Form 1, Form 4 and draft disposition;

(c)   answer any title queries and obtain anything further required by the purchasers. (Compare with **10.2**.)

14.17   The purchasers' solicitors then have the disposition engrossed and return it to the sellers' solicitors for signature, with the draft for comparison, and blank form of particulars of signing and witnesses. The Forms 1 and 4 are typed in principal form. Everything is prepared for settlement as before.

14.18   At settlement the sellers' solicitors hand over in exchange for the price:

(a)   the signed disposition, draft and particulars of signing;

(b)   Form P16 report;

(c)   letter of obligation (in terms of **14.8**). They also exhibit the draft letter of obligation to the purchasers' solicitors to enable them to check the principal;

(d)   the title deeds and any other relevant papers;

(e)   the receipted state for settlement;

(f)   A Form 11A report, which brings down the report to a date as close as possible to settlement. This should be applied for by the seller at least three working days before settlement. Sellers' solicitors who have applied for, but not yet received, a Form 11A report at settlement, may obtain a telephoned or faxed report from Register House, at a small fee. This allows the sellers' solicitors to grant a letter of obligation with an easy conscience (**14.8**).

14.19   The purchasers' solicitors then send off to the Keeper:

(a)   Forms 1 and 4, the latter in duplicate;

(b)   the disposition;

(c) the various papers stipulated in **14.11**. A GREEN address label, provided by the Keeper with Land Register forms, should be used when sending application for registration. Applications for Renfrew, Glasgow and Dumbarton only should be sent to Cowglen.

The Keeper checks off the deeds against the Form 4, and acknowledges receipt by returning the duplicate Form 4, which also bears the new title number and the date of the registration, both of which can be regarded as conclusive.

The purchasers' solicitors then settle up the odds and ends of the transaction as they would have under the old system; they answer any question the Keeper may have.

14.20   Assuming that everything is in order, the Keeper will send out in due course a land certificate, Form 6, which discloses the following:

(a) **The registered number of the title.**

(b) **A statement of indemnity.**   'Subject to any specific qualification ... a person who suffers loss as a result of any of the events specified in 12(1) of the above (ie 1979) Act shall be entitled to be indemnified in respect of that loss by the Keeper of the Registers of Scotland in terms of that Act.'

(c) **Section A – the property section.**   A description of the property and a coloured plan based on the Ordnance Survey Scale 1/1,250 for densely populated urban areas; 1/2,500 for less densely populated urban areas and farms; 1/10,000 for hill farms, mountains and moorland.

(d) **Section B – the proprietorship section.**   The name and designation of the proprietor, the date of registration (ie when the real right was created), the price and the date of entry.

(e) **Section C – the charges section.**   Details of charges affecting the property whether previously existing or created by the proprietor. There is also a separate charge certificate. (Form 7, see **16.2.**)

(f) **Section D – the burdens section.**   A verbatim note of all land obligations affecting the property, in so far as still relevant and existing. The Keeper discards what he considers all irrelevant information, such as narrative and ancillary clauses, descriptions, old and useless burdens, such as details of roads that have long since been formed, and retains only the relevant ones.

The Keeper is walking a tightrope in this respect, for what may be considered to be irrelevant, may turn out to be painfully relevant (see leasehold casualties) and the Keeper will be responsible for any loss in respect of lost rights. (See Chapter 21.)

14.21   When the purchasers' solicitors receive the land certificate, they should read it to confirm it is in order and then discharge the letter of obligation (assuming that all other items on it have been met) and return it to the sellers' solicitors.

14.22 This wonderful document completely takes the place of the title deeds, and can be brought up to date in future, as and when required. If it is lost an office copy can be obtained from the Keeper who prepares this from the Title Sheet. You can, in theory at least, tear up all the title deeds – but before you do so remember (1) it is better to keep them until the first sale, just in case there has been a mistake that has been overlooked (2) they belong to the owner of the house who may very well want to keep them and (3) the deeds may have archival interest to the local archivist who should be allowed to see any old documents before they are shredded.

14.23 If the purchasers sell the property in the course of registration, a difficult situation arises. The Keeper can be requested to return the title deeds, but this only delays the registration. Alternatively, the Keeper prefers to supply photocopies of the title deeds, but this is an expensive and time-wasting procedure. The Keeper in a circular to the profession suggested that, if there is any likelihood of the property being sold before registration is complete, the applicants' solicitors should take photocopies of the deeds presented before sending them. This is not very satisfactory either. This problem has become less acute as registration delays have decreased.

In any event, when the sellers' solicitors do get the title, or photocopies of them, they are sent to the purchasers' solicitors, and in all other respects the transaction proceeds as a normal dealing of a registered interest (see Chapter 15).

14.24 Armed with the land certificate and after a great deal of hard work, the lawyer's job is now a great deal easier – the millenium is in sight!

In summary, it might be said that the main difference between this transaction and a sasine transaction is that there is a greater burden on the sellers' solicitors in a land registration transaction. If they do not ensure that the papers presented to the Keeper are in order, they will have to rectify these sooner or later, under the terms of the letter of obligation. The purchasers' solicitors are essentially the 'middlemen' between the sellers' solicitors and the Keeper.

14.25 Inevitably the details requested in the various forms will change from time to time, and it is proposed by the Land Register (Scotland) Amendment Rules to change the presentation Forms 1, 2 and 3 in 1995. The changes in the new forms are:

(a) Solicitors will be asked to state if they have lodged a plan of the subjects to be registered, or, failing that, a deed containing a full bounding description and measurements. This is to help sort out the number of disputes in which the Keeper inevitably becomes involved, and which take up so much of his staff's time. The biggest single difficulty the Keeper has to deal with are discrepancies between legal title, and the ground actually being occupied. This question will help the Keeper to identify any possible problem a bit earlier.

(b) Solicitors will be asked if a P16 report is lodged with the deeds. If not, and the boundaries are therefore vague, they will be asked questions about the extent of the 'occupational boundaries'.

(c) They will be asked about the possibility of there being any leasehold casualties.

(d) In line with the provisions of the Companies Act 1989, s 112, if any party to registration is a company, it will be asked to state whether or not the company is a charity or a company dealing with its own directors, in which case the ultra vires doctrine (now largely superseded) revives.

(e) The questions about limited companies, and their powers (*vires*), will be simplified somewhat.

(f) The question about matrimonial consents et cetera will be amended. The provision of the Law Reform (Miscellaneous Provisions) (Scotland) Act 1990, which permitted consents et cetera to be granted retrospectively, will entail the dropping of the second question.

The forms are optically readable, to save time, and are available from Meadowbank House free of charge. The old P16 Form is still available.

14.26 It is probable that when the Land Registers (Scotland) Bill is passed (and at the time of writing it is struggling through the parliamentary processes) solicitors will require to lodge applications for registration in both the Sasine and Land Registers, accompanied by the appropriate fee.

The reason for this is that the profession is owing the Keeper some £5 million, which is not an acceptable level of debt for any commercial undertaking, which the Agency now is. Efforts are being successfully made to recoup this sum, and the necessary legislation allowing the Keeper to charge fees 'up front' will be passed in the near future. Solicitors will therefore, quite sensibly, be required to make the same arrangements for payment of registration dues as they do for the payment of stamp duty.

Deeds presented without the appropriate fee will be returned. You have been warned!

Chapter fifteen

THE DEALING

'Once a property is registered, subsequent transfers are much simpler to effect, thus providing scope for lower conveyancing costs.'
(Keeper's Report 1993–94)

15.1 A dealing is a second registration and subsequent registrations of the same subjects, together with a transfer of a part of a registered holding (see Chapter 16), securities, discharges or other deeds granted affecting the subjects, at any time after, or contemporaneously with, the first registration (as opposed to part of the subjects only).

15.2 The forms which I refer to in this chapter are:

Form 2 (Blue)	– application for registration of a dealing
Form 4	– inventory writs
Form 6	– land certificate
Form 12	– application for report over registered subjects (similar in purpose to the Form 10 in a first registration)
Form 13	– continuation of Form 12 (similar to the Form 11 in a first registration).

15.3 The missives are completed exactly as previously, in the compendious form, which includes the obligation for dealings in land:

'In exchange for the purchase price there will be delivered a duly executed disposition in favour of the purchasers and there will be exhibited or delivered to the purchasers

(i) a land certificate (containing no exclusion if indemnity under section 12(2) of the Land Registration (Scotland) Act 1979), (ii) all necessary links in title evidencing the sellers' exclusive ownership of the subjects of offer and (iii) a Form 12 report brought down as near as practicable to the date of settlement and showing no entries adverse to the sellers' interest. The cost of said report shall be the responsibility of the purchasers.

In addition, the sellers will furnish to the purchasers such documents and evidence as the Keeper may require to enable the interest of the purchasers to be registered in the Land Register without exclusion of indemnity under section 12(2). The land certificate to be issued to the purchasers will disclose no entry, deed, or diligence prejudicial to the purchasers' interest, other than such as are created by, or against the purchasers, or have been disclosed to and accepted by the purchasers prior to the date of settlement. Nothwithstanding the delivery of the disposition above referred to, this clause shall remain in full force and effect and may be founded upon.'

The sellers' obligation is thus to provide a valid disposition, a clear title in the form of a land certificate without restriction of indemnity, and clear searches in the shape of Forms 12 and 13 reports.

15.4 The land certificate is sent to the purchasers' solicitors together with:

(a) a draft Form 12 (not a Form 10 which is applicable only prior to registration). Form 12 is a report over registered subjects;

(b) any other certificate (eg planning and roads), affidavits, links in title et cetera that may be required;

(c) draft letter of obligation.

The title deeds, of course, need not be sent as they are replaced by the land certificate.

15.5 The purchasers' solicitors inspect the various sections of the land certificate. This is a matter of comparative simplicity, because the land certificate contains all relevant information that would have previously required to be extracted from the title deeds. Everything now is nicely printed in a central document, and you don't have to hunt through a mass of spidery handwriting, on crumbling paper, to discover the land obligations affecting the land. This makes it all the more imperative that you read the land certificate very carefully – there are no excuses available if you don't.

The purchasers' solicitors also draw up a draft disposition. This document is simplicity itself, because you need only state the postal address of the property and the number of the land certificate, which provide a sufficient description. You do not require a traditional conveyancing description, nor need you mention the deeds referred to for the land obligations they contain, nor need you put on a warrant of registration. The disposition thus becomes a very short document. It is perhaps paradoxical that as missives have got longer and longer, the disposition, which is still the primary deed of transfer, has shrunk to almost nothing.

The disposition need contain only the following:

the narrative clause – granter, grantee, and consents, and the consideration;

the dispositive clause – words of transference, destination of grantee, postal address of subjects, land certificate number;

ancillary clauses – date of entry, warrandice, stamp duty mitigation certificate, if appropriate, non-supersession clause; testing clause.

A sample disposition might therefore read:

I, Allister McAllister (design) in consideration of the price of FIFTY NINE THOUSAND NINE HUNDRED POUNDS (£59,900) paid to me by JAMES MEIKLE (design) HEREBY DISPONE to the said James Meikle and his executors and assignees All and Whole the subjects 3 Miller Drive, Paisley, Renfrewshire, registered under Title Number 0000; with entry on Thirty first October Nineteen hundred and ninety four; and I grant warrandice; and I certify that the transaction hereby effected does not form part of a larger transaction or of a series of transactions in respect of which the amount or value or the aggregate amount or value of the consideration exceeds sixty thousand pounds: the missives of sale which I have concluded with the said James Meikle and which are constituted by letter dated ... will form a continuing and enforceable contract notwithstanding the delivery of these presents except in so far as fully implemented thereby, but the said missives shall cease to be enforceable after a period of two years from the date of entry, except in so far as they are founded on in any court proceedings which have commenced within the said period: IN WITNESS WHEREOF (Testing Clause)

Note: There is no description of the property, no reference to burdens, no parts and pertinents, no assignation of writs or rents, no obligation of relief and no warrant of registration.

15.6 The Form 2 (blue) and Form 4 are filled up in accordance with the printed form of instructions. This Form 2 is substantially the same as Form 1 (pink) (see **14.8**), and nothing further need be added in this respect. The draft Form 2 is returned to the sellers' solicitors for approval together with:

(1) draft letter of obligation, duly approved;

(2) draft Form 12 (application for report over registered subjects) duly approved;

(3) the draft disposition;

(4) the land certificate and other papers sent by the sellers' solicitors;

(5) draft Form 4 (inventory of writs).

15.7 The sellers' solicitors revise the disposition and return it to the purchasers' solicitors, who in turn have this document engrossed and send the typed deed and draft back to the sellers' solicitors for signature by their clients. The draft disposition is also returned for comparison purposes.

15.8 The sellers' solicitors send Form 12 to Meadowbank House or Cowglen, as appropriate, for a 12A report which they exhibit to the purchasers' solicitors. The latter should satisfy themselves as to the sufficiency of the report, as with an interim report in pre-registration procedures. If there is a significant time gap between obtaining the Form 12 report and settlement this report should be brought down to a date nearer settlement by sending a Form 13 to the Keeper for a more current report, observing a three-working day period.

15.9 Settlement duly takes place and the disposition, Form 2 (duly signed), Form 4, land certificate and such other papers as are required (see **14.13**) are sent to Meadowbank House. In due course the land certificate is returned, with the purchasers' name inserted in the proprietorship section. The letter of obligation, which is in the terms following, is returned to the sellers' solicitors.

With reference to the settlement of the above transaction today, we hereby (1) undertake to clear the records of any deed, decree or diligence – other than such as may be created by or against your clients – which may be recorded in the Personal Register in the period from*   to†   inclusive (or to the earlier registration of your clients' interest in the above subjects) and which would cause the Keeper to make an entry on, or qualify his indemnity in, the Land Certificate to be issued in respect of their interest; and (2) confirm that, to the best of my knowledge and belief, as at this date the answers to the questions numbered 1 to 8 in the draft Form 2 adjusted with you (in so far as these answers relate to my client or to my client's interest in the above subjects) are still correct.

*Insert date of certification of Form 12 report, or if a Form 13 report has been instructed, the date of certification of that report. If there is a significant time gap between obtaining the Form 12 report and settlement, the report should be brought down to a date nearer settlement by sending a Form 13 to the Keeper, who will return a more up-to-date report.

†Insert a date 14 days (or such other period as may be agreed) after settlement.

15.10   The land certificate and other relevant papers are kept carefully either by the client or as instructed by the client. If the land certificate is misplaced, an office copy can be obtained from the Land Register (see **16.7**). If a land certificate is irretrievably lost, a substitute one can be requested from the Keeper. The Keeper is, however, reluctant to issue one unless satisfied by due inquiry and certification that every reasonable effort has been made to locate the land certificate, which accordingly can be viewed as irretrievably lost, as distinct from misplaced.

15.11   The Form 2 has been changed in line with the Form 1 (see **14.25**).

15.12   Statutory instruments made in 1994 (SIs 2866–68) end the authorised use of imperial units and measurements used to describe length, area, volume and mass after 30 September 1995. Imperial measures cannot therefore be used on plans, except as a supplementary indicator, apart from acres, which are specifically allowed in use for land registration.

Chapter sixteen

SOME OTHER REGISTRATION PROCEDURES

'As regards turnround times for Transfers of Part, in the last Report it was reported that the legal profession had intimated, through the Joint Consultative Committee of the Agency and the Law Society of Scotland, its preference for the current policy of attempting to ensure conformity with the legal extent and the fenced position as picked up by the Ordnance Survey. The continuation of this policy means that turnround time is an inappropriate measure of performance and the sole measure is output. In that respect output exceeded intake by slightly over 6%.'
(Keeper's Report 1993–94)

Application for registration of a transfer of part of registered holding

16.1 This procedure is similar to that under Chapter 15 ('blue form' procedure) which refers to the transfer of an entire landholding. Thus if A bought a house in 1993, registered the title, and then re-sold the house in 1989, the proper procedure is the 'blue form' procedure.

If, however, a builder bought a two-acre field in 1993, registered the title and then sold off the field in 20 plots with houses, then the appropriate procedure for each house purchase is 'yellow form'.

Again the yellow form is largely similar to the pink and blue forms (1 and 2) and there are similar official notes for its completion. The transaction will follow the same course as a 'blue form' transaction (see Chapter 15). Again the forms will be changed in the near future.

The disposition, however, is slightly different, as the proper conveyancing description must be prepared for the plot of land being split off the larger, registered, subjects.

If you refer to the sample disposition of 3 Miller Drive, Paisley, in **15.4**, and then assume that part of the (presumably large) garden is being sold for the building of a small house, then the disposition would read along these lines:

I, JAMES MEIKLE (design) in consideration of the price of £X paid to me by JEREMIAH JONES (design) HEREBY DISPONE to the said JEREMIAH JONES and his executors and assignees ALL AND WHOLE that plot of ground in the County of Renfrew containing one-tenth of an acre Imperial Measure delineated and shown within the boundaries coloured red on the plan annexed to this Disposition; being part of the subjects registered under Title number REN 0000. (Thereafter insert any new land obligations relating to the new holding: the date of entry; warrandice; stamp duty clause; non-supersession clause; and testing clause.)

Considerable difficulties in registration are caused by builders lodging estate plans with the Keeper, of proposed building estates, and then not adhering to them. This is not done maliciously, it's just that it's easy to draw a site plan in the office, but hard to mark out the site accurately on the ground, and the boundary markers are often misplaced, or run over by a JCB. The fence is then placed in a position different from the site plan, and this is the boundary that is picked up by the Ordnance Survey when it maps the site. For this reason the Keeper will take some time to produce a land certificate, as it will be necessary to obtain an Ordnance map of the estate, and to see that all the land certificates in the estate are consistent with each other.

Charges over land under registration procedures

16.2 The first thing to point out is that if you frame a new security over unregistered land without a transfer of ownership for valuable consideration in an operational area, this security is registered in the General Register of Sasines, which continues to run in parallel with the Land Register. Thus, for example, if A has a loan from Y Building Society, but discharges this and creates a new security in favour of Z Building Society, then both of these deeds are registered in the General Register of Sasines. Similarly if A dispones a half interest in his house to the spouse for 'love, favour and affection', that is not a valuable consideration and the disposition is registered in the General Register.

If, however, you buy a house for valuable consideration in an operational area, you must register the title (pink form) and register any simultaneous or subsequent security, using the blue form procedure (Form 2).

You will see that the notes for the blue form say that this form is to be used among other things for:

standard security over the whole of the interest;
standard security over part of the interest in one registered title;
discharge of a registered standard security (a discharge of an unregistered security will be registered in the General Register of Sasines).

The standard security is sent to the Land Register, with a blue form and the land certificate, and any existing charge certificate (which is prepared by the Keeper to conform with land registration Form 7), and any other writs which may be necessary (such as links in title, but see explanatory notes for fuller details).

The charge thus created is entered into section C of the land certificate (the charges section). A charge certificate (Form 7) is also prepared, which is made to agree with the title sheet. The certificate certifies that the lender is a registered creditor in the heritable security on the date of registration. The standard security is also annexed to the charge certificate. Where a limited company is creating the security, a copy of the certificate of registration of charge in the Register of Charges (which is mandatory under the Companies

Act 1985, s 410 ff) should be sent to the Keeper within 21 days of the registration of the standard security in the Land or Sasine Registers. Where separate solicitors act for the lender, as is usually the case, a letter of obligation is given to them by the borrowers' solicitors in the following terms:

(a) *First registration or purchase of registered interest with immediate grant of a standard security.*

With reference to the settlement of the above transaction today, we hereby undertake to deliver to you within twelve (or as appropriate) months of this date a Land Certificate issued by the Keeper of the Registers of Scotland in favour of our clients, showing the interest of our clients as registered proprietors of the above subjects, which Land Certificate shall be unaffected by any deed, decree, or diligence – other than such as may be created by or against your clients – given effect to in the Land Register in the period from*
to†   inclusive, or to the earlier date of registration of clients' Standard Security over the above subjects, and further will disclose the Standard Security granted in favour of your clients; provided that it is presented for registration in the Land Register within fourteen days of this date.

*Date of certificate 10/11/12/13.
†Fourteen days after settlement.

Further we (1) undertake to exhibit to you along with the said Land Certificate all deeds, documents and other evidence which were submitted to the Keeper in support of our clients' application for registration of their interest as heritable proprietors of the above subjects; and (2) confirm that, to the best of our knowledge and belief, as at this date the answers to the Questions numbered 1 to 8 in the draft Form 2 adjusted with you – insofar as these relate to our clients or to our clients' interest in the above subjects – are still correct.

I further undertake to exhibit to you within fourteen days of this date the duplicate Form 4 lodged with my clients' application for registration with the Keeper's acknowledgement thereon.§

Yours faithfully,

§Where purchasers' solicitors lodge the purchasers' application with the Keeper; or where there are two lenders, one of whom will present that application.

(b) *where borrower is already registered proprietor of the interest to be secured.*

With reference to the settlement of the above loan transaction today, I hereby (1) undertake to clear the records of any deed, decree, or diligence – other than such as may be created by or against your clients – which may be recorded in the Personal Register or to which effect may be given in the Land Register in the period from*   to†   inclusive (or to the earlier date of registration of your clients' interest in the above subjects) which would cause the Keeper to make an entry on, or qualify his indemnity in, the Title Sheet relating to my clients' interest in the above subjects; and (2) confirm that, to the best of my knowledge and belief, as at this date the answers in Questions numbered 1 to 8 in the draft Form 2 adjusted with you – insofar as these answers relate to your client or to my clients' interest in the above subjects – are still current.

I further undertake on behalf of my clients, to deliver to you within two months a clear Search in the Companies and Charges Register in terms of the Memorandum adjusted between us down to the date occurring 21 days after today's date.

Yours faithfully,

*Insert date of Form 12/13 Report.
†Insert date fourteen days from settlement.

Form 5   Application for noting an over-riding interest or for entry of discharge of an over-riding interest or of additional information

16.3   An over-riding interest is defined in s 28(1) of the 1979 Act which is the definition section (see **14.13**). Reference should be made to this subsection, but the interest is generally an interest in the land concerned, enjoyed, by a third party, and not constituted by a deed recorded in the General Register of Sasines.

Some examples given are:

(a)   the interest of a lessee under a long lease, provided that the leasehold interest has not been registered in the Land Register. On registration the interest ceases to come within the definition of an over-riding interest;

(b)   a croft;

(c)   the dominant tenement in a servitude;

(d)   a public right of way.

Such over-riding interests are generally to be notified to the Keeper on the pink, blue or yellow forms as appropriate, and they are noted on the title sheet.

Any interest or discharge of an interest not thus notified, should be notified on Form 5, in terms of the Land Registration (Scotland) Rules 1980, r 13.

Form 8   Application for land or charge certificate to be made to correspond with the title sheet (Land Registration (Scotland) Rules 1980, r 16)

16.4   Where a certificate has been in existence for some time, without any dealings taking place, the Keeper may be requested in a Form 8 to bring it up to date with his title sheet.

Form 9   Application for rectification of the Register (Land Registration Rules 1980, r 20)

16.5   Where it appears to any party that there is a mistake in the land certificate, however trivial or however fundamental, the Keeper may be requested to rectify this mistake. Reference is made to s 9 of the Land Registration (Scotland) Act 1979.

Form 14   Application to ascertain whether or not the subjects have been registered

16.6 This form may be used in the course of a normal transaction but it is more usual to obtain this information from the relevant part of the Form 10. (See **14.6.**)

Form 15   Application for an office copy of a land certificate or charge certificate or any part of one of these

16.7 An office copy of the title sheet kept by the Keeper may be requested if a land certificate is in constant use or is misplaced. The office copy may be of the whole title sheet or any part of it or of any document referred to in it. If a land certificate is irretrievably lost, see the comments in **15.10**.

Rectification of boundaries

16.8 When the boundary disclosed on the deed plan and the boundary shown on the Ordnance Survey plan do not agree, as will happen from time to time, an agreement in terms of the Land Registration (Scotland) Act 1979, s 19, may be signed by the parties concerned and registered. This agreement should also contain a plan showing the agreed boundary. The agreement is registered in the Land Register, in the case of registered interests, or in the Sasine Register, in the case of unregistered interests. (For style see **14.5.**)

Legal and occupational extents of boundaries

16.9 The Forms 1, 2 and 3 pose the question 'Is there any person in possession or occupation of the subjects or any part of them adversely to the interest of the applicant?' The main purpose of this question is to elicit whether legal and occupational extents correspond, and whether there may be a competition in title with, for example, a neighbour.

16.10 The transfer of an interest which is held under a long lease is also a registerable event. A long lease is defined in the Land Tenure Reform (Scotland) Act 1974, as being a lease over 20 years duration. In practice, many commercial leases will be for a long period, because only by registering a lease may a security over that lease be created. The LTR (S) Act 1974, s 12, also prohibited the creation of leases of residential property for a period exceeding 20 years. This is therefore a matter principally for commercial leases, although a pre-1974 residential long lease may still be registered, if it hasn't been already.

Similarly an assignation of a registered long lease, or a sub-lease, or a sub-under-lease, or a standard security over any part of the property contained in the registered lease, may be registered.

If an unregistered long lease has less than 20 years to run, but its length was originally over 20 years, it may still be registered. Thus (writing in 1995) a lease for a 25-year period, granted say in 1980, may still be registered although it has only a life of a further ten years.

The registration of a long leasehold interest proceeds in exactly the same way as the registration of a right of ownership, although one must apply for the registration of an assignation et cetera, and not of a disposition.

16.11 The Keeper and his staff are very helpful, and are willing to discuss any problems that you may have. If it is a general question, ask for the Group Services for the appropriate division at Edinburgh or Cowglen, but if it is a specific question, ask for the appropriate County Register, and specify the Title Number, or the property involved. The telephone numbers are – Meadowbank House 0131 659 6111 and Cowglen 0141 306 4400.

In return the legal profession owe consideration to the Keeper's staff. In particular, you should:

(a) Not bombard the Keeper with stupid or hypothetical questions. The story goes that the stupidest question ever asked was 'does a title in Paisley have to be registered?'

(b) Fill in the correct forms carefully and accurately. Don't forget to sign applications for reports and registration. Check all writs carefully before sending them – that they are properly signed, stamped, completed, and that the testing clauses are in order.

(c) Not forget to send duplicates of forms where these are specified.

(d) Check that you have up-to-date forms. New forms were introduced in 1989, and these in turn are to be replaced in 1995. The Keeper will still accept old forms, but he may have to ask supplementary questions. This wastes everyone's time. Why don't you just throw out your stock of old forms, and get some new ones.

(e) Obtain quick copies of deeds that you do not have. Do not expect the Land Register to obtain these itself, just because it's in the same building as the Sasine Register. It won't, as this would impose an intolerable extra workload. Keep copies on file of all important deeds sent to the Register, in case a re-sale is necessary before the land certificate is sent.

(f) Make sure that if you have a note that the Keeper has already seen a common title in connection with another earlier application, quote that title number to the Keeper.

(g) Pay fee notes promptly. If the Land Registers (Scotland) Act 1995 is passed, please note to send a cheque for registration dues with the application.

Part three

TRANSFERS OF SPECIAL SUBJECTS

Part Five

Chapter seventeen

TRANSFERS OF SUPERIORITIES

'One of Jersey's leading lawyers is using an obscure feudal title, which has been in his family for years, to try and win legal control of a £1 billion development site on the island.

Tradition says that the rights extend as far as the seigneur could ride his horse into the sea at low tide. Mr Falle is asserting that the feudal rights over the foreshore, which boasts the island's main power station, a fuel farm, and a large area of reclaimed land, include ownership.

If Mr Falle wins, the States – the island's parliament – has been advised by lawyers that he would own everything built on the land in perpetuity.'
(*The Times*)

17.1 Scotland and the Channel Islands remain the last bastions of feudalism in the civilised world, and as long as they do, we shall be subjected to picturesque mediaeval claptrap and blackmail by title raiders, that is to say purchasers who buy these titles solely to squeeze out of the carcass what they can get. Their reasons for doing so are narrated at **17.9**.

17.2 We have to date dealt with the transfer of title of a reasonably average detached house. You will have noticed that there are four main parts of the sale:

(a) negotiation;

(b) completion of missives;

(c) examination of title and transfer to title;

(d) settlement.

The same pattern can be distinguished in the transfer of a number of special kinds of subjects, although obviously there are differences of emphasis depending on the nature of the property involved.

Superiorities

17.3 When land is completely in the ownership of the superiors, they are said to own the *dominium plenum*. If they sell it, or any part of it, they may either:

(a) sell the *dominium plenum* or any part of it without dividing it into different strata of ownership (generally known as a 'freehold' conveyance); or

(b) sell the *dominium plenum* wholly or partially into two strata of ownership – the superiority (or *dominium directum* or direct ownership) which the seller retains, and the feu (or *dominium utile* or useful ownership) which is sold to the purchaser.

17.4 When a sale is made by the landowners either of the *dominium plenum* or of the *dominium utile*, the method of sale is similar to the method already outlined in this book. In **case (a)** above, an offer to purchase or sell is made, and accepted. A disposition is then prepared, agreed and signed and delivered. The disposition is granted subject to any land obligations the sellers may wish to impose. Please note that a disposition is the competent deed for this transfer, because it is a transfer, pure and simple, and nothing is created. If it was this would require a deed of creation.

In **case (b)** however, two new strata of ownership in the same property are created (the superiority and the feu), and this requires a deed of creation. An agreement to sell and buy is negotiated and a feu disposition, or feu contract or feu charter is prepared by the sellers' solicitors (this is the normal rule – see Table of Fees General Regulations 7(2)) agreed, signed and delivered. These three deeds are deeds of creation and are generally referred to as 'feu writs' or 'feu grants'. They actually create a superiority and a feu out of a whole and single ownership and confer different rights and duties on the parties to them.

17.5 Once a superiority has been created it can be bought and sold in the same way as a feu (to the sale of which the last sixteen chapters have been devoted). The competent deed is a deed of transfer (a disposition) and not a deed of creation or feu grant. Nothing in this case is created.

Sales of created superiorities are relatively uncommon, but do occur from time to time. In the past, superiorities were bought as a sound perpetual investment, both for the feuduties payable annually, and for the chance of an occasional fee for granting a waiver of a land obligation, eg the prohibition of using a house for certain commercial purposes (see *Bowmaker* 1965 SC 163). The price payable for the sale of a superiority is negotiable and as a rule of thumb is generally about twenty times the annual feuduty, but this very much depends on the negotiating powers of the parties, and the circumstances.

In addition, the owners of a feu may wish to purchase their superiority and consolidate the superiority and the feu in terms of the C (S) Act 1874, s 6 and Sch C and the C (S) Act 1924, s 11 and Sch G.

17.6 Purchase of the superiority should not, however, under any circumstances be confused with redemption of the feuduty under the terms of the Land Tenure Reform (Scotland) Act 1974, ss 4 to 6, which is merely a cancellation of a monetary payment as opposed to an extinction of the right to enforce land obligations.

A firm of English property owners recently bought the superiorities of a number of houses in Bearsden from the builders. They then wrote to the various feuars offering 'to extinguish the feuduty at a price of ten times the annual rent (sic) together with contribution of £35 towards legal costs and expenses'.

If the firm had really been intending to sell the superiority and grant a disposition of the superiority to the feuar, then this would have been a fair offer, for a certain amount of legal work is involved. But the firm appears to have become hopelessly muddled between feuduties and English ground rents, and was not sure if it intended to redeem the feuduty or sell the superiority.

If it intended the former there is of course a simple procedure for this, and indeed an inalienable right to the feuar to require a redemption. Redemption is made at a variable multiplier of the feuduty (around eleven or twelve times the feuduty on November 1994: see **7.28**) and no legal fee is payable to the superior for this.

17.7   A sale of the superiority is not a sale of a right of possession, thus many of the clauses in an offer for the feu are inapplicable. The offer is a very simple document making no mention of planning, roads, affidavits, moveable property included, rateable value or maintenance. The form of disposition of a superiority of land is very similar to a disposition of the feu of the same land, and indeed the unwary may be tricked. The only sure sign of a superiority disposition is the warrandice clause which reads:

'And I grant warrandice subject to the current feu rights, but without prejudice however to the rights of the grantee to quarrel or impugn the same on any ground not inferring warrandice against me.'

17.8   A sale of the *dominium plenum* or undivided ownership of land is effected again by a disposition, which again is little different from a disposition either of a superiority or a feu. In fact the only way you can truly distinguish a disposition of the *dominium plenum* from a disposition of the feu is by reference to the title of the granters, to see what they own and to ensure that the disposition transfers these rights intact.

17.9   Most superiorities have now passed into institutional hands – pension funds, assurance companies, friendly societies – who regard them as a sound rather than a spectacular investment.

The benefits of buying estates that have largely been feued off are:

(a) a high income return from feuduties;

(b) a regular flow of feuduty redemptions in terms of LTR (S) Act 1974, ss 4 to 6 (see **7.28**);

(c) payments from granting waivers of feuing conditions;

(d) a likelihood that little pockets of land in the estate have been left unfeued, and thus still belonging to the superior. Such pockets may be of considerable value nowadays. Consider the pension fund that recently sold a small stretch of private road to a builder for access – price £35,000!

Title raiders are now buying estates that have been largely feued off, and picking the carcasses clean. Consider the profitable operation of a title raider in the Aberdeen area, who discovered that the estate he had bought had formerly gifted land to the county council for the building of a school. Incredibly a formal title to the land had never been taken, presumably because people in those days thought that once land was owned by a county council it would never revert to private hands.

The council built the school, and houses for teachers, which latterly became unnecessary, and the council sold them off. The council could, of course, produce no title in their favour, and gave each purchaser a disposition by the council backed by an insurance indemnity.

The title raider, who had obviously done his homework, then pounced, claiming that the land was still his. Further the houses were his, because what is built in the ground belongs to the ground (*aedificatum solo solo cedit*). He was right of course; the insurance company presumably paid up, and there were red faces all round. For another example of a title raider's activities see *Hamilton v Grampian Regional Council* 1995 GWD 8–443, where it was held that the closure of a school, built on land given by the superiors, operated as a statutory irritancy, and the land reverted to the superiors.

The building of houses on ground you don't actually own is a risky business, as the Scottish Office found out. In anticipation of an oil boom on the West Coast, which has not come yet, they bought land at Portvadie in Argyll and built a deep harbour there. They also built a splendid village for the expected workforce, which never arrived, called Polphail. Unfortunately they did not acquire the land, which is believed to be in the ownership of a company registered in the Netherlands Antilles. Meanwhile the village is a rotting eyesore on what used to be one of the most beautiful parts of Argyll, and no one can do anything about it.

This should be compared with, but not confused with, the activities of the people who try to exercise leasehold casualties (see Chapter 21) which is another unwelcome survival from another age, which could easily be reformed, but has not been.

The Scottish Law Commission has suggested that the power of the superior be removed, but nothing has yet been done. It is to be hoped that this mediaeval detritus will not be allowed to survive into the new millenium.

Chapter eighteen

SALES AND PURCHASES OF FLATS IN TENEMENT BUILDINGS

'The "broom cupboard" sold in the summer of 1987 for £36,500 wasn't just an estate agent's fanciful description of a small studio flat but a real life former broom cupboard which was converted into a 9 ft by 7 ft "town flat" in a building close to Harrods. It had no cooking facilities and was marketed as a weekday residence for "the professional who likes to eat out".'
(*Daily Mail*)

'It would assist the members of the [Property Managers] Association greatly if the [legal] profession could ensure that purchasers of property are made fully aware of their obligations in terms of the deed of conditions and counselled to keep for future reference the copy deed of conditions which their solicitor sent to them.'
(Letter from James A Millar, Secretary of the Association, 1994 JLSS 445)

18.1 A tenement of flats in separate ownership is to some extent an alien concept in Scots law, in that the owner of a flat owns only a slice of air space surrounded by walls, ceiling and floor, and not the ground. There is also the question of the ownership of the structure of the tenement.

The position in Scots law (where not amended by agreement) is fully summarised by Professor Kenneth Reid in 18 *Stair Memorial Encyclopaedia* paras 227–251. General information on tenements, in Glasgow at least, can be found in Frank Wordsall's superb book *The Tenement, A Way of Life* (Chambers 1989).

Briefly the common law of tenement provides that each flat owner should own and maintain the parts of the tenement nearest their own flat. Thus the top flat owners are the owners of the roof above them, and the ground floor flat owners are the owners of the ground below them. The owners of each flat own the walls which bound the flat, and the floor and ceiling to the centre of the joists, and the common passage and stairs are the property of all owners. While this may appear perfectly logical in theory, it doesn't really work in practice. Thus for example, if there is a storm and some roof tiles are blown off, water will eventually penetrate the roof beams. An expensive repair is urgently called for, otherwise the water will percolate through the building to the detriment of all owners. Yet the cost is borne only by the top floor owners and, if it is prohibitive, they may neglect the repair.

It is therefore more practical to have as much of the tenement in mutual ownership as possible, with repairs being paid for by all owners in the tenement, in order that the structure is kept in good order and repair at the expense of all owners.

18.2 When missives for the first sale of a flat in a tenement building have been completed, a disposition is prepared in favour of the purchasers, as with any other sale. The property transferred is (a) the ownership of the flat itself and (b) a fractional right to the commonly-owned parts of the building. These common parts are, as a general rule, the solum, foundations, outside walls, gables, roof, attic, chimneyheads (but not the pots), the entrance, close, staircase, hatchway to the roof, rhones, gutters, all pipes, wires and sewers, the back garden ground and the walls surrounding it, the coal cellars and the street back lane and pavement in so far as not maintained by the regional council. In more modern buildings these common parts may be extended to such common property as landscaped gardens, car parking areas, door entry systems, lifts and television aerials and satellite dishes.

There then follow the burdens and land obligations applicable to the ownership of the flats in the tenement, which are outlined in **18.4**.

18.3 If the owners of a tenement building, which is currently in their sole ownership, decide to dispose of the flats individually, there are two approaches to the problem:

(a) the burdens can be detailed at length in every single disposition of every flat. This creates an enormous amount of repetitive work, and does not necessarily ensure uniformity, as a disposition granted in 1975 may vary from one granted in 1980, by accident or design. If therefore a dispute arises as to, say, common maintenance you may have to inspect every disposition granted to ascertain the true position;

(b) preferably therefore advantage should be taken of the provisions of the C(S) Act 1874, s 32, which permits a deed of conditions to be granted setting forth the burdens at length. This deed is granted before the first sale is made and the deed is registered in the Register of Sasines or Land Register. That deed is then simply referred to in future dispositions for the burdens it sets out. This deed is not one of those referred to in the C(S) Act 1924, s 3, and the granter must therefore have a registered title ('be infeft'). In terms of the LR(S) Act 1979, s 17, the burdens become real as soon as the deed of conditions is recorded, unless s 17 is specifically disapplied, in which case the burdens (as was the case before the 1979 Act came into force) only become real when a flat is conveyed to another person. A disapplication of this kind may be appropriate when the tenement owners wish to reserve the right to change conditions in the future, but it is thought that the circumstances where this might happen are pretty limited.

18.4 The standard deed of conditions is still that prepared between the wars by the Royal Faculty of Procurators in Glasgow, although this is now a bit dated in its phrasing. This deed sets out a precise pattern of common ownership and maintenance, and its clauses may be summarised as follows:

Preamble. This sets out the name of the granter and the description of the property in question. It states that the granter wishes to set forth the burdens and conditions applying to each flat, which are as follows:

One.   The common parts of the building are defined (see **18.2**).

Two.   It is declared that these are to be held in common for the use and benefit of all proprietors, and kept in good repair.

Three.   Only the flats themselves and their fixtures and fittings are to be in individual ownership, and the owners shall keep them in good condition, for the benefit of all.

Four.   The small garden plots at the front are usually given in ownership to the owners of the ground floor flats, unlike the back gardens which are in common ownership.

Five.   The coal cellars are, as appropriate, distributed among the various owners.

Six.   The feuduties and ground annuals are apportioned (not allocated usually: see **7.28**) among the various owners.

Seven.   There is to be a common insurance policy against loss by fire, storm, impact, property owners' liability, and so on. The amount of the insurance is to be decided on by the proprietors of the building in meeting (see **eight**) and the premium apportioned among the owners in the same way as the other common charges (see **ten**). This is very much preferable to each flat having its own insurance, or not as the case may be. Experience shows that 'seamless' insurance cover of the building is infinitely easier to handle in the event of damage to the whole building. The alternative is to have various insurers, with varying liabilities, haggling over the reinstatement. Note the further comments on insurance below at **18.8**.

Eight.   Any owner in the building may at any time call a meeting of owners on seven days' notice. A quorum for the meeting is fixed in the deed. The owner of each house has one vote. The meeting (if properly constituted) can order repairs, renewals or redecoration, make regulations for the preservation and enjoyment of the building (eg stair cleaning) which regulations are binding on all owners, whether they agree or not, decide insurance details, and appoint or dismiss factors and fix their remuneration.

Nine.   The factors, when appointed, shall exercise these powers on behalf of the owners, subject to any limit of expenditure set by the owners.

Ten.   The expenses of maintaining and repairing the building are divided amongst all owners (contrast the common law position: see **18.1**) If all the houses are of equal size, the repair costs are divided equally. If the houses are not of equal sizes, or if there are shops in the building, the common charges are generally divided in the ratio the rateable value of the flats bears to the rateable value of the whole building. This is generally taken as the rateable value when rates were last charged on domestic properties, but this may present a problem when there have been extensive alterations.

Eleven. The factors are empowered to collect all proportions of feuduty, ground annual, insurance premiums, expenses and their fees from the owners and to pay accounts incurred on behalf of the owners.

Twelve. If one proprietor feels that certain work should be done, but cannot get the approval of a majority of the proprietors, that proprietor may refer the matter to arbitration (see **nineteen**). If the arbiter sanctions the repairs, this decision is then binding on all owners, whether consenting or not.

Thirteen. Any owner who is aggrieved by a decision of a meeting, may appeal that decision to the arbiter, who is generally someone appointed by the local sheriff court, or by the Dean of the local legal faculty.

Fourteen. No houses are to be sub-divided or used for trade purposes or for schools, or for the teaching of music – especially, for some reason, singing! Each flat shall be used as a house for one family only.

Fifteen. There is a prohibition against keeping hens and pigeons, and any other animal to be kept should not constitute a nuisance, as determined by the other owners in the building – this time without there being recourse to arbitration.

Sixteen. The top floor owners are not permitted to build storm or attic windows, lest this should weaken the communally-owned roof.

Seventeen. No owner shall put up notices outside the building or decorate the interior differently from the commonly-agreed scheme of decoration, nor make structural alterations.

Eighteen. Each owner shall allow the other owners in the building and their tradesmen access to their houses for the purpose of repairing common parts of the tenement which can only be reached by entering privately owned property. If this is a reciprocal obligation, there can be no logical objection to it, otherwise it can make work, particularly to ceilings and floors, very difficult.

Nineteen. All disputes arising (except under **fifteen**) are referred to arbitration and the arbiter's decision is binding. The arbiter may take skilled advice and apportion the costs of the arbitration as considered appropriate.

Twenty. These burdens are declared to be real burdens to be referred to in all future conveyances.

18.5 If you are involved in preparing a deed of conditions for a building firm, say, you will probably find that the owner has nominated the first factors, whose appointment should subsist until all the flats are sold, when the owners may make their own decision. It would be advisable for you to liaise closely with the factors in the preparation of the deed, as the factors will probably want rather more modern conditions relating to their powers. They will, for example, want a fairly realistic deposit or float from the owners to ease their cash flow problem. Factors do not like to order repairs and then wait endlessly to get paid for them. When an owner sells, the factor will deduct the amount of any outstanding accounts from that owner's float, and refund the balance on sale of the property.

18.6   When an offer to purchase a flat is made to the owner, the offer should include not only the flat itself but also the common rights of property. When describing the flat, great care must be taken – 'left' and 'right' are ambiguous words. Thus I am standing inside the building looking at you on the street, I will think I am in the leftmost flat. You on the other hand will think I am in the rightmost flat, and in a way we're both correct. It is always preferable to use compass points. Similarly floors tend to be numbered in different ways, so you should say 'first floor above street or ground level'.

It may also be stated in the offer that 'the liability for the maintenance of the tenement shall be assessed on an equitable basis' (see **18.4. Ten**) and 'that the conditions regulating the rights and obligations of the proprietors are normal for a tenement property and contain nothing unusual or unduly onerous'. In particular, when the purchase is of a top floor flat, careful solicitors will require evidence that the maintenance of the roof is shared by all proprietors in the building, and not just by the two top floor proprietors. To satisfy themselves they will have to read through every disposition of parts of the tenement, unless there is a deed of conditions. Where there is no deed of conditions, this may entail reading through all dispositions granted in the tenement to see that each flat has a liability for roof repairs.

As these statements are very much a matter of opinion, the sellers' solicitors may simply send you the titles referred to for burdens, and invite you to satisfy yourself within a certain time limit. This is quite a reasonable suggestion.

18.7   In the case of flats, the clause number seven of the offer (printed at Appendix II.11.7(Ib)) is of particular relevance, because local authority notices and orders tend to apply more readily to flats than to houses standing in their own ground. For an example of the dangers lurking see the property certificate printed at **18.16**.

The most obvious danger is that there may be a repairs notice, requiring the houseowner to rectify the defect within 28 days, in terms of the Housing (Scotland) Act 1987, s 108. Worse still, there may be a closing order under s 114 of the same Act, or a demolition order under s 115. Section 108 corresponds to and replaces the Housing (Scotland) Act 1969, s 24, and still tends to be referred to as 'a section 24 notice', as everyone knows what that means. Section 24 notices were served fairly liberally, in Glasgow at least, to enable maximum grants to be obtained for the refurbishment of tenements, but the incidence of these has dropped away.

Where such a notice is revealed by a letter from the district council, you should check (a) does it prejudicially affect the property? (if it does, you should take advantage of the provision in missives, and suggest to your clients that they rescind, and save themselves a lot of problems); (b) has the necessary work been done and paid for? (if it has, you should see that the notice is withdrawn); (c) if the work has been done, but not paid for, part of the purchase price should be placed on deposit in joint names at settlement and used to pay the account when it is received.

18.8 Insurance presents a constant difficulty in tenements, and most tenements are believed to be substantially under-insured, simply because the proprietors will not agree to realistic values. It is perhaps understandable that a person who bought a flat for £20,000 should find an insurance valuation of £50,000 simply extortionate. Yet the larger valuation is probably justified because it is a reinstatement value – the cost of repairing the damage, which can be very expensive in tenements built of traditional building materials. The Golden Rule, as ever, is 'Fire insurance is cheap – it is always better to be over-insured than under-insured'. Again do not forget the doctrine of 'average' – if there is partial destruction (eg your kitchen goes on fire) and you are under-insured, the insurers may determine that you were carrying a proportion of the risk yourself, and pay out only part of the claim, leaving the remainder with you.

Check if there is a common policy over the whole tenement –a good idea as it provides 'seamless' insurance – but if the common policy for the tenement seems to be on the low side, persuade your clients to take out extra insurance. Also, lenders on the flat may not wish to accept a common policy if it is too low, and will insist on instructing their own insurance.

18.9 Traditionally the interest of a new owner of a flat should be endorsed on the common policy, as should the interest of a lender. You write to the insurance company and ask 'to endorse the interest of James and Mary Bloggs as proprietors and the Black Country Building Society as heritable creditors *primo loco*' on the policy. In modern practice, however, this is too unwieldy and policies are taken in the name of the factors on behalf of all owners and heritable creditors of flats in the tenement and it is not then necessary to notify a change of ownership to the insurance company.

18.10 The factors will submit an account to owners half-yearly at Whitsunday and Martinmas, detailing the payments made on their behalf (including repairs to the common parts, insurance premiums, ground burdens, cleaning expenses, fees, et cetera) and dividing these among the owners in the proportions set out in the deed of conditions. When a flat changes hands, the factors will apportion the account between the sellers and purchasers around the date of entry. The sellers' portion is then deducted from the float and the balance is refunded. The purchaser is, of course, required to pay a float to the factor to cover future expenses.

The agreed reference to the House of Lords in the case of *David Watson v Woolwich Equitable Building Society* 1992 SLG 48, indicates that when a lender repossesses a house on default of the borrower, then there is no obligation on the lender to recompense the factor for expenses incurred by the factor prior to default. This has caused considerable difficulties for factors, as the same reasoning could be applied to arrears incurred by a normal seller. A prudent conveyancer should insist on having confirmation from the factor that common charges have been paid to the date of entry.

18.11   Blocks of flats built in recent years have beeen built to a far higher specification than the traditional tenement. The deeds of condition should reflect this, and regulate the use, maintenance and repairs of lifts, landscaped gardens and amenity areas, garages, car parks, common television aerials and satellite dishes.

It is therefore recommended that when a sale is agreed, the sellers' agents should write to the factor in terms similar to:

The Property Managers Association, Scotland, Limited

To Solicitors

Please complete and send this Form to the Property Factor on completion of Missives of Sale of Flat, Shop etc. in tenement property.

COMMON FACTORS PRO-FORMA

DETAILS OF CHANGE OF OWNERSHIP

FOR THE APPORTIONMENT OF COMMON CHARGES

FOR PROPERTY FACTORED BY:- Messrs Brittain & Brown

ADDRESS OF PROPERTY:– 23 Dundee Street, Glasgow

FLAT POSITION:– 1st Floor North

NAME OF SELLER:– Euphemia Flange

SELLERS' SOLICITORS:– Messrs Edwards & Bennett, Glasgow

DATE OF ENTRY:– 16th December 1994

SELLERS' NEW ADDRESS:– per solicitor

NAME OF PURCHASER/S:– Mr & Mrs FitzHenry

PURCHASER/S SOLICITORS:– Messrs Kyle & Strathdee, Glasgow

Information required by Sellers' Solicitors   Please tick as required

Please send

(1) details of Common Insurance Policy

(2) copy of last cumulo Ground Burdens Receipt

(3) copy of last Common Charges Receipt.

The factors are also requested to confirm that no substantial work has been instructed but not yet done.

18.11   *Part three. Transfers of Special Subjects*

18.12   To prevent argument, it is usual to provide in missives (see Appendix II.12, clause 5) that the cost of any work instructed or done before the date of entry, is the responsibility of the seller or the purchaser may, if this is not the case, rescind without penalty. The factors (above) are requested to provide details of any such work. Where the work is major this of course may be a matter of negotiation between the parties.

18.13   When the title of a flat being sold requires to be registered in the Land Register, the procedure is little different from that for a detached house. The most important difference is that you do not apply for a P16 report, even in a first registration, as the Keeper will not issue these for flats or buildings with 'a shared solum'.

18.14   The principles outlined in this Chapter also apply to large houses that are being horizontally divided and to 'four in a block' houses, which are known in Glasgow as 'cottage flats' for some reason. In such cases there will, however, be a garden to divide into separate ownership (it is unusual to put the whole garden into common ownership) and a right of access over the garden ground to each house must be reserved, usually by making the paths into common property. There should also be a servitude right in favour of the upper house over the garden on the lower house, permitting ladders to be placed for window cleaning and other maintenance.

18.15   The collector's department should also be advised on the change of ownership in order that the council tax may be apportioned around the date of entry between purchaser and seller. A form for this purpose is available from the appropriate council.

18.16

Example of a property certificate

SUBJECTS: 64 MILLION DOLLAR COURT, GLASGOW.
Date of Certificate: 1/10/94   Property Certificate No. 999/999
COMBINED DISTRICT AND REGIONAL SEARCH

With reference to your recent enquiry regarding the above noted please find detailed below information gathered from Searches of the publicly available records from the District Council Departments of Planning, Building Control, Environmental Health and Housing, together with the Regional Departments of Planning, Roads, Water and Sewerage. Searches are from January 1986 onwards.

DISTRICT SEARCH
Town and Country Planning (Scotland) Acts as Amended and associated Planning Legislation

Policies
1.   The subjects lie within a Land Use Policy Area zoned for Mixed use, as defined by Glasgow Central Area Finalised Draft Local Plan Approved May 1991.

Proposals
2.   There are no proposals by the District Authority under the Town & Country Planning (Scotland) Acts which would affect the subjects.

     However, please note that the subjects lie in close proximity to the following sites, identified as having opportunity for development, as defined by Glasgow Central Area Local Plan, Finalised Draft May 1991:
     Site 9, City Halls, Candleriggs/Albion Street – Refurbishment for leisure/cultural use;
     Site 10, Former Cheesemarket, Albion Street/Walls Street – Refurbishment/redevelopment for residential/retail/office use;
     Site 16, Former Goldbergs Store, Candleriggs – Redevelopment/refurbishment for residential/retail/office use (consent granted, see application no. 02848/91 below);
     Site17, Property at Bell Street/Candleriggs/Trongate – Redevelopment/refurbishment for residential/office use.

Planning Applications
3.   Please note the following Planning Applications which may have relevance with regard to the subjects:

     01020/88   Demolition, redevelopment and conversion of commercial premises to provide private housing development comprising 117 flats, shops, car parking, landscaped courtyard, formation of vehicular access and external alterations at site on Wilson Street. Approved on conditions 21 April 1989.

02114/88   Demolition of building, erection of 30 flats (including 2 shops and 2 offices), formation of basement carpark, conversion of workshops/offices to 16 flats, use of warehouse as art gallery (including photographic studio and conference room), shop, restaurant and extension of licensed restaurant, at 62–100 Albion Street/51 Bell Street/25–27 Blackfriar Street/5–19 Walls Street. Approved on conditions 31 October 1989.

01148/90   Demolition of existing buildings and erection of 5-storey building comprising retail units at ground and first floor, with residential on 2nd, 3rd and 4th floors in the form of 54 flats, with basement servicing and car parking and landscaped courtyard area at 14–54 Glassford Street/17–57 Hutcheson Street/63–69 Wilson Street. Approved on conditions 22/3/91.

00718/91   Demolition behind retained facade including complete demolition of 96 Trongate with erection of new facade and building. Construction of extension to facade on Candleriggs and use of ground floor for retail use and upper floor offices, at 76–104 Trongate. Approved on conditions 25 June 1991.

02848/91   Partial demolition of listed buildings (facade retention), demolition of buildings within the conservation area, refurbishment of remaining buildings and new build infill to provide 97 residential flats, offices, shops, leisure centre, landscaping and basement car parking, at the Goldbergs Building (3–69 Candleriggs, 5–33 Wilson Street, 106–122,124,132 & 142 Trongate, 44–74 Brunswick Street). Approved on conditions 10 January 1992.

461/94   Use of former market hall as shop with associated internal and external works at, 80 Albion Street/Walls Street. No decision, application registered 24 February 1994.

Designations, Directions, Notices or Orders
4. Subjects listed as a building of Special Architectural or Historic Interest   No
5. Subjects situated in a Conservation Area   Yes
 The subjects lie within Glasgow Central Conservation Area.
6. Subjects affected by Article 4 Direction   Yes
 The subjects are affected by an Article 4 Direction, which has the effect of removing permitted development rights. Within the designated Glasgow Central Conservation Area planning permission is required for the following Classes of Development (Town and Country Planning(General Permitted Development)(Scotland) Order 1992 As Amended):-
 Class 7 – The erection, construction, maintenance, improvement or alteration of a gate, fence, wall or other means of enclosure.
 Class 9 – The stone cleaning or painting of the exterior of any building or works.

*Class 14 – The provision on land of buildings, moveable struc-
tures, works, plant or machinery required temporarily in connection with and for the duration of operations being or to be
carried out on, in, under or over that land or on land adjoining
that land.*

*Class 15 – The use of land (other than a building or land within the
curtilage of a building) for any purpose, except as a caravan site or
an open air market, on not more than 28 days in total in any calen-
der year, and the erection or placing of moveable structures on the
land for the purposes of that use.*

*Class 27 – The carrying out on land within the boundaries of a pri-
vate road or private way of works required for the maintenance or
improvement of the road or way.*

*Class 28 – The carrying out of any works for the purposes of
inspecting, repairing or renewing any sewer, main pipe, cable or
other apparatus, including breaking open any land for that purpose.*

*Classes 30,31 and 32 – (relating to Development by Local
Authorities).*

*Classes 38,39,40,41 and 43 – (relating to Development by
Statutory Undertakers).*

*Class 67 – (relating to Development by Telecommunications Code
System Operators).*

7.	Subjects situated in a Site of Special Scientific Interest	No
8.	Subjects situated in an Area of Special Advertisement Control	No
9.	Subjects affected by a Tree Preservation Order	See below

*The subjects are not affected by a Tree Preservation Order.
However, please note that within a Conservation Area it is an
offence to fell or lop any tree without notifying the District
Council Planning Department six weeks before it is intended to
carry out the work.*

10.	Subjects affected by an Enforcement Notice	No
11.	Subjects affected by a Stop Notice	No
12.	Subjects affected by a Breach of Condition Notice	No
13.	Subjects affected by an Execution and Cost of Works Notice	No
14.	Subjects affected by a Waste Land Notice	No
15.	Subjects affected by the location of an Ancient Monument	No

Other Legislation

16. A Search has also been carried out for Orders, Notices, Declarations and Agreements under the following Acts:-

Outstanding

Public Health (Scotland) Act 1897
Section 20(1)   Notice requiring Removal of Nuisance   No

Clean Air Act 1956/68 [as amended by the Clean Air Act 1993]
Section 18(1)   Subjects situated within a Smoke Control Area   Yes

Building (Scotland) Acts 1959/70 [as amended by the Housing (Scotland) Act 1974]

Section 10	Work without warrant or in Contravention of Conditions of Warrant	No
Section 11	Requirements for an existing Building to conform to Building Standards Regulations	No
Section 13	Dangerous Buildings	No

Civic Government (Scotland) Act 1982

Section 87(1)	Statutory Repairs Notice	No
Section 87(3)	Emergency Repairs Notice	No
Section 90(5)	Lighting of Common Stairs etc Notice	No
Section 92(6)	Cleaning and Painting of Common Stairs Notice	No
Section 95(2)	Private Open Spaces Notice	No
Section 96(1)	Statues and Monuments Notice	No

Housing (Scotland) Act 1969

Section 24	Compulsory Repairs Notice	Yes – see below

Housing (Scotland) Act 1974 [as inserted by Section 10 of the Housing (Financial Provisions)(Scotland) Act 1978]

Section 14(A)	Improvement Order	No
Section 44	Agency Agreement/Voluntary Grant	No

Housing (Scotland) Act 1987

Section 88	Improvement Order of Houses Below Tolerable Standard	No
Section 89	Housing Action Area for Demolition Declaration	No
Section 90	Housing Action Area for Improvement Declaration	No
Section 91	Housing Action Area for Demolition and Improvement Declaration	No
Section 106	Improvement or Repair Agreement (Agency Agreement/Voluntary Grant)	No
Section 108	Compulsory Repair Notice	Yes – see below
Section 114	Closing Order	No
Section 115	Demolition Order	No
Section 157	Management Order relating to House in Multiple Occupation	No
Section 160	Multiple Occupancy Management Code Works Notice	No
Section 161	Works Notice relating to House in Multiple Occupancy	No
Section 162	Notice requiring Provision of Fire Escape	No
Section 166	Overcrowding Direction Notice	No

Housing (Scotland) Act 1969 and 1987
Action has been taken under Sections 24 and 108 of the
above acts in respect of the subjects. SPH Property Search
have written to City of Glasgow District Council for further
information and will advise accordingly.

REGIONAL SEARCH
Town and Country Planning (Scotland) Acts as Amended and associated Planning Legislation

17. There are Policies, Proposals and Recommendations of relevance to the subjects as noted in the Consolidated Strathclyde Structure Plan, corrected edition 1991 as approved by the Secretary of State and as revised by the Written Statement 1990 Update with modifications approved by the Secretary of State on 10th September 1992.

    The Written Statement of the 1992 Update of the Strathclyde Structure Plan was approved on 26th May 1994. The Update deals with the balance of supply and demand for private housing land in the period 1992–99.

    The Structure Plan recommends (Recommendation R2, R3b, R3c) that Glasgow city centre be designated a *Renewal Area*, requiring action in the fields of housing, derelict and degraded land, and planning blight both to improve employment opportunities and maintain the process of renewal.

Roads (Scotland) Act 1984
18. The road and footway ex adverso the subjects have been taken over and are maintained by the Regional Authority.
19. The subjects lie approximately 500 metres from the proposed Townhead-London Road Link as defined by Strathclyde Transport Policies & Programmes No.8 1992–97. This scheme involves 0.6km of dual 3-lane 11.0m carriageway with Special Road Status and 1.1km dual 2-lane 7.3m (All Purpose) carriageway including a tunnelled section between Cathedral Street and Duke Street. The scheme will improve accessibility between the motorway network and the eastern side of the City Centre and the East End by providing more direct connections to Ingram Street/George Street and Gallowgate/London Road. The Link Road will result in traffic relief to High Street and Castle Street and enable environmental improvements to be achieved in the area between the Cathedral and Strathclyde University precinct, and at Glasgow Cross. The scheme will ease congestion in the Townhead section of the ring road and will be of substantial benefit to buses in the north east of the Central Area. Please note that as amended by the Transport Policies and Programmes TPP No.8A this scheme is now not included in the 1993–98 Roads Capital Programme.

Sewerage (Scotland) Act 1968
20. A public sewerage pipe which is maintained by the Regional Authority lies ex adverso the subjects.

Water (Scotland) Act 1980

21. A public water pipe which is maintained by the Regional Authority lies ex adverso the subjects.

Notes:
1. This enquiry does not consider whether all necessary consents have been obtained. Purchasing agents are advised to obtain the necessary documentation from the vendors.
2. The information contained in this Certificate is based on public record information and is accurate 3 days prior to issuing the Certificate.

Signed

Stirrat Park Hogg
[SPH Property Search is a division of Stirrat Park Hogg,
Chartered Town Planners, 113 St George's Road, Glasgow G3 6JA
Greater Glasgow Tel: 0141-353 2680 Glasgow District Tel: 0141-353 2681
Fax: 0141-331 2425]

Chapter nineteen

PURCHASING OF PUBLIC SECTOR HOUSING

'I believe that right to buy sales will remain very attractive to many tenants. On average the weekly mortgage payments to buy a house under the right to buy legislation, at current interest rates, could be only £2–£3 a week greater than the average standard rent. Home ownership is within reach of many thousands more households.'
(Lord James Douglas-Hamilton quoted in *The Herald*)

19.1 A right to tenants to purchase the house they are occupying was given by the Tenants' Rights Etc (Scotland) Act 1980 as amended by the Tenants' Rights Etc (Scotland) Amendment Act 1984. This legislation has been consolidated in the Housing (Scotland) Act 1987, Part III (ss 44–84). Prior to 1980, however, some local authorities were prepared to sell their housing stock to tenants voluntarily, and such sales proceeded in the manner already outlined, for private sales, in prior chapters. Not all local authorities by any means were prepared to do this, and the main 1980 Act introduced a right for the tenant to buy, whether the local authority consented or not. The amending Acts merely circumvented certain difficulties that had arisen from the objection of recalcitrant councils.

The main Act also introduced a statutory procedure for sales under the Act, and this only is dealt with in this Chapter.

19.2 The procedure is fully detailed in the Housing (Scotland) Act 1987, which should be carefully studied before undertaking a transaction in this area. The application to purchase must be made on an official form which is available from the local authority concerned, with *Notes for Guidance to Tenants on the Completion of the Application*. A helpful booklet 'Your Right to Buy Your Home' is also available from The Scottish Office Environment Department, Room 401, St, Andrew's House, Edinburgh EH1 3DE.

19.3 Tenants who have occupied a publicly provided house on a secure tenancy for at least two years have a right to purchase such housing provided by:

(a) a district or islands council;

(b) a new town development corporation;

(c) the Scottish Special Housing Association;

(d) the Housing Corporation;

(e) A regional council;

(f) A registered housing association.

Also included are a variety of other authorities, the most important being, a housing co-operative, a police authority, a fire authority, the prison service, the armed forces, a health board, the Forestry Commission, a State hospital, the Commissioners of Northern Lighthouses, HM Coastguard, the United Kingdom Atomic Energy Authority, the Ministry of Defence, and any other authority prescribed by the Secretary of State by order.

19.4 There are three kinds of occupation for the two-year period which the authority must take into account – (1) a house occupied by the applicant as tenant; (2) a house occupied by the applicant as husband or wife of the tenant and (3) a house occupied by the applicant of which one or both of his or her parents were tenants.

19.5 Houses which are subject, not to a tenancy agreement, but a service agreement requiring the occupier to occupy the house for the better performance of his or her duties, and which must be surrendered on termination of the employment (eg houses in parks) are not included, as there is no secure tenancy. (See *Naylor v Glasgow District Council* 1982 LTS/TB/129.) Further a house which is provided with certain services (eg sheltered housing for the elderly or infirm) is not susceptible to purchase in terms of the Act.

19.6 The tenant who is qualified to purchase should first complete the official application and send it to the authority concerned by recorded delivery, keeping a copy. When the form is received the authority will arrange for the house to be valued by the district valuer, who is the official government valuer for a number of such purposes including assessment of gross annual values and valuation for capital transfer tax. Alternatively the valuation can be made by another valuer, nominated by the landlord and accepted by the tenant, so the valuer should be informed of any such improvements at the time of inspection.

19.7 The authority concerned should issue an offer to sell within two months of the application, or a notice of refusal if it considers the applicant not to be qualified to purchase for any reason (eg if it is not a secure tenancy, or is sheltered housing, is specially designed for use by the elderly, or if it is required by an islands council for educational purposes). A notice of refusal may be referred to the Lands Tribunal by a disgruntled applicant, and the Tribunal may order the authority to make the offer if it is satisfied that this should be done.

19.8 The offer to sell should then be checked to see that it contains the subjects intended. The authority should sell all rights possessed by them (see *Annott v Midlothian District Council* 1982 LTS/TR/191). The offer should also stipulate the valuation made, the discount applied to the valuation, and the price thus reached. Further the offer may contain conditions stipulated by the authority. Any of these matters can be referred to the Lands Tribunal. For examples of decisions on unreasonable conditions see *Clark v Shetland Islands Council* 1981 LTS/TR/599, 598, 597, 594, all summarised in 1984 JLSS 469, and *McLeod v Ross and Cromarty District Council* 1981 LTS/TB/150.

19.9 The time limits here are quite crucial. If the tenant is satisfied with the offer, an acceptance should be sent within two months. If the tenant needs a loan from the selling authority, the time limit in that case is only one month. If the authority will not alter conditions to which the applicant objects, the applicant may refer the matter to the Lands Tribunal, the time allowed being one month, starting from a date one month after the tenant wrote to the authority asking it to amend the offer to sell.

19.10 If the authority does not issue an offer to sell within two months of the application to buy, the matter may be referred to the Land Tribunal which will investigate the matter, and which may, in the last resort, issue an offer on behalf of the defaulting authority.

19.11 When the valuation of the house has been agreed, a discount is then deducted in respect of the application being made to purchase by a secure tenant. It is, incidentally, a general principle that a tenanted house should be sold at a discount, because vacant possession can be given to no one but the tenant. The basic discount after two years' occupation is 32% and the discount rises by 1% for every year's tenancy to a maximum of 60%. In the authority's discretion a period of occupation prior to a break of between 12 and 24 months may be taken into account. The reason for the break should be stated on the application.

In the case of a flat, the basic discount is 44% of the value, rising by 2% each year to a maximum of 70%. A flat is defined as 'a separate and self-contained set of premises whether or not on the same floor, forming part of a building from some other part of which it is divided horizontally'. This definition includes the traditional tenement and 'four-in-a-block' type of houses, as well as high-rise flats.

19.12 When agreement has been reached, and missives concluded, the transaction then proceeds, as previously outlined, to settlement. The applicant has a recorded title and may sell at any time thereafter. However there is a financial penalty if a sale is made within three years of purchase. If a sale is made within one year of purchase, all discount is refundable, and this figure then decreases by 33⅓% a year until it reaches nil at the end of the third year. The purchaser grants a standard security over the property in favour of the authority for the amount of the discount plus interest, which security ranks second to any security granted by the purchaser in respect of a loan to purchase the property. If the purchaser then defaults on repayment of the discount, or part of it, the authority may then enforce its security. On the expiry of the three-year period, it is not necessary to record a discharge of the security. If the owners insist on receiving a discharge, they will be expected to pay the legal discharge fee of the council.

19.13 If an application is made by one person only, a valid consent must be received from any non-entitled spouse, although the title may of course still be taken in joint names. Similarly if there are any other joint tenants, who are not included in the title, their consents must also be given.

19.14   If the tenant requires a loan to purchase, application to lending institutions should be made as in the normal case, but if two refusals are received, the authority is under an obligation to provide a loan based on the applicant's income and other circumstances. Please remember that in these circumstances there is only one month for acceptance of the offer to sell (see **19.9**). Applications for loans therefore should be made as soon as the application to purchase is submitted, for time is very tight. As mentioned in **19.12**, the standard security in favour of the lender has the first ranking. Finally, if the authority does not offer a loan sufficient for the purchase to be made, the tenant may on payment of £100 reserve an option to purchase the house at the price currently fixed at any time within two years of the date of the original application to purchase.

19.15   There have been many complaints about long delays in processing applications, which were caused by a variety of reasons – title difficulties, in many cases councils had never completed the conveyancing formalities after compulsory purchase of land for building, staff shortages, and huge numbers of applications. This fortunately has settled down now.

19.16   When a house which was bought from a public authority in this manner is re-sold, the procedure is exactly the same as with any other house. If the house is disposed of within three years of its acquisition date, however, it is necessary to repay the discount (or part of it) and obtain a discharge of the standard security signed to protect the discount (**19.12**). Acquisition and disposal are defined respectively as the date on which the purchaser and the council complete missives.

19.17   While this scheme has proved to be very attractive to many, there are certain matters to be made clear to a potential purchaser. The new owner, in particular, will become responsible for repairs and insurance of the property, and should be advised of this new liability. In the case of high-rise flats particularly, repairs may be higher than expected, as recladding of the building or expensive lift repairs may be needed.

Further, many local authority houses were built of suspect materials and by unsatisfactory methods, which might give rise to a high level of repairs. The valuer's report will issue a warning where this is the case, and the purchaser must then decide whether to proceed or not. (For an example see the case of *Forsyth v Scottish Homes* 1990 GWD 10–558.)

19.18   In the case of *Clydebank District Council v the Keeper of the Land Register* (LTS/LR/1992/1) the Lands Tribunal found that in terms of sections 72 and 73 of the 1987 Act the sale of the subjects by an executor terminated the liability to repay to the council a proportion of the statutory discount on the purchase price of a house, and that the Keeper had acted correctly in cancelling the entry in the Land Register relating to the standard security for the amount of the discount. The missives had been concluded on 13 August 1990, the owner died in February 1991, and the disposition was registered on 5 November 1991.

19.19 There has now been introduced the complex rent to mortgage scheme, which allows tenants to buy their homes for a weekly outlay roughly equivalent to the rent paid. The rent to mortgage (RTM) scheme divided the purchase price into two lump sums – the Initial Capital Payment (ICP) and the Deferred Financial Commitment (DFC).

The value of the house is discounted in the same way as in the right to buy (RTB) scheme, but the discounts are 15% less. Thus for a house the minimum discount is 17% going up by 1% a year to a maximum of 45% after 30 years' tenancy. In a flat the similar figures are 29% minimum: 2% a year increase: 55% maximum.

The ICP is normally financed by a building society or bank or other financial institution loan (loans from the landlord are not available), and the tenant becomes the owner on paying this, and as such responsible for insurance and maintenance. The DFC does not have to be repaid until the house is sold or the owner dies. The rent is reduced to 90% of the present rent.

In as much as the former tenant becomes the owner on payment of the ICP, no rent is now payable and the owner is responsible only for the mortgage payment and the insurance and maintenance of the property. The DFC is payable on the sale of the house, or the death of the tenant turned owner. The monthly outgoings should thus be approximately equal, and the rent is transferred to a mortgage payment.

19.20 Where elderly people are the tenants, they will be helped sometimes by younger relatives. This is, of course, in order, but the position of the younger relatives must be protected. Some authorities will allow the young relatives to appear on the deeds, in the destination clause, and you should enquire if this is possible. If not, the older persons should make wills in favour of the young relatives, to protect their position against other relatives, with preferential or equal claims on the estates, who have not been involved in the purchase.

19.21 Where the landowner has sold the land on which the house in question has been built to the district council, and has retained a right of preemption, that right may be exercised when a tenant is offered the house in terms of the right to buy legislation. Thus the landowner, rather surprisingly, but probably correctly in terms of the statute, benefits from the discounted rate, and not the tenant. This is yet another example of the superior benefiting, and was surely not the will of Parliament? (See *Ross & Cromarty District Council v Patience* 1995 GWD 18–858.) Taken with another recent case, *Hamilton v Grampian Regional Council* (1995 GWD 443), one can see that the feudal system is still flourishing in Scotland, and ought to be quietly laid to rest.

Chapter twenty

SALE AND PURCHASE OF BUSINESS

'How the price (360p a share) was finally arrived at reflects precious little credit on the Low board and its advisers ... it is not the job of any board to recommend to its shareholders one opening offer (225p a share) which, within weeks, proves to be £100m less than that bidder is actually willing to pay for the business.'
(Alf Young – *The Herald* (discussing the sale of Wm Low to Tesco in 1994))

20.1 I think that I should first of all explain what this Chapter sets out to do, and what it does not set out to do. I have printed at the end of the Chapter a simple offer for a small retail business. My main effort will be to show that such a business is simply a collection of assets, bound together by the good-will of the business, and that the sale of the business is really only a transfer of the various assets, with certain safeguards built in for the purchasers.

I shall ignore businesses run as limited companies, for such organisations are outwith the scope of this subject. I shall merely leave the topic with the suggestion that the differences between a small retail business and, say, British Petroleum, is one of scale. I know that I shall be accused of over-simplification, but both businesses are collections of assets, and whereas the small business's transport is represented by one bicycle, BP's transport is represented by a hundred super tankers, five hundred petrol tankers, ten thousand cars and so on. When either business is sold, these assets are valued and the total forms part of the price to be paid by the intending purchasers.

20.2 The assets of a business are: the heritable property, whether owned or leased, the stock-in-trade, the trade fittings and fixtures, work-in-progress (but not particularly with retail businesses), money owing, vehicles, the trade name, trade marks, copyrights, patents et cetera, and any licences of franchises owned by the business. All of these assets are wrapped up in the good-will of the business. The liabilities of the business, which are deducted from the valuation of the assets, are basically money owing to suppliers, employees, the taxman and so on. And lastly, we have the people of the business, who are probably an asset in a good business and a liability in a bad business, but not always so.

Heritable property

20.3 The property of the business is valued by a surveyor, and the offer should make the usual stipulations for the purchase of heritage; that is date of entry, clauses dealing with heritable and moveable property, non-supersession clauses, clauses dealing with property enquiry certificates and outstanding notices and so on. It should be remembered that there are certain statutory requirements for commercial property, particularly the Health and Safety at Work Acts, and the offer should stipulate that all requirements under these Acts have been met, particularly fire requirements, otherwise the purchasers may be faced with making extremely expensive alterations. Where the property is leasehold, the lease will be valued bearing in mind, among others, these considerations: (a) the remaining life of the lease, (b) the rent being charged, (c) the frequency of rent reviews and the terms of the rent review clause, (d) the use permitted by the lease, (e) the planning position of the property, (f) restrictions of assigning and sub-letting, (g) the general fairness of the lease to the tenant, and (h) the location and trading prospects of the site.

Precaution should be taken that there are no outstanding liabilities to the landlord for, eg rent and dilapidations of the property (the cost of restoring the property to the condition it was in when it was first let). As well as receiving permission from the landlord for the assignation of the lease or sub-let, a certificate should also be received from the landlord confirming that there are no outstanding liabilities, and that the proposed use of the property is approved.

The stock-in-trade

20.4   This is valued, at cost except in the case of old or slow-moving stock, by agreement of the parties. If so wished, a valuation can be made by a person specialising in stocktaking, with the account being divided equally between the parties. The stocktaking should obviously be done as near to the date of sale as possible, perhaps in the evening or on a Sunday afternoon.

Trade fittings and fixtures

20.5   These include counters, scales, cash registers et cetera. Some of these items are expensive to buy and may be on hire purchase or other credit arrangement. This should be clarified in the offer to buy, and if the item is owned by a finance company, arrangements for the transfer of the item should be made subject to the amounts still payable under the contract. It should be carefully noted that value added tax is payable on second-hand trade fittings and fixtures.

Thus if a price is quoted for these, without mention of VAT, it will be taken to mean that the price is VAT inclusive. With VAT at 17½% the VAT content is 7/47ths of the total. The purchasers should therefore get a receipt from the sellers showing the VAT content, in order that they may claim this as an input on their own return.

The purchasers of a business relying largely on telephone orders, will also want to acquire the telephone number(s).

Bearing in mind that most '*Winston v Patrick* cases' have been about central heating or other mechanical applicances, it is as well that the offer shall contain a fairly tight condition about the working order of any such plant, and the liability of the sellers to pay for any repairs. To avoid bad feeling, the purchasers should inspect the mechanical equipment concerned, and arrange for the sellers to pay for any necessary repairs, before parting with any money. The contractual position should, however, also be preserved, by including the various provisions dealing with non-supersession.

Work-in-progress

20.6   This refers particularly to business people like solicitors or builders who do work and get paid at the end of that work. If the business is transferred while the work is continuing, a valuation should be made of the work done but not yet paid for, and that forms an asset of the business.

Money owing to the business

20.7   The debts owing to the business are generally retained in the ownership of the sellers, who collect them as and when they can. If the sellers are emigrating or retiring, however, this may not be appropriate, and the purchasers may take these over. The purchasers should then pay the sellers for this asset, and it should be remembered that the debts should be assigned to the purchasers, and the assignation intimated to each debtor, both to satisfy the technical rule that 'the right of a creditor in a debt is fully transferred by an assignation followed by an intimation' (*Gloag on Contract*, 2nd edn, p 74) and to let the debtor know who the creditors are. The intimation can simply be printed on the account when it is rendered.

Similarly the purchasers of a business can have the benefit (or liability) of any court actions in which their predecessors were engaged, or the benefit of any court decrees that they hold (see quotation supra). The valuation of the business should reflect the likely outcome of the case.

Vehicles

20.8   Vehicles being taken over are valued at date of sale, by reference to *Glass's Guide*, a trade publication containing current values. These figures will probably have to be obtained through someone in the motor trade. Again care must be taken to ensure that there is no outstanding debt on these vehicles, or alternatively that the debt is allowed for in the price.

The trade name

20.9   Some trade names are beyond value and form a very valuable part of the business; others are of very doubtful value, and may be changed on takeover. Where an individual or partnership or limited company trades under a name that is not its own, details of the ownership of the trade names must be disclosed on letterheads and by a notice displayed in the place of business. This provision of the Business Names Act 1985 (formerly Companies Act 1981, ss 28 to 30) replaces the provisions of the Registration of Business Names Act 1916, which provided for such names to be registered in the Register of Business Names. That useful register is now discontinued, although an unofficial register is kept privately.

It should be noted that neither the old nor the new register conferred any right of ownership in a name, as was mistakenly thought. The old register was in fact designed to reveal the name of enemy aliens who might be trading under assumed names when anti-German feeling was at its height during the First World War. Unchallenged ownership of a trade name can only be acquired by use, and both registers provide the useful information as to when a name was first used.

A trend emerged in the 1980s for companies to take over other companies whose principal assets are their strong brand names (eg Rowntree Mackintosh). This led to some companies placing a valuation on their brand names in their balance sheet (eg Guinness). Some doubt of the value of brand names emerged in the Nineties, when first Marlboro, a strong brand name, began to discount its goods because of competition from 'own name' brands. The notion grew that the public was in fact paying extra for the brand names, and this led to supermarkets introducing 'own name' brands which were packaged similarly to branded goods, but which sold for rather less. This was exemplified in the 'cola war' of 1994, when Sainsbury's eventually had to repackage its cola, so that it would not be confused with a well-known brand. As I write, this war is still rumbling.

Intellectual property

20.10   A small retail business is unlikely to own any patents, trademarks or copyrights, but a small electronics business, for example, might own all three, and be completely dependent on their existence. It is important therefore to check (a) that the sellers own the right, (b) that they are validly registered, (c) their remaining years of life and the date of renewal in the case of a trade or service mark, (d) that they are properly assigned and intimated, in the case of trade marks and patents, to the appropriate registrar. The specialist advice of a chartered patent agent should probably be sought, as a mistake in this direction could be catastrophic.

Licences and franchises

20.11   Many businesses depend almost entirely on a licence or franchise for their existence. There is little point in buying the business unless you can be sure the licence or franchise can be transferred to the purchasers. The purchasers may therefore wish to insert a suspensive condition making the purchase dependent on getting a transfer of the licence or franchise. The commonest example of the former is a hotel or shop licensed to sell alcohol, and of the latter, a business which owns a franchise outlet of one of the franchise companies (eg MacDonalds, Wimpys, Dyna–Rod, Pronuptia, the Pancake House, Holiday Inns et cetera).

An application for transfer of license must be made to the licensing board set up by each district council under the Licensing (Scotland) Act 1976. These boards meet quarterly, and an application for transfer must be submitted before the last date for submission, which date is intimated in the local press – usually it is a month before the board meets. The offer should therefore, unless circumstances dictate otherwise, be suspended in action until a day or two after the next licensing board meeting.

If there are to be objections, which are fairly rare to transfers unless the transferee is of doubtful character, the purchasers will be told well in advance, and are given a chance to meet the objections. If no such indications are received, the parties can get on with arranging the formalities of the licence being transferred.

The purchase of a business which depends on a franchise will depend on the consent of the franchisers, who will probably prove extremely fussy about the ability of the purchasers to run the business. Please remember that the franchisers, and other franchisees, will lose heavily if one of the franchises is badly run, especially in the case of a food shop.

Various other activities require a licence, eg road haulage, post offices, bookmakers and so on. The rules for the transfer of these licences are quite complicated, and specialist advice should probably be sought. In addition the Civic Government (Scotland) Act 1982 provides that metal dealers must have a licence. The same Act also provides that each district council may adopt a licensing system for any of the following activities: the operation of taxis and private hire cars, second-hand dealing, boat hire, street trading, private markets, operation of places of entertainment, late-hours catering, window cleaning, and sex shops. Requirements vary widely from area to area and enquiries should be made of the appropriate district council when dealing in any of these areas.

Incidentally, if you think that my spelling is a bit variable I would refer you to the Penguin Dictionary of Troublesome Words: 'Licence, License. In British usage the first is the noun, the second the verb – "a licence to sell wines" but "licensed premises". In America "license" is preferred for both noun and verb.'

Franchises are licences privately granted authorising the licensee to use the business style of the licensor. See articles by the author on the topic in Scottish Law Gazette, March 1985, p 7 and June 1986. Note the case under Article 85 of the Treaty of Rome where international franchises were considered and broadly ratified (under conditions) by the European Court – *Pronuptia de Paris GmbH v Pronuptia de Paris Irmgard Schillgallis* (1986) CMLR 414.

Goodwill

20.12   Goodwill has been defined as 'the probability that the old customers will revert to the old place': *Crutwell v Lye* (1810) 17 Ves 335 at 346 per Lord

Eldon. But perhaps it is something more prosaic as suggested by Dr Samuel Johnson remarking on the sale of Thrale's Brewery in 1781 – 'We are not here to sell a parcel of boilers and vats, but the potentiality of growing rich beyond the dreams of avarice.'

Goodwill is the only asset so far that cannot be precisely valued, and its valuation will vary widely from case to case. To some extent it will also vary with the purchasers' opinion as to whether it is a good business that can be extended, or it is a poor business that will require an investment of time and money to bring it round. You must always be careful, especially in small businesses, of highly personal goodwill that will simply disappear when the sellers leave. Customers or clients of a business are often resentful of having their custom being taken for granted, and sold like a pound of butter, as Saatchi and Saatchi discovered when they bought, in the 1980s, an advertising agency in the United States for $450m; almost immediately they lost the three main clients of the business and consequently $300m of annual billings. You will probably wish to discuss this valuation with an accountant who will base his valuation largely on past figures, which is as good a basis as any. Generally speaking, people do return to the old place despite a change of ownership, unless they are antagonised. Goodwill is treated as heritable property for stamp duty purposes.

With no particular apologies I would mention that Saatchi and Saatchi had more troubles in 1994–95, when the founder of the business (Maurice Saatchi) was effectively sacked. He has set up a new business, and taken many clients with him. This underlines the dangers of a business where the only real assets are the goodwill and the staff. Please remember that both can simply walk out of the door. I will deal with this further under 'people'.

Value

20.13 The valuation of a business is part art and part science. An accountant will work it out almost exactly, but a good businessman will pay less, and a fool will pay more. All in all it is a matter of negotiation (see quotation at head of chapter). You can pay an asset valuation, but what if there is a pile of assets making a loss, or needing replaced largely? A multiplier of income is probably a fair starting point for negotiations. Another starting point, and probably a more accurate one, is what it would cost your clients to set up a similar business, taking into account the initial losses your clients would probably suffer.

People

20.14 As I indicated earlier, a business is largely at the mercy of its employees. A good business which is being sold will probably have high calibre employees whom the purchasers will wish to retain. A bad business may have been brought to its knees by its employees, and the purchasers are unlikely to feel a great compulsion to inherit these liabilities.

Good employees may be hard to retain. They may feel upset at the business being sold over their heads, and the owner disappearing with a large sum. They may even decide that they could do the same thing, and will leave to start up their own businesses. Apart from advising on and drawing up service contracts, there is not much the solicitor can do here. It is more of a personnel management exercise, or 'golden handcuffs' to give them their vulgar name – that is a good reward to stay faithful to the employer.

If an employee is under contract for a number of years, and the employers are afraid that the employee is going to be disruptive and uncooperative, yet they are unwilling to cancel the contract, and let the employee move to another firm, they can give the employee 'gardening leave' ie pay the employee to do nothing.

Unhelpful staff are rather easier to lose, but the rights conferred on them on redundancy or dismissal under the various Employment Acts may make this an expensive exercise for the purchasers.

It is no longer competent to provide in the sale agreement that the sellers shall dismiss employees before takeover, and pay their compensation, in order that the purchasers may re-engage only such of those as they wish to keep. (See Transfer of Undertakings (Protection of Employment) Regulations 1981, SI 1981/1794 and possibly also the redundancy provisions of the Employment Protection (Consolidation) Act 1978, s 94.)

Formerly a clause would normally be put into a contract to the effect that the purchasers of a business would require the sellers to terminate all contracts before the sale and the sellers would deal with the employees' redundancy and unfair dismissal claims. The purchase would then re-employ such employees as might be required, as new employees without accumulated rights.

Under the Transfer of Undertakings (Protection of Employment) Regulations 1981, SI 1981/1794 this process is no longer possible. The rather poor drafting of these regulations originally caused considerable speculation as to their meanings, and at one stage the Scottish and English Employment Appeal Tribunals managed to find different interpretations of the same United Kingdom regulations. The matter has now been put beyond doubt by the House of Lords case *Litster v Forth Dry Dock & Engineering Co Ltd* 1989 SLT 540, (1989) IRLR 161, HL. In this case, employees had been dismissed by the receivers of the business an hour before the transfer of the business took place. The Court of Session held that the employees were not therefore (as stated in the Regulations) 'employed immediately before the transfer'.

The House of Lords held that the Court of Session had erred in this literal interpretation of regulation 5(1), which would allow the transferor of a business to dismiss employees a short time before the transfer becomes operative. Where the transferor is insolvent, as Lord Keith of Kinkel (a Scottish judge in the House of Lords) pointed out, this would leave the employees with only a worthless claim for unfair dismissal against the transferor.

Lord Keith continued by saying that the European Court, in a number of decisions and particularly in *P Bork Internationals A/S v Foreningen af Arbejdsledere i Danmark* (1989) IRLR 41, had ruled that where employees have been dismissed by the transferor for a reason connected with the transfer, at a time before the transfer takes effect, then the employees are to be treated as still employed by the undertaking at the time of the transfer. Thus as Lord Templeman further said, the courts of the United Kingdom are under a duty to follow the practice of the European Court by giving a purposive construction to EC Directives, and to Regulations issued for the purpose of complying with the Directives. The meaning of the term 'purposive construction' is that the purpose of the relevant Directive is not thwarted or evaded. (For a discussion on this topic see the article by Roderick Mackenzie in Property Law Bulletin 1994, p 7.)

A clause therefore which purports to require the sellers of a business to dismiss all employees before transfer, and to be responsible for the employees' claims, is not competent. The claim against the purchasers will be for either unfair dismissal or redundancy. Now, in order for it to be redundancy alone, the purchasers will have to show that the dismissal is an 'economic, technical or organisational one' entailing changes in the work force. The meaning of these words is not at all clear. An economic reason must be a reason relating to the running of the business, not a reason relating to the price obtainable on the scale of that business. It should also be borne in mind that establishing an economic, technical or organisational reason is not in itself enough, and you must then go on and establish that the reasons for dismissal were fair in terms of the Employment Protection (Consolidation) Act 1978, s 58(3).

Employees dismissed for these reasons will also generally be entitled to a redundancy payment. (*Anderson and McAlonie v Dalkeith Engineering Ltd* (1984) IRLR 429.) Consultations with workers' representatives must take place before any transfer, with a view to reaching agreement about changing conditions.

It has to be said that most businesses and mergers result, sooner or later, in job losses – whatever pious intentions are expressed at the time of the happy event. The effect can hopefully be achieved by natural wastage, but the purchasers of a business who intend to trim the workforce should bear these provisions in mind, and should adjust the price to be paid in accordance with the potential liability that is acquired with the business.

What of the departing sellers? Hopefully they will have made enough to enjoy a well-earned retirement, but whether they have or not, they should be subjected to a restrictive covenant to prevent them from returning to business to compete with the purchasers. The covenant should be neither too loose to stop the sellers from competing unfairly, nor too tight to be declared unenforceable by the courts. See the case of *Scottish Farmers v McGhee* 1933 SC 148 and many subsequent cases on the topic.

Lastly some other terms in use in this area of practice include:

'**Golden Hello**' – where an employee is induced to change jobs by a 'headhunter' (recruitment agent) the employee is usually rewarded by an additional incentive. This is to cover the danger of the employee moving from a job for life, only to find that things are not working out, and thus having to leave. This happens frequently.

'**Golden Parachute**' – an executive has a contract which provides extra rewards in the event of a hostile takeover of a firm, leading to dismissal.

'**Poison Pill**' – a company makes provisions for certain things to happen in the event of a hostile takeover, which will make the company less attractive to a purchaser.

20.15   The question of creating a monopoly situation under the Fair Trading Act 1973, or of falling foul of Articles 85 and 86 of the Treaty of Rome, relating to the creation of monopolies or the abuse of a dominant position, should always be borne in mind. From October 1990 the European Commission alone is responsible for vetting all cross-border mergers where the companies concerned have a joint turnover of 5 billion ECUs, unless three-quarters of the total turnover is earned in one member state. Where these conditions are not fulfilled, the national authorities, such as the Monopolies and Mergers Commission has jurisdiction. This has the effect of clearing up the confusion where a merger might face vetting both in Brussels and by a national body. While these provisions are relevant mainly to large companies, they could also apply where two quite small companies merge, and thereby control a quarter of the home market. If there is any doubt about this, the Office of Fair Trading and the appropriate office in Brussels should be consulted.

20.16 The sale agreement should, where necessary, call upon the sellers to grant warranties that the situation is as they have stated. The purchasers will also do 'due diligence' ie thorough inspection of old records, which may cut down the need for elaborate warranties. Warranties may not be very effective unless there are also indemnities to cover them. For this reason agreements for the sale of large companies are very lengthy and complex, there being alone about 30 different kinds of tax liability that may arise after the sellers have received their money. This is, however, outwith the scope of this work, and is dealt with in other specialist publications. (See Butterworth's *Encyclopaedia of Forms and Precedents* for many helpful styles of offer for a variety of situations.)

20.17

Offer of a business – contract to be completed by acceptance

Messrs Talle, Darke & Hansom,
Solicitors,
33 Watson Street,
AYR

6 November 1994

Dear Sirs,

On behalf of our client Mr Art Sidewright ('the purchaser') we hereby offer to purchase from your client Mr Humphrey MacKerrell ('the seller'):

(1) the shop property at 44 Angus Avenue, Ayr together with all the heritable fittings and fixtures therein;

(2) the goodwill of the business of Fishmonger and Poulterer carried on therein by the seller under the name 'Seafresh';

(3) the fittings and equipments hereinafter specified; and

(4) the non-perishable stock-in-trade;

and that at the price and on the terms and conditions following:

1. The price for the heritable property shall be THIRTY SEVEN
   THOUSAND POUNDS (£37,000) STERLING payable as at the
   date of entry aftermentioned. The price for the goodwill shall
   be SEVEN THOUSAND FIVE HUNDRED POUNDS (£7,500)
   STERLING payable as at the date of transfer aftermentioned.

2. The seller will sell as at the date of transfer and at the price
   of THREE THOUSAND POUNDS (£3,000) STERLING to the purchaser the whole trade fixtures and fittings, trade utensils
   and equipment which shall include counters, refrigerators,
   cash registers and scales. By acceptance of this Offer the
   seller warrants that there are no hire purchase or credit sale
   agreements, diligences, liens or charges of any kind affecting
   any of these moveable items, and that the title of the seller
   thereto cannot be reduced or affected at the instance of third
   parties. It is further understood that this price is inclusive of
   Value Added Tax and that the seller will account for this and
   will hand over a valid receipt to the purchaser within two
   weeks of payment of the price.

3. The purchaser will take over the non-perishable stock-in-trade
   of the business as at the date of entry and transfer, at a price
   to be agreed between the parties. Failing agreement the
   Valuation shall be referred to a neutral Valuer to be agreed
   between the parties.

4. The date of entry to the heritable property and the date of
   transfer of the goodwill and other subjects of sale shall be at
   the commencement of business on Thursday, 28 December
   1994.

5. The following conditions shall apply with reference to the heritable property:

(a) It is understood that the Rateable Value is £1,800 and that
    the share of the ground burdens apportioned on the subjects
    does not exceed £2.50 per annum. It is understood that the
    property is liable for one-eighth of the common charges of the
    whole tenement in which it is situated. The current rates,
    ground burdens and common charges and other outgoings will
    be apportioned as at the date of entry.

(b) In exchange for the price the seller will deliver a valid
    Disposition of the shop premises in favour of the purchaser
    or his nominees, and will deliver or exhibit a valid mar-
    ketable title with Searches in the Property Register for not
    less than Forty years and in the Personal Registers for the
    prescriptive period showing clear records.

(c) It is understood that the minerals are included in the sale
    only in so far as the seller has right thereto.

(d) It is understood that there are no burdensome or unusual con-
    ditions, servitudes or wayleaves affecting the subjects and

that there are no Orders affecting the subjects under the Town and Country Planning (Scotland) Act or the Public Health Acts or other Acts or any Notices or Orders by the Regional, District or other authority affecting the subjects. Full Planning Permission for the present use has been granted and not revoked.

(e) It is understood that there are no conditions of Title which would prejudice the free use by the purchaser of the premises for trading purposes.

(f) It is understood that the premises meet the requirements of the Offices, Shops and Railway Premises Act; Health and Safety at Work Act and all other statutory provisions applicable thereto and that a Fire Certificate has been issued and not withdrawn or revoked.

(g) It is understood that the roadway *ex adverso* the subjects of sale and the sewer service the same have been taken over and are maintained by the Local Authority.

(h) The subjects of purchase shall include the refrigerated cold store, and the refrigeration system, all thermostats, pipes, plant, valves, pumps, time clocks, laggings, and vents. It is understood that the purchaser or his engineer shall be entitled to inspect the said equipment in the week before the date of transfer, and satisfy himself that it is in full working order. In the event of any repair being necessary, the purchaser shall be entitled to withhold a reasonable part of the price pending execution of the required repairs.

[The purchaser may also wish to insert other clauses for heritable property, such as a clause dealing with local authority notices et cetera.]

6. The following conditions shall apply with reference to the sale of the goodwill.

(a) The seller will be entitled to the whole sum due in respect of sales of stock prior to the date of transfer and be liable to meet the cost of all stock ordered and delivered to the shop prior to that date.

(b) The seller will maintain the business as at present between the date of acceptance of this Offer and the date of the transfer but shall not order stock for delivery after the date of transfer without the consent of the purchaser.

(c) All outgoings of the business shall be apportioned as at the date of transfer, and the seller will be entitled to all book debts owing to the business prior to the date of transfer, and will be responsible for their collection. The purchaser will assist the seller to collect such book debts, but without recourse to legal proceedings.

(d) The seller shall indemnify the purchaser against all liabilities whatever of the business incurred or arising in connection with the business transactions carried out prior to the date of transfer.

(e) The Books of Account relating to the business shall become the property of the purchaser on the date of transfer, but they shall for a period of six months thereafter be open to the inspection by the seller or his agents at all reasonable times for entries relating to the period prior to the date of transfer and twenty-one days thereafter.

(f) The seller will not in any way carry on directly or indirectly (unless with the written consent of the purchaser) within one year after the date of transfer and within one mile of 44 Angus Avenue either on his own account or as a partner with, or in the name of, or as a servant or agent to any person or persons, firm or company, the business of Fishmonger or Poulterer within the said area.

7.   The whole subject of Offer will be maintained by the seller in good condition and repair to the date of entry and transfer and adequately insured against fire, theft and other usual risks to the said date.

8.   This offer and the missives following hereon will form a continuing and enforceable contract notwithstanding the delivery of the Disposition, except in so far as fully implemented thereby, but the said missives shall cease to be enforceable after a period of two years from the date of entry except in so far as they are founded on in any court proceedings which have commenced within the said period. A clause to this effect may be included in the Disposition at the purchaser's option; and the purchaser may require the seller to deliver a letter to the purchaser, after delivery of the Disposition, also to this effect.

9.   This Offer is for immediate acceptance only.

Yours faithfully,

Adopted as holograph

SHORT, FATTE & UGGLY

Note: From this point completion of the contract will be reached by exchange of letters until all points are resolved and *consensus in idem* has been reached.

Chapter twenty-one

ASSIGNATIONS OF LEASES

'During the course of the year the Agency made a total of 18 payments, totalling £62,779.96 in respect of indemnity claims. Of this amount over £55,000 was paid out in respect of 3 claims, 2 of which were a result of omissions from, or misleading information in Agency reports, and the third was in respect of leasehold casualties omitted from the title sheet.'
(Keeper's Report 1992/93)

21.1 In certain areas it was traditionally the practice to grant long leases (or tacks to use the old Scottish term) of property, rather than feudal rights. The lease would usually be for a period of 99 or even 999 years. If you buy a leasehold property with some 800 years of the lease to run, it may seem little different from a feu, but it is quite a different concept, and there are certain differences of emphasis. The most obvious difference is that you never own the property, and the lease will come to an end one day, no matter how remote that day may be.

Thus certain unfortunate tenants on Seafield Estates, in the North-east, are faced with losing their houses simply because their leases are about to expire, and they are being asked to pay substantial sums to buy houses that they had considered as their own. It is perhaps difficult to understand why this miscomprehension has arisen, but that is the way things stand, and no statutory relief has been offered.

21.2 It is perhaps also unfortunate that advantage was not taken of the provisions of the Long Leases (Scotland) Act 1954, Part I, which allowed such tenants to convert their leases into feus on a small payment to the landlord in compensation. Sadly the benefits of that Act ceased to be available after 1 September 1959, and have never been renewed.

The model village of Eaglesham in Renfrewshire was largely let on long leases by the Earl of Eglinton, who had, however, to sell the village some years later to make up for his disastrous losses when he staged a jousting tournament at his castle on one of the wettest days apparently ever remembered. The rentals charged were one or two old shillings per house, with the only notable condition being a requirement on the villagers to pay for a piper for the Earl when required.

The successors to Eglinton Estates were happy enough to convert their leases into feus, and will, I believe, still do so, if asked by anyone who has not yet done so. Not so Seafield Estates, who rest on their contracts.

21.3 When a leasehold property is sold, the land is not sold, merely the right to occupy it for a certain number of years. A disposition is not therefore the competent deed, it is an assignation of the lease in the form provided by the Registration of Leases (Scotland) Act 1857, Sch A.

An assignation of lease takes this form:

I, (*name and address of seller*) IN CONSIDERATION of the price of (*price*) paid to me by (*name and address of purchaser*) of which price I hereby acknowledge the receipt HAVE SOLD and DO HEREBY ASSIGN to the said (*purchaser*) the tenant's right and interest to and in a Tack (*specify details of the Tack*); and further I assign in so far as necessary my title thereto which is recorded (*specify Register and date of registration*); Together with (first) the parts privileges and pertinents of the Leasehold rights hereby assigned; and (second) my whole right, title and interest present and future therein; WITH ENTRY as at (*date*); And I grant warrandice (*Stamp Duty clause if appropriate*); the missives of sale which I have concluded with the said (*purchaser*) and which are constituted by letters dated (*detail*) will form a continuing and enforceable contract notwithstanding the delivery of these presents, except in so far as fully implemented thereby, but the said missives shall cease to be enforceable after a period of two years from the date of entry, except in so far as they are founded on in any court proceedings which have commenced within the said period: IN WITNESS WHEREOF

Similarly if money is borrowed on the security of the long lease, the competent security was a bond and assignation in security, in terms of Sch B to the 1857 Act. Nowadays, of course, in terms of the C & FR (S) Act 1970, s 9 it is competent to grant a standard security over any interest in land, including a leasehold interest.

It should, however, be made perfectly clear that, as a practical matter, no institution will lend money over a leasehold property of which the lease has only a few years to run as this does not constitute a reasonable security, nor over an unregistered lease.

21.4 Purchasers acquiring a lease should be satisfied that the landlord's title to the land is a good one, and therefore that the lease is competent. Further, all assignations of the lease should be checked as if these were normal dispositions. (See earlier remarks on noting of title in Chapter 7.)

A search over the lease (not over the property which is a distinctly separate interest) should also be seen. Searches over both lease and property can of course be requested, but the sellers may not be willing to produce the latter which is not really their concern.

21.5 It was a requirement of the Leases Act 1449, s 18, that to qualify for the protection of that Act, the tenants must enter into possession of the land. This had the effect that a lease could not be used as security for money borrowed. This difficulty was circumvented by the Registration of Leases Act 1857, s 1, which provided that a probative lease for a period of 31 years or more might be registered in the General Register of Sasines, thereby giving the tenants a real right. Any lease of less than 31 years was regarded as not being of sufficient importance to be so registered, but the Land Tenure Reform (Scotland) Act 1974, Sch 6, has reduced that qualification period to 20 years.

Conversely, however, the 1974 Act, s 8, forbids the creation of future leases of residential property for periods exceeding 20 years. It is thus unlikely that residential leases will be registered any more, and the remarks that follow on registration would therefore seem to apply mainly to commercial leases.

21.6 It should be noted, however, that it is still competent to register long residential leases created before 1974 which have not yet been registered. If the lease is in an area which has been declared operational for land registration, the lease or a transfer of it for value must now be registered in the Land Register. The forms and procedures used are as for dispositions of feudal property. (See Chapters 13 to 16.)

21.7 The advent of land registration has thrown up another difficulty with long leases that was not appreciated before, and which is fully discussed by Colin Miller in his paper 'Conveyancing: Points to Ponder', Law Society PQLE Papers of Missives and General Conveyancing Course, February 1985. Mr Miller points out that the Keeper of the Land Register has taken the view that it is not, and never has been, competent to use a deed of conditions to regulate leasehold property, on a strict reading of the C (S) Act 1874, s 32. Further the Keeper takes the view that it is not competent to impose land obligations by reference in an assignation or partial assignation of a lease, as would be the case with a disposition. Any such obligations referred to in an assignation are therefore incompetent, and would be only personal obligations upon the tenants, and that the only safe way to proceed in such transactions is to set forth at length the conditions of title in each and every assignation – something which has never apparently been done.

21.8 The Law Reform (Miscellaneous Provisions) (Scotland) Act 1985, s 3, however provides that it is retrospectively competent to impose conditions and make stipulations by reference to a previous deed which upon recording in the Register of Sasines or registration in the Land Register become binding upon singular successors of the tenants. Mr Miller also points out that this piece of retrospective legislation is to cure difficulties raised by the Keeper, but it does not seem to apply to deeds of conditions.

21.9 An unexpected feature of long leases which has cropped up in the last few years, (note the quotation at the head of this chapter) has been the incidence of leasehold casualties. It should be explained that casualties were double payments of feu duty or rent which occurred every nineteenth year, or on the sale of the property. Feudal casualties were abolished in 1914, by the Feudal Casualties (Scotland) Act 1914.

Unfortunately, however, this Act did not cover leasehold casualties. It had been generally assumed that these had been cancelled by the 1914 Act, or had otherwise dropped away, but this has not turned out to be the case.

A leasehold casualty is an additional payment of rent occurring on certain events. An example of this is as follows:

> As also to pay to the said (Landlord) and his successors proprietors of the said subjects or his or their assignees the sum of twelve pounds of additional rent for the first year's possession at the entry or succession of every heir to the said subjects and <u>one full year's rent or value of the said subjects</u> including all buildings erected or to be erected thereon according to the actual value thereof at the time for the first year's possession or entry of every assignee or singular successor and that within a year and a day from the date of the heir assignee or singular successor succeeding or acquiring right or

possession or of the right or possession opening to or devolving upon him, her or them;

You will note that I have underlined the part dealing with full year's rent or value, which is the critical part, it being claimed that this is intended to reflect inflationary changes, although at the time of the granting of the lease, inflation was not really known to any extent.

On the basis of this clause the landlord made a claim for a payment of several thousand pounds, on the basis of the 'full year's rent or value' being the amount of the rateable value on the property.

In this case a member of the Keeper's staff had omitted the leasehold casualty from the land certificate, presumably believing it to be a matter that had then become redundant – this being several years ago, when virtually everyone would have thought similarly. It turned out not to be, and a claim was received from the landlord for the loss of the casualty payment, and was paid.

It is understood that there are many such casualty rights throughout Scotland, and that 'Title Raiders' are buying estates and enforcing these casualty rights. They are, of course, totally within their legal rights to do so, if the clauses support them and are specific.

What is wrong is the legal position. These payments should have been abolished in 1914 together with feudal casualties, and, as a matter of the greatest urgency, they should be abolished now. It is suggested that a scheme of commutation of leasehold casualties be drawn up, as was the case in 1914 with feudal casualties, and that leasehold casualties should no longer exist. Alternatively, the Feudal Casualties (Scotland) Act 1914 gave power to the court to promulgate an Act of Sederunt for the abolition of other casualties, including leasehold casualties. This power has never, to date, been used.

Chapter twenty-two

COMMERCIAL LEASES

'Lease Terms: The building is being offered to let on the basis of a 25 year full repairing and insuring lease with upward only rent reviews at five yearly intervals. The incoming tenants will be responsible for the landlords' legal expenses together with stamp duty and VAT incurred in connection with the grant of the lease.'
(Developer's Circular)

'A leading City (London) law firm is being sued for £7.5 million over a blunder allegedly made in drafting a guarantee. The action is being brought .... on behalf of 2,700 investors ... who complain that because of the guarantee they are only receiving a third of the rent promised.

The main purpose of the guarantee was to ensure that even if the buildings were not let, investors would still receive rental income for the first five years. In the event the guarantee failed to do the one thing it was supposed to do – protect the investors in the event of the developers of the building, who promised to pay the rent, going bust.'
(*Financial Mail on Sunday*)

22.1 The modern commercial lease is a repairing, renewing and insuring lease (RRI); that is, these obligations are placed on the tenants by agreement. This is a basic practice which has become customary (see quotation above). Whatever else you may be able to negotiate with the landlord, you are very unlikely to be able to negotiate out of this stipulation.

22.2 The modern commercial (or full repairing, renewing and insuring lease) is a formidable creature, and was, until recently, entirely unmoderated by any statutory relaxation of its strict terms, with the exception of the modest security of tenure given by the Tenancy of Shops (Scotland) Acts 1949 and 1964. The contents of such a lease are entirely governed by negotiation between the parties. The terms are fixed usually by the landlord, and agreed by the tenants. There are none of the safeguards of security of tenure, and of compensation payable on outgoing afforded to tenants in England by the string of Landlord and Tenants Acts, 1929 to 1988.

There was enacted the Law Reform (Miscellaneous Provisions) (Scotland) Act 1985, which protected tenants from an irritancy arising from late payment of rent, as in the case of *Dorchester Studios (Glasgow) Limited v Stone* 1975 SLT 153. It also protected the tenants from an irritancy relating to non-monetary breaches of the lease. At s 5 it produced the most bizarre legal animal yet. Burdened and benefited proprietors, entitled spouses and non-entitled spouses, to name but four recently created legal animals, are fairly clearly-definable legal concepts, but the concept of a 'fair and reasonable landlord' who 'in all the circumstances of the case' would not have terminated a lease, is vague beyond belief.

In his annotations of this Act, Professor Joseph Thomson says that 'it is to be hoped that the uncertainty surrounding "the fair and reasonable landlord" test will not be the occasion for protracted litigation'. This approach was tried successfully in *Lothian Chemical Co Ltd v City of Edinburgh District Council* 1995 GWD 4–197.

22.3 But what are fair and reasonable landlords? It could be argued that the landlords are merely attending to their duties on behalf of their investors, and it is right and proper that the landlords should follow a consistent management philosophy, and that they should not let the tenants away with too much for the sake of their investors, and indeed, for the sake of the tenants themselves. Alternatively, you could argue that fair and reasonable landlords are benign characters, not getting too upset about minor breaches of the rules, and turning a blind eye to breaches of the conditions of leases; but if a tenant neglects an essential repair, the whole property may suffer, and that is not being a fair and reasonable landlord at all.

22.4 And if the Act does not create a matching concept of a 'fair and reasonable tenant' can we perhaps invent one? Tenants who always pay their rent in time, perform the various other obligations posed by the lease, are good traders and attract customers to the development, are an example of this. These tenants are otherwise known as a 'good covenant', and needless to say are a highly sought-after commodity. A good covenant can more or less dictate terms to the landlord, within the restraints mentioned above, whereas a lesser covenant has to take more or less the terms the landlord dictates.

22.5 Thus when we have negotiations for a lease, much depends on the respective bargaining powers of the two parties. You may have two kinds of negotiation: (a) competitive, or win/lose, negotiation where one party is intent on imposing its will on the other party, and if it does not succeed in any respect, it will simply stop negotiations; and (b) co-operative, or win/win, negotiations where both parties are prepared to concede certain points to the other, and, without breaking the basic pattern of the leasing scheme, the landlord is prepared to allow certain deviations from it.

The former pattern of 'negotiation', which is less common nowadays, because leases that are too strict have proved to be counter-productive when they come to a rent review, requires the lawyer to do little more than to report to the client on the possible impact of the conditions imposed, and to outline the costs involved, which are liable to be extensive.

But if we take the second possibility, of co-operative negotiation, it is here that the skilled leasing lawyers come into their own. Wit is pitted against wit, each striving to get the best deal for their clients, and at the end of the day both should feel that they have done a good job for their clients. You can take satisfaction that you have acted like good lawyers should, instead of like an unskilled office junior, whose only job is to take the bad news to the client.

22.6   What then, in sensible negotiations, are some of the major points that good lawyers should be looking for? First of all the lease should be clear and comprehensible, not repetitive or ambiguous, in a logical order, with an index and side headings, and have a clear definition section at the beginning. Solicitors for both parties should keep their clients continuously informed of the progress of negotiations. You may feel that this is unnecessary, as the client doesn't understand what is going on, but it is very important to keep the client informed, in this sphere of law as all others. This is as much a matter of self-protection as anything else.

22.7   The rent payable is a matter for negotiation; the tenants should not necessarily be expected to accept the landlord's first figure. You will be kept advised on this, as on other matters, by a competent surveyor. Whether or not value added tax is payable on the rent is a competent matter for negotiation. Basically, to a VAT-registered company, whether or not it pays VAT on the rental is neither here nor there, because it can claim it back, and the only loss is that it had to pay the tax rather earlier, with a cash-flow benefit to the landlord, and detriment to the tenants. Where tenants are not VAT registered, as with a bank or other financial institution, it is distinctly detrimental to have VAT imposed, as it is just a straight 17.5% rent increase, which cannot be reclaimed. As such companies are generally good covenants, however, some solution can usually be found with co-operative negotiation.

22.8   Machinery for reviewing the rent must be established. Landlords are entitled to have the rent adjusted to cover the fall in the value of money, but the tenants should not yield completely to the landlord. This is purely a matter for negotiation – the length of the review break and so on – but there are important drafting considerations too. There should be resisted by the tenants any attempt to impose a condition that any restriction on use shall be disregarded on a rent review (see **22.12**). On the other hand, the tenants should insist on the insertion of 'disregards' for rent review purposes of the tenants' occupancy and the goodwill the tenants have created, and of improvements made by the tenants. It is bad enough to improve someone else's property, without having to pay additional rent in respect of those improvements.

22.9   While on a longish lease it is quite acceptable that the tenants shall pay for repairs, there should be excluded repairs of latent defects that were not reasonably foreseeable at the outset of the lease, and which not even a competent survey of the premises would have revealed. These defects seem to arise mainly in the much-maligned buildings of the 1960s when, as it turns out, all sorts of dubious materials were used and poor building practices followed. Asbestos and concrete which dissolved ('concrete cancer') cladding which separates from the building, and high alumina cement are among the most likely building materials to cause latent defects.

22.10   The insurance provisions should be fair, and if in doubt the insurances of the property should be checked over by a broker. While the tenants can be reasonably expected to pay premiums, and while the landlords can fairly expect also to instruct the insurances, care should be taken that all risks that need to be covered are in fact covered, and that those that are not requiring cover, are not. The premiums should also be competitive, and the risks should be insured with a sound company. The position as to destruction of the property, and the insurance provisions against it, should be fair to the tenants. Ideally the tenants would want the Scottish law of *rei interitus* to apply, as in the case of *Cantors Properties (Scotland) Limited* 1980 SLT 165, and to be able to abandon the lease in the event of destruction of the property, but it is now fairly well established that the landlord will wish to contract out of this provision. An unwelcome recent development has been the need to instruct cover against terrorist damage.

22.11 As heritable securities are generally taken over registered leases, the lending institutions will generally want clauses contained in the lease which will protect their interests in the event of an irritancy, or bankruptcy or liquidation of the tenants. These clauses will rarely be resisted by landlords, as the 'muscle' of financial institutions is hard to resist, and also because they would simply cease to lend if they lost their security in the event that the tenants became insolvent, or failed to pay their rent in time. It should be borne in mind that no security can be created over a lease that is not registerable, that is to say with a lease period of 20 years or less, as opposed to a lease for a period greater than 20 years, but which has less than 20 years of that period left to run.

22.12 The tenants must ensure that every contemplated use of the premises is allowed by the lease, and is permitted under Town and Country Planning legislation. The tenants should ensure that not only does this permission exist, but is applicable to the whole length of the lease, and is not personal to another party. If planning permission is to be obtained, the lease should be made subject to the permission being obtained, and in terms acceptable to the tenants. Further the solicitors for the tenants should ensure that the use contemplated is acceptable in terms of the title deeds and that there are no restrictions which would adversely affect the use proposed by the tenants. From the landlords' point of view, restrictions on other uses should not be disallowed by the lease, lest this should affect the level of rent to be fixed on review, on the basis that the restriction makes the lease hard to transfer, and therefore of less value. If a restriction on use is imposed, this should not be stated in the lease to be disregarded on a future review of the rent, as the impact on the rent payable could be quite dramatic.

22.13 The tenants' solicitors should also inspect the title deeds, as if the property was being purchased, and searches should be obtained to show that the landlord truly is the owner of the property and that there are no securities over the property, or if there are that the consent of the security holder to the lease is obtained. The consent of the superior, or of any head landlord, to the proposed lease arrangement and to the proposed usage of the property should be obtained, if required. The same care should be taken when leasing a property, as when purchasing it, in seeing the appropriate planning and building certificates and any permission required from the superior.

22.14 Details of the landlords' management charges should be obtained and be seen to be reasonable. Where, as the modern practice is, a shopping development contains, say, an ice rink, the tenants should not incur any share of the charges involved in running the rink.

22.15 From the tenants' point of view, there should not be too severe restrictions on assigning and sub-letting the lease. In addition, the tenants should be assured that in the event of an assignation of the lease being allowed that the original tenants are released from any further liability under the lease. In England there is a doctrine of privity, which imposes this liability on the original leaseholder. Landlords may well try to impose this concept to Scotland by negotiation and by inserting a joint and several liability on the original tenants and all assignees. It should be resisted, as the consequences for the original tenants can be very considerable.

From the landlords' point of view, it is also desirable to have a fair degree of freedom to assign or sub-let, as if the lease is unduly restrictive in this regard, this too may have a detrimental effect on the level of future rent reviews. Landlords will, reasonably, wish to ensure that a future tenant is as good a covenant as the old tenant.

Generally, throughout the lease the tenants should be protected against any temptation on the landlords to spend the tenants' money freely, and safeguards should be built in that all expenditure should be incurred 'reasonably'. Further, the ascertainment of what is reasonable spending, and what is not, should be referred to an arbiter.

22.16 The tenants should be allowed quiet possession of the whole subjects of lease, provided that the terms of the lease are adhered to. The tenants should also reserve such rights over adjoining areas of ground, belonging to the landlords, as may be required, particularly from the point of view of access, and support of buildings, and for the leading of services to the premises leased.

22.17 It is certainly reasonable that the tenants should keep the subjects decorated, in a lease of any length. This obligation should not be too onerous, however, nor should it be inappropriate. If the tenants have a particular 'house style' the lease should not be framed in such a way as to be inimical to this. Also the tenants should not accept an out-of-date decoration clause, which requires them, for example, to paint the woodwork with 'three coats of oil-based paint' and to apply distemper to the walls. Just try and get oil paint and distemper in your local supermarket!

22.18 The landlords may attempt to get personal guarantees from the directors of a lease to a limited company if it is considered that the covenant of the company is not good enough, and that the company is not financially secure. This is a perfectly acceptable practice, and is not unfair. Having said that, the tenants' solicitors should automatically resist the attempt, but if the tenants are a small or newly-established company, it is not unreasonable for the landlords to protect their own interests if the tenant company is quietly dissolved at the first sign of trouble. What is important from the guarantor's point of view is that it is released when the tenants assign the lease, and that it be kept informed of any aberrant practices by the tenants which, if continued, might lead to an irritancy of the lease, such as slow payment of rent. A time limit on the guarantee may also be included.

22.19 The lease should specify the landlords' fixtures, bearing in mind that fixtures brought onto the premises may be deemed to have become heritable by the operation of the rule in *Brand's Trustees v Brand's Trustees* (1876) 3 R (HL) 16 and *Scottish Discount Co Ltd* 1986 SLT 123. As should be the general practice disclosed in a number of conflicting cases following *Winston v Patrick* 1981 SLT 41, central heating and ventilation plant should always be inspected before taking over premises, to ensure that they are in good working order.

22.20 Lastly, after a long recital of the obligations of the tenants, all of which must be paid for by the tenants, the expenses of preparation of this document by the landlords' agent are fairly and squarely placed on the tenants' shoulders. Of course you may console the tenants by saying that if they did not pay for these now, they would only have to pay for them in the future in the form of an increased rent, for in this world there is no such thing as a free lunch. The tenants will probably reply that while they admit that, were the case otherwise, the payment would probably be spread over a number of years. I would suggest that the tenants' solicitors attempt to limit these expenses at the outset, and tell the clients what they must expect to pay.

Better still, if you can negotiate out of paying the landlords' expenses at all, you should enjoy, but need not expect, the gratitude of the clients. It really comes down to curbing the free spending of your clients' money, and your clients should not be expected to pay a very fancy price for a long, word-processed lease.

Be sure to warn the tenants at the outset of the negotiations of the cost of all this – the stamp duty, the recording dues, the landlords' expenses, the management charges, your expenses, as well as the first rental payment due in advance, and the fitting out costs. If you fail to do this you may find that the tenants seek to make a saving of the only thing under their control, and delay to pay your fee!

22.21 In England the tenant is held responsible for the terms of the lease even after the lease has been assigned to someone else. This is known as 'privity of contract', and it does not apply in Scotland. Landlords may, however, try to slip the provision into the contract by making the tenants jointly and severally liable with their successors. Tenants should resist this maneouvre.

22.22 These are only some of the major considerations of negotiation and drafting a lease. No practitioner in this field should be without a copy of M J Ross and D J McKichan's invaluable *Drafting and Negotiating Commercial Leases in Scotland* (Butterworths, 2nd Edn, 1993).

Chapter twenty-three

SITE ASSEMBLY

'The next step was to buy all the land as quietly as possible. The site stretched for a quarter of a mile between the underground stations at Warren Street and Great Portland Street, along the north side of Euston Road, which until the 18th century had been the northern boundary of London ... an area which Joe Levy (property developer) extravagantly describes as "a derelict bloody den of disease".'

'Joe Levy was forming a consortium of estate agents. He knew that if his firm alone were to attempt to buy from all the many different owners, freeholders, leaseholders, and subleaseholders, his intention might become apparent and there would be two great dangers. Owners might dream up an exaggerated idea of the value, to him, of their properties, or some small time property dealers might compete against him in order to hold him to ransom. In either case his ultimate profit on the redevelopment could either be slimmed down or wiped out entirely.'

(The Property Boom – Joseph Marriott, on the redevelopment of the Euston station site)

23.1 Commercial conveyancing is reasonably similar to domestic conveyancing, in that the same sort of documentation applies. There the similarity ends because commercial conveyancers handle huge sums of money, deal probably with several lenders, floating charges, ranking of securities, and go into other esoteric matters like leverage (borrowing) and mezzanine financing (a debt half secured by a security over the borrowers' assets and half by shares in the borrowing company). A good commercial conveyancer should, however, have a sound grounding in the basics of domestic conveyancing, and then the other bits can be grafted on.

While I feel that this chapter will introduce many basic concepts of commercial conveyancing, I should, however, stress that this chapter makes no claim to be anything but introductory, although I hope that it will be usefully so.

23.2 First it is important to note that the conveyancing aspects of commercial deals do not differ radically from domestic conveyancing. There are the four main stages – (1) negotiation; (2) missives; (3) examination of title; and (4) settlement. The real difference lies in the fact that the lawyer in a commercial transaction must liaise with a number of other people, and know fairly well what they are attempting to do. It should be remembered that it is the lawyers who must complete the evidence of the agreement, with their own signature on the missives, and therefore they must be amply satisfied that everything leading to the agreement seems to be in order.

I shall turn to the these aspects later, but first it may be useful to look at some of the metaphorical creatures in the metaphorical jungle of commercial conveyancing.

The landowner

23.3 The first persons with whom we must deal are the persons who own the land, and who are now being stalked by the developer. In most cases the developer will wish to acquire the landowner's interest absolutely, and the landowner will then be paid and will disappear. Developers do not like third parties to have any interest in their developments, as such interests may prove awkward at a future date. Some landowners, however, will not sell their land, but will grant a ground lease to the developer. This lease will be for a long number of years and will require the developer to build the building and to pay a ground rent to the landowner. The developer then subleases the building to the tenants, and his profit is the difference between the two rentals (known as the profit rental), less – of course – the expenses of development.

The landowner will enjoy an annual rental income, probably increasing regularly, and at the end of the lease period, the land and buildings will revert to the landowner, or more probably to unknown descendants. This right is known as a reversion.

As such arrangements tend to be for a period exceeding the normal life-span, one may assume that in the intervening period the developer will have sold the reversion to a pension fund or similar body, which invests in the long term, and has invested what should be a handsome sum elsewhere. The small landowner is unlikely to reach such an agreement with a developer, and only powerful and experienced landowners are likely to reach such arrangements. For the rest, it is the case of a lump sum in their hands, and off to the Bahamas.

The developer

23.4 The developer is the person who makes the whole thing happen; the co-ordinator, profit maker, and let it not be forgotten, the risk-taker. The developer runs considerable risks, and in return expects a substantial return. A sensible developer will employ a team of experts. They include:

(a) The lawyer: The lawyer completes all the documents and in such role should be the key adviser in the development. No detail should escape the lawyer's notice, for all may have a vital bearing on the documentation and, indeed, in any disputes that may follow. The lawyer should clearly establish the brief before commencing – is the lawyer engaged merely for clerical functions, or to provide commercial expertise? It is, I understand, a common source of liability claims when the lawyer thought that the job was to supply clerical services, but in fact the developer expected to be provided with commercial development expertise as well. When I talk of lawyers here I mean solicitors, but of course an advocate may also be called in at any stage to advise, or indeed may have to be. The lawyer is also responsible for the site assembly, where the development is made up of several parcels.

(b) The valuation surveyor: A valuation surveyor (as opposed to a quantity surveyor who provides a quite different service although belonging to the same institute – the Royal Institute of Chartered Surveyors) is the expert on the price of land – the price at which it may be bought, and the price at which the development may be rented to provide the maximum return to the developer.

(c) The architect: The architect's primary task is to design and supervise the building of an attractive and useful development which conforms to all the requirements of the planning and building authorities. The architect may also provide useful advice on planning and environmental aspects, in conjunction with a planning consultant or otherwise.

(d) The planning consultant: The planning consultant and architect will negotiate with the district council planning department, bearing in mind the requirements for a successful development, and also that it is unlikely that this can be completed nowadays in the teeth of opposition from the planning department. The planning position wished by the developer should be a material, suspensive, condition of purchase.

(e) The environmental consultant: The environmental consultant will advise on the environmental audit to be carried out before purchase, and the carrying out of the required cleaning of a contaminated site. This process is referred to as BATNEC – best available treatment at not excessive cost. The environmental consultant may come from any discipline, but most probably will have a planning or scientific or engineering background. An environmental audit should be made a material condition of purchase, and be the subject of a suspensive condition.

The purchase of land should be the subject of a suspensive environmental clause, along the following lines:

> 'the purchaser shall receive, in respect of the site, ground support and geotechnical survey reports (all including soils and minerals survey reports and a site survey report in terms satisfactory to them) in which regard the purchasers will be the sole judge and whose judgement shall not be challengeable.

> The purchasers will also carry out an environmental audit to allow them to satisfy themselves no dangerous or deleterious substances have been used on, disposed of, dumped, released, deposited or buried at the site and that the site is not adversely otherwise affected by the terms of the Public Health (Scotland) Act 1897, Control of Pollution Act 1974, Environmental Protection Act 1990 (all as amended or varied or substituted from time to time) or any other legislation concerning the protection of human health or the environment or the treatment or disposal of dangerous substances.'

(f) The accountant: The accountant will give advice generally on financial matters and particularly on the many complex taxation problems that may arise. The accountant is also responsible for due diligence reports on any property-owning companies bought as part of the site assembly.

(g) The civil engineer: Initially the engineer will take test bores and will assess the ground conditions both for contamination and building purposes. The engineer will sink test bores to make sure that the ground is sufficiently stable to support the building envisaged. No contract should be entered into by the developer without it being made a material, suspensive, condition that if test bores, or environmental audit, prove unsatisfactory, the developer may withdraw. The potential cost of making an unstable site suitable for building is horrific. After the site has been assembled the engineer may well work with the architect to ensure the structural safety of the building, and other matters like lift shafts. In addition a mechanical engineer may be called in to assess moving plant, such as lift machinery and so on.

(h) The quantity surveyor: The quantity surveyor (QS) will again work with the architect. Broadly the architect will produce plans of the building and the QS will prepare Bills of Quantity, which will be handed out to potential tenderers for the building work.

(i) The insurance broker: The insurance broker will advise on all insurance aspects from the first acquisition of property, through the building work, until the tenants are in possession of the new building. This covers an enormous range of potential insurable risks.

(j) The financier: The developer will have to buy the land, pay substantial professional fees, and then pay the cost of the building before any significant return is received. Temporary financing will therefore be necessary, and no doubt some form of security over the ground will also have to be given.

The planning and building departments of the district council

23.5 The obtaining of a building warrant is relatively simple, provided the various complex building regulations are followed. This can be safely left to the architect, the quantity surveyor and the builders. Planning is much less simple as other considerations enter, particularly aesthetic and political considerations, which should quite properly enter, but which do not make life any easier, as they are imprecise and unspecified.

Thus the developer may find that the sub-standard building that is to be demolished is, in fact, a little-known work of someone famous, and that listed building consent is required, and various preservation societies are opposed to the development. The co-operation of a planning department is most important, without it being necessary to concede to all their points. Basically these departments are reasonable to deal with, and they will not block a useful development – one which provides 'planning gain', in the form of cleaning up an eyesore or providing jobs etc – and which increases rates income. The district council, possessing compulsory purchase powers as it does may prove to be vital.

There was an example in Glasgow recently of the district council saving a major development by compulsorily purchasing a small piece of land in disputed ownership, which dispute was preventing access to the development. There are also numerous other examples of councils helping the developer by stopping up streets or closing rights of way and so on. As a quid pro quo for help rendered, the council may enter into an enforceable agreement with the developer under s 50 of the Town and Country Planning Act 1972. Thus the parties might agree that while the developer is building on the site anyway, something else – eg a public toilet – shall be built, thereby saving the council expense. The s 50 agreement is enforceable and can be recorded or registered.

An example of a very simple agreement of this kind follows:

Section 50

WHEREAS the first party are planning Authority for the District of in terms of the Town and Country Planning (Scotland) Act 1972; AND WHEREAS the second party are the heritable proprietors of ALL and WHOLE that piece of ground part of the farm and lands of   in the Parish of and County of and comprising the south-east part of the field or enclosure? numbered on the Ordnance Survey Map of the said County of all as the said piece of ground is delineated and coloured red on the plan annexed and subscribed as relative hereto;

AND WHEREAS an application has been made to the first party by the second party for permission to erect a dwellinghouse on the said area of ground outlined in red on the plan annexed and executed as relative hereto;

AND WHEREAS the first party are disposed to grant the said planning permission subject to the second party entering into an Agreement with the first party in terms of Section 50 of the Town and Country Planning (Scotland) Act 1972; THEREFORE the parties have agreed and do hereby agree as follows, videlicet:-

(First) The second party hereby undertake that the dwellinghouse to be erected on the said subjects outlined in red on the said plan shall be used in all time coming by a person connected with or employed in agriculture and the dependents of any such person;

(Second) The second party further undertake that the said dwellinghouse shall not be sold in all time coming other than to a person so employed in or connected with agriculture;

The parties hereby agree that in the event of any disputes or differences of opinion arising as to the provisions of these presents or the interpretation thereof, such disputes or differences shall be referred to the Secretary of State for Scotland, or such other person or persons as may be nominated by him, and the decision of the Secretary of State, or his nominee as the case may be, shall be final and binding; But the provisions contained in this clause shall be without prejudice to the right of the first party to enforce these presents or any provision thereof or any condition of the planning permission to be granted in respect of the said dwellinghouse against the second party or anyone deriving title from him;

The second party hereby obliges himself to meet the recording dues of this Agreement and any other outlays and administrative expenses incurred by the first party in connection herewith;

The parties hereby grant consent to registration hereof for preservation and execution as well as for publication.

The demolishers

23.6 The demolishers level the site for the builders. The developer should ensure that the price charged for this service reflects the value of any reusable material on the site, eg tiles, steel, wood, copper etc.

The builders

23.7 The builders are obviously in charge of building work. It is important that they do their work properly and promptly, under the supervision of the architect. The buildings contract is in standard form and should provide that the builders shall pay a penalty for every day late in completion. This should, of course, be a genuine estimate of loss incurred through lack of use, and consequently rental or deemed rental – it must not be merely punitive. Conversely, a bonus may be payable to them if they finish the work early.
Examples of typical, if simplified, clauses are given below:

Penalty (or properly 'liquidate damages') clause. The parties bind themselves and their respective representatives whomsoever to implement and fulfil the whole terms of this agreement, each to the other, under a penalty of £X sterling (or £X per day) to be paid by the party failing, to the party observing or willing to observe his part, and that over and above performance.

Force majeure. The sellers shall not be responsible for prevention or delay in production transport to and delivery into the XY Terminal, storage in the XY Terminal, loading into trucks from XY Terminal, transport to place of delivery of the goods, or any part thereof, whether in country of origin, in XY, in the country of delivery or in transit, occasioned by any executive or legislative act done by or on behalf of any government, act of God, war, blockade, hostilities, strike, lockout, riot, or civil commotion, combination of workmen, breakdown of machinery, fire, floods, earthquakes, or any other causes whatsoever beyond the reasonable control of the sellers or the producer. Sellers shall advise buyers if delivery is prevented or delayed by any such cause and sellers have the option either to cancel the contract or to extend the delivery period by such times as is required to effect delivery.

Arbitration. Any difference or question that may arise between the partners or their representatives or creditors or trustees in bankruptcy as to the meaning of the terms of this agreement, or as to the rights and liabilities of the parties to the agreement, or in the winding up of the partnership, or any other matter or claim relating to or arising out of the partnerships or any affairs thereof, whether during its subsistence, or after its termination, is hereby referred to the arbitration of (here state a person's name or an office-bearer who shall choose an arbiter); (if the arbiter's decision is to be final state here 'the terms of the Administration of Justice (Scotland) 1972 section 3 are hereby excluded from this agreement to arbitration').

Mediation. The parties attempt in good faith to resolve through negotiation any dispute arising out of or relating to the contract. If a dispute shall arise which cannot be resolved between the duty manager and the supervisor, the chief executives of the parties shall attempt in good faith to resolve the dispute. They shall meet within 5 days of the date (the 'breakdown date') of failure of the duty manager and supervisor to resolve the issue and if they are unable to resolve the issue within 10 days of the breakdown date either party may request to resolve the dispute through mediation conducted by a mediator appointed by the Law Society of Scotland by sending a written request to that body with a copy to the other party. The mediation procedure shall be determined by the appointed mediator in consultation with the parties. The fees and expenses of the mediator shall be borne equally by the parties. If the dispute has not been resolved within 14 days of the commencement of the mediation hearings or if no mediation has been commenced within 30 days of the breakdown date the provisions of this clause shall be of no effect.

Whether a dispute is resolved in court, by arbitration or by mediation is the question to be met by the parties. It is as well to think of this at the outset, when the parties are on co-operative terms, rather than when a dispute breaks out and they can't even agree the time of day. Each has its merits, but, on the other hand, court proceedings are perceived to be expensive and too bound up in archaic rituals. Arbitration should be quicker and cheaper, but too often degenerates into a court without gowns. Therefore mediation would seem to be the ideal answer, but the concept has not fully caught on in Scotland yet, although it is enthusiastically used in the United States, and increasingly in England, at the instigation of a Lord Chancellor from the Scottish Bar!

23.8 The letting agents. These may be the same people as the valuation surveyors mentioned earlier, but not necessarily. They obtain tenants for the building. A really clever developer with a good development may 'pre-let' it, that is let it out before it is even complete. This will obviously make the developer's life much easier.

23.9 The tenants. They provide the income which should reward the developer's efforts. Once the development is let, the developer will want as little to do with tenants as possible, and accordingly all maintenance and other obligations are passed to the tenants (see Chapter 22). The only obligation remaining upon the developer then will be to ensure that the rent cheques arrive promptly.

23.10 The fund. The development is now complete, and let. The developer is drawing rents. Developers, as a class, are not collectors of rent. They prefer to develop, sell, and move on to the next development.

On the other hand a good building, full of responsible tenants, all on full repairing leases, and subject to frequent rent reviews and an eventual reversion, presents an admirable investment opportunity to a pension fund or life assurance company with plenty of money to invest in solid investments. The developer therefore sells on to one such, and is happy. The acquiring fund is also happy for it has a sound investment with an attractive yield and prospects of increases. Further, if the leases are properly drawn up, it need never trouble itself with the tenants and can safely leave a managing agent in charge of the building – at the expense of the tenants naturally!

23.11   The development.   Having identified, I hope, the principal players, I would now like to look at the various problems which may face the developer. In the exercise at the end of the chapter, I have sought to provide examples of some of the simpler problems that face the developer.

It is implicit in the developer's job that a messy collection of buildings and pieces of land are acquired and bit by bit a site is assembled for development. This technique is known as 'site assembly' and perhaps the simplest example of this is to be found in the game of Monopoly. You may remember that if you own Fleet Street you can demand a substantial rent; but if you also acquire The Strand and Trafalgar Square, you have all the reds and the rents double. You can then start developing the site, and by the time you have built hotels, the rents are enormous. This is of course a simplification, but I hope you will see the point.

In real life the process is obviously much more complex. Sites have to be assembled laboriously, subject to many conditions of purchase and usually without letting anybody know that the process is going on. If the secret is released, prices will inevitably rise, and as the acquisition is nearly complete, the persons with the 'ransom strip' can demand almost anything they want, as they can otherwise block the development. For this reason the developer has to work in a cunning and covert fashion. Property and interests in property have to be acquired bit by bit, a property here, the landlord's part of a lease there – to await the termination of the lease. Businesses or property companies must be bought for their property content, and be run both to divert suspicion and to provide the developer with a bit of income. Properties must be bought in name of nominees or associated companies.

The properties have to be bought subject to suspensive conditions – conditions that suspend the implement of the agreement until the conditions are met – such as a grant of planning permission or the transfer of a licence, or satisfactory test bores or environmental audit (see **23.4**).

At all time natural caution must be tempered with stealth and it may be that buildings may have to be bought without planning permission, as an application for this might reveal the master plan. Here careful advice on planning is certainly necessary. The duty of the lawyer in site assembly is to obtain for the developer a good and clear title to the entire development, with all third party interests – so far as possible – eradicated.

23.12   The negotiations with the planning authorities do not primarily concern the lawyer, and I shall pass over these, as I will pass over the building of the property. The next problem is therefore to let the building to good tenants. It is a lucky developer who can get a single tenant for the whole development, and most have to be content with a number of tenants, and the standard lease of the development must therefore allow for multi-ownership.

The whole concept of ownership of commercial property subject to tenancies is, as I have attempted to point out, to shift the entire responsibility for the buildings to the tenants. Thus the practice has grown up in commercial leasing for the leases to be on a full repairing, renewing and insuring basis.

Because of the immense power and ability of developers to choose their tenants at leisure, this is generally accepted practice.

You act for a Mr John Buzz, who has been engaged in property development on a small scale for several years. He now informs you that he wants to put through a larger development which will, if successful, provide a sum of money which will enable him to retire. For some months now Mr Buzz has quietly been acquiring a block at the corner of Sardinia Terrace and Lombardy Street (see Plan A attached) which is in a rather run-down part of town, but which is nevertheless near a lot of housing. Mr Buzz has accordingly entered into a tentative agreement to build a supermarket on the cleared site and then to let this to Prontomart Limited, a well-known national supermarket chain (see Plan B attached).

Furthermore, assuming that everything else goes to plan, Mr Buzz has an understanding with the Long Life Assurance Company Limited that it will buy the site as an investment of pension funds, and will therefore then become the landlords of Prontomart.

This will provide Mr Buzz with a sizeable sum which will enable him to retire in some comfort.

There are however a number of problems to be overcome, and you are asked to provide general or specific advice on these:

23.12.1 Referring to Plan A, which shows the existing site, you will notice that there is at the corner of Sardinia Terrace and Lombardy Street a plot of ground with two large trees. These trees are the subject of a Tree Preservation Order under the Town and Country Planning (Scotland) Act 1972, s 58. However, they overhang Lombardy Street, and the falling leaves in autumn make the road slippery. Furthermore, the roots are intruding under Number 1 Sardinia Terrace causing difficulties in the foundations. Advise Mr Buzz as to the possibility of his being allowed to remove these trees legally, and substitute a landscaped area. (Hint: T & CP Act 1972, s 58.)

23.12.2 The bottom floor of the house at Number 1 Sardinia Terrace is a shop which is tenanted by a Mr Hammer. Mr Hammer is opposed to the development as, he says, he will not be able to obtain a new shop property at an equally advantageous rent. Further he says that the new supermarket will ruin his business anyway. Has Mr Hammer any security of tenure? (Hint: Tenancy of Shops (Scotland) Act 1949, as amended.)

23.12.3 Between Numbers 2 and 3 Sardinia Terrace, there runs a right of way to the public park. This is quite extensively used by children from the nearby school as a way to the swings. Mr Buzz wants to build over this right of way, and is quite prepared to provide an alternative route. Can Mr Buzz have the right of way closed? (Hint: T & CP Act 1972, s 203 ff.)

23.12.4 The public house, the Dog and Ferret, has two full-time employees, Ron and Fred (known to the clientele as Fido and Ferdie), whose belligerent and unhelpful attitude has ensured that over the years the public house has not been very successful. Can Mr Buzz ask the seller to dismiss Ron and Fred before Mr Buzz takes over, and, if not, what are Mr Buzz's liabilities in this matter to Ron and Fred? (Hint: see **20.14**).

23.12.5   The superiors are the Diamond Insurance Group, and the title conditions are that the houses shall be used as houses for the occupation of one family only. Some years ago a Minute of Waiver was granted over Number 3 Sardinia Terrace, permitting this to be used as a private nursery school. It has, in fact, never been used as such. Mr Buzz has told the Diamond Insurance Group of his plans, and they have refused to allow the property to be used for the building of a supermarket. Advise Mr Buzz. (Hint: see C & FR(S) Act 1970, s 1.)

23.12.6   The planning department of the district council has told Mr Buzz that if it grants planning permission for the supermarket it would 'very much like' if he would build a public toilet in the position shown on Plan B, while he is building the store. If he agrees to do this, can that agreement be binding on Mr Buzz and his successors? (Hint: see T & CP Act 1972, s 50.)

23.12.7   Advise Mr Buzz on his liability for: (a) stamp duty, (b) capital gains tax, (c) income tax on rental income received prior to the development being started, and (d) VAT on the sales made in the public house and on any commercial rents received. (Hint: see taxation textbook.)

23.12.8   Advise Mr Buzz in general terms on the terms of the lease to be granted by him to Prontomart Limited. (Hint: see Chapter 22.)
      The entire law of landlord and tenant is therefore completely replaced by the terms of the lease. Unlike in England there is no statutory interference with this process, barring the relatively mild security of tenure provisions of the Tenancy of Shops (Scotland) Act 1949, as amended, and the prohibition of automatic irritancies contained in the Law Reform (Miscellaneous Provisions) (Scotland) Act 1985. There is thus no security of tenure beyond the terms of the lease, no machinery for fixing fair rents, and no compensation for improvements made by the tenant. The lawyer for the tenant must therefore proceed with great care and try to get some sort of safeguard for the tenant if at all possible.
      The entire topic of commercial leasing is a complex one, and is dealt with in a general manner in Chapter 22, but for a fuller discussion I can confidently refer you to Ross and McKichan on *The Negotiation and Drafting of Commercial Leases in Scotland* (2nd Edn). Any lawyer who embarks on commercial leasing without reference to this book is either very good or very foolish.

23.13   There follows a fairly simplified example of a succesful site assembly, which hopefully will show some of the problems that can arise.

PLAN A

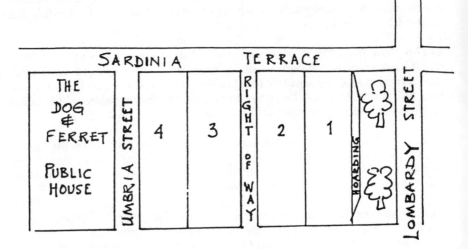

PLAN B

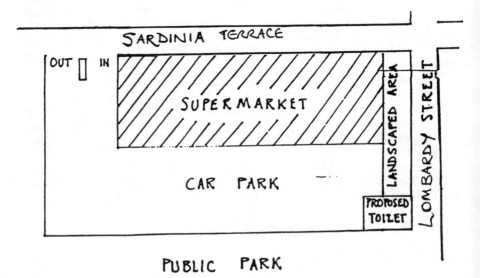

Chapter twenty-four

BUYING FROM A BUILDER

'Despite the land rush last year saw 17,330 new housing starts in Scotland – a 22% increase on the previous year (1993) and a figure which outperformed every other UK region.

'It has been estimated that some 5,000 acres of land in Glasgow is derelict – some 9% of all the land within the city boundary ... a higher spend on decontamination and site preparation would unlock new sites, strengthen urban communities and ease the pressure on the green belt. And we would not need so many motorways.' (Stewart McIntosh – *The Herald* 1995)

24.1 We have until now been discussing the purchase of 'second-hand' housing. Your clients may well wish to buy a new house, and the procedure is similar, but there are some very important differences; for a start, the purchasers usually have almost no bargaining power, and have to sign a printed missive, produced by the builder, and not susceptible to any alterations, other than very minor ones. The terms of this agreement favour the builder, not unnaturally, and it behoves the solicitor to make sure that the settlement takes place on the date when it is agreed, otherwise strict penalties are incurred.

24.2 Before entering into an agreement, the purchasers should ensure that the houses are not built on an environmentally unsound site. This may sound rather dramatic, but there have been numerous instances of builders, even in good faith, building on sites which latterly turn out to be heavily contaminated. It should be said that local authorities are now much more vigilant in this respect, and gradually will not grant planning permission if the site is environmentally unsound. The following case was cited in a pamphlet entitled 'Buyer Beware!' published by Friends of the Earth:

'57 families were evacuated from a housing estate in Portsmouth. The families were given 24 hours to leave their homes after dangerous levels of asbestos were found in air and soil samples. The houses had been built on a former Ministry of Defence landfill site. The landfill had been covered with clean topsoil to prevent contamination but the capping proved inadequate.'

Potentially contaminative uses of the land are as follows: agricultural, extractive industry, energy industry, production of metals, production of non-metals and their products, glass-making and ceramics, production and use of chemicals, engineering and manufacturing processes, food processing industry, paper, pulp and printing industry, textile industry, rubber industry, infrastructure, waste disposal, gas work sites, landfill sites, metal industries, sewage works and sludge tips, chemical works, docks and wharfs, tar, oil and petroleum depots, scrap yards, tanneries, railway sidings and depots. For further details see the pamphlet mentioned above – 'Buyer Beware!'.

Even when the site appears to be an attractive 'green field' site, it should be remembered that it may have been used for some other purpose in the past, particularly in war time. The history of 'brown field' sites – that is sites that have been previously occupied – should always be carefully checked. Unfortunately plans for district councils to maintain a register of contaminated land within their district were abandoned.

The builders should be able to provide sufficient evidence of the prior uses of the land, or treatment that has been done to the site, but if they do not, certain information as to past uses can be obtained from the local library, or from asking a specialist surveyor or planning consultant to investigate the history of the land. The conveyancer may also be able to shed some light from the title deeds, but the ironic aspect of land registration is that the whole purpose of the land certificate is *not* to give the history of the title. Therefore if you wish to find out who owned the site in years gone by, investigations have to be made in the old Sasine Register.

If your clients cannot be satisfied as to the prior uses of the site by the information given by the builders, or from their own enquiries, they are better not to purchase. The purchase may prove to be an unpleasant one, and the house may eventually turn out to be unsaleable. Prospective buyers should also make enquiries about any history of flooding in low lying areas.

24.3 The typical builders' missive describes a property, and the description of the property should be checked, and in particular the boundaries of the property. In land registration areas, considerable difficulty has been caused to the Keeper by properties not being laid out as they were stated to be in estate plans submitted to the Keeper prior to sales. For this reason, land certificates of new houses are often delayed until all the land certificates in the site are prepared, so that they can be fully consistent with each other. The plan of the house should not be a standard estate plan, with the relevant house coloured in – this is not sufficient for land registration, and remember that the whole country will be subject to land registration by 2003.

The standard for descriptions is stated in an article by Alistair Rennie, the Deputy Keeper, in the January 1995 JLSS 16, where it is suggested that the appropriate obligation should read:

'In exchange for the price the seller will deliver a duly executed disposition in favour of the purchaser and will exhibit or deliver a valid marketable title together with a Form 10 Report brought down to a date as near as practicable to the date of settlement and showing no entries adverse to the seller's interest, the cost of said report being the responsibilty of the seller. In addition, the seller, at or before the date of entry and at his expense, shall deliver to the purchaser such documents and evidence as the Keeper may require to enable the Keeper to issue a land certificate in the name of the purchaser as the registered proprietor of the whole subjects of offer and containing no exclusion of indemnity in terms of section 12(2) of the Land Registration (Scotland) Act 1979: such documents shall include (unless the whole subjects of offer only comprise part of a tenement or flatted building) a plan or bounding description sufficient to enable the whole subjects of offer to be identified on the Ordnance map and evidence (such as a Form P16 Report) that the description of the whole subjects of offer as contained in the title deed is *habile* to include the whole of the occupied extent. The land certificate to be issued to the purchaser will disclose no entry, deed or diligence preju- dicial to the purchaser's interest other than such as are created by or against the purchaser prior to the date of settlement. Notwithstanding the delivery of the disposition above referred to this clause shall remain in full force and effect and may be founded upon.'

Builders' solicitors may be reluctant to give such an obligation, but this is the standard of information that should be provided in every case.

24.4 The price is stated, and the date of entry is given, not as a precise date, but as the date on which it is certified as complete. A small deposit may be payable upon signing of missives, which deposit is subtracted from the final purchase price. It is generally provided that the settlement shall be by tele- graphic transfer, and if the purchaser fails to make payment, interest is payable at a commercial price on the balance outstanding. After a certain time the contract may be brought to an end by the builder. No partial pay- ment of the price is generally permitted, and the keys are not available until full settlement is made.

24.5 The offer states briefly the principal feuing conditions, such as reserva- tion of minerals, use of the house and garden, formation of roads, fencing, provisions as to the ownership, use and maintenance of open amenity spaces, reservation of servitude and wayleave rights for mains services, and the usual obligations of the seller in sasine and land register transactions. To avoid disputes arising this selection of conditions is stated to be 'without prejudice to the generality' – which is that the conditions to be included in the feu grant shall be 'in conformity with similar titles given off on this and other of (the builders') estates and will be subject to a deed of conditions contain- ing such conditions as (the builders) consider appropriate for the preserva- tion of amenity.' A deed of conditions is prepared in terms of the Conveyancing (Scotland) Act 1924, s 9, and lays down the standard condi- tions for the whole estate. The feu grant can therefore be kept relatively short, because it refers to the deed of conditions for the conditions contained.

24.6 The builders will usually apply for and warrant that necessary plan- ning permissions, building warrants and the like have been obtained, but will not give an obligation to produce these. Furthermore, the superior's con- sent should also be obtained, particularly where an older building has been knocked down or converted, as there may be an old feuing condition that is inconsistent with the modern use.

The builders however give an obligation to produce a completion or habi- tation certificate from the local authority. Settlement should not be made until this is exhibited, and the transfer from builder to purchaser is available for delivery. (See *Gibson & Hunter Home Designs Ltd* 1976 SC 23 for a case when it was not, and the terrible consequences that flowed from this failure, both for the purchaser who lost the house and the money, and for the legal profession generally.)

24.7   The builders will reserve the right to vary the building materials to materials of a similar specification, in accordance with the circumstances, without affecting the price.

24.8   All extras on the building price, such as additional fittings to the basic specification, should be carefully checked, as should all discounts and incentives offered, in order that the purchasers may comply with the conditions for obtaining these.

24.9   The provision of searches in the Sasines Register is similar to the normal obligation, but the builders will not continue the search to disclose any security created by the purchasers. In land registration cases, the obligation is the same as is normally given.

24.10   The builders will give a probable completion date, but they will not warrant this, nor pay any sort of damages if this date is not met. Thus a penalty clause and a *force majeure* clause is not appropriate, which would force the builders to pay damages if the house is not ready by a certain date, but exempting the builders for any failure caused by certain events such as war or strikes.

24.11   Larger builders are usually members of the National House Building Council, and as such offer an NHBC Certificate to cover the house against defects arising over a ten-year period (see **7.33**). A small builder may not be a member of the NHBC, which implies no disrespect, in which case a certificate of inspection will be produced from the independent architect who supervised the development, stating that the development is complete in accordance with the plans. The architect should possess full indemnity insurance cover, in the event that a mistake is made.

24.12   When a purchase is made from a large builder, a 'package' is being bought and stamp duty is payable on the total price of the heritage, less any moveable items included.

When a plot is bought separately, and a house is then later built on it, stamp duty is broadly only payable on the purchase of the land. Thus if a plot is bought at £20,000 and a house is then built on it at a price of £50,000, stamp duty would only be payable on the price of the plot. As the current threshold for stamp duty is £60,000, there is therefore no stamp duty, instead of £700, which would have been payable if the items had been purchased simultaneously.

This useful device must not, however, be used artificially, and the Stamp Office has produced a statement of practice (SP 10/87 of 22.11.87) restating the Inland Revenue's views on this matter.

In the purchase of a new house each party will generally pay their own fees, but certain builders may offer incentives, including a contribution to the purchasers' fees. This should be carefully checked.

APPENDICES

APPENDICES

Appendix I

A PURCHASE OF PROPERTY IN 1994 (GENERAL REGISTER OF SASINES)

1 Letter from George Gizzard to Henry Pink (15 August 1994)

123 Chancery Row,
LONDON.

15 August 1994

GG/BP/P60

Henry Pink, Esq,
Solicitor,
42 Registration Row,
GLASGOW.

DEAR HENRY,

James and Jane Meikle

You may remember that we met at the Final of the Black Country Building Society Golf Competition at Lytham in the summer.

I wonder if you would look after young friends of mine, James and Jane Meikle, who are being sent to Edinburgh by their firm. They are looking for a house, not too far from the city centre, but with a bit of a garden.

I gather that the Meikles have spoken to 'the Black Country' and they are quite happy to finance them in Scotland. They should have a good amount from the sale of their house and should be looking for a house around the £60,000 bracket.

Can you please confirm that you can act in Edinburgh and will help them, and I shall then give them your name and address.

I hope you are keeping well, and perhaps I will see you again next summer. I hear the Final is at Turnberry next year.

Yours sincerely,

GEORGE GIZZARD (signed)

Note: This letter is an introduction only, and while it gives some idea of the Meikles' financial status, Gizzard does not risk any personal liability if the Meikles default. If solicitors instruct others to act on behalf of their clients, there is a duty on the instructing solicitors to meet the second solicitors' fees, if the clients don't. (See Solicitors (Scotland) Act 1980, s 30 – while this Act refers specifically to Scottish solicitors, morally the stipulation also covers other solicitors, et cetera.) Gizzard is much too wily to fall into that trap. Pink should consider checking for possible money laundering, but the Meikles are borrowing most of the money from the building society, and the balance is coming from their sale through Gizzard.

Please note that Gizzard maintains a happy relationship with at least one building society – this is always a good idea.

2   Letter from Henry Pink to George Gizzard (16 August 1994)

42 Registration Row,
GLASGOW.

HP/PH/C1234

16 August 1994

George Gizzard Esq,
Messrs Gizzard, Gullet & Co,
123 Chancery Row,
LONDON.

DEAR GEORGE,

Thank you for your letter of 15 August. It was pleasant to hear from you again.

I shall be pleased to act for the Meikles, would confirm that I can deal in Edinburgh, and am obliged to you for the introduction. Can you please ask them to telephone me to discuss tactics?

I doubt if I shall qualify for the Golf Trophy next year or indeed any other year. I am playing so badly that I wish I could get my slice back!

Yours sincerely,

HENRY PINK (signed)

Note: A firm, instant reply that says all that requires to be said. It is imperative that Pink should meet the Meikles to ascertain their finances, bona fides et cetera before becoming their solicitor and lending the firm's name to the Meikles' contracts.

There are also one or two other things that are different between Scotland and England that require to be explained, particularly the Scottish practice of completing a binding preliminary contract, as opposed to the English practice of having a non-binding preliminary contract.

It was formerly the custom for English solicitors introducing business to Scottish solicitors to claim 'agency' – that is a percentage of the fee in respect of the instructions – and vice versa.

While one cannot be definite, I think this practice has more or less come to an end. There is certainly no mention of the question here.

3   Minute of meeting between Mr Pink and Mr and Mrs Meikle – 19 August 1994

Meeting the Meikles and noting that they had selected a number of houses from *The Scotsman* to look at, and discussing these in light of their requirements.

(Engaged 30 minutes)

Note: It is a feature of Mr Pink's business that he keeps clear notes of all meetings and telephone calls. This is a practice that cannot be praised too highly, due to the general fallibity of the human memory. As the work is charged on a 'time spent and work done' basis (see Appendix 1.39) it is obviously a useful practice to record time spent at such meetings.

4   Note of telephone conversation between Mr Pink and Mr Meikle (1 September 1994)

Noting that the Meikles liked the house at 3 Barrie Drive, Edinburgh, being sold by Messrs Able, Grand, Brain & Co. This was around their price bracket and they wanted to bid about £60,000 for the house and about another £2,000 for carpets and curtains.

Explaining to Mr Meikle the incidence of stamp duty and that they would not be liable for stamp duty if they kept the price at £60,000 maximum, but there was no liability for duty on the moveables.

Noting entry to be 31 October 1994. Further noting that the title is to be in joint names. Explaining in detail the advantages of a 'survivorship' destination, and being instructed to take one.

(Engaged 10 minutes)

Note: This letter quotes stamp duty rates in force in 1994.

5   Note of telephone conversation between Mr Pink and Messrs Able, Grand, Brain & Co (1 September 1994)

Intimating to Mrs Brain the Meikles' interest in the property at 3 Barrie Drive, and noting that no closing date fixed yet.

Obtaining details of council tax band and agreeing moveables to be contained in offer. Asking for details of the house to be sent as soon as possible. Noting that these would be sent this morning by FAX.

Stating that we would send a surveyor from the Black Country Building Society, who would telephone Mr and Mrs McAllister, the sellers, first.

(Engaged 5 minutes)

6   Note of telephone conversation between Mr Pink and Mr Burslem of the Black Country Building Society (1 September 1994)

Informing Mr Burslem that the Meikles had now found the house that they wanted, and asking for a survey to be done forthwith. Noting that this would be done by Mr Hanley.

We would ask the Meikles to call this afternoon at the society to sign application forms et cetera.

(Engaged 5 minutes)

7   Note of telephone conversation between Mr Pink to Mr Meikle (1 September 1994)

Telling Mrs Meikle what we had done, and asking them to go to building society to complete application form.

Discussing different kinds of mortgages available to them, and suggesting that, in light of the possibility of their moving in two years, and having good incomes and substantial pension plans, the pension fund method would probably be slightly better for them than the endowment or repayment methods.

Reminding them forcefully that they should cover the amount of the loan under a s 226A policy, which would repay the loan if one or other died prematurely, without affecting the death benefit payable under the pension scheme.

(Engaged 15 minutes)

Note: A brisk flurry of work to lay groundwork for the offer. Note the wide range of impartial advice given in these entries by the solicitors. The firm is, of course, authorised by the Law Society to give financial advice.

8   Details of house received from Able, Grand, Brain & Co (2 September 1994)

Messrs Able, Grand, Brain & Co,
Solicitors,
109 Sasine Place,
EDINBURGH EH 1 XY.   Ref: Mrs Brain

DX ED 444

Telephone No: 0131–222–3333 (8 lines)

Particulars of semi- detached villa at 3 Barrie Drive,
Edinburgh.

Seller:	Mr and Mrs McAllister
Viewing:	by arrangement through Messrs Able, Grand, Brain & Co.
Price:	Offers around £60,000
Entry:	Around end of October/early November
Council Tax band:	D
Feuduty:	£5 per annum to be redeemed by seller.

This is a pleasant mordern house, built around 1953 by
Millhaugh Developments Co Ltd in the grounds of a man-
sion house. Secluded garden, garage and outhouse.
Convenient for shops, transport and schools.

Gas-fired cental heating, carpets, curtains and blinds are
for sale, which are of the highest quality.

Accommodation

Ground Floor

Hall: With small cloakroom off with w.c. and w.h.b. c/h
radiators (2). Fitted carpets.

Lounge: Airy and spacious room with feature fireplace.
c/h radiators (2). Fitted carpets.

Dining Room: Another spacious public room with double
glazed sliding doors to patio and rear garden. Wall
lights. c/h radiator. Fitted carpets.

Study: Small, comfortable room, which can be used as
a 'snug' in winter. Ample shelving for books. c/h
radiator. Fitted carpets.

Kitchen: Fully modernised kitchen with built-in
Pollywolly hob and split level oven. Kitchen is connected to dining room and has ample cupboards and

work tops. Venetian blinds and extractor fan. c/h radiator and 8 × 13 amp power points. New vinyl flooring.

<u>Note</u> The washing machine and dishwasher are not included in the sale of the house and will be removed by the seller.

<u>First Floor</u>

<u>Bedroom 1.</u>   Faces to east for morning sunshine. Fitted wardrobes. c/h radiator. Fitted carpets. Bathroom with shower en suite.

<u>Bedroom 2.</u>   Double size. Some fitted wardrobes. c/h radiator. Fitted carpets.

<u>Bedroom 3.</u>   Small room with cam-ceiling. Suitable for child's bedroom or playroom. c/h radiator and fitted carpet.

<u>Bedroom 4.</u>   A good single bedroom with c/h radiator and fitted carpet.

<u>Bathroom:</u>   Coloured suite. Vinyl tiled floor. Half tiled walls. Medicine chest. Heated towel rail. Bath, w.c., w.h.b. and bidet.

All offers for the property should be made to Messrs Able, Grand, Brain & Co, from whom further details are also available.

<u>Note</u> The above details are believed to be correct, but their accuracy is not warranted.

Note: Slightly laconic details, compared to some, but they do tell you all you need to know without breaking into purple prose. They presumably do not offend against the Property Misdescriptions Act (see Chapter 2). Measurements of rooms may be inserted, but unless strictly accurate that can be dangerous. The principal difficulty is that measurements tend to be given in feet and inches, while carpets are supplied in metres. Note the disclaimer at the end, but the law of misrepresentation still applies in exaggerated cases of misstatement. Note how items which might or might not be included in the sale are clearly dealt with. This is an admirable practice.

It is appreciated that even in the hard days of 1994, a semi-detached house in Edinburgh would probably cost more than £60,000, but this price is chosen to expain the point about stamp duty.

9   Note of telephone call Mr Burslem to Mr Pink (2 September 1994)

Mr Burslem of Black Country Building Society phoned to say survey was clear, and they were prepared to lend Mr Meikle £40,000 on security of house at 3 Barrie Drive. Mr Hanley, the surveyor, had commented critically on the state of the outside woodwork, and suggested that this be painted forthwith to prevent rot.

(5 Minutes)

10 Note of telephone call Mr Pink to Mrs Meikle (2 September 1994)

Informing Mrs Meikle of results of survey and obtaining their go-ahead to lodge offer as arranged. Explaining that, although the survey report was intended to be helpful to purchasers, this survey was principally for the benefit of the building society, and that if they wished further details they should instruct their own structural survey. Noting that they were prepared to take the risk of not obtaining a full structural survey.

(12 Minutes)

Note: The correct way in which Mr Pink has given all the details to the Meikles, and obtained clear instructions to proceed. Never forget that the client is the person who pays the price!

11 Offer by Messrs Brown, Jarvie & Walker on behalf of Mr & Mrs Meikle

42 Registration Row,
GLASGOW.

3 September 1994

Messrs Able, Grand, Brain & Co,
Solicitors,
109 Sasine Place,
EDINBURGH EH1 XYZ

DEAR SIRS

On behalf of our clients, James and Jane Meikle, residing at 300 Brookmans Ave, Brookmans Park ('the purchasers'), we hereby offer to purchase from your clients, Mr and Mrs McAllister, ('the sellers'), that semi-detached dwelling house at and forming Number 3 Barrie Drive, Edinburgh, ('the subjects of sale') with the garden ground effeiring thereto, the garage and outbuildings thereon, the whole heritable fittings and fixtures in and about the premises and with all rights and pertinents, on the following terms and conditions, namely:

(1) The price shall be SIXTY TWO THOUSAND POUNDS (£62,000) ('the price') payable on the date of entry here-

inafter mentioned, which price shall include the items contained in condition (2) hereof.

(2) The price includes all fitted carpets, curtains, blinds, curtain rods and rails and electric fittings, including all bulbs and bulbholders, and ornamental wall lights in the hall. It is understood that the value of £2,000 shall be allocated to these items. The sale shall also include the following items, insofar as they are in existence in the subjects – all non-carpet floorcoverings, curtain rails, rods and pelmets, all door handles and door knobs, all light flexes, bulbs and bulbholders, shades and ceiling roses, all fluorescent light castings, the door bell and burglar alarm system, all decorative panels, mirrors, shelves, cabinets, towel rails, furniture shelves, fire surrounds, other units and accessories to the extent that they are presently attached or fixed to the floors, ceilings or walls, all stair clips, rods and eyes, all gas fires, storage heaters, fireplaces and grates, all fitted units, cupboards, sinks, water closets, baths, showers, bidets and other sanitary ware, all built in wardrobes and cupboards, all television and radio aerials and satellite dishes, all venetian, roller and other blinds, all central heating systems and plant, all plants, trees, shrubs, stock and ornaments in the garden and common areas generally, all boundary walls, fencing and gates, all garages, garden huts and outhouses.

(a) It is warranted that the said items belong absolutely to the sellers and none is subject to any hire purchase, leasing, loan or other similar agreement.

(b) The central heating system (if any), burglar alarm system (if any), and any electronically operated and/or mechanically operated items among the said items will be in good working order at the date of entry. The purchasers shall be entitled to inspect any of these items in the seven days prior to the date of entry to satisfy themselves as to their condition. If not in good working order at or before the date of entry, the sellers will be solely responsible for having them put into such order, provided that notice of the defects is given within seven days of the date of entry.

(3) The conditions contained in Schedules I & II hereto are to be read as an integral part of this offer, so far as applicable to property of this nature.

(4) With prejudice to the generality of the terms of this offer, your clients will exhibit all necessary permissions and guarantees for refurbishment and reconstruction works, if any.

(5) Entry and actual vacant possession will be given on 31 October 1994 or such other or earlier date as may be agreed between the parties ('the date of entry').

(6) The Council Tax Band is Band 'D', and the annual allocated feu duty is £5, which shall be redeemed by your clients in terms of Section 5 of the Land Tenure Reform Act, 1974.

(7) This offer, unless previously withdrawn, will remain open for acceptance reaching us here no later than 1 pm on Monday, 6 September 1994.

Yours faithfully,

'ADOPTED AS HOLOGRAPH
BROWN, JARVIE & WALKER'

(Note: ADD SCHEDULES I and II AT THIS POINT. To keep this book within a human scale these are not printed in full. They would be similar to the material contained in Appendix II.11.)

Notes (1) Please note the 'labelling' of the principal features of offer. This practice makes the offer very much easier to produce, and also the labels are totally self-explanatory. When labelling, please avoid ambiguous monstrosities like 'party of the first part'.

(2) Note the elaborate specification of what is included in the sale. This is to spell out to the sellers what it is intended that they should leave. Most of these items are, in fact, heritable, and should be left anyway, but some people will try to remove as much as they can. This will not stop them, of course, but at least it spells out unambiguously what should be left, and makes a court action for recovery relatively easy.

(3) Note the provision for the central heating. This is designed to prevent the following – the central heating was installed some years ago; it has never been maintained; it is dangerous; it is inspected after entry, and a claim is lodged with the sellers; it emerges that the sellers have disappeared with the money. For that reason I always suggest that the heating be inspected before the date of entry, preferably by a heating engineer, and the cost of repairs is withheld from the purchase price. Not everyone would agree with this course.

(4) The Council Tax Band 'D' is for properties valued at £45,000–£58,000 on 1 April 1991.

(5) This offer is made prior to the enactment of the Requirements of Writing (Scotland) Act 1995, and the letter is therefore 'adopted as holograph'.

12 Note of telephone call Mrs Brain to Mr Pink (13 September 1994)

Noting offer appeared to be acceptable but sellers had gone away for the weekend and instructions could not be obtained. It might therefore be difficult to comply with the time limit which would therefore be deleted along with other small qualifications relating to payment of interest at overdraft rate and the redemption of feuduty.

(10 Minutes)

Note: The sellers' solicitors should always try to discuss any revisions they propose to make with the purchasers' solicitors. This communication is frequently made by FAX nowadays.

13 Telephone call Mr Pink to Mr Meikle (3 September 1994)

Informing Mr Meikle of telephone call and probable acceptance of offer, but cautioning that nothing was concluded until written acceptance received.

Noting that Mr and Mrs Meikle would stand Mr Pink a lunch and bottle of champagne if they got the house! Agreeing a fee with Mr Meikle.

Note: It is totally correct to keep the clients informed, and considerate not to keep them in the dark, over a weekend particularly.

The display of bonhomie from the clients is typical at the time of triumph. It doesn't usually last. Now is the perfect time to talk to the clients about fees or any other matter that may not be so easy to broach at a later date.

14 Sending copy of offer to Mr and Mrs Meikle with a short covering letter (3 September 1994)

Note: The letter merely confirms the telephone call and is short and to the point. It is of course sent by first class post, like all important documents. The old cliché, about not spoiling the ship for a halfpennyworth of tar, applies at this stage.

15 Formal letter of acceptance of offer subject to qualifications
(7 September 1982)

109 Sasine Place,
EDINBURGH.

6 September 1994

Messrs, Brown, Jarvie & Walker,
Solicitors,
42 Registration Row,
GLASGOW.

DX GW 1002

DEAR SIRS,

On behalf of our clients, Alistair and Fiona McAllister, residing at
3 Barrie Drive, Glasgow, we hereby accept your offer of 3
September, 1994 to purchase the detached dwelling house, 3
Barrie Drive aforesaid with the ground effeiring thereto, the
garage and outbuildings thereon, the heritable fittings and fixtures in and about the premises and with all rights and pertinents on the terms and conditions therein stated, but subject to
the following qualifications, namely:

(1) Payment of the purchase price in full on the date of entry,
     as stated in our offer, are of the essence of the contract. In
     the event of the purchase price or any part thereof remain-
     ing outstanding as at the date of entry then, notwithstanding
     consignation or the fact that entry has not been taken by the
     purchasers, the purchasers shall be deemed to be in material
     breach of contract and that whether our clients have offered
     vacant possession except as against payment of the full pur-
     chase price any interest due as aftermentioned. In the event
     of failure to pay the purchase price or any part thereof as
     aforesaid interest will accrue in favour of our clients at the
     rate of 5 per cent per annum above the Bank of Scotland
     base lending rate from time to time from the date of entry
     until full payment of the purchase price is made, or in the
     event of our clients exercising the option to rescind the con-
     tract until such time as our clients shall have completed a
     resale of the subjects and received the resale price; and, fur-
     ther, interest shall run on any shortfall between the pur-
     chaser price hereunder and the resale price until such time
     as the shortfall shall have been paid to our clients.

     In the event that the said purchase price is not paid in full
     within fourteen days of the said date of entry the sellers
     shall be entitled to treat the purchasers as being in material
     breach of contract as aforesaid and our clients shall be enti-
     tled, but not bound, to rescind the missives in giving prior

written notice to that effect to the purchases at any time after expiry of the said fourteen-day period. In the event of our clients exercising their option to rescind then our clients shall be entitled to proceed to resell and a rescission by our clients shall be entirely without prejudice to our clients' right to claim damages from the purchasers for the material breach of contract and, without prejudice to the generality of our clients' right to claim damages computed in accordance with the law of damages, under the following heads of claim:

(a) Any capital loss sustained by our clients on the resale of the property being the difference between the purchase price under these missives and the resale price under any such resale.

(b) Any estate agency marketing or other advertising expenses properly incurred in connection with the resale.

(c) Any legal expenses properly incurred in connection with the resale.

(d) Any expenses in connection with cancellation of removal of furniture, storage of furniture and transfer or retransfer of furniture incurred as a result of the purchasers' breach of contract.

(e) Interest at the rate of 5 per cent above the Bank of Scotland base lending rate from time to time on the purchase price in terms of these missives or on such part of said purchase price as has not been paid to our client either by the purchasers or as a result of any resale from the date of entry hereunder until our clients shall have received payment of the whole purchase price from said resale or from the purchasers in the event of your clients requiring to make up a shortfall by way of damages.

(f) Reimbursement of the arrangement fee payable to the Bank in respect of any overdraft necessarily arranged as a result of your clients' failure to honour the contract.

The damages which may be claimed by our clients by law or by virtue of this clause shall be deemed to be exigible by our clients notwithstanding that they may exercise their option to rescind the contract and for this purpose our clients' claim to interest as part of these damages under sub-paragraph (e) of this clause.

The provisions of this clause shall not have effect in any period during which the delay in settlement of the purchase price is the fault of the sellers or their agents.

This clause shall be deemed as the ruling clause in the event of any discrepancy between it and any other clause herein or in your offer.

(2) Clauses 8 and 17 are deleted as no such works have been carried out.

(3) While the position stated in the relevant clauses of your offer are believed to be correct, the sellers shall not be obliged to obtain any certification from the Superior or co-proprietors in respect of title conditions or alterations, nor from the Regional Council in respect of the roads, pavements, water supply and sewers. In the event that the roads and footpaths *ex adverso* the subjects have not been taken by the Local Authority, there are no outstanding liabilities in respect of same.

(4) The feuduty has been redeemed and a receipt for the redemption will be delivered at settlement.

(5) The time limit contained in the said Offer is deleted.

Yours faithfully,

'ADOPTED AS HOLOGRAPH
ABLE, GRAND, BRAIN & CO'

Note: The interest clause takes up most of the acceptance, thanks to the case of *Lloyd's Bank*. The remainder is a tidying up exercise. So commonly used is the interest clause that it would seem to be sensible for it to be in the offer, but old habits die hard.

16   Note of telephone call Mr Pink to Mr Meikle (7 September 1994)

Informing Mr Meikle that the copy offer had been faxed to them at business and that acceptance has been received. Explaining that the clause about mineral rights is a mere technicality and that it does not mean that they are liable to have people digging coal in their back garden. Obtaining instructions to conclude the agreement.

(Engaged 10 Minutes)

Note: Again, the facts are presented clearly to the clients, and instructions obtained. The 'minerals' clause always causes difficulty to the public – it is high time that the suggestion of the Halliday Committee, that the necessity be dropped **(3.31)**, is implemented.

17 Formal acceptance of qualifications and conclusions of agreement by purchasers' solicitors to sellers' solicitors (7 September 1994)

42 Registration Row,
GLASGOW.

7 September 1994

Messrs Able, Grand, Brain & Co,
Solicitors,
109 Sasine Place,
EDINBURGH

Dear Sirs

On behalf of our clients, we hereby accept the qualifications contained in your qualified acceptance of 6 September 1994 of our offer to purchase the subjects at 3 Barrie Drive, Glasgow, and now hold the bargain concluded.

Yours faithfully,

'ADOPTED AS HOLOGRAPH
BROWN, JARVIE & WALKER'

Note: This letter concludes the agreement, and displays completed *consensus in idem*. The word 'bargain' is a legal word – it does not indicate that either side has got a bargain. Better not to use it, in case of misunderstandings with clients?

18   Letter by Mr Pink faxed to Mr and Mrs Meikle (7 September 1994)

42 Registration Row,
GLASGOW.

HP/MM/M231   7 September 1994

James and Jane Meikle,
Crisp Computers Limited,
321 Tel-el-Kebir Street,
GLASGOW.

FAX 0141-777-1234

DEAR MR and MRS MEIKLE,

<u>3 Barrie Drive, Edinburgh</u>

I now enclose a copy of the acceptance of your offer, subject to certain qualifications which we discussed, and of our acceptance of these qualifications on your behalf. This now concludes the agreement between you and the McAllisters for the purchase of this house.

I would confirm that this is now a binding contract on both parties and is not 'subject to contract'.

Will you please tell the Black Country Building Society that you have bought the house, and ask them to process the loan?

I shall contact you again as and when necessary.

Yours sincerely,

H. PINK

Note: Not every firm would favour the personal approach of this letter as opposed to a formal business letter but the former has become quite common practice in the last few years. You would obviously adhere to firm's practice here, as in all other things.

Apart from that, this letter leaves the Meikles exactly in the picture. In the unlikely event of the Meikles claiming that Pink acted contrary to instructions, Pink has plenty on file to prove the contrary. The importance of recording one's conversations, et cetera, cannot be over-stressed. The proof is any such action would probably be in 12 to 18 months' time, by which time the memory has faded to an almost calamitous extent.

'Subject to contract' is an English term indicating that the contract is non-binding. This should always be explained to clients coming from England.

19   Letter from Able, Grand, Brain & Co to Brown, Jarvie & Walker sending title deeds et cetera (9 September 1982)

109 Sasine Place,
EDINBURGH.

9 September 1994

Messrs, Brown, Jarvie & Walker,
Solicitors,
42 Registration Row,
GLASGOW.

DEAR SIRS

<u>Mr and Mrs McAllister</u>
<u>Mr and Mrs Meikle</u>
<u>3 Barrie Drive, Edinburgh</u>

We now enclose the Title Deeds of the property, as shown in the inventory enclosed in duplicate. Please receipt one copy of the inventory and return it to us.

We also enclose draft Discharge of a Security, draft Letter of Obligation, and draft Memorandum for Continuation of Search. As our clients are a married couple, no matrimonial affidavit is required.

We shall be pleased to hear from you.

Yours faithfully,

ABLE, GRAND, BRAIN & CO.

20 Enclosures

(a) Inventory of writs

INVENTORY OF WRITS

of

3 BARRIE DRIVE,
EDINBURGH.

1   Feu Contract between Alpin McAlpine and another and Hugh
     McHugh and recorded GRS (Glasgow) 3 February 1884.

2   Disposition by John Evans and Gareth Evans, Trustees of
     Evan Evans in favour of Millhaugh Development Co Ltd
     dated 3 et cetera and recorded said GRS 24 June 1952.

3   Feu Charter by Millhaugh Development Co Ltd in favour of
     Gregor McGregor dates 3rd July and recorded said GRS 10
     July 1953.

4   Extract Registered Trust Disposition and Settlement of
     Gregor McGregor dated 5 July 1965 and registered said BCS
     10 July 1953.

5   Certificate of Confirmation in favour of Donald McDonald
     dated 4 October 1978 with dockets in favour of William
     McWilliam dated 10 November 1978, all registered BCS 25
     November 1978.

6   Notice of Title in favour of William McWilliam recorded said
     GRS 3 March 1979.

7   Disposition by William McWilliam to Alistair and Fiona
     McAllister dated 3rd June and recorded said GRS 16 June
     1981.

8   Standard Security by Alistair and Fiona McAllister to Ben
     Wyvis Building Society recorded said GRS 16 June 1981.

9   Certificate from Lothian Regional Council as to roads, et
     cetera dated 13 September 1985 and as to water et cetera
     dated 25 September 1985.

10   Certificate from City of Edinburgh District Council re plan-
     ning dated 5 August 1994.

11   Feu-duty Redemption Receipt by Millhaugh Development Co
     Ltd, dated 19 June 1981.

(b)   Draft memorandum for continuation of search

MEMORANDUM FOR CONTINUATION OF SEARCH
against
3 BARRIE DRIVE,
GLASGOW.

Search:

(1)   In the Register for the County of Midlothian from 17 June
1981 to date to disclose recording of
(1)   Discharge by Ben Wyvis Building Society
(2)   Disposition by Alistair and Fiona McAllister to James
and Jane Meikle
*(3)   **Standard Security by James and Jane Meikle in favour
of Black Country Building Society.***

(2)   In the Personal Register against
(1)   Alistair and Fiona McAllister, residing formerly at 173
Cathedral Street, Glasgow, and now at 3 Barrie Drive,
Edinburgh from 17 June 1981 to date of Sasine
Certificate
and
*(2)   **James and Jane Meikle residing at 300**   **approved
Brookmans Avenue, Brookmans Park,**   **BJ & W**
Hertfordshire, for
Five years to date of Sasine Certificate.*

***SEARCH ALSO REQUESTED IN THE COMPUTERISED PRESENT-
MENT BOOK***
Interim Report and Account requested by return.

Note: The words in bold italic represent the amendments made by the purchasers' agents on behalf of the purchasers and the building society.

Search in the computerised presentment book which provides a relatively
up-to-date search. This is not indemnified by the Keeper. (See Appendix
I.35(a).)

(c)   Draft letter of obligation

ABLE, GRAND, BRAIN & COMPANY,
Solicitors,
109 Sasine Place,
EDINBURGH.

Messrs Brown, Jarvie & Walker,
Solicitors,
42 Registration Row,
GLASGOW.

DEAR SIRS,

Mr Alistair and Mrs Fiona McAllister
Mr James and Mrs Jane Meikle
3 Barrie Drive, Edinburgh

With reference to the settlement of this transaction today, we hereby undertake *(1)* to deliver to you within twelve months following the date hereof Searches in the Property Register and Personal Register duly brought down to the date fourteen days after the date hereof in terms of the Memorandum thereof adjusted between us which searches shall be (a) clear of any entry deed or diligence which is either prejudicial to the validity of or is an encumbrance upon the title of our clients and (b) will disclose the disposition or other deed in favour of your client provided it is recorded in the Register of Sasines within fourteen days of the date hereof; *and (2) to deliver to you within six months following the date hereof a duly recorded Discharge of Standard Security granted by the Ben Wyvis Building Society in favour of our clients.*

Yours faithfully,

Approved B J & W
20/9/82

Notes: See note to **(b) Draft memorandum for continuation of search** on the previous page.

This letter is written along the lines suggested by the Law Society in a circular of 30 January 1995, and meets the requirements of a classic letter of obligation (see Chapter 8). It also gets around the difficulties presented by the case of *Warners v Beveridge & Kellas* (again see Chapter 8).

(d) Draft discharge of standard security

WE, BEN WYVIS BUILDING SOCIETY, incorporated under the Building Societies Acts, and having our Chief Office at Ben Wyvis House, Three hundred and twenty three Sauchiehall Street, Glasgow IN CONSIDERATION OF TWENTY TWO THOUSAND POUNDS (£22,000) paid by Alistair McAllister and Fiona McAllister residing formerly at One hundred and seventy three Cathedral Street, Glasgow, and now at Three Barrie Drive, Edinburgh, DO HEREBY DISCHARGE a Standard Security for Eight Thousand Pounds by the said Alistair McAllister and Fiona McAllister in our favour recorded in the Register for the County of Midlothian on Sixteenth June, Nineteen hundred and eighty one: IN WITNESS WHEREOF

REGISTER on behalf of the within-named ALISTAIR McALLISTER and FIONA McALLISTER in the REGISTER for the COUNTY of MIDLOTHIAN

Solicitors   *approved*
Edinburgh, Agents.   *B J & W*
                                                                                  20/9/82

Notes: For other forms of discharge see Professor Halliday's *Conveyancing Law and Practice* (1987) W Green & Son Ltd, volume 3, chapter 40.

The sellers' solicitors have sent a comprehensive collection of documents in plenty of time to enable full settlement to take place on 31 October – provided that the purchasers' agents don't sleep on things. Should they do so, the blame lies on their shoulders alone, if the 'penalty' clause becomes operative.

Please note that as many questions on title as possible are met before they are even asked. This is commendable practice. In particular, local authority certificates re planning and roads were obtained ahead of sale. The roads and water certificates are a bit old, and some solicitors might ask for more up-to-date ones. The facts about the public nature of a road, are, however, perfectly obvious, and road-widening schemes, if any, tend to be public knowledge.

To keep this book to a manageable size, the various title deeds et cetera have not been printed in full. They are, however, listed in the inventory of writs (see Appendix **I.20(a)**) and noted in skeletal form in the Notes on Title (see Appendix I.25).

Further reference should perhaps be made to the search. This is 'brought down' to 16 June 1981, which was the date on which the McAllisters' disposition and standard security were recorded. That is to midnight on that date, so that the search has to be re-stated on the following date to show what (if anything) the McAllisters have been doing with the property in the interim.

The letter of obligation now leaves the purchasers no alternative but to lodge the disposition for registration as soon after settlement as possible.

We also ask for an interim report now – that is a report to the latest possible date, which is probably well before the date of the request. This is, of course, the gap which the letter of obligation has to cover. If necessary a further interim report may be obtained at a time nearer settlement.

The Personal Register search is against all who have had an interest since the date of the closing of the search. For these purposes we shall assume that this is only the McAllisters. Technically the lenders should perhaps also be searched against, but in practice this is not usually done in the case of well-established building societies, who would not permit an inhibition to be placed against them.

The lender is under a statutory obligation (C & FR (S) Act 1970, Sch 3, cond 11(5)) to grant a discharge on repayment of a loan, and this duty cannot be stopped by an inhibition.

The handwritten alterations (indicate by *bold italic* type) on these drafts indicate the purchasers' agents' revisals. These are as follows:

(1) **Search** – the sellers' agents do not know the purchasers' loan arrangements or the purchasers' personal details. It is for the purchasers' agents to add these.

(2) **Letter of Obligation** – the loan is generally not repaid until the price is paid to the sellers' agents. A Discharge is not therefore deliverable at this date, because the loan has not been repaid to the building society. To resolve this vicious circle, the sellers' agents undertake to repay the loan and deliver the Discharge with a certain time limit. The sellers' agents have forgotten to insert this and the purchasers' agents quite properly have added it.

(3) **All documents** – are marked as revised and initialled by the purchasers' agents. This is customarily done in red pen.

21 Inter-office memorandum from Mr Pink to G Brown, trainee solicitor (10 September 1994)

Here is the file for the Meikles' purchase and the title deeds, et cetera. Will you please deal with these? Please keep me informed. Please deal with the Meikles through me.
H.P.

Note: Delegation is all-important, but should be distinguished from abdication, which is not good practice. The instructing solicitor should give clear instructions to the assistant, and the assistant should keep the instructor completely informed. They should discuss the business concerned on a regular basis, and the correspondence should be signed (if not written) by the partner of the firm.

It is a matter of circumstances whether the assistant should or should not communicate or meet with the clients directly. If the relationship is a personal one, as in the present case, the partner will probably wish to keep in touch with the clients. This is to a large extent a matter partly of the personal relationship that should exist between solicitors and clients and partly a matter of protection of goodwill which might be syphoned away by an unscrupulous assistant – or lost by an incompetent assistant.

In any event the precise relationship between solicitor and assistant should be clearly established, and maintained. Obviously the quality of this relationship varies widely from firm to firm.

22 Letter from Messrs Brown, Jarvie & Walker to Black Country Building Society (15 September 1994)

The General Manager,
Black Country Building Society,
Black Country Buildings,
STOKE-ON-TRENT.

DEAR SIRS,

James and Jane Meikle
Roll No XY 1234567/A
Mortgage for £40,000 over 25 years

Thank you for your letter of 14 September 1994 instructing us to act on the society's behalf in this mortgage. We shall be pleased to do so and shall let you have a request for the cheque in due course.

In particular we note that it is a special condition of the loan that the outside woodwork be painted within six months and we shall obtain Mr and Mrs Meikle's undertaking to this effect.

Yours faithfully,

BROWN, JARVIE & WALKER

Note: Again, for the sake of brevity, the loan instructions have been omitted. This is generally a printed document, and the contents vary from society to society. The conditions should be carefully read and be complied with. Not to do so is a breach of trust, and probably negligent. Note *Bristol & West Building Society v Kramer & Co* The Times, 6 February 1995.

Please note the condition regarding the outside woodwork. In certain cases the society may keep back part of the loan until such work us done, but this tends to be a rather cumbersome exercise, and can leave the borrowers with liquidity difficulties – especially if they have to pay for the work as it is done, yet not get the rest of the loan until after it is done. In this case the society only seeks an undertaking that the work shall be done and the Meikles, being sensible people, will doubtless ensure that this is the case.

23   Inter-office memorandum from Mr Pink to G Brown (5 September 1994)

Here are the loan papers which I have acknowledged.
H.P.

24   Inter-office memorandum from G Brown to Mr H Pink (20 September 1994)

Here are the Titles and file together with Notes on Title, Draft Disposition, Draft Affidavit, Draft Standard Security and Draft Assignation of Policy. Hope these are all right. I also enclose the sellers' agents' drafts, which I have revised.
G.B.

25 Notes on title

NOTES OF TITLE

of

3 Barrie Drive, Edinburgh

<u>Seller:</u>   Alistair & Fiona McAllister.
<u>Purchaser:</u>   James & Jane Meikle
<u>Sellers' Solicitors:</u>   Able, Grand, Brain & Co
<u>Price:</u>   £62,000 (including £2,000 of moveables)
<u>Entry:</u>   31 October 1994
<u>Loan:</u>   £40,000 from Black Country Building Society.
Pension Mortgage

A   <u>Description of Subjects:</u> (Also see plan attached)

ALL and WHOLE that part of ground lying in the County of Midlothian containing .084 acre and bounded as follows:

<u>West:</u> by centre line of Barrie Drive, 28' 10".
<u>South:</u> by Plot IV, 135' 1" along line of mutual gable, wall or fence.
<u>East, North & East again:</u> by property of Trustees of Evan Evans respectively 27' 10", 8' 10", 12' 5" along centre line of mutual wall or fence.
<u>North:</u> by Plot II, 115' 4" along centre line of mutual wall or fence.

All as the said plot is described in delineated and marked 'Plot III' on the plan annexed to Writ No 3 hereof. (Copy plan with these notes). Being part of the Lands of Lothian containing 22.42 acres described in Feu Contract No 1 hereof between Alpin McAlpine and others and Hugh McHugh.

B   <u>Writs referred to for burdens</u>

1.   Feu Contract between Alpin McAlpine, Solicitor, 123 Princes Street and George Squair of the one part and Hugh McHugh of the other part dated 1, 3, 4 and 31 January, and recorded G.R.S. (Midlothian) 3 February 1884.

<u>Superiors:</u> Alpin McAlpine and others as pro indiviso owners.
<u>Feuars:</u> Hugh McHugh and his heirs and assignees.
<u>Subjects:</u> The house and lands of Lothian, being 22.42 acres
   of which the subjects now transferred from part.
<u>Burdens:</u> (1)   Feuar bound to erect one villa of specified construction to be approved by the Superiors. Remainder of land to remain unbuilt on, and to be kept as parkland, shrubberies, and other associated uses.
   (2)   The whole area to be walled or fenced to the satisfaction of the Superiors.
   (3)   Nothing to be done in the subjects which

would constitute a nuisance, all in the sole
discretion of the Superiors.

(4)	Feuars bound to keep the house insured
against damage with a reputable British
insurance firm and to use the proceeds of any
claim for rebuilding.

(5)	No liquor ever to be made or sold on the
ground.

(All declared real liens and burdens).

Date of Entry: Martinmas 1883 notwithstanding date of Deed.

Tenendas: Feu

Feuduty: £23 per annum payable in equal portions at
Whitsunday and Martinmas. Duplication each 19th year
after Whitsunday 1884.

Assignation of Writs: Writs relate to larger area but will be
made available when required.

Assignation of Rents: as from date of entry.

Relief: Superiors to relieve feuars of all duties and casualties
payable to their superiors in all time coming and of all
public and parochial burdens exigible prior to said terms
of entry.

Warrandice: Absolute

Consent to Registration: for preservation and execution

2.	Disposition by John Evans and Gareth Evans, the
Trustees of Evan Evans in favour of Millhaugh Development
Co Ltd, dated 3rd, 7th and 9th and recorded said G.R.S. 24
June 1952.

Consideration: £10,000   Stamp duty: £100

Subjects: 5 acres part of 22.42 acres described above.

Burdens: 1. Disponees to fence off area purchased entirely at
their own expense, and if adjoining areas are
purchased for building purposes, they shall be
entitled to recover one-half of the cost from the
adjoining properties.

2. The layout of the Housing Estate to be built and
details of the external appearance of the houses
to be approved by disponees or successors.

Entry: 25 June 1952

Assignation of Writs: The writs relating to 22.42 acres are
assigned but not delivered and will be made available
when required. The right of the disponees to examine all
prior writs and searches is assigned.

Deduction of Title: Last vested in Evan Evans on 3 May 1947.
Link in title – Will by Evan Evans dated 5th May 1947
and recorded Books of Council and Session 7 October
1949.

3.	Feu Charter by Millhaugh Development Co Ltd, in favour
of Gregor McGregor dated 3 July and recorded said G.R.S. 10
July 1952.

Mid-Superior: Millhaugh Development Co Ltd
Feuar: Gregor McGregor
Consideration: Feuduty of £15 per annum
Stamp: Nil.
Subjects: See description at front.
Burdens: as in 1 and 2.
Additional Burdens:

1. Minerals reserved to Superiors (not coal) with power to work and carry away, without entering on ground. Provision for damages caused by workings.
2. Reservations to Superiors of right to lay and use sewers et cetera in plot, under liability of restoring surface.
3. Dwellinghouse to be erected on plot subject to certain building conditions. To be used as private dwellinghouse only with no sub-division or occupation by more than one family.
4. House, and fences to be maintained. No other buildings on plot without Superior's consent as to plans. All fences et cetera between adjoining plots are mutual.
5. Unbuilt on ground to be used for garden ground at front and vegetables or drying green at back.
6. Roadway and footpath to be formed and maintained until taken over by Local Authority. Similarly drains to be formed and maintained.
7. Superiors may use roads, footpaths and sewers et cetera without liability.
8. No manufacturing or trade, or profession and no sale of liquor. Doctor or Dentists may have consulting rooms with approval of Superior provided no nuisance is created.
9. No poultry etc. or dog breeding.
10. Insurance for full value, and proceeds of claim to be used for repairs. Receipts to be shown to Superiors if called for.
11. Superiors may depart from feuing plan.

All declared real liens and burdens.
Irritancy Clause: Providing for irritation on non-payment of feuduty or breach of feuing conditions.
Declaration: That Superiors are not bound to convey other parts of the land under these conditions.
Entry: 7 July 1953.
Tenendas: Feu
Reddendo: £15 per annum in equal portions at Whitsunday and Martinmas
Assignation of Rents: Obligation of Relief: Warrandice: Usual clauses.

C   Prescriptive Title:

4. Feu Charter No.3 hereof (referred to for burdens).

*5. Extract Registered Trust Disposition and Settlement by Gregor McGregor dated 5 July 1965 and registered B.C.S. 17 September 1978 (outwith prescriptive period).
  (1) In event of Mrs Georgina McPherson or McGregor surviving for more than 30 days, she is appointed Executor and is sole beneficiary.
  (2) If not, Donald McDonald and Rodger Rodger are appointed Trustees for following purposes:
      1,2,3 administrative and legacy provisions.
      4,   whole residue to William McWilliam, whom failing to his children.
  (3) Wide power to Trustees.

*6.   Certificate of Confirmation in favour of Donald McDonald issued from Commissariat of Glasgow, 4 October 1978 (outwith prescriptive period).
  As Executor of Gregor McGregor who died on 1 September 1978.
  Item – house at 3 Barrie Drive, with full description as required at that time.
  Docquet in terms of the Succession Act 1964, s 15 nominating William McWilliam as person entitled to property in terms of No 6, dated 10 November 1978.

*7.   Notice of Title in favour of William McWilliam recorded said G.R.S. 3 March 1979 (outwith prescriptive period).
Subject: .084 acres at 3 Barrie Drive as described.
Burdens: As in Nos 1,2 and 3 hereof.
Deduction of Title: Last vested in Gregor McGregor per No. 5 hereof, from William McWilliam derived right by No. 7 hereof.
Subscribing Solicitor: Euan McEwan, 322 West Regent Street, Glasgow.

8.   Disposition by William McWilliam to Alistair McAllister dated 3rd June and recorded said G.R.S. 16 June 1981. (FOUNDATION WRIT)
Consideration: £37,000   Stamp Duty: £740 (2%)
Subjects: 3 Barrie Drive (as described)
Burdens: see Nos. 1,2 and 3 hereof.
Entry: 11 June 1981.
Usual formal clauses – all in order.

This is the foundation writ for prescription – the first outwith ten-year period. Strictly speaking there is no need for the trainee to trouble with the writs 5,6, and 7, but the trainee is keen to learn what is included in a title. Time will have an effect on this keenness to do unnecessary work!

9. Standard Security by Alistair McAllister in favour of Ben Wyvis Building Society recorded GRS 16 June 1981.
    Capital and interest loan of £22,000 over 25 years.

D Search (over 3 Barrie Drive)
   Property Register:
   From 1 July 1953 to 16 June 1981.
   Disclosures:

10/7/52	Feu Charter No. 3.
3/3/79	Notice of Title No. 7.
16/6/81	Disposition No. 8 to McAllisters.
16/6/81	Standard Security No. 9.

Personal Register:

1/7/48–10/7/53	Millhaugn Development Co Ltd
3/3/73–3/3/79	Gregor McGregor & his Trustees
16/6/76–16/6/81	William McWilliam
	ALL CLEAR

Continue – Property Register 17/6/81 to disclose recording in favour of James Meikle.
   Personal Register – Alistair & Fiona MacAllister for five years to date of sale.

E Miscellaneous:

10. Letters from Lothian Regional Council dated 13 September 1985 certifies that roads, footpaths, and sewers are maintained by Regional Council, and 25 September 1985 that there is mains water and sewage.

11. Letter from Midlothian District Council dated 5 September 1984 certifying:

(1) No outstanding Notices under Building (S) Acts 1959 and 1970
(2) No outstanding Notices under Civic Government (Scotland) Act 1982.
(3) No notices under Edinburgh District Council Confirmation Act 1991.
(4) No notices under Housing (Scotland) Act 1987.
(5) Property situated in a Conservation area.
(6) Affected by an Article 4 declaration.
(7) Affected by a window policy.
(8) No other Notices under T & CP A 1972 and T & CP (General Development) (Scotland) Order.
(9) In area zoned for residential purposes.
(10) No outstanding Planning Notices.

12. Feuduty Redemption Receipt by Millhaugh Development Co Ltd dated 19 June 1982.
Feuduty redeemed at 18 June 1981.

Observation on Title
1. Note slightly unusual feudal relationship. Successors of Alpin

McAlpine and others are superiors of 22.42 acres, and successors of Hugh McHugh are feuars. Feuars sold their undivided interest in 5 acres to Millhaugh, who are now feuars to the extent of 5 acres. This area of 5 acres was divided into housing plots of which Millhaugh are superiors and houseowners are feuars.

Arising from this:

(a) What about feuduty over 22.42 acres of £23 per annum? We should see current feuduty receipt for this. What is duplication every 19th year?

(b) What about feuing condition that 22.42 acres is for one villa only?

2. Get their draft State for Settlement and Rates receipt.
3. Request interim Report on Search. Search is from 1952, the 40-year period. Not necessary to see the prior estate search?
4. Insurance – the building society will cover the property with a Policy from the Disastrous Fire Insurance Co Ltd when loan is paid out.
5. Note declaration in writ 3, which eliminates all rights of third parties to enforce feuing conditions. (*Turner v Hamilton* (1890) 17 R 494.)

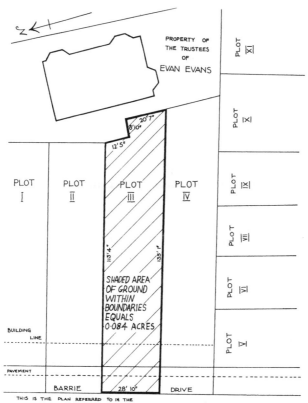

THIS IS THE PLAN REFERRED TO IN THE FOREGOING FEU DISPOSITION BY MILLHAUGH DEVELOPMENT COMPANY LTD. IN FAVOUR OF EVAN EVANS

" B. BRUSH " DIRECTOR "L. LAMB" SECRETARY

26 Draft Disposition

I ALISTAIR McALLISTER and FIONA McALLISTER both residing formerly at One hundred and Seventy three Cathedral Street, Glasgow and now at Three Barrie Drive, Edinburgh, heritable proprietors of the subjects hereinafter disponed IN CONSIDERATION of the sum of SIXTY THOUSAND POUNDS (£60,000) paid to me by JAMES MEIKLE and JANE MEIKLE equally, residing at Three hundred Brookmans Avenue, Brookmans Park, Hertfordshire of which we acknowledge receipt and discharge them HAVE SOLD AND DO HEREBY DISPONE to the said James Meikle and Jane Meikle equally between them and the survivor of them and to his her or their executors and assignees whomsoever, heritably and irredeemably, ALL and WHOLE the plot of ground known as Three Barrie Drive Edinburgh, lying in the County of Midlothian being the subjects containing eighty four decimal or one thousandth part of an acre or thereby described in a delineated and marked 'Plot III' on the plan annexed to Feu Charter by Millhaugh Development Company Limited in favour of Gregor McGregor dated Third July and recorded in the Division of the General Register of Sasines applicable to the County of Midlothian Tenth July Nineteen hundred and Fifty three; but always with and under the declaration, reservations, real burdens and land obligations specified in (One) Feu Contract between Alpin McAlpine and another of the one part and Hugh McHugh of the other part dated First and subsequent dates of January and recorded in the said Division of the General Register of Sasines on the Third February Eighteen hundred and eighty four; (Two) Disposition by John Evans and another, the Trustee of Evan Evans in favour of Millhaugh Development Company Limited dated Third and subsequent dates and recorded in the said Division of the General Register of Sasines on Twenty fourth all days of June Nineteen hundred and fifty two, (Three) the said Feu Charter by Millhaugh Development Company Limited dated and recorded as aforesaid; WITH ENTRY as at the Thirty first day of October Nineteen hundred and ninety four; and we grant warrandice; the missives which we the granters hereof have concluded with the said James Meikle and Jane Meikle and which are constituted by letters dated Third, Sixth and Seventh September Nineteen hundred and Ninety Four will form a continuing and enforceable contract notwithstanding the delivery of these presents, except so far as fully implemented thereby, but the said missives shall cease to be enforceable after a period of two years from the date of entry except in so far as they founded on in any court proceedings which have commenced within the said period; and we certify that the transaction hereby effected does not form part of a larger transaction or of a series of transactions in respect of which the amount or value or the aggregate amount or value of the consideration exceeds Forty thousand pounds; IN WITNESS WHEREOF.

REGISTER on behalf of the within-named JAMES MEIKLE in the Register of the County of Midlothian.

Solicitors, Glasgow, Agents.

27   Draft standard security by James and Jane Meikle

I, JAMES MEIKLE and JANE MEIKLE both residing at 300
Brookmans Avenue, Brookmans Park, Hertfordshire, WHEREAS
the expression set out below shall have the meanings and effects
respectively set opposite to them, namely:

The Society	BLACK COUNTRY BUILDING SOCIETY having its Chief Office at Black Country Buildings, Stoke-on-Trent
The Advance	Forty Thousand Pounds
The Term of Years	Twenty five
The Interest Rate	X per cent per annum or such other rate as shall be from time to time applicable
The Subjects	The property known as Three Barrie Drive, Edinburgh more fully described below.

HEREBY UNDERTAKE TO PAY jointly and severally to the Society
all sums due and that may become due by us to the Society in
respect of any further advances that may be made by the Society
to us with interest computed in accordance with the practice of
the Society at the Interest Rate by calendar monthly payments of
the Monthly Payment during the repayment period commencing
on the date specified for such purpose in a Certificate served or to
be served by the Society upon us, and each subsequent payment
at successive intervals of one calendar month until the whole
sums hereby secured are paid and satisfied; and we agree that a
certificate under the hand of an officer of the Society authorised
by the Board of Directors of the Society for that purpose shall be
sufficient to ascertain and constitute conclusively the amount due
to the Society at the date of the Certificate in respect of the
Advance and any further advances hereby secured and interest
thereon; FOR WHICH WE GRANT A STANDARD SECURITY in
favour of the Society over the Property being All and Whole that
plot or area of ground lying in the County of Midlothian containing Eighty four decimal or one thousandth parts of an acre or
thereby Imperial Standard Measure being the subjects described
in and disposed by and shown within the boundaries coloured red
and marked 'Plot III' on the plan annexed and signed as relative
to Feu Disposition granted by Millhaugh Development Company
Limited in favour of Gregor McGregor dated the Third and
recorded in the Division of the General Register of Sasines applicable to the County of Midlothian the Tenth both days of July,
Nineteen hundred and fifty three; Together with the dwellinghouse known as Three Barrie Drive, Glasgow, and the whole
other buildings and erections thereon, free ish and entry there-

from and thereto, the parts, privileges and pertinents thereof and our whole right, title and interest present and future therein; the Standard Conditions specified in Schedule 3 to the Conveyancing and Feudal Reform (Scotland) Act 1970 as varied by the Deed of Variations made by the Society dated and registered in the Books of Council and Session on the Thirtieth day of November, Nineteen hundred and seventy and any lawful variation thereof operative for the time being shall apply and I grant warrandice; and we consent to registration hereof and of any such certificate as aforesaid for execution: IN WITNESS WHEREOF (et cetera)

REGISTER on behalf of the within named BLACK COUNTY BUILD-ING SOCIETY in the REGISTER of the COUNTY OF MIDLOTHIAN

Solicitors, Glasgow, Agents.

28   Draft assignation of life policy by James and Jane Meikle

I, JAMES and JANE MEIKLE residing at Three hundred Brookmans Avenue, Brookmans Park, Hertfordshire

CONSIDERING that we have agreed to grant these presents as additional security for the whole sums including interest due under a Standard Security granted or about to be granted by us the said James and Jane Meikle in favour of THE BLACK COUN-TRY BUILDING SOCIETY, having its Chief office at Black Country House, Stoke-on-Trent (hereinafter with its successors and assignees referred to as 'the Society'), Do hereby IN FURTHER SECURITY of the provisions (hereinafter called 'the said provi-sions') contained or referred to in the said Standard Security ASSIGN, CONVEY and MAKE OVER to and in favour of the Society redeemably as aftermentioned yet irredeemably in the event of a sale by virtue of the powers hereinafter referred to ALL and WHOLE the following Policy of Assurance, videlicet:

Policy Number:	1234567 XYZ
Date:	1 September 1994.
Name of Insurance Company:	Longlife Assurance Company
Name of Insured:	James and Jane Meikle
Amount Insured:	Forty thousand pounds with profits
Date of Maturity:	15 September Two Thousand and Nineteen (2019)

together with the said sum(s) contained in the said Policy(ies) and all bonuses, additions and all other sums which may accrue thereon and our whole right, title and interest, present any future, in and to the said Policy(ies); with full power to the Society to exercise all the powers, rights and remedies competent to the Society under the said provisions in so far as relevant thereto; And we reserve power of redemption subject to the said provisions; which Policy and the foregoing Assignation we warrant absolutely: IN WITNESS WHEREOF

Note: This is an assignation of the life policy taken out to provide for repayment of the loan in the event of the death of either borrower. There will be a death benefit under their pension plans, but these are not assignable to the Building Society, who will therefore require this policy.

29 Draft notice of assignation

Longlife Assurance Company,
Longlife House,
Charlotte Square,
Edinburgh.

SIRS

Please note the following Assignation of a Policy issued by your company:

Life Assured and Policy Holder:	James Meikle and Jane Meikle, 300 Brookmans Avenue, Brookmans Park, Hertfordshire.
Assignees:	Black Country Building Society, Black County Buildings, Stoke-on-Trent.
Policy Number:	1234567 XYZ
Sum Assured:	£40,000 with profits
Date of Policy:	1 September 1994
Date of Maturity:	1 September 2019

Please acknowledge receipt by returning the enclosed duplicate of this notice with your receipt thereon.

Yours faithfully,

SOLICITORS FOR BLACK COUNTRY BUILDING SOCIETY

30 Draft affidavit under MH(FP) (S) Act 1981, section 8(2)

Note: This being a security by a married couple, no affidavit is necessary. An affidavit would otherwise be required. See Appendix III.1.

31 Draft letter of undertaking by the Meikles to building society

The Black Country Building Society,
Black Country House,
Stoke-on-Trent.

DEAR SIRS,

With reference to the loan of £40,000 being made by you to us over 3 Barrie Drive, Edinburgh, we hereby undertake that we shall have repainted the outside woodwork of the house at 3 Barrie Drive, Edinburgh, within six months of our taking entry on 31st October 1994.

Yours faithfully,
ADOPTED AS
HOLOGRAPH
JAMES MEIKLE
JANE MEIKLE

32 Inter-office memorandum from H. Pink to G. Brown (24 September 1994)

Thank you for your memo of 20 September 1994. I now return the various papers that you handed to me. All your notes and drafts appear to be in order. Please proceed to return title, et cetera to sellers' agents. Please also write (in my name) to Mr Meikle explaining to him what is happening, when you can put him fully in the picture.

Did they not tell you at the University that casualties such as duplication of feuduties, were abolished by the Feudal Casualties (Scotland) Act 1914? Unfortunately they failed to abolish lease-hold casualties at the same time. H.P.

Note: Mea culpa! The legal profession, rather optimistically, expects the universities to teach students every detail of law, quite irrespective of constraints of time.

This Act in 1914 also allowed for an augmentation to be made of the feuduty as compensation for the last duplication. As a deed of augmentation would have been recorded if this had happened, presumably the feuduty has not been augmented. So be it. A lot of people had a great deal more to think about after 1914 than augmentations of feuduty.

Unfortunately Pink is right about leasehold casualties, which are still a present menace. (See Chapter 21.)

33   Letter from Messrs Brown, Jarvie & Walker to Messrs Able, Grand, Brain & Co (1 October 1994)

DEAR SIRS

James and Jane Meikle
Alistair and Fiona McAllister
3 Barrie Drive, Edinburgh

We refer to our previous correspondence in this matter and now return the title deeds and other papers sent by you on 9 September 1994.

We also enclose our Draft Disposition for revisal and return.

Our observations on title are as follows:

1.   Please let us have an Interim Report on Search.

2.   Please let us have your Draft State for Settlement and confirmation that you have informed the Council Tax office of the change of ownership.

3.   Please exhibit a recent receipt for cumulo feuduty of £25 per annum.

4.   We note the undischarged feuing conditions in the Feu Contract of 1884 to the effect that this land is to be unbuilt upon. Please comment.

5.   Please confirm that the moveable property is not affected by any hire purchase credit sale leasehold or other similar agreement.

Yours faithfully,

BROWN, JARVIE & WALKER

Note: Again, a nice polite, businesslike letter, albeit containing a delayed action bomb at paragraph 4. The sellers' agents have only themselves to blame for this – they should have cleared up this obvious title defect when they bought the house. Thus the importance of noting title and studying even old and boring deeds. It is to be hoped that the superiority has not been bought my a commercial superior who will no doubt be looking for a pound of flesh.

This letter is kept short – if there is nothing else worth asking, why ask it?

34. Reply from Messrs Able, Grand, Brain & Co to Messrs Brown, Jarvie & Walker (7 October 1994)

DEAR SIRS

Alistair and Fiona McAllister
James and Jane Meikle
3 Barrie Drive, Glasgow

We thank you for your letter of 1 October, and now return your Draft Disposition which has been revised.

We could deal with your observation seriatim:

1. We enclose Interim Report.

2. We enclose draft State of Settlement. We are notifying the Regional Collector of the change of ownership.

3. We also enclose the cumulo feuduty receipt that you request.

4. We would contend that this residential development was built by Millhaugh Development Co Ltd, with the full knowledge of the Superiors, and indeed under their noses, so to speak. The house was built in 1952, and we would therefore contend that the breach of a feuing condition, if there was one, is cured by acquiescence.

Yours faithfully,

ABLE, GRAND, BRAIN & CO.

Note: Not a particularly elegant reply to a civil question and one might suspect that the original question has touched a raw nerve. The answer does however outline the operation of the law of acquiescence, and is probably correct, although acquiescence is notoriously hard to establish (see 6 *Stair Memorial Encyclopaedia* – conveyancing section). Undoubtedly, however, a waiver of discharge of this condition should have been obtained before the house was built, or since then. The matter should be put beyond doubt now. It is perhaps unfortunate that feuing conditions are not subject to negative prescription, as this would avoid much uncertainty.

The word 'seriatim' is just a fancy way of saying 'in the same order that you raised them' and is perhaps more frequently used in civil court pleadings than in conveyancing correspondence.

The sellers' solicitors should inform the council tax authority of the change of ownership, in order that the sellers are no longer liable for council tax on this house.

35 Enclosures with letter No. 34

(a) Interim Report on Search

General Register of Sasines
Report from Search Sheet 141000

Note of Entries

affecting

Subjects:
                          3 Barrie Drive, Edinburgh
                          County of Midlothian
                          From 17 June 1981
                          To   1 August 1982
                                (Both inclusive)
                          No Deed

                                        'A. Maxwell'
                                        Deputy Keeper

Inhibitions and Adjudications
                          From 17 June 1981
                        To   4 October 1982
                             (Both inclusive)
                        Clear

                                        'A. Maxwell'
                                        Deputy Keeper

Date: 05 Oct 94   Time: 12:10:37   Report by: Anthony Perry

Registers of Scotland Presentment Book

This search is not covered by the Keeper's indemnity.

Every deed is subject to withdrawal prior to entry in the Minute Book.

Search of Edinburgh between 01.08.94 and 03.10.94

For the name: Meikle
Subjects: 3 Barrie Drive
Date: Cty   Numb   Name/Address

No deeds found which match selection criteria
............END REPORT.............

(b) Draft State of Settlement

STATE FOR SETTLEMENT
in connection with sale of
3 Barrie Drive, Edinburgh.

Price: £62,000 (including moveables of £2000)
Entry: 31 October 1994
Seller: Mr & Mrs McAllister (Messrs Able, Grand, Brain & Co)
Purchaser: Mr & Mrs Meikle (Messrs Brown, Jarvie & Walker)
1994
31 October   Price per Missives   £62,000.00

36   Letter from Brown, Jarvie & Walker to Able, Grand, Brain & Co (15 October 1994)

DEAR SIRS,

<u>James and Jane Meikle</u>
<u>Mr and Mrs A McAllister</u>
<u>3 Barrie Drive, Edinburgh</u>

We refer to your letter of 7th October and now enclose the Disposition for signature, a Schedule for completion to show the date and place of signing, and the witnesses' full names and addresses, and the Draft Disposition for comparison.

We also return the Interim Report on Search and draft State for Settlement both of which are in order.

Further, we return the earlier Search and cumulo feuduty receipt, both of which are in order.

We note what you say about acquiescence, and agree with your viewpoint.

Please contact us when the deed has been signed, and you are in a position to settle.

Yours faithfully,

BROWN, JARVIE & WALKER

Note: What a climbdown! As previously said, there probably has been acquiescence, but I have no hesitation in saying that his important matter should not be left to chance, and a written agreement to the development should have been received. Not all solicitors are as easy as Brown, Jarvie & Walker, and at some future date this problem may be raised again and pecked to death, Brown, Jarvie & Walker may then have to obtain a waiver, and will regret their charitable attitude towards some fairly slack earlier conveyancing.

37   16 October 1994

Attendance with Mr and Mrs Meikle at this office when they signed (1) Standard Security (2) Assignation of Policy and (3) Letter to Building Society undertaking to do certain work.

Generally advising them as to progress and confirming that we could see no difficulty in settling at 31 October 1994.

Note: It might be safer to advise Mrs Meikle to take independent legal advice before signing. See *Mumford v Bank of Scotland* The Times, 4 August 1994.

38   Letter from Brown, Jarvie & Walker to head office of Black Country Building Society dated 18 October 1994

DEAR SIRS

<u>James and Jane Meikle – Loan No. XYZ 1234567/A
Endowment Mortgage for £40,000</u>

We now enclose Certificate of Title signed by us and shall be obliged if you will let us have your cheque for £40,000, being the amount of the loan, in time for settlement on 31 October 1994.

We would confirm that we have obtained Mr and Mrs Meikle's undertaking to have the outside woodwork painted within six months of 31 October 1994.

Please send the funds to our Clients' Account with the Bank of Alba, Glasgow Chief Office. National number 130.24.66. Clients Account number 1234567.

Yours faithfully,

Note: The exact contents of the Certificate of Title vary from society to society, but generally the solicitors certify that the title is in order for a building society loan and provide such further details as are requested.

The timing is crucial. The cheque should be received in good time for settlement, but not too far before. If a building society cheque is not presented within seven days of receipt, it generally has to be returned to the Society, for re-issue on a later date.

Nowadays a lot of loan funds are telegraphically transferred into the solicitors' clients' account. I have never found this to be as smooth a process as is suggested. For some reason a transfer even between two branches in the same Scottish city still has to go through London.

Otherwise all such correspondence sending or requesting money, or indeed, of any importance, should be sent by first class post or the excellent DX system.

A building society's cheque may be treated as 'cleared funds' (see **10.17**).

Ensure the report on title covers all matters contained in the instructions (Appendix I.22).

39   Letter from Brown, Jarvie & Walker to Mr and Mrs Meikle (20 October 1994)

DEAR MR and MRS MEIKLE,

Purchase of 3 Barrie Drive, Edinburgh

We refer to your recent meeting with Mr Pink and would confirm that we are now in a position to settle your purchase.

Can you please let me have your cheque for £22,732.75 at least by the end of the week in order that this may clear your bank in time for settlement?

This sum is made up as undernoted in our business account and statement.

Yours sincerely,

Note referred to:

1. Business Account
    Fee in connection with concluding Missives, examining title and preparing conveyance

	Fee on purchase	£450.00
	+ VAT @ 17.5%	78.75
Outlays		£528.75
	Amount	
Recording dues of		
Disposition and	132.00	
Standard		
Security (£7)	22.00	
Post and Incidents	50.00	
(incl. VAT £7.44)		
		204.00
Amount of Account		£732.75

Note: Please see earlier notes on fees and stamp duty et cetera. While the fee note is fairly heavy, please note that the government (not the solicitor, who is only an unpaid, unthanked collector) collects in VAT no less than £86.19 as a result of this move, and there is no stamp duty on this transaction. Mr Pink had, at least, the good sense to give an idea of this account at the outset – if you don't do this, the result may come as a terrible shock to the clients, especially the stamp duty which not everyone knows about. A disgruntled purchaser once suggested to me that stamp duty was an additional charge for the solicitors' postages! This is in fact covered in 'post and incidents'. The fairness or otherwise of the fee charged I shall leave to others to decide!

2. Statement

1994 Purchase price of house and moveables		£62,000.00
£40,500.00		
	Deduct:	
	Building Society Loan	40,000.00
		£22,000.00

Note: The cheque from the client should always be requested in sufficient time to enable it to be cleared with reference to early strictures about uncleared funds and dishonoured cheques. The client may feel that this shows a lack of trust on the solicitors' part – if so, you must explain the Accounts Rules to them. The solicitors must not write a cheque unless they have sufficient cleared funds in clients' accounts to meet that cheque. A building society cheque may be taken as cleared funds for this purpose.

40 22 October 1994

Attendance with Mr and Mrs Meikle who handed over their cheque. Handing this to cash room with a request that it be immediately presented.

H.P.

41 Inter-office memorandum from Mr Pink to Mr Brown (26 October 1994)

Please note that building society cheque has arrived today, and we got the Meikles' cheque last week. Please proceed to settle.

H.P.

42 28 October 1994

Telephoning Able, Grand, Brain & Co to arrange settlement.

Note: Try not to arange entry on Saturday or Sunday or on holidays. Reference to a good diary should prevent this mistake.

The rule for settlement is 'the cheque goes to the Disposition'.

43 Slip for settlement

Hand over signed cheque

Collect

Keys
Receipted state for settlement
Disposition, particulars of signing and draft
Signed letter of obligation
Discharge of security and their Keeper's letter
Title deeds
Letters re roads and planning

Note: The discharge of the existing security is presented by the sellers at registration, but to keep matter in step, the sellers' agents normally hand over the completed discharge of settlement, together with their letter to the Keeper requesting registration. The purchasers' agents send off these papers with their own to the Keeper. In due course the recorded discharge is returned to the sellers' agents who deliver it to the purchasers' agents per their letter of obligation.

44 Note of telephone call from Mr H Pink to Mr James Meikle (29 October 1994)

Telephoning Mr Meikle to tell him all is safely settled and asking him to collect keys from us.

45 Inter-office memorandum from G Brown to H Pink (1 November 1994)

Please note I settled Meikles' purchase on Monday. I shall now clear up odds and ends.

G B

Well done!

H P

46 Completion

(a) Testing clause added to disposition

IN WITNESS WHEREOF these presents are signed by me the said Alistair McAllister and Fiona McAllister at Edinburgh on twenty fifth October, Nineteen hundred and Ninety Four two in presence of these witnesses Gregor Townsend and Robert Wainwright, both Trainee Solicitors of Forty two Registration Row, Glasgow.

(b) Letter to Keeper prepared for disposition and standard security. This and the Warrants of Registration are signed by the purchasers' solicitors (disposition) and Building Society's solicitors (standard security), who are of course the same firm in this case. The discharge and the sellers' solicitors' request for registration are also sent to the Keeper in the same envelope (see **47** and **48**). The Keeper should record these three writs in logical sequence – if not, the doctrine of accretion should validate the deeds even though recorded in wrong order.

(c) The writs will be returned in due course, duly recorded and, in the meantime, with a slip requesting the Registration dues. You pay these out of funds retained for this purpose (see **39**). Obviously an up-to-date note of recording dues is necessary. These can be found in the current issue of the *Scottish Law Agents Society Memorandum Book* (available from the Society), or from the *Scottish Law Directory* (T & T Clark Ltd) or Butterworths' *Blue Book*, all produced annually and totally indispensable. Do not rely on an old directory and keep an eye on the *Scots Law Times* for any changes in fees et cetera.

(d) Please note that the recording dues paid by the clients in advance of recording are clients' money, and should be kept in clients' account until they are paid to the Register.

(e) Again, the execution formalities are prior to the coming into force of the Requirements of Writing (Scotland) Act 1995 which requires only one witness. A statutory instrument with the style of testing clause to be used after 1 August 1995 will be promulgated.

(f) The sooner the writs are sent to the Register the better, to comply with the terms of the Letter of Obligation which requires registration within 14 days. (Appendix I.20(c).)

47(a) Form accompanying disposition

C.P.B. 2

REGISTERS OF SCOTLAND EXECUTIVE AGENCY 01
APPLICATION FOR RECORDING IN SASINE REGISTER

Typewriter Alignment Box Type XXX in centre	Please complete this form in **BLACK TYPE** using **WHITE RESPONSE AREAS** in accordance with the guidance notes.	Typewriter Alignment Box Type XXX in centre

1. Presenting Agent Name, Address and RE No. (If any) (See Note 1) BROWN JARVIE & WALKER 42 REGISTRATION ROW GLASGOW G1 32M	KEEPER OF THE REGISTERS OF SCOTLAND EXECUTIVE AGENCY MEADOWBANK HOUSE 153 LONDON ROAD EDINBURGH EH8 7AU TELEPHONE 031 659 6111 DX ED 300 EDINBURGH

2. F.A.S. Number (digits only)	3. Agents Tel. No. (include S.T.D. Code)	4. Agents Reference
5555	0141-234-1243	HP/G

5. Name of deed in full (See Note 2)	6. County (See Note 3) Mark X if any other county
DISPOSITION	MIDLOTHIAN

7. GRANTERS Surname (See Note 4)	Forename(s)
a) McALLISTER Surname	ALISTAIR & FIONA Forename(s)
b) and/or company/firm or council, etc	Place X in box if more than 2 granters c)

8. GRANTEES Surname (See Note 4)	Forename(s)
a) MEIKLE Postal address of First Grantee (See Note 5) 300 BROKKMANS AVENUE, BROOKMANS PARK Surname	JAMES & JANE Forename(s)
b) and/or company/firm or council, etc	Place X in box if more than 2 grantees c)

9. a) Subjects (See Note 6) Postal Address	or	b) Other (See Note 6) Name of Subjects
House Name		
Street No. 3 BARRIE DRIVE		
Town EDINBURGH	Extent of land (if known)	

10. Consideration/Amount of loan - if in writ (See Note 7)	Value/Amount of loan - if not in writ
a) £ 60,000	b) £

11. TYPE OF PROPERTY (Place X in box) (See Note 8)	12. SPECIAL REQUESTS (See Note 9)	13. Additional Information
Domestic ✓	Preservation	
Commercial/Leasehold	Preservation/Execution	
Land only	No. of Extracts required (if any)	
Other	Duplicate Plan(s)	

I/We certify that the information supplied on this form is accurate and correct to the best of my/our knowledge.

14. Date 31/10/94	15. Signature of presenting party	Insert No. of accompanying application forms (See Note 10)

PRINTED FOR HMSO SCOTLAND, S40/0652, M600, 4/91, 155/01

47(b) Form accompanying standard security

C.P.B. 2

REGISTERS OF SCOTLAND EXECUTIVE AGENCY 01
APPLICATION FOR RECORDING IN SASINE REGISTER

Typewriter Alignment Box Type XXX in centre	Please complete this form in **BLACK TYPE** using **WHITE RESPONSE AREAS** in accordance with the guidance notes.	Typewriter Alignment Box Type XXX in centre

1.	Presenting Agent Name, Address and RE No. (If any) (See Note 1) BROWN JARVIE & WALKER 42 REGISTRATION ROW GLASGOW G1 32M	KEEPER OF THE REGISTERS OF SCOTLAND EXECUTIVE AGENCY MEADOWBANK HOUSE 153 LONDON ROAD EDINBURGH EH8 7AU TELEPHONE 031 659 6111 DX ED 300 EDINBURGH

2. F.A.S. Number (digits only)	3. Agents Tel. No. (include S.T.D. Code)	4. Agents Reference
5555	0141-234-1243	HP/G

5. Name of deed in full (See Note 2)	6. County (See Note 3)	Mark X if any other county
STANDARD SECURITY	MIDLOTHIAN	

7.	GRANTERS Surname (See Note 4)	Forename(s)
a)	MEIKLE Surname	JAMES & JANE Forename(s)
b)	and/or company/firm or council, etc	Place X in box if more than 2 granters c)

8.	GRANTEES Surname (See Note 4)	Forename(s)
a)		
	Postal address of First Grantee (See Note 5)	
	Surname	Forename(s)
b)	and/or company/firm or council, etc BLACK COUNTRY BUILDING SOCIETY	Place X in box if more than 2 grantees c)

9. House Name	a) Subjects (See Note 6) Postal Address	or	b) Other (See Note 6) Name of Subjects
Street	No. 3 BARRIE DRIVE		
Town	EDINBURGH	Extent of land (if known)	

10.	Consideration/Amount of loan - if in writ (See Note 7)	Value/Amount of loan - if not in writ
a) £		b) £ 40,000

11. TYPE OF PROPERTY (Place X in box) (See Note 8)	12. SPECIAL REQUESTS (See Note 9)	13. Additional Information
Domestic ✓	Preservation	
Commercial/ Leasehold	Preservation/ Execution	
Land only	No. of Extracts required (if any)	
Other	Duplicate Plan(s)	

I/We certify that the information supplied on this form is accurate and correct to the best of my/our knowledge.

14. Date 31/10/94	15. Signature of presenting party	Insert No. of accompanying application forms (See Note 10)

PRINTED FOR HMSO SCOTLAND, 8409652, M600, 4/94, 155391

48 Form accompanying discharge

C.P.B. 2

REGISTERS OF SCOTLAND EXECUTIVE AGENCY 01
APPLICATION FOR RECORDING IN SASINE REGISTER

Typewriter Alignment Box Type XXX in centre	Please complete this form in **BLACK TYPE** using **WHITE RESPONSE AREAS** in accordance with the guidance notes.	Typewriter Alignment Box Type XXX in centre

1. Presenting Agent Name, Address and RE No. (If any) (See Note 1)

ABLE, GRAND, BRAIN, & COMPANY
109 SASINE PLACE
EDINBURGH EH1 XYZ

KEEPER OF THE REGISTERS OF SCOTLAND
EXECUTIVE AGENCY
MEADOWBANK HOUSE
153 LONDON ROAD
EDINBURGH EH8 7AU

TELEPHONE 031 659 6111
DX ED 300 EDINBURGH

2. F.A.S. Number (digits only) **3.** Agents Tel. No. (include S.T.D. Code) **4.** Agents Reference

4444   0131-123-4321   MB/ABC

5. Name of deed in full (See Note 2)   **6.** County (See Note 3)   Mark X if any other county

DISCHARGE   MIDLOTHIAN

7. GRANTERS Surname (See Note 4)   Forename(s)

a) Surname   Forename(s)

and/or company/firm or council, etc   Place X in box if more than 2 granters

b) BEN WYVIS BUILDING SOCIETY   c)

8. GRANTEES Surname (See Note 4)   Forename(s)

a) McALLISTER   ALISTAIR & FIONA
Postal address of First Grantee (See Note 5)

3 BARRIE DRIVE, EDINBURGH
Surname   Forename(s)

and/or company/firm or council, etc   Place X in box if more than 2 grantees

b)   c)

9. a) Subjects (See Note 6) Postal Address   or b) Other (See Note 6)

House Name

Street No. 3   BARRIE DRIVE   Name of Subjects

Town   EDINBURGH   Extent of land (if known)

10. Consideration/Amount of loan - if in writ (See Note 7)   Value/Amount of loan - if not in writ

a) £   b) £ 22,000

11. TYPE OF PROPERTY (Place X in box) (See Note 8)   **12.** SPECIAL REQUESTS (See Note 9)   **13.** Additional Information

Domestic ✓   Preservation

Commercial/Leasehold   Preservation/Execution

Land only   No. of Extracts required (if any)

Other   Duplicate Plan(s)

I/We certify that the information supplied on this form is accurate and correct to the best of my/our knowledge.

14. Date   **15.** Signature of presenting party   Insert No. of accompanying application forms (See Note 10)

31/10/94

49   Letter from Messrs Brown, Jarvie & Walker to Mr & Mrs Meikle (1 November 1994)

DEAR MR *&* MRS MEIKLE

Purchase of 3 Barrie Drive, Edinburgh

I refer to our recent telephone call when I confirmed that this transaction had been settled, and requested you to collect the keys from here.

I would now confirm settlement in writing. The building society cheque has been collected, the price paid over, all necessary papers completed and sent for recording in Edinburgh.

The disposition in your favour and the standard security you signed in favour of the Black Country Building Society will be returned to me duly recorded, in about six to eight weeks. I shall then send these and the other title deeds to the building society, who will keep them until the loan is repaid. You may, however, request these on loan if you wish to increase your loan, or if there is (say) any question as to the terms of the deeds.

Lothian Regional Council has been informed of the change of ownership, by the sellers, and will in due course send you an account for the proportion of Council Tax due by you from 31 October 1994 to 31 March 1995, which please pay either in one sum or by monthly bankers' order.

The building society and assurance company will have sent you a bankers' order for the payment due.

The building society instalment is subject to MIRAS (Mortgage Interest Relief at Source) and you will pay the building society a sum nett of tax, and no allowance will therefore be made in your PAYE.

The property is insured against loss by the building society. You should, however, make your own arrangements for contents insurance, if you have not already done so.

I am obliged to you for entrusting your business to my firm and shall be pleased to give you any further information you may require.

Yours sincerely,

H PINK

Note: This letter seems to say enough to keep the client informed. Some would argue that it should say more, some that it says too much. It is a matter of judgment in the circumstances.

It is always polite and sensible to thank the clients for their custom – clients should never be taken for granted.

50   Letter from Brown, Jarvie & Walker to Longlife Assurance Company (1 November 1994)

Longlife Assurance Company,
Longlife House,
Charlotte Square,
EDINBURGH.

DEAR SIRS

Mr & Mrs Meikle
The Black Country Building Society
Policy No. 1234567 XYZ

We enclose Notice of Assignation of the above policy, in duplicate. Please return the duplicate to us with your receipt of the principal marked thereon.

Yours faithfully,

Note: An absolutely essential step which converts the society's personal right in the policy to a real right. The form of notice is shown (in draft) at **29**.

The insurance company is entitled to charge a small fee for this service (25p) under the Policies of Assurance Act 1867, but never do, for administrative reasons. You should not even offer this fee, as it will be refused.

51   Inter-office memo from G. Brown, legal trainee to secretary (1 November 1994)

Please make a diary entry for this file:
(a)   in two weeks, *re* return of duplicate Notice of Assignation
(b)   in eight weeks, *re* return of deeds from Record

G.B.

Note: The Law Society encourages the use of such diary entries, to prevent things from 'falling asleep' and claims from arising. It is also very good practice, to be highly commended. See Appendix VII.

52   Letter from Longlife Assurance Company to Brown, Jarvie & Walker (8 November 1994)

(This returns the receipted Notice of Assignation, and is put alongside the policy and Assignation in the title deeds.)

53 Receipt of recorded Disposition and Standard Security from HM Register of Sasines (16 December 1994)

(These are checked to make sure they are properly recorded and are also put with the title deeds, et cetera.)

54 Letter from Able, Grand, Brain & Co to Brown, Jarvie & Walker (18 December 1994)

DEAR SIRS,

Mr & Mrs McAllister
Mr & Mrs Meikle
3 Barrie Drive, Edinburgh

We enclose the duly recorded Discharge in favour of Mr McAllister in terms of our Letter of Obligation.

Please acknowledge receipt and mark our Letter of Obligation as being thus far implemented.

Yours faithfully,

ABLE, GRAND, BRAIN & CO

55 Reply from Brown, Jarvie & Walker to Able, Grand, Brain & Co (20 December 1994)

DEAR SIRS,

Mr & Mrs Meikle
Mr & Mrs McAllister
3 Barrie Drive, Edinburgh

We thank you for your letter of 18 December 1994 enclosing the recorded Discharge.

We have marked your Letter of Obligation as being thus far implemented, and shall be pleased to receive the Search in due course.

Yours faithfully,

BROWN, JARVIE & WALKER

Note: The Discharge is put with the rest of the titles. The Search should follow within three to four weeks.

56   Letter from Able, Grand, Brain & Co to Brown, Jarvie & Walker (12 January 1995)

DEAR SIRS,

Mr & Mrs McAllister
Mr & Mrs Meikle
3 Barrie Drive, Edinburgh

We have now received, and enclose, the Search. Please return our Letter of Obligation duly marked as implemented.

Yours faithfully,

ABLE, GRAND, BRAIN & CO

57   Reply from Brown, Jarvie & Walker to Able, Grand, Brain & Co (13 January 1995)

DEAR SIRS,

Mr & Mrs Meikle
Mr & Mrs McAllister
3 Barrie Drive, Edinburgh

Thank you for letting us have the Search. We now return your Letter of Obligation, duly marked as implemented.

Yours faithfully,

BROWN, JARVIE & WALKER

Note: The Search should, of course, be checked to see that the discharge, disposition and standard security are all duty recorded, and that there are no inhibitions, etcetera against the sellers.

The letter of obligation is then pen stroked across its face, and the words 'Implemented Brown Jarvie & Walker – 13/1/95' are added.

The Search should be put with the rest of the title deeds and sent to the building society.

58 Letter from Brown, Jarvie & Walker to Black Country Building Society (13 January 1995)

The General Manager,
The Black Country Building Society,
Black Country Buildings,
STOKE-ON-TRENT.

DEAR SIRS,

<u>Mr & Mrs Meikle</u>
<u>Roll No. XY 1234567/A</u>
<u>Endowment Mortgage for £40,000 over 25 years</u>

We now enclose the title deeds et cetera of the above property, conform to the Inventory enclosed in triplicate.

Please acknowledge receipt by returning one copy of the Inventory with your receipt thereon.

Yours faithfully,

BROWN, JARVIE & WALKER

Note: Send everything you can to the building society. The practice varies from society to society. Some societies like the title deeds as soon as the purchase is settled, and the rest to follow; others prefer the whole lot at the end. Most societies will provide a Form of Inventory which should be used. If not, something equivalent to **20(a)** is appropriate.

In all cases follow the society's instructions carefully.

59 Letter from Black Country Building Society to Brown, Jarvie & Walker (21 January 1995)

(Simply enclosing receipted inventory of titles.)

60 Note from Mr Pink to cash room of Brown, Jarvie & Walker (21 January 1995)

Please check that there are no stray balances here. If not, please close the file and put it away.

H.P.

Note: Finis!

Appendix II

A FIRST REGISTRATION IN THE LAND REGISTER IN 1995
(See Procedural Table II)

Sale of 3 Miller Drive, Glasgow (1995)

1   Note of telephone conversation between Henry Pink and John James (1 March 1995)

Attendance on telephone with Mr James. Noting that he was moving to London, and would therefore wish to sell his house at 3 Miller Drive, Glasgow, which we had bought for him in 1987.

Offering to market the property for him but noting that he had a business associate who was interested around the asking price of £75,000. Stating that the sale would cost about £550 in fees plus VAT and outlays, but we would send a written estimate.

2(a)   Henry Pink to John James (1 March 1995)

42 Registration Row,
GLASGOW.

1 March 1995

John James Esq,
3 Miller Drive,
GLASGOW,
G31 6BX.

DEAR MR JAMES,

3 Miller Drive, Glasgow

I refer to our telephone conversation today and now enclose a written estimate for work to be incurred in connection with your proposed sale at a price of say £75,000.

This is in accordance with my telephoned estimate today. As this is a sale, there are no stamp duty dues payable by you, and the only outlays are on reports and registration dues of the discharge of your standard security.

I hope that this will be in order and I shall be pleased to have your instructions.

When replying, could you please let me know if you are unmarried?

Yours sincerely,

HENRY PINK

Note: The fee quoted here is not in any way a suggested fee, it is merely what my accountant would call a 'ballpark figure' provided as an example. Each transaction must be treated on its merits, and in accordance with the guidelines laid down by the Law Society of Scotland, in the General Regulations in the Law Society's table of fees. Care should be taken to include all foreseeable outlays, and especially the VAT.

A first registration involves extra work for the solicitors involved and may justify a 'positive weighting' of fees – 25% extra was permitted under the old Scale of Fees.

Conversely a second registration should involve less work, and therefore a 'negative weighting' – again, this was formerly 25%.

A loophole is left for extra work involved if the transaction goes all wrong (see Note 1 on form).

On a sale only transaction, don't forget the recording dues of discharge. If the Land Registers (Scotland) Bill becomes law, such fees will be paid 'up front' on sending the deeds.

The form is no longer available from the Law Society, but most firms have their own similar forms. In his report of 1995 the ombudsman is particularly emphatic concerning the need for accurate fee estimation.

2(b) Domestic Conveyancing Charges quotation form

DOMESTIC CONVEYANCING CHARGES

Solicitor's Firm's Name BROWN JARVIE & WALKER

Address 42 REGISTRATION ROW, GLASGOW

Telephone No 0141-333-3436

NOTE: This form, which has been approved by The Law Society of Scotland, is an indication of charges on the basis of details presently known and on the assumption that the transaction(s) will not prove to be substantially more complex or time-consuming than expected. If the matter does not proceed to completion, work done and payments made up to that point will remain chargeable.

Client's Name JOHN JAMES ESQ

Address 3 MILLER DRIVE, GLASGOW

Telephone No 0141-611-4321

Address of property to be sold:

3 MILLER DRIVE, GLASGOW

Recorded
First Registration
Registered

Price £ _____ Name of Building Society or other lender BLACK COUNTRY

Amount of existing loan £ _____

Repayment/Endowment

Address of property to be bought:

Recorded
First Registration
Registered

Price £ _____ Name of Building Society or other lender _____

Amount of existing loan £ _____

Repayment/Endowment

NOTES

1. The proposed fee is for a normal transaction involving the normal amount of work. In the event of the work required involving more than normal time or being of an unusually complex nature the proposed fee may require to be increased. You will be advised of any such development in the course of the transaction.

2. The Quotation shows V.A.T., Stamp Duty and Recording Dues at the current rate. If the Government should vary these duties or dues during the course of the transaction the increase will be passed on to you.

3. In addition to the above you may have to provide for payments to other parties, eg your building society or other lenders for their survey fee and your own surveyor if you employ one.

4. If Press Advertising is not included as an estimate you should bear this item in mind as it can be substantial and depends on the number of advertisements and the newspaper.

5. You will be responsible for any other incidental outlays (eg proportion of Rates at settlement, cost of photography, travelling expenses, notice of change of ownership, Extracts or Quick Copies of prior Deeds), which might arise during the course of the transaction and these will be paid from your Client Account.

6. In the first instance Solicitors are entitled to deduct all proper outlays, fees and expenses from the proceeds of sale or any loan received at settlement. In the event that there is a debit at balance of your Client Account and there is unreasonable delay in settling this balance the Firm, at their sole discretion, reserve the right to charge interest at 1% per month (APR 12.68%) compound, at monthly stops on any debit balance.

7. If it should arise that a lender or other party interested in the transaction requires to engage his own solicitor and by Contract or otherwise you are responsible for his fees and outlays in connection with the transaction, the above Quotation will not apply and will become subject to revisal.

8. In a purchase transaction in the event that you require for your own protection to arrange a Search in the Register of Sasines the cost of the Search will be in addition to the sum quoted above.

9. The Proposed Fee is based on the price, and where applicable, the loan stated. Variation in price or loan will result in a variation in the Fees. Minor variations may be ignored.

Everyone should have a family lawyer.

FEES FOR SERVICES

Commission on Sale %	£ _____
Fee for Missives	£ 50
Conveyancing of Property–Sale	£ 400
Conveyancing of Property–Purchase	£ _____
Preparation of Standard Security	£ _____
Discharge of Standard Security	£ 50
Posts and Incidents	£ 50
Our Charges	£ 550

In addition we will have to make a number of payments to the Government and Others, including at present rates:—

VAT on our Charges	£ 96.25
Stamp Duty	£ _____
Recording or Registration of Disposition	£ _____
Recording or Registration of Standard Security	£ _____
Recording or Registration of Discharge	£ 33.00
Search–estimated–or Form P16	£ 100.00
Local Authority for Certificates	£ _____
Advertising–Property Centre	£ _____
Advertising–Press–estimated	£ _____
Miscellaneous–See Note 5	£ 30.00
Payment to Others	£ 259.25

SUMMARY

Our Charges	£ 550.00
Payment to Others	£ 259.25
TOTAL	£ 809.25

Signed Brown Jarvie & Walker Dated 01/03/95

3   John James to Henry Pink (2 March 1995)

3 Miller Drive,
GLASGOW.

2 March 1995

Henry Pink Esq,
Solicitor,
42 Registration Row,
GLASGOW.

DEAR MR PINK,

Thank you for your letter. Your estimate is quite acceptable and I shall be obliged if you will carry on. I am pretty certain Lachie McLachlan will buy the house, and he has been to see his Solicitor.

I was married to my wife Agnes in August 1990. Do you not remember, you were at my wedding? Why do you need to know anyway?

Yours sincerely,

J. JAMES

Note: Mr Pink is indeed a lucky man to keep his clients!

4   Memo note Henry Pink to his secretary Veronica Vanburgh (2 March 1995) and reply

Please see Mr James's letter of 2 March. Why didn't you remind me I was at his wedding?

H P

I was still at school in August 1990.

V V

Note: Mr Pink is also a lucky man to keep his staff!

5   Memo from Henry Pink to his trainee Wendy Robertson (2 March 1995)

Wendy – Please take over this transaction, I think it is to do with Land Registration, with which I still have not come to terms. You'll know all about this from University. Here is the file for the purchase in August 1985. Please keep me informed as to progress.

H P

Note: Despite being a bit short in current legal knowledge, Mr Pink at least admits his limitations and remains a master of clear firm delegation. It is also good to produce the purchase file. As a guide, files should be kept for at least ten years. Please note that Glasgow became an operational area for land registration on 30 September 1985, and that the title is presumably a sasine title.

6   Reply – Wendy Robertson to Henry Pink (3 March 1995)

Thank you. I have written for the title deeds and to Mr James and for Local Authority Certificates, and 10A and P16 Reports.

W R

Note: see **6(a)**, **6(b)**, **7, 8, 9** and **10**.

6(a)   Application to Keeper (for reply see 11b)

Form P16

REGISTERS OF SCOTLAND

APPLICATION TO COMPARE A BOUNDING DESCRIPTION[1] WITH THE ORDNANCE MAP

Applicant's reference: HP/WR

FROM

Brown Jarvie & Walker
Solicitors
42 Registration Row
Glasgow
FAS 5656

FOR OFFICIAL USE
Index Map
C.O.

TO

Keeper of the Registers of Scotland

Meadowbank House
153 London Road
EDINBURGH   EH8   7AU

Telephone: 031-659 6111

I/we apply for the boundaries of the subjects[2]

3 Miller Drive, Glasgow

delineated on the plan annexed[3]
to be compared with the Ordnance Map.

Signature.... *Brown Jarvie & Walker* .... Date ...03/03/95......

Notes

1. The bounding description must sufficiently define the extent of the subjects to enable the Keeper to identify them on the Ordnance Map. This may be achieved by supplying the Keeper with —

    (a) a plan with boundaries of stated lineal dimensions or boundaries which can be measured from an adequate scale appearing on the face of the plan, the position of the property being tied by stated measurements to road junctions or other features which are depicted on the Ordnance Map, or

    (b) such a plan, together with a postal address, but without the position of the property being so tied to features which are depicted on the Ordnance Map, or

    (c) a written description which includes measurements and refers to adjoining subjects by name or street number and not by the name of the owner, together with a postal address.

2. Insert postal address.

3. Delete whichever is inapplicable.

FOR RESULT SEE OVERLEAF

Notes: (1) The FAS No. is the Keeper's computerised account number for this firm.

(2) Attach a coloured plan of the property.

6(b)   *Appendices*

6(b)   Application to Keeper (for reply see 11a)

REGISTERS OF SCOTLAND
(Land Registration (Scotland) Rules 1980 Rule 24(1))

APPLICATION FOR A REPORT PRIOR TO REGISTRATION
OF THE SUBJECTS DESCRIBED BELOW[1,2,3]

Applicant's reference: HP/WR

Telephone: 041–204 3213

	FOR OFFICIAL USE
	Search Sheet No.
	Date of Receipt
	Report Number

FROM   Brown Jarvie & Walker
        Solicitors
        42 Registration Row
        Glasgow
        FAS 5656

TO

        Keeper of the Registers of Scotland

        Meadowbank House
        153 London Road
        EDINBURGH EH8 7AU

        Telephone: 031-659 6111

I/We apply for a report

(I)   on the subjects described below, for which an application for registration in the Land Register is to be made, from

        (a)   the REGISTER OF SASINES (County of_____ The Barony and Regality of Glasgow _____)

                and

        (b)   the LAND REGISTER
                stating whether or not registration of the said subjects has been affected

DESCRIPTION   3 Miller Drive, Glasgow
OF SUBJECTS[4]

                edged red on the accompanying Plan[5,6]
                ~~being (part of) the subjects described in~~[5,7]_____

OFFICE   If the subjects have been registered, the Keeper is requested to supply an Office Copy of the Title Sheet[5,8]
COPY

[1]   To be completed in duplicate.
[2]   No covering letter is required and an existing Search should not be submitted.
[3]   No charge is made for this Report.
[4]   The description must be sufficient to allow the subjects to be identified in both Registers and, if lengthy, may be on a separate sheet.
[5]   Delete if inapplicable.
[6]   A plan need not be attached if a verbal description will sufficiently identify the subjects.
[7]   Describe by reference to a writ recorded in the Register of Sasines.
[8]   The fee payable for an Office Copy will be intimated.

Notes: (1) See Note 1 above – form is sent in duplicate.

(2) A plan is usually sent with this form. If no plan is available, a description should be given.

7 Brown Jarvie & Walker to Black Country and Midlands Building Society (3 March 1995)

42 Registration Row,
GLASGOW.

3 March 1995

The General Manager,
Black Country & Midlands Building Society,
Black Country Buildings,
STOKE-ON-TRENT.

DEAR SIRS,

Mr John James
Roll No. XY 1234567/A

Please note that Mr James is proposing to sell his house in connection with his return to England.

Please let us have title deeds to enable the sale to be arranged.

Yours faithfully,

BROWN, JARVIE & WALKER

Note: The Black Country Building Society and the Midlands Building Society amalgamated in 1989. This makes little practical difference except in the wording of the Discharge, where title must be deduced. (See **18c**.)

8 Brown, Jarvie & Walker to John James (3 March 1995)

Ref: HP/WR/VV/1759

42 Registration Row,
GLASGOW.

3 March 1995

John James Esq,
3 Miller Drive,
GLASGOW.

DEAR MR JAMES,

3 Miller Drive, Glasgow

Thank you for your letter of 2 March. It is important that Mrs James should sign an Affidavit under the Matrimonial Homes (Family Protection) (Scotland) Act 1981 to renounce her occupancy rights as a non-entitled spouse under this Act.

Could she therefore please call at this office to sign an Affidavit before a Notary Public at the earliest opportunity?

Can you please let us know if there have been any alterations to the house that would require permission from the District Council and from the superior?

Yours faithfully,

BROWN, JARVIE & WALKER

Notes: (1) This technical little letter should get around the embarrassment over Mr Meikle's marriage.

(2) Mrs Meikle could also consent to the Disposition which would release her occupancy right. This is probably preferable, as it does not involve stamp duty complications, nor the service of a Notary Public. See Appendix III, Forms 2 and 3.

(3) The question in the last paragraph is appropriate. Note that Mr James does not answer it and see **21(a)**! The sellers' solicitors are really under a professional duty to obtain this information.

9   Brown, Jarvie & Walker to Strathclyde Regional Council (3 March 1995)

42 Registration Row
GLASGOW

3 March 1995

The Chief Executive,
Strathclyde Regional Council,
20 India Street,
GLASGOW G2 1DU.

DEAR SIR,

Mr & Mrs James
3 Miller Drive, Glasgow

In connection with the sale of the property at 3 Miller Drive, Glasgow, please forward a Certificate confirming that the roads, footpaths and sewers *ex adverso* the subjects have been taken over and have been maintained by the Regional Council.

We enclose a cheque for £XXXX and look forward to hearing from you when convenient.

Yours faithfully,

BROWN, JARVIE & WALKER

Note: First, make sure that there is not such a certificate already with the titles.

10 Brown, Jarvie & Walker to Glasgow District Council (3 March 1995)

42 Registration Row,
GLASGOW.

3 March 1995

The Town Clerk,
City of Glasgow District Council,
City Chambers,
GLASGOW G2 1DU.

DEAR SIR,

Mr & Mrs J James
3 Miller Drive, Glasgow

In connection with the sale of the property at 3 Barrie Drive, Glasgow, please forward when convenient, the usual planning certificate. We enclose cheque for £XXXXX in payment of your fee.

Yours faithfully,

BROWN, JARVIE & WALKER

Note: These certificates have been applied for in ample time, which is the best practice. The firm could also have written to SPH and got a combined certificate slightly cheaper, and rather quicker. Please note the relatively high cost of the roads certificate. The purchasers should therefore preserve it carefully for when they come to sell.

10(a) *Appendices*

10(a) **P16 Report – Reply from Keeper – all in order (see 14.3)**

FOR OFFICIAL USE

**RESULT OF COMPARISON OF BOUNDING DESCRIPTION WITH
THE ORDNANCE MAP**

1.   ~~The subjects are not identifiable on the Ordnance Map.~~

2.   The boundaries of the subjects coincide with those on the Ordnance Map.

3.   ~~The boundaries do not coincide with those on the Ordnance Map. Please see print herewith.~~

Signature *Fergus Ferguson*

Date   05/03/95

NOTES

1.   THE ABOVE INFORMATION HAS BEEN ISSUED IN RESPECT OF THE SUBJECTS DESCRIBED OVERLEAF. IT DOES NOT
     NECESSARILY REPRESENT THE SUBJECTS PRESENTLY COMPRISED IN THE TITLE.

2.   PLEASE ENSURE THAT THIS FORM ACCOMPANIES ANY APPLICATION FOR FIRST REGISTRATION OF THE SUBJECTS
     DESCRIBED OVERLEAF.

PRINTED IN SCOTLAND FOR HMSO BY (13161) Dd.0287015/4658-20 C500 9/88
20p EACH £2.00 PER 25 (EXCLUSIVE OF VAT) ISBN 0 11 493365 0

Form 10A

REGISTERS OF SCOTLAND	Report No.

(Land Registration (Scotland) Rules 1980 Rule 24(1))
REPORT PRIOR TO REGISTRATION

REGISTER OF SASINES

1. Prescriptive progress of titles

Deed	Recording date
Feu Charter to Gregor McGregor	10th July 1968
Notice of Title to William McWilliam	3rd March 1984
Disposition to Alistair McAllister	16th June 1984
Disposition to John James	3 May 1985

2. Statement of Securities recorded within 40 years prior to the date of certificate and for which no final Discharge has been recorded.

    Standard Security Black Country Building Society   3 May 1985

3. Statement of Discharges (of Securities) recorded within the 5 years prior to the date of the certificate.

4. Deeds, other than transfers or deeds creating or affecting securities, recorded within the 40 years prior to the date of the certificate.

    Certified correct to 5th March 1995   Initials

LAND REGISTER

The subjects have not been registered
The subjects have been registered under Title Number. . . . . . .
An Office Copy is enclosed as requested
The subjects are in course of being registered under Title
Number . . .
An Office Copy will be sent in due course
Certified correct to 5th March 1995   Initials

Note: Glasgow became operational for Land Registration on 30 September 1985, ie after the last sale.

REGISTER OF INHIBITIONS AND ADJUDICATIONS	FOR OFFICIAL USE
No Deed	Nat. Grid ref.

8805971 10M 9/85 R.P.

Notes: (1) The Discharge of 1985, not having been recorded within the 5 year period, is not now mentioned at Paragraph 3.

(2) This document takes the place of Search and Interim Report and broadly provides the information detailed on **14.6**.

(3) This report is brought down to the settlement date by a Form 11. A fee of £10 plus VAT is payable for a Form 11 Report and a Form 13 Report.

(5) There are no entries in the Personal Register.

11   Mair & Kildare to Brown, Jarvie & Walker (5 April 1995)

Mair & Kildare,
Solicitors,
35 Magister Street,
PAISLEY PA1 4ZZ.
DX PA5000

7 March 1995

Messrs Brown, Jarvie & Walker,
Solicitors,
42 Registration Row,
GLASGOW G1 3XX.

DX GW500

DEAR SIRS,

On behalf of our clients, Lachlan and Jean MacLachlan of 3
Glenlivet Road, Glasgow, (hereinafter called 'the Purchaser') we
hereby offer to purchase from your client Mr John James the
heritable proprietor, (hereinafter called 'the Seller') the subjects
comprising the dwellinghouse known as and forming 3 Miller
Drive, Glasgow; together with (one) the whole parts, privileges
and pertinents; (two) the whole common, mutual, and exclusive
rights of property; (three) all necessary rights of access; (four)
the heritable fittings and fixtures; (five) the central heating system; and (six) the Seller's whole right title and interest in and to
the said subjects (hereinafter called the subjects), which term
shall include any part of the said subjects; and that on the following terms and conditions:

1.   The price will be SEVENTY SIX THOUSAND FIVE HUNDRED
     POUNDS (£76,500) (hereinafter called 'the price'). The price
     will be apportioned between the heritable property
     (£75,000) and the moveable property included in the sale
     (£1,500). The price shall be payable on the date of entry.

2.   Entry to and vacant possession of the subjects will be given
     on 18th April 1995 (hereinafter called 'the date of entry') or
     such other and earlier date as may be agreed between the
     contracting parties.

3.   (a) The price shall include the following specific items,
         whether heritable or moveable in character, as viewed by
         the Purchaser:

         the carpet in the dining room, the refrigerator, two elec-
         tric fires in the hall and dining room, the hob and split
         level oven, all non-carpet floor coverings, all curtain
         rails, rods and pelmets, all door handles and door knobs,

303

all light flexes, bulbs and bulbholders and ceiling roses, all fluorescent light casings, the door bell and burglar alarm system, all decorative panels, mirrors, shelves, cabinets, towel rails, furniture shelves, fire surrounds, other units and accessories to the extent that the foregoing are presently attached or fixed to the floors, ceilings or walls, all stair clips, rods and eyes, all gas fires, storage heaters, fireplaces and grates, all fitted units, cupboards, sinks, water closets, baths, showers, bidets, and other sanitary ware, all built in wardrobes and cupboards, all television and radio aerials and satellite dishes, all venetian, roller, and other blinds, all central heating systems and plant, all plants, trees, shrubs, stock and ornaments in the garden and common areas generally, all boundary walls, fencing, and gates, and garages, garden huts and outhouses.

(b) It is warranted that the said items belong absolutely to the Seller and none is subject to any hire purchase, leasing, loan or other similar agreement.

The said central heating system, burglar alarm system and any electrically operated and/or mechanically operated items among the said items will be in good working order on the Date of Entry.

4. The seller will inform the Council Tax Office of the change of ownership.

5. As at the Date of Entry there shall be no allocated monetary ground burdens exigible from the Subjects. Any unallocated burdens exigible from the Subjects do not exceed £10 per annum.

6. (a) The minerals are included in the sale or alternatively there are adequate rights of support and adequate provisions in the title of the Subjects for compensation for subsidence and/or any damage to the surface of the Subjects or any buildings comprised therein caused by or arising from mineral workings past present or future.

(b) There are no unduly onerous conditions or restrictions in the title of the Subjects and the title conditions have been adhered to. There are no conditions in the said title which restrict the present use of the Subjects. There are no unimplemented building or feuing conditions (other than those of a continuing nature).

(c) There are no servitudes, wayleaves or rights in favour of third parties affecting the Subjects.

(d) There are no overriding interests (as defined by the Land Registration (Scotland) Act 1979) affecting the Subjects.

7. (I) The Seller warrants that as at the Date of Entry and as at the date hereof:

    (a) there are no notices, orders, proposals or others served or intimated by the relevant local authority or any other authority under any public, local or other statute (or regulation, order or other thereunder) affecting or likely to affect the Subjects;

    (b) there are no outstanding notices, orders, undertakings or others issued by or given to the relevant local authority or any other authority or body in respect of repairs, renewals, improvements, demolition or other works to the Subjects;

    (c) the Subjects are in an area zoned for residential purposes in the Development Plan; they are not affected by any planning schemes or redevelopment proposals at the instance of or contemplated by the relevant local authority; they are not listed as being of Special Architectural or Historic Interest and they do not lie within a Conservation Area;

    (d) the roads, footpaths and sewers *ex adverso* the Subjects have been taken over for maintenance by the relevant local authority and there are no road widening or other road proposals affecting the Subjects; and

    (e) the Subjects are adequately served by a mains water supply and mains drainage and sewerage systems.

    (II) Written evidence of the foregoing will be exhibited or delivered to the Purchaser on or prior to the Date of Entry.

    (III) If the matters warranted herein are not as stated, the Purchaser shall be entitled to rescind without penalty from the missives of which this offer forms part ('the Missives').

8. If any alterations or other works have been carried out to the Subjects for which Planning Permission or Building Warrant would have been required, all necessary Planning Permissions, Building Warrants and Completion Certificates will be delivered on the Date of Entry together with the Superior's consent or waiver if such consent or waiver was required. The Seller warrants that all works have been carried out strictly in accordance with such Planning Permissions, Building Warrants and Superior's consent or waiver.

9. The Seller warrants that the Seller is not aware of any applications or proposed applications for Planning Permission or

Building Warrant in respect of other subjects in the vicinity of the Subjects in respect of which the relevant works have not been completed at the date hereof. If the Seller becomes aware of any such applications prior to the Date of Entry the Seller shall notify the same to us forthwith and the Purchaser shall at the Purchaser's option have ten working days to resile from the Missives by notice in writing to the Seller's Solicitors if such application would adversely affect the Purchaser's use and enjoyment, or the value, of the Subjects.

10. (a) If any Specialist treatments have been carried out to the Subjects, the Seller warrants that such treatments have been carried out by reputable tradesmen and a valid guarantee in terms acceptable to the Purchaser exists and will be delivered along with the relative survey report at the Date of Entry. Further the Seller will execute and deliver at the Date of Entry a valid assignation of all rights under such guarantee.

    (b) If double glazing, central heating or a burglar alarm system have been installed in the Subjects then the Seller will deliver at the Date of Entry any guarantee in respect thereof and will, if requested by the Purchaser, execute and deliver at the Date of Entry a valid assignation of all rights under such guarantee.

11. The Seller will maintain the Subjects and the specific items hereinbefore mentioned in their present condition (fair wear and tear excepted) until settlement of the transaction on the Date of Entry. The risk of damage or destruction to the Subjects or any part thereof and the specific items hereinbefore mentioned will remain with the Seller until settlement of the transaction on the Date of Entry. If the Subjects or any part of them are destroyed or materially damaged on or prior to the Date of Entry or if there is any material deterioration or change in the Subjects between the time when they were viewed by the Purchaser and the Date of Entry, the Purchaser will be entitled to resile without penalty.

12. At the Date of Entry the Seller will in exchange for the Price: –

    (a) deliver a duly executed disposition in favour of the purchaser and will exhibit or deliver a valid marketable title together with a Form 10 Report brought down to a date as near as practicable to the date of settlement and showing no entries adverse to the Seller's interest, the cost of said report being the responsibility of the Seller. In addition, the Seller, at or before the date of entry and at his expense, shall deliver to the Purchaser such docu-

ments and evidence as the Keeper may require to enable
the Keeper to issue a land certificate in the name of the
purchaser as the registered proprietor of the whole subjects of offer and containing no exclusion of indemnity in
terms of section 12(2) of the Land Registration
(Scotland) Act 1979: such documents shall include
(unless the whole subjects of offer only comprise part of
a tenement or flatted building) a plan or bounding
description sufficient to enable the whole subjects of offer
to be identified on the Ordnance map and evidence (such
as a Form P16 Report) that the description of the whole
subjects of offer as contained in the title deed is *habile* to
include the whole of the occupied extent. The Land
Certificate to be issued to the Purchaser will disclose no
entry, deed or diligence prejudicial to the Purchaser's
interest other than such as are created by or against the
Purchaser, or have been disclosed to, and accepted by,
the Purchaser prior to the date of settlement.

Notwithstanding the delivery of the disposition above
referred to this clause shall remain in full force and
effect and may be founded upon.

(b) If the Seller is a Company:–
   (i) exhibit or deliver clear Searches in the Company
     Charges Register and Company files against all lim-
     ited companies (or other corporate bodies) interested
     in the Subjects within the prescriptive period brought
     down to 22 days after the company or companies
     concerned ceased to be infeft in the Subjects. In the
     event of such Searches disclosing any Floating Charge
     currently affecting the Subjects, there will be deliv-
     ered to the Purchaser on the Date of Entry a
     Certificate of Non-crystallisation of such Floating
     Charge granted by the holders thereof. Such Searches
     so far as against the Seller, after being brought down
     as aforesaid will be delivered to the Purchaser not
     later than two months after the Date of Entry;
   (ii) deliver to the Purchaser a letter signed by two of the
     Directors of the Seller in terms of the draft letter set
     out in Schedule 1 hereof.

(c) It is a condition of the bargain that during the period
commencing with the delivery to the Purchaser of the
Disposition (in favour of the Purchaser referred to in
clause 6 above) and ending with the effective recording
of the said Disposition in the Land Registers or the
Register of Sasines, the Seller shall hold the title to the
subjects of sale, so far as not effectively transferred to
the Purchaser by delivery of the said Disposition, in trust
for the disponees in the said Disposition and at the

Purchaser's option there shall either be included in the said Disposition a declaration to this effect or there shall be delivered at settlement along with the said Disposition a probative declaration by the Seller to this effect.

13. Notwithstanding delivery of the said Disposition (and except as otherwise hereinbefore provided), the missives shall remain in full force and effect for a period of two years from the date of delivery of the said Disposition and thereafter only insofar as they are founded on in any court proceedings which have commenced within the said period. At the option of the Purchaser or the Seller, immediately following upon delivery of said Disposition there shall be exchanged letters between the Seller's solicitors and the Purchaser's solicitors in the form set out in Schedule 2 hereof confirming the foregoing. Further, at the option of the Purchaser a clause to that effect shall be contained in the said Disposition.

14. The Seller will provide such reasonable evidence as shall be satisfactory to us in all respects that as at the Date of Entry there are no subsisting occupancy rights under either the Matrimonial Homes (Family Protection) (Scotland) Act 1981 (as amended) or the Family Law (Scotland) Act 1985 prejudicial to the Purchaser or the nominees of the Purchaser affecting the Subjects. Any spouse of the Seller shall sign the Disposition hereinbefore referred to giving consent to the dealing implemented by the delivery of the said Disposition.

15. The Seller warrants that the Subjects are not affected by any transfer of property order under the Family Law (Scotland) Act 1985.

16. The Seller will, prior to the Date of Entry, disclose his new address to the Purchaser.

17. Notwithstanding any rule of law to the contrary, the *actio quanti minoris* shall be available to the Purchaser.

18. If the subjects are a flat in a tenement, the following conditions shall apply:–

    (a) The said dwellinghouse forms part of a tenement and the usual parts of the said tenement are held in common by all of the proprietors thereof, including without prejudice to the foregoing generality the roof, outside walls, the foundations, the solum on which the said tenement is erected and the back green or court thereof. The cost of maintenance, repair and renewal of the common parts is borne in equal shares by all of the proprietors of the said

tenement. The common charges will be apportioned
between the Purchaser and the Seller as at the said Date
of Entry.

(b) The Seller will be liable for the cost of all common
repairs instructed or undertaken prior to the Date of
Entry whether completed or not. The Seller warrants
that there are no common repairs in contemplation, or
under tender but not yet instructed.

19. This offer is open for acceptance unless sooner withdrawn
until 10am on Friday 9th March 1995 and if an acceptance
has not been received by us by then this offer shall be
deemed to be withdrawn.

Yours faithfully,

This and the five preceding pages together with Schedules 1 and
2 adopted as holograph

MAIR & KILDARE

M & K

Note: This offer was prepared and signed 'adopted as holograph' prior to the
coming into force of the Requirements of Writing (Scotland) Act 1995 on 1
August 1995.

Schedule 1

This is the draft letter referred to in Condition 12(b) of the foregoing Offer.

To: Messrs Mair & Kildare,
Solicitors,
35 Magister Street
Paisley   Date:

WE,   both Directors of
Limited ('the Seller') hereby certify and warrant after due and
diligent enquiry (i) that no deeds of any kind which are capable
of being recorded in the Register of Sasines or Land Register in
respect of or affecting
('the Subjects') have been granted by the Seller other than as are
disclosed in the Search (including Interim Reports on Search) in
the Sasine Register or Land Register exhibited to you as Solicitors
for ('the Purchaser') (ii) that no Floating Charge, Debenture or
other security document which is capable of being registered in
the Companies Charges Register has been granted by the Seller
other than as are disclosed in the Search (including Interim
Reports on Search) in the Companies Register exhibited to you
and (iii) that the Seller is solvent and no steps have been or are
about to be taken by us or to the best of our knowledge and belief
by any third party to commence liquidation proceedings which
would prejudice the validity of the Disposition of the Subjects now
being granted to the Purchaser or to appoint a Receiver or otherwise place the Seller in a position whereby it cannot execute and
deliver to the Purchaser a valid and unobjectionable title.

We further agree and acknowledge that in the event of the
Purchaser incurring any loss, damage or expense as a result of
any of the matters included in the foregoing certificate and warrant being untrue or proving to be unfounded we shall be liable
personally and individually, and jointly and severally to make
good all such loss, damage and expense to the Purchaser.

M & K

Schedule 2

These are the draft Non-Supersession Letters referred to in Condition 13 of the foregoing Offer.

A. Letter from Purchaser's Solicitors to Seller's Solicitors.

DEAR SIRS,

AB Purchaser
CD Seller
Address of Subjects

Notwithstanding delivery of the Disposition relative to the above
subjects, which has already taken place, we on behalf of the
Purchaser, hereby AGREE that the Missives relative to the sale
of the above subjects dated
will remain in full force and effect as provided therein.

Yours faithfully

B. Letter from Seller's Solicitors to Purchaser's Solicitors.

DEAR SIRS,

CD Seller
AB Purchaser
Address of Subjects

We hereby acknowledge receipt of your letter dated
relative to the above subjects, and on behalf of the Seller confirm
that the Missives relative to the sale of the above subjects dated
        will remain in full force and effect as provided therein.

Yours faithfully

M & K

Note: Although these letters are provided for in the missives, as an extra pre-caution against a *Winston v Patrick* situation, I obtain the impression that they are used less and less. Certainly they are not exchanged in this transaction.

Notes: (1) This is a pretty good example of the standardised wordprocessor offer, which has the advantage of being better looking than an offer with a photocopied schedule of conditions, of being quickly prepared, and of covering a lot of eventualities. On the other hand, parts of the offer are inappropriate (eg the large parts covering a company seller and the sale of a tenement). Care must be taken with such offers, as they are dynamite in the wrong hands – for instance I recently saw a residential offer being used for a commercial property, for which it was quite inappropriate. If you are using such an offer, it should not be issued uncritically.

(2) While the recurrence of a *Winston & Patrick* situation is covered in law, I would have doubts about the result in practice. While the central heating clause is fine, what happens if a defect in the heating is not noted for a few days? By that time the seller has been paid, and is safely outwith the jurisdiction. For what it is worth, I would advise a clause allowing an inspection of the heating before entry, and if there is any defect, then pressure can be put on the seller by refusing to settle until arrangements are agreed to rectify the defect. Compare alteration clause in Appendix I, 11/2b.

(3) The offer stipulates that the purchaser be informed of any material development to adjoining subjects. Of course, one has no rights to a view, unless one owns the land over which the view is, but the purchaser does not want to buy a house in a nice settled area, only to find that it becomes a building site after the move takes place.

(4) The selling company clause is inappropriate, as is the tenement clause. It is the seller's decision whether they will be deleted or not – it is probably better to delete them, just in case a problem arises.

(5) Note how labels are attached to everyone and anything at the outset of the offer. This is perfectly sound drafting practice, and avoids tiresome repetition and possible mistakes, which is commendable. Note, however, the labels should be clear and self explanatory – eg 'Seller', 'Purchaser' and so on. Avoid jargon words like 'party of the first part' which are ugly and not at all self explanatory. I am also less than happy that a married couple should be referred to as 'the Purchaser' – it would only take a little extra effort to refer to them as 'the Purchasers', and to make the required grammatical amendments.

(6) Please note that obligation contained at 12(a) which is in the style recommended by the Deputy Keeper in an article – 'Land Registration Update' January 1995 JLSS 15.

(7) Further note clause 12(c) which states that the Disposition shall be held by the seller in trust for the purchaser. This is to get around the difficulty raised in the case of *Sharp v Thomson* 1994 GWD 19–1181, which decision was in May 1995, sustained on appeal.

12 Office memo from Henry Pink to Wendy Robertson (6 March 1995)

Here is McLachlan's offer for 3 Miller Drive. I am getting too old for this game. What happened to the old five clause offer? What does it all mean? Please prepare acceptance for my signature.

H.P.

Note: Particularly note how law reform and systematic legal education have changed things a bit. Pink has been a conveyancer for some thirty years, and Wendy Robertson is only a year or so out of University. She probably now knows more about registration of title and other modern developments. But Pink is no fool. He keeps himself up-to-date by attending courses and reading comprehensively. He will keep a pretty close eye on Wendy Robertson, bearing in mind the Law Society's recommendations in Appendix VII.

13 Letter received from Black Country & Midlands Building Society (7 March 1995)

Letter enclosing title deeds, and a note of deduction of title for the discharge, which should be followed (see **18c** in this Appendix).

14 File Note (7 March 1995)

Meeting with Mr and Mrs James and going through offer with them. Basically they approved the price, the entry date and the moveables (with one small exception) and said they would leave 'all the rest' to us.

W.R.

Note: This is a most important note to make in case the James's ever challenge the Agents' right to have made the acceptance, or any part of it. The note would not be very good evidence, but it is much better than nothing. It is really quite extraordinary what disappears from even the best human memory.

15   Acceptance from Brown, Jarvie & Walker to Mair & Kildare (9 March 1995)

BROWN, JARVIE & WALKER,
Solicitors,
42 Registration Row,
Glasgow G1 3XX.

Messrs Mair & Kildare,
Solicitors,
35 Magister Street,
Paisley PA1 4ZZ.

DX PA5000

URGENT COURIER DELIVERY

9th March 1995

DEAR SIRS,

On behalf of our client Mr John James of 3 Miller Drive, Glasgow, (hereinafter called 'the seller') we hereby accept the offer dated 7th March 1995 made on behalf of Mr and Mrs MacLachlan (hereinafter called 'the Purchasers') to purchase the detached dwellinghouse at 3 Miller Drive, Glasgow, as described in your offer, and that at the price of SEVENTY SIX THOUSAND FIVE HUNDRED POUNDS (£76,500) and that on the terms and conditions contained in your said offer to purchase, but subject to the following qualifications:-

A. Payment of the purchase price in full on the date of entry is of the essence of the contract. In the event of the purchase price or any part thereof remaining outstanding as at the date of entry, then notwithstanding consignation or the fact that entry has not been taken by your clients, your clients shall be deemed to be in material breach of contract and further, interest will accrue at the base lending rate of 4 per centum per annum above The Royal Bank of Scotland plc base lending rate from time to time until full payment of the price is made or in the event of our clients exercising their option to rescind the contract until such time as our clients shall have completed a resale of the subjects and received the resale price and further interest shall run on any shortfall between the purchase price hereunder and the resale price until such time as the shortfall shall have been paid to our clients. In the event that the said purchase price is not paid in full within fourteen days of the date of entry, our clients shall be entitled to treat your clients as being in material breach of contract and to rescind the missives on giving prior written notice to that effect to your clients without prejudice to any rights or any claims competent to our clients arising from the breach of contract by your clients including our clients' rights to claim all losses, damages and expenses sustained as a result of your clients' breach of contract including interest on the price calculated as set out in this clause. For the purposes of computation of our clients' loss, the interest element of that loss shall be deemed to be a liquidate penalty provision exigible notwithstanding the exercise by our clients of their option to rescind the contract for non-payment of the price or any repudiation of the contract by your clients. This clause shall have effect always provided that any unreasonable delay in settlement is not attributable to us or our clients.

This clause, where inconsistent with clauses 1 and 2 of your offer, shall be the ruling clause of the two.

B. The time limit in your Offer (if any) shall be withdrawn.

C. While it is to be believed that the position is as stated in Condition 6 of your Offer, no Superior's certificate in any respect shall be made available.

D. In Condition 11 of your Offer, the word 'the Purchaser' where it occurs in the last line shall be deleted and 'both parties to this contract' shall be substituted.

E. With reference to clause 6 of your Offer, the title deeds shall be dispatched to you at the earliest opportunity, and your clients shall have seven days to intimate any objection to their terms, failing which they will be deemed to have satisfied themselves.

F. Clauses 12 (b) and 18 will be deleted as inappropriate.

G. Double glazing was fitted to the windows throughout four years ago, but the Company has gone out of business, and the Guarantee is thought to be worthless.

H. An acceptance of the terms of this letter shall be received in this office by 12.00 pm on Monday 12th March 1995 failing which this letter, if not sooner withdrawn, shall be treated pro non scripto.

We shall be pleased to receive your acceptance of these qualifications and conclusion of the agreement.

Yours faithfully,

BROWN, JARVIE & WALKER

cc Mr James

Notes: (1) Letters of the Alphabet are used for conditions to distinguish them from the numbers used in the offer.

(2) An interest clause is inserted, which is apparently heavily in favour of the seller. This is drafted along the lines suggested in an article in November 1993 JLSS 450 following the case of *Lloyds Bank plc v Bamberger* 1993 SCLR 727.

There is a longer suggested style in that article, which could be used. The shorter form has the advantage of being more general in its specification of damages, while the larger clause specifies them, and omits such matters as an arrangement fee for overdrafts – which can be as high as £1000. It is however quite fair, and its terms will be accepted by the vast majority of purchasers. It is only prejudicial to a purchaser who is careless in his arrangements, or unlucky. Where it might be prejudicial is if it doesn't suspend the sanctions on the seller's default. It might save time, therefore, for purchasers to make this quite standard clause part of an offer.

(3) To comply with the time limit, a courier service is used. The offer time limit is nevertheless cancelled, and a new time limit inserted.

(4) To provide a Superior's Certificate is usually a frustrating and expensive exercise. The purchasers should be left to satisfy themselves in this respect. But see Chapter 17 on superiors.

(5) If you allow the purchasers too long to note the title, the danger is that the day before settlement they will raise some objection. In this case the purchasers are allowed seven days from receipt of title to intimate any objections.

(6) A Guarantee is only as good as the Guarantor! A reputable firm would in turn be guaranteed by a trade or indemnity organisation.

(7) In Condition D, what is sauce for the goose is considered sauce for the gander.

(8) The letters 'cc' are an instruction to the typist to make an additional copy and to send it to the persons named. The letters actually mean 'carbon copy', but nowadays it is usually a photocopy.

16   Letter from Mair & Kildare to Brown, Jarvie & Walker (11 March 1995)

DEAR SIRS,

On behalf of our clients Lachlan and Jean McLachlan, we hereby accept the qualifications contained in your letter of 9 March 1995, being a qualified acceptance of our offer, dated 7 March 1995 for the purchase of the property at 3 Miller Drive, Glasgow.

We are accordingly holding the bargain between our respective clients as concluded on the basis of (1) our offer (2) your acceptance (3) this letter.

Yours faithfully,

MAIR & KILDARE

Notes: This letter concludes the missives, both parties being *in idem* (in the same thing). The conclusion of missives initiates a sequence of events from the seller as follows:

(a) inform client (see Appendix **I.18**);
(b) inform building society of sale and ask for amount required to redeem mortgage at that date;
(c) send title deeds to purchaser's agent;
(d) make future diary entries to ensure that transaction does not 'fall asleep'.

Letters (a) and (b) are self-explanatory and are not reproduced here.

17   File Note (5 March 1995)

Attendance with Mrs James and explaining to her carefully the importance of the MH(FP)(S) Affidavit and advising her that she was at liberty to seek separate advice before signing the affidavit if she was at all unsure. Noting that Mrs James had worked in a law firm, understood exactly what the Affidavit was, and had no intention of claiming her rights as a non-entitled spouse.

W R

Note: Mrs James has had the position carefully explained to her, which is good. This Act had an impeccable social purpose, but it does create some difficulties in perfectly normal conveyancing transactions. On the question of dealing with non-entitled spouses, please see the case of *Mumford* The Times, 4 August 1994. The Affidavit is in form of Appendix III.1, or could be incorporated into the disposition.

18   Letter from Brown, Jarvie & Walker to Mair & Kildare (11 March 1995)

DEAR SIRS,

We refer to the conclusion of the agreement for sale and now enclose the following:

(a) the title deeds of the property per inventory;
(b) draft discharge of our client's loan;
(c) Form 10A Report and draft Form 11;
(d) draft letter of obligation;
(e) feuduty redemption receipt;
(f) matrimonial affidavit.

We shall be pleased to receive your draft disposition in due course, together with your draft Forms 1 and 4.

Yours faithfully,

BROWN, JARVIE & WALKER

Notes: (1). Please compare this letter with the equivalent letter (Appendix I. 19/20) in the Sasine Register Transaction.

(2). The title deeds are sent, whether relevant or not. This is not really necessary. See relevant title deeds as listed in **21(i)**.

18(a)   **Inventory of Writs enclosed with 18**

INVENTORY OF WRITS

of

3 Miller Drive,
GLASGOW.

1. Feu Contract between Alpin McAlpine and other and Hugh McHugh and recorded GRS (Glasgow) 3 February 1884.

2. Disposition by John Evans and Gareth Evans. Trustees of Evan Evans in favour of Millhaugh Development Co Ltd dated 3 et cetera and recorded said GRS 24 June 1952.

3. Feu Charter by Millhaugh Development Co Ltd in favour of Gregor McGregor dated 3 July and recorded said GRS 10 July 1968.

4. Extract Registered Trust Disposition and Settlement of Gregor McGregor dated 5 July 1965 and registered said BCS 10 July 1953.

5. Certificate of Confirmation in favour of Donald McDonald dated 4 October 1978 with dockets in favour of William McWilliam dated 10 November 1978, all registered BCS 25 November 1978.

6. Notice of Title in favour of William McWilliam recorded said GRS 3 March 1979.

7. Disposition by William McWilliam to Alistair McAllister dated 3 June and recorded said GRS 16 June 1984.

8. Standard Security by Alistair McAllister to Ben Wyvis Building Society recorded said GRS 16 June 1981.

9. Disposition by Alistair McAllister to John James recorded said GRS 3 May 1985.

10. Standard Security by James Meikle to Black Country Building Society recorded said GRS 3 May 1985.

11. Certificate from Strathclyde Regional Council as to roads, et cetera dated 13 August 1982.

12. Feu-Duty Redemption Receipt by Millhaugh Development Co Ltd dated 19 June 1981.

18(b)   **Draft letter of obligation enclosed with 18**

DRAFT LETTER OF OBLIGATION

Messrs Mair & Kildare,
Solicitors,
35 Magister Street, Paisley.

1995

DEAR SIRS,

Mr John James
Mr and Mrs McLachlan
3 Miller Drive, Glasgow

With reference to the settlement of the above transaction today, we hereby (1) undertake to clear the records of any deed, decree or diligence (other than such as may be created by or against your clients) which may be recorded in the Property or Personal Registers, or to which effect may be given in the Land Register in the period from*   to†   1995 inclusive (or to the earlier registration of your clients' interest in the above subjects) which would cause the Keeper to make an entry on, or qualify his indemnity in, the Land Certificate to be issued in respect of that interest; and (2) confirm that, to the best of our knowledge and belief, as at this date, the answers to the questions numbered 1 to 14 in draft Form 1 adjusted with you (in so far as the answers relate to my client or to our clients' interest in the above subjects) are still correct.

Yours faithfully,

Note: The dates are inserted at the time of settlement and are (a) the date of the Form 11 Report and (b) 14 days after settlement.

*Insert date of certification of final Form 10 or 11 Report.
†Insert date 14 days after settlement.

18(c) **Draft discharge of standard security** (enclosed with 18) (see original security at Appendix **I.26**)

WE, BLACK COUNTRY and MIDLANDS BUILDING SOCIETY incorporated under the Building Societies Acts having the Chief Registered Office at Black Country Buildings, Stoke-on-Trent IN CONSIDERATION of the sum of TWENTY FIVE THOUSAND POUNDS being the whole amount secured by the Standard Security aftermentioned now or formerly paid by JOHN JAMES residing at Three Miller Drive, Glasgow HEREBY DISCHARGE the Standard Security for the sum of Twenty five thousand pounds by the said John James in favour of the Black Country Building Society of Black Country House, Stoke-on-Trent recorded in the Division of the General Register of Sasines applicable to the County of the Barony and Regality of Glasgow on Third May Nineteen hundred and eighty five; which Standard Security was last vested in the said Black Country Building Society as aforesaid and from whom we acquired right by Transfer of Engagements dated Tenth October Nineteen hundred and ninety one between the said Black Country Building Society and Midlands Building Society of Midlands House, Cradley Heath, West Midlands and confirmed by the Building Societies Commission under section 95(3) of the Building Societies Act 1986 the Twenty First June Nineteen hundred and ninety one and Registration Certificate of said confirmation by the Building Societies Commission issued from the Central Office of the Registry of Friendly Societies: IN WITNESS WHEREOF these presents are sealed with the Seal of the Society on
the   day of
                    and countersigned by
Authorised Officer in the presence of these witnesses

Securities Clerk   Authorised Officer
Black Country Buildings   by authority of the Board
Stoke-on-Trent   of Directors

Securities Clerk
Black Country Buildings
Stoke-on-Trent

SEAL

Notes:
(1) Please see the deduction of title by the new building society linking up with the Security granted to the old society.
(2) The building society will normally supply all of these details – if not, ask for them.
(3) Note – no Warrant of Registration; this deed is not recorded in the General Register of Sasines, but in the Land Register.

19 Note from Wendy Robertson to Veronica Vanbrugh – Diary entries to be made (11 March 1995)

3 Miller Drive, Glasgow
Please make the following diary entries:
11 March – Titles sent out.
28 March – Draft disposition received.
4 April   – Check file to ensure that everything is on course.
11 April   – Submit Form II for Report. Make arrangements for settlement.
18 April   – Settlement.

Note: This is very important for the busy law office. The secretary will make these entries both in her own diary and in the diary of the person dealing ('Double-diary system'), and on the appropriate date will let the person dealing with this have the file for action. At all costs the horrors of a last minute rush should be avoided.

20

Note: At this point the purchasers' solicitors should be kept busy for a week or two. They must note the title precisely as before (see Appendix **I.25**) bearing in mind that they must (a) satisfy themselves as to title and (b) satisfy the Keeper that the title is registerable without exclusion of indemnity. As I mention in the text, the first registered transaction is not easy, and the Solicitors may charge accordingly; it is the second and subsequent registrations that become easy, because there is no need to examine a prescriptive title.

Make sure, however, that the purchasers' solicitors do not take too long – see above.

21(a)   Letter from Mair & Kildare to Brown, Jarvie & Walker (28 March 1995)

DEAR SIRS,

Mr & Mrs L. McLachlan
Mr James
3 Miller Drive, Glasgow

We refer to our previous correspondence and return the title deeds and your various drafts, all duly approved. We also enclose our draft Disposition and draft Forms 1 and 4 for your approval and return.

Kindly attend to the following observations:

(1) Please let us have the Form 11 Report at settlement.

(2) Please confirm that there are no outstanding liabilities for any moveable items included in the sale.

(3) Please let us have your State for Settlement.

(4) Please let us have the usual letter confirming that there are no outstanding notices.

(5) Please let us see a Building Warrant, Completion Certificate, and Superior's consent in relation to the garage built approximately seven years ago.

Yours faithfully,

MAIR & KILDARE

Note: (1) The enquiries on title are few. This is basically because all the queries have been answered before they are asked. This is precisely the way in which it should be done. I am also assuming that Mair & Kildare are not the kind of firm who ask a lot of questions purely for the sake of trying to show how clever they are.

(2) In modern conveyancing transactions it might be said that the missive stage is now more important than the examination of title stage.

(3) Note that there is no mention of apportionment of Rates, which is not now applicable to domestic properties.

(4) Question 5 is going to cause a flutter at Brown, Jarvie & Walker. They didn't know about the garage!

21(b)   Note of telephone call. Wendy Robertson to Mrs James (2 March 1995)

Asking Mrs James about the building of the garage. Noting she did not know if it had a Building Warrant or Completion Certificate, as they were not married then. Noting that Mr James was abroad for the next 10 days on business (10 minutes).

21(c)   Note from Wendy Robertson to Henry Pink (29 March 1995)

Please note situation here with no details of Building Warrant or Completion Certificate, and Mr James out of country. What do you suggest?

21(d)   Note from Henry Pink to Wendy Robertson (29 March 1995)

Try CRGP for a Letter of Comfort. It's all we can do in the time left. See article in JLSS February 1994, p 46. Millhaugh will give a superior's certificate fairly quickly.

Note: This service may not be preferable to obtaining a Letter of Comfort from the local authority. It depends on the circumstances. In an emergency like this the CRGP service will be better.

21(e)

Telephoning CRGP and explaining position to them. Noting that they would survey the property as soon as possible and let us know if they would issue their letter which has the same effect as a Letter of Comfort, and which is insured against inaccuracy. (29 March 1995)

21(f)

Telephoning Mair & Kildare and explaining that we propose to get CRGP Report. Noting that they would accept this. (29 March 1995)

21(h)   **Purchasers Draft Form I**

FORM 1   Rule 9(1)(a)

Form of application for first registration

REGISTERS OF SCOTLAND EXECUTED AGENCY	**FORM 1**	***Please complete in BLACK TYPE*** Typewriter Alignment Box
(Land Registration (Scotland) Rules 1980 Rule 9(1)(a)	)	No covering letter is required Type XXX in centre

APPLICATION FOR FIRST REGISTRATION

1 **Presenting Agent, Name and Address (see Note 1)**

MAIR & KILDARE
35 MAGISTER STREET
PAISLEY DX PA 5000

Keeper of the Registers of Scotland
Meadowbank House
153 London Road
EDINBURGH EH8 7AU
Telephone: 0131 659 6111

Part A

2 **FAS No.** (see Note 2)	3 **Agent's Tel No** (include STD Code)	4 **Agent's Reference**
5555	0141 898 1324	JHS/AA

5 **Name of Deed** in respect of which registration is required	6 **County** (see Note 3)	Mark X in box if more than one county
DISPOSITION	GLASGOW	

7 **Subjects** (see Note 4)

Street No.	3	Street Name	MILLER DRIVE		
Town	GLASGOW			Post code	G99 1AA
Other					

8 **Name and Address of Applicant** (see Note 5)

1. Surname   Forename(s)
   McLACHLAN   LACHLAN

Address
3 GLENLIVET ROAD, GLASGOW

2. Surname   Forename(s
   McLACHLAN   JEAN

Address
3 GLENLIVET ROAD, GLASGOW

and/or company/firm or council, etc.   Mark X in box if more than 2 applicants
N/A

Address

9 **Grant/Party Last Infeft** (see Note 6)

1. Surname   Forename(s)
   JAMES   JOHN

2. Surname   Forename(s)

and/or company/firm or council, etc   Mark X in box if more than 2 granters
N/A

10 **Consideration** (see Note 7)	**Value** (see Note 8)	**Fee** (see Note 9)	**Date of Entry**
75000	75000	A 176.00	18 APRIL 19957

11 If a Form 10 Report has been issued in connection with this Application, please quote Report No.   A/12345689

12 I/We apply for registration in respect of Deed(s) No in the inventory of Writs (Form 4). I/We certify that the information supplied in this application is correct to the best of my/our knowledge and belief.	**FOR OFFICIAL USE**

Signature   **Date**

Notes 1–9 referred to are contained in Notes and Directions for completion of Applications for First Registration

PART B

Delete **YES** or **NO** as appropriate
N.B.   If more space is required for any section of this form, a separate sheet, or separate sheets, may
be added.

---

1.   Do the deeds submitted in support of this application include a plan   **YES/NO**
illustrating the extent of the subjects to be registered?
If **YES**, please specify the deed and its Form 4 Inventory number:

If **NO**, have you submitted a deed containing a full bounding description   **YES/NO**
with measurements?

If **YES**, please specify the deed and its Form 4 Inventory number:

N.B.   If the answer to both the above questions is **NO** then, unless the
property is part of a tenement or flatted building you must submit a
plan of the subjects properly drawn to a stated scale and showing
sufficient surrounding features to enable it to be located on the
Ordnance Map. The plan should bear a docquet, signed by the
person signing the Application Form, to the effect that it is a plan
of the subjects sought to be registered under the attached
application.

---

2.   Is a Form P16 Report issued by the Keeper confirming that the boundaries   **YES/NO**
of the subjects coincide with the Ordnance Map being submitted in support
of this Application?

If **NO**, does the legal extent depicted in the plans or descriptions in the   **YES/NO**
deeds submitted in support of the Application cohere with the ocupational
extent?

If **NO**, please advise:–

(a)   the approximate age and nature of the occupational boundaries, or

(b)   whether, if the extent of the subjects as defined in the deeds is larger   **YES/NO**
than the occupational extent, the applicant is prepared to accept the
occupational extent as viewed, or

(c)   whether, if the extent of the subjects as defined in the deeds is   **YES/NO**
smaller than the occupational extent, any remedial action has been
taken.

---

3.   Is there any person in possession or occupation of the subjects or any part   **YES/NO**
of them adversely to the interest of the applicant?
If **YES**, please give details:

---

4.   If the subjects were acquired by the applicant under any statutory   **YES/NO**
provision, does the statutory provision restrict the applicant's power of
disposal of the subjects?
If **YES**, please indicate the statute:

---

5.   (a)   Are there any charges affecting the subjects or any part of them,   **YES/NO**
except as stated in the Schedule of Heritable Securities etc. on page
4 of this application?
If **YES**, please give details:

(b)   Apart from overriding interests are there any burdens affecting the   **YES/NO**
subjects or any part of them, except as stated in the Schedule of
Burdens on page 4 of this application?
If **YES**, please give details:

(c) Are there any overriding interests affecting the subjects or any part of them which you wish noted on the Title Sheet? **YES/NO**
If **YES**, please give details:

(d) Are there any recurrent monetary payments (e.g. feuduty, leasehold casualties) exigible from the subjects or any part of them? **YES/NO**
If **YES**, please give details:

6. Where any party to the deed inducing registration is a Company registered under the Companies Acts

Has a receiver or liquidator been appointed? **YES/NO**
If **YES**, please give details:

If **NO**, has any resolution been passed or court order made for the winding up of the Company or petition presented for its liquidation? **YES/NO**
If **YES**, please give details:

7. Where any party to the deed inducing registration is a Company registered under the Companies Acts can you confirm

(a) that it is not a charity as defined in section 112 of the Companies Act 1989 and **YES/NO**

(b) that the transaction to which the deed gives effect is not one to which section 322A of the Companies Act 1985 (as inserted by section 109 of the Companies Act 1989) applies? **YES/NO**

Where the answer to either branch of the question is **NO**, please give details:

8. Where any party to the deed inducing registration is a corporate body other than a Company registered under the Companies Acts

(a) Is it acting *intra vires*? **YES/NO**
If **NO**, please give details:

(b) Has any arrangement been put in hand for the dissolution of any such corporate body? **YES/NO**
If **YES**, please give details:

9. Are *all* the necessary consents, renunciations or affidavits in terms of section 6 of the Matrimonial Homes (Family Protection) (Scotland) Act 1981 being submitted in connection with this application? **YES/NO**

N.B. If sufficient evidence to satisfy the Keeper that there is no subsisting occupancy rights in the subjects of this application is not submitted with the application then the statement by the Keeper in terms of rule 5(j) of the Land Registration (Scotland) Rules 1980 will not be inserted in the Title Sheet or will be qualified as appropriate without further enquiry by the Keeper.

10. Where the deed inducing registration is in implement of the exercise of a
     power of sale under a heritable security

     Have the statutory procedures necessary for the proper exercise of   **YES/NO**
     such power been complied with?

11. Where the deed inducing registration is a General Vesting Declaration or a
     Notice of Title pursuant on a Compulsory Purchase Order

     Have the necessary statutory procedures been complied with?   **YES/NO**

12. Is any party to the deed inducing registration subject to any legal   **YES/NO**
     incapacity or disability?
     If **YES**, please give details:

13. Are the deeds and documents detailed in the Inventory (Form 4) all the   **YES/NO**
     deeds and documents relevant to the title?
     If **NO**, please give details:

14. Are there any facts and circumstances material to the right or title of the **YES/NO**
     applicant which have not already been disclosed in this application or its
     accompanying documents?
     If **YES**, please give details:

SCHEDULE OF HERITABLE SECURITIES ETC.
N.B. New Charges granted by the applicant should not be included

SCHEDULE OF BURDENS

21(i)   *Appendices*

21(i)   Draft Form 4 prepared by Purchaser's Agent

FORM 4   Rule 9(2)

Form of inventory of writs

REGISTERS OF SCOTLAND EXECUTIVE AGENCY   FORM 4
(Land Registration (Scotland) Rules 1980 Rule 9(2))

Typewriter Alignment Box
Type XXX in centre

INVENTORY OF WRITS RELEVANT TO APPLICATION FOR REGISTRATION *(see Note 1)*
(to be completed in duplicate)

MAIR & KILDARE
35 MAGISTER STREET   *(see Note 2)*
PAISLEY

DX PA 5000

Title Number(s)
(to be completed for a dealing with
registered interests in land.)

N/A

Subjects *(see Note 3)*   3 MILLER DRIVE
                               GLASGOW

Registration County   GLASGOW

Applicant's Reference   HP/WR

Please complete Inventory overleaf as in this specimen

Item No.	Please mark 'S' against writs submitted	Writ	Grantee	Date of Recording
		Particulars of Writs *(see Note 4)*		
		Land Certificate*		
		Charge Certificate*		
1	–	Feu Charter	Upright Builders Ltd	2 May 1938
2	S	Feu Disposition	Smith	4 Feb 1939

*Delete if inapplicable

Notes 1–4 referred to are contained in Notes and Directions for Completion of Inventory of Writs Relevant to Application for Registration.

FOR OFFICIAL USE ONLY
            APPLICATION NUMBER   DATE OF RECEIPT   TITLE NUMBER

The writs marked "S" on this inventory were received on the Date of Receipt stamped on this page.

Item No.	Please mark 'S' against writs submitted	INVENTORY Particulars of Writs (see Note 4) Writ	Grantee	Typewriter Alignment Box Type XXX in centre Date of Recording
–	–	Land Certificate*		
–	–	Charge Certificate*		
1	S	Feu Contract	Hugh McHugh	3 Feb 1884
2	S	Disposition	Millhaugh Development	24 June 1955
3	S	Feu Charter	Gregor McGregor	10 July 1968
4	S	Extract Will of	–	10 July 1982 (BCS)
		Gregor McGregor	–	
5	S	Confirmation	Donald McDonald	26 Nov 1982 (BCS)
6	S	Notice of Title	William McWilliam	3 March 1984
7	S	Disposition	Alistair McAllister	16 June 1984
8	S	Disposition	John James	3 May 1985
9	S	Standard Security	Black Country	3 May 1985
–	–		Building Society	
10	S	Disposition	Lachlan McLachlan	
11	S	Feuduty Redemption		
		Receipt d.10/6/84		
12	S	Discharge	John James	
13	S	Standard Security	Widnes Building Society	

*Delete if inapplicable

22   Reply by Brown, Jarvie & Walker to Mair & Kildare (1 April 1995)

DEAR SIRS,

John James
Mr and Mrs McLachlan
3 Miller Drive, Glasgow

Thank you for your letter of 28 March. We have revised your Draft Disposition, Draft Forms 1 and 4, and return these.

We would deal with your enquiries as follows:
(1) We shall send Form 11 to the Keeper on 11 April.
(2) We have now received and enclose letters from the District Council re planning et cetera, and the Regional Council re roads.
(3) We are obtaining the other information that you require.
(4) We enclose our draft State for Settlement.

Yours faithfully,

BROWN, JARVIE & WALKER

Note: The District Council and Regional Council Certificates are not printed here, as they are quite routine. For an example of the former see **18.16**.

23(a)   Draft state for settlement prepared by sellers' solicitors

STATE for SETTLEMENT
in connection with sale of
3 Miller Drive, Glasgow.

Price: £76,500 (including moveables of £1,500).

Entry: 18 April 1995.

Seller: Mr John James (Messrs Brown, Jarvie & Walker).

Purchaser: Mr and Mrs Lachlan McLachlan (Messrs Mair & Kildare).

18 April 1995	Price per Missives	£76,500.00
	Sum due by Purchaser	£76,500.00

Note: Council tax is dealt with by the following letter, 23(b).

23(b) Strathclyde Regional Council – Council Tax Notification

STRATHCLYDE REGIONAL COUNCIL
COUNCIL TAX

Strathclyde
FINANCE

<u>NOTIFICATION OF THE CHANGE IN OWNERSHIP OF A DWELLING HOUSE</u>

CLIENTS NAME :-___JOHN JAMES____
PROPERTY ADDRESS :-___3 MILLER DRIVE____
___GLASGOW____
_____
_____

REF No. (if known) :-_____–_____

I have acted in the sale/~~purchase~~ of the above mentioned property and would confirm the undernoted details :-

1. The date the property was sold/purchased :-___18 APRIL 1995___

2. My clients ~~previous~~/new address :-___per this form___
_____
_____
_____
_____

3. The name of the purchasers/sellers :-___BROWN JARVIE & WALKER___

AND THEIR

Agents Name :-___MAIR & KILDARE___
and Address :-___35 Magister Street___
___PAISLEY___
_____
_____
_____

SIGNED :-_____   DATE :-_____
Name and Address :-___42 Registration Row___
___GLASGOW___
_____
_____

24   Letter from Brown, Jarvie & Walker to Building Society (3 April 1995)

DEAR SIR,

<u>Mr John James</u>
<u>3 Miller Drive, Glasgow</u>
<u>Roll No XY1234567/A</u>

We enclose Discharge of Standard Security and Retrocession of Life Policy which please have executed for the Society. Please then let us have this, on the understanding that we shall hold it as delivered until the loan is repaid.

Please cancel the Fire Insurance on repayment of the loan, as client is moving elsewhere.

Please also let us have a note of the amount required to redeem the loan on or around 19 April 1995.

Yours faithfully,

BROWN, JARVIE & WALKER

25   Letter from Brown Jarvie & Walker to Mair & Kildare (7 April 1995)

DEAR SIRS,

<u>Mr John James</u>
<u>Mr & Mrs L McLachlan</u>
<u>3 Miller Drive, Glasgow</u>

We refer to our letter of 1 April 1995 and now enclose the Letter of Comfort that we have received from CRGP and letter from superiors.

We trust these are acceptable to you.

Yours faithfully,

BROWN, JARVIE & WALKER

26(a)   Letter from CRGP to Brown, Jarvie & Walker (6 April 1995)

CRGP,
12 Lynedoch Place,
Glasgow G3 6AB.

Brown Jarvie & Walker,
Solicitors,
42 Registration Row,
Glasgow.

DEAR SIRS,

LETTER OF COMFORT
Subjects: 3 Miller Drive, Glasgow

We refer to the inspection carried out by us at the above address yesterday.

From a cursory and non-disruptive survey, so far as we are able to ascertain after taking all reasonable steps on that behalf, we are satisfied the extension/alteration has been constructed and carried out generally in accordance with the requirements of building regulations. We do not anticipate that the District Council would have any ground of which to take any further action in this instance, with regard to any breach of the Building (Scotland) Acts 1959/70 with regard to the said extension/alteration.

Yours sincerely,

C.R.G.P.

26(b)   Letter from Millhaugh Development Limited to Brown, Jarvie & Walker

DEAR SIRS,

3 Miller Drive, Glasgow

Further to our recent telephone conversation regarding request for superiors consent for the erection of a garage retrospective feu superiors consent, we grant this subject to the following condition:–

1. All statutory consents are to be obtained as may be required.

Our fee in connection with this matter is £50.00 plus VAT, totalling £58.75.

Yours faithfully,

MILLHAUGH DEVELOPMENTS LIMITED

27   Note of telephone call from local office of Building Society (7 April 1995)

To: Wendy Robertson
From: Veronica Vanbrugh

Black Country Building Society telephoned today. Amount to settle on 18 April is £25163.58. Daily rate thereafter is £11.23.

V.V.

Note: If the transaction is settled on 18 April, the money should be received by the Building Society by 20 April at latest. Interest accrues daily, so the daily rate must be added to the repayment sum if the loan is repaid late.

Mr James may be upset to find he owes more than the original loan, but it is of course an endowment loan and he is forgetting that he is repaying no principal (see **12.10(b)**).

28   Note from Veronica Vanbrugh to Wendy Robertson (8 April 1995)

Please note diary entry today to send Form 11 and make arrangements for settlement.

V.V.

Thanks. Please send Form 11 to Register. Please check that we have the following on file:

(a)   draft state for settlement (approved by other side);
(b)   draft letter of obligation (approved by other side);
(c)   discharge and retrocession executed by Building Society and with testing clause complete;
(d)   matrimonial affidavit signed by Mrs James;
(e)   disposition signed by Mr James;
(f)   Please check we have returned draft Disposition to Mair & Kildare;
(g)   Letter of Comfort and superior's letter.

All present and correct.

V.V.

Thanks.

W.R.

Note: What a wonderfully efficient pair Wendy and Veronica are! This is, I'm afraid, all too often, a perfection unachieved.

29 Note of telephone call from Wendy Robertson to John James (9 April 1995)

Attendance on telephone call with Mr James and noting that he was moving out on 14 April and would drop the keys into Mr Pink's house on way South although Mrs James is staying in Glasgow for a few more days.

Informing Mr James that he should cancel all Bankers' Orders for Building Society payments et cetera, with effect from 19 April.

Note: This is good practice again.

30 Note of telephone call from Mair & Kildare to Wendy Robertson (17 April 1995)

Mair & Kildare have ten settlements tomorrow and regret they can't settle this personally. They will send cheque by Hot Wheels, the courier agency.

W.R.

31   Letter from Brown, Jarvie & Walker to Mair & Kildare (18 April 1995)

DEAR SIRS,

John James
Mr and Mrs McLachlan
3 Miller Drive, Glasgow

We have received your cheque for £76,500 and therefore now enclose:

1. The keys (two sets);
2. the signed disposition and particulars of signing (you already have the draft);
3. the prior writs;
4. out letter of obligation and draft for comparison and return;
5. feuduty redemption receipt;
6. receipted state for settlement and draft for comparison and return;
7. the matrimonial affidavit signed by Mrs James and draft for comparison and return;
8. discharge of standard security and draft for comparison and return.

Please confirm that these papers are all in order and return our drafts.

Yours faithfully,

BROWN, JARVIE & WALKER

Note: The letter of obligation is draft **18b**. The dates to be inserted in the blanks are 13 April 1995 (date of Form 11 Report) and 2 May 1995 (14 days after settlement).

32   Letter from Mair & Kildare to Brown, Jarvie & Walker (19 April 1995)

DEAR SIRS,

Mr and Mrs L. McLachlan
Mr John James
3 Miller Drive, Glasgow

Thank you for your letter of 18 April 1995 and would confirm that the settlement papers are all in order.

We return your draft letter of obligation, state for settlement and discharge.

Yours faithfully,

MAIR & KILDARE

33   Letter from Brown, Jarvie & Walker to John James (19 April 1995)

DEAR SIR,

<u>Sale of 3 Miller Drive, Glasgow</u>

We have now completed the sale of your house and have pleasure in enclosing cheque for £50,369.42 as undernoted.

We shall send your assurance policy and other papers within a few days.

We trust that you had a successful move to London, and are obliged to you for your instructions in this case.

Yours faithfully,

BROWN, JARVIE & WALKER

<u>Note referred to</u>:

Amount received at settlement	£76,500.00
<u>Less</u>: Repayment of your loan	£25,163.58
	£51,336.42
<u>Less</u>: Fees and outlays for our quotation of 1/4/90 and receipted account herewith	967.00
Sum due to you	£50,369.42

34   Letter from Brown, Jarvie & Walker to Building Society (19 April 1995)

DEAR SIRS,

Mr John James
<u>Sale of 3 Miller Drive, Glasgow</u>
<u>Roll No. XY1234567/A</u>

We now enclose cheque for £25,163.58 in repayment of the above loan. Please acknowledge receipt.

Yours faithfully,

BROWN, JARVIE & WALKER

Note: As the cheque from Mair & Kildare can be treated as 'cleared funds' this money might also be telegraphed by the firm's bank to the society's bank.

35 Letter from Mair & Kildare to Brown, Jarvie & Walker (19 April 1995)

DEAR SIRS,

<u>Mr and Mrs McLachlan</u>
<u>Mr John James</u>
<u>3 Miller Drive, Glasgow</u>

Please note that when our clients went to the house yesterday, they found that the central heating radiators were not working at all well. We are notifying you, in terms of the Missives, that we are holding your clients responsible for repairing the defects.

Yours faithfully,

MAIR & KILDARE

Note: The writer of this letter is obviously contemplating a re-run of *Winston v Patrick* or World War III, or something similar!

36 Telephone call by Wendy Robertson to Mrs James (20 April 1995)

Telephoning Mrs James at the Forte Crest Hotel and telling her of the contents of the letter received today. Suggesting that she go round and see the McLachlans to ascertain the extent of the damage. Telling her that I would investigate contractual provisions, but I didn't think they were particularly promising.

W.R.

35 Telephone call by Mrs James to Wendy Robertson (23 April 1995)

Mrs James informed me that she had been round to the property and inspected the damage. The reason the heating would not work properly was an air lock! Mrs James had a key with her and bled the radiators, which then worked perfectly. Mrs James then had a cup of tea and left. She says that the McLachlans have the house very nice, but she doesn't like their hall carpet.

W.R.

Note: Another crisis defused; another reputation not made. This little story (which is true) shows that a personal visit is often worth a ton of solicitors' letters.

This reminds me of another true story – a Glasgow legal firm dissolved in some acrimony. The usual panoply of legal remedies were exercised, inhibitions, arrestments, interdicts and so on, for there is nothing worse than a legal partnership gone sour, except perhaps a marriage, but even then there is a chance of the couple kissing and making it up.

Eventually good sense prevailed, and the protagonists met after work for a beer. Within twenty minutes the dispute was settled, and they ended the night playing snooker!

38   Letter from John James to Brown, Jarvie & Walker (23 April 1995)

DEAR SIRS,

Thank you for your letter enclosing cheque for £50,369.42 and for your very efficient handling of this sale.

I am settling down in London again, but I hope that my firm will send me back to Glasgow to do a new factory soon.

In the meantime, I have recommended your services to Jim Parsley, who is going to Glasgow to take my place.

Yours sincerely,

JAMES MEIKLE

Note: Virtue brings its own rewards!

39   Letter from Brown, Jarvie & Walker to Longlife Assurance Company (23 April 1995)

DEAR SIRS,

John James
Policy No 1234567 XYZ

We enclose Notice of Retrocession of the above Policy in duplicate. Please return the duplicate to us with your receipt of the principal marked thereon.

Yours faithfully,

BROWN, JARVIE & WALKER

Note: See Appendix **I.29** and **50** (notes). The names in **29** are simply changed.

40   Letter from Mair & Kildare to Brown, Jarvie & Walker (30 April 1995)

DEAR SIRS,

Mr & Mrs L. McLachlan
Mr John James
3 Miller Drive, Glasgow

We have today received the Land Certificate, without exclusion of indemnity, and enclose your Letter of Obligation marked as implemented.

Yours faithfully,

MAIR & KILDARE

Note: This was acknowledged by a note and a compliment slip. A full letter is not necessary.

41   Note by Wendy Robertson to Veronica Vanbrugh (3 May 1995)

Veronica: Please let me have Mr James' file for the sale of 3 Miller Drive. *Wendy.*

Wendy: Here it is. *Veronica.*

Veronica: Returned with thanks. I have checked everything is in order. Please close the file and put it away. *Wendy.*

Appendix III

SOME FORMS UNDER THE MATRIMONIAL HOMES (FAMILY PROTECTION) (SCOTLAND) ACT 1981

1   For use in both sale and security transactions where the subjects are not a matrimonial home within the meaning of the Matrimonial Homes (Family Protection) (Scotland) Act 1981 as amended by the Law Reform (Miscellaneous Provisions) (Scotland) Act 1985, s 13 (See 1986 JLSS 214).

I, AB (design), proprietor of the subjects known as *(the subjects of sale/the security subjects), do solemnly and sincerely swear/affirm as follows:

With reference to *the sale of the subjects of sale to
/*the grant by me of the standard security over the security subjects in favour of   the *subjects of sale/security are not a matrimonial home in relation to which a spouse of mine has occupancy rights, the expressions 'matrimonial home' and 'occupancy rights' having the meanings respectively ascribed to them by the Matrimonial Homes (Family Protection) (Scotland) Act 1981 as amended. Sworn/affirmed by the above-named at

on the   day of   in the presence
of XY (design)
Notary Public
(*Delete where inapplicable)   (*Witnesses – see note 4*)

Notes:
1.   The 'dealing' referred to in the forms of consent in respect of a loan should, for consents signed after 30th December 1985, be 'the granting of the security' as opposed to 'the taking of the loan'.

2.   In cases where Registration of Title is applicable, the Keeper formerly required a statement from the applicant's solicitor to the effect that the relative consent, renunciation or affidavit as delivered at or before delivery of the disposition as standard security. Since the passing of the Law Reform (Miscellaneous Provisions) (Scotland) Act 1985 it has been competent to deliver consents retrospectively, and this question has been dropped from the new Forms 1, 2 and 3.

3.   The term 'Notary Public' includes any person duly authorised in the law of the country (other than Scotland) in which the swearing or affirmation

takes place to administer oaths or receive affirmation in that other country.

4. Witnesses are also required if the Affidavit is to be registered in the Books of Council and Session.

5. It is not competent for an Attorney to grant the consent et cetera on behalf of the constituent.

6. Since the LR(MP)(S) Act 1985 it has been competent to grant the affidavits and renunciations retrospectively.

Exempt from Stamp Duty by virtue of Finance Act 1949, Part IV, Section 35, Schedule 8, Part (1)(2).

2   For use where the title to the matrimonial home stands in the name of one spouse only.

FORM OF RENUNCIATION OF OCCUPANCY RIGHTS

I, A (design) spouse of B (design) hereby renounce the occupancy rights to which I am or may become entitled in terms of the Matrimonial Homes (Family Protection) (Scotland) Act 1981 as amended in the property known as   being intended to become a matrimonial home as defined in the said Act: And I hereby swear/affirm that this renunciation is made by me freely and without coercion of any kind: And I declare these presents to be irrevocable.

Given under my hand at   this
day of   19   in the presence of (design)
Notary Public, and in the presence of these witnesses:–

............................Witness

...........................Full name
                                                    ....A
...........................Address

.........................Occupation

...........................Witness

..........................Full name
                                                    ....NP
..........................Address

.........................Occupation

Note: Liable for fixed Stamp Duty of 50p under the Head of Charge 'Release or Renunciation' as set out in the First Schedule to the Stamp Act 1891.

3 Consent by a non-entitled spouse to a sale of the matrimonial home by the entitled spouse (as provided in The Matrimonial Homes (Forms of Consent) (Scotland) Regulations 1982).

SCHEDULE 1

CONSENT TO BE INSERTED IN THE DEED EFFECTING THE DEALING

(The following words should be inserted where appropriate in the deed. The consenter should sign as a party to the deed.)

… with the consent of A.B. (*designation*), the spouse of the said C.D., for the purposes of the Matrimonial Homes (Family Protection) (Scotland) Act 1981 as amended …
[To be attested].

SCHEDULE 2

CONSENT IN A SEPARATE DOCUMENT

I, A.B. (*designation*), spouse of C.D. (*designation*), hereby consent, for the purposes of the Matrimonial Homes (Family Protection) (Scotland) Act 1981 as amended, to the undernoted dealing with the said C.D. relating to (*here describe the matrimonial home or the part of it to which the dealing relates: see Note 1*).
Dealing referred to: –
(*Here describe the dealing: see Note 2.*)
[To be attested].

Note 1
The expression 'matrimonial home' is defined in section 22 of the Matrimonial Homes (Family Protection) (Scotland) Act 1981 as follows: –

'"matrimonial home" means any house, caravan, houseboat or other structure which has been provided or has been made available by one or both of the spouses as, or has become, a family residence and includes any garden or other ground or building attached to, and usually occupied with, or otherwise required for the amenity or convenience of the house, caravan, houseboat, or other structure.'

Note 2
The expression 'dealing' is defined in section 6(2) of the Matrimonial Homes (Family Protection) (Scotland) Act 1981 as follows: –

'"dealing" includes the grant of a heritable security and the creation of a trust but does not include a conveyance under section 80 of the Lands Clauses Consolidation (Scotland) Act 1845.'

Note 3
The consent is not liable to Stamp Duty.

Appendix IV

1 Organisation of the Registers of Scotland

With the introduction of Registration of Title into:
(1) the County of Renfrew on 6 April 1981
(2) the County of Dumbarton on 4 October 1982
(3) the County of Lanark on 3 January 1983
(4) the County of the Barony and Regality of Glasgow on 30 September 1985
(5) the County of Clackmannan from 1 October 1992
(6) the County of Stirling from 1 April 1993
(7) the County of West Lothian from 1 October 1993 and
(8) the County of Fife from 1 April 1995, the Department now comprises the Land Register of Scotland and the 14 other Registers which already existed and which are grouped under four offices with which they are historically and administratively connected, namely the Sasine Office, the Deeds Office, the Chancery Office and the Horning Office.

Office	Registers
Sasine Office	Register of Sasines
Deeds Office	Register of Deeds
	Register of Protests
	Register of English and Irish Judgments
Chancery Office	Register of Service of Heirs
	Register of the Great Seal
	Register of the Quarter Seal
	Register of the Prince's Seal
	Register of Crown Grants
	Register of Sheriffs' Commissions
	Register of the Cachet Seal
Horning Office	Register of Inhibitions and Adjudications
	Register of Entails
	Register of Hornings (abolished by the Debtors (Scotland) Act 1987, s 89)

2   Administration of the Sasine Office

For administrative purposes the Sasine Office is divided into 5 Districts each handling the registration work for a county or a group of counties. The counties are those which applied prior to the reforms introduced by the Local Government (Scotland) Act 1973 and the Local Government etc (Scotland) Act 1994. These counties are mapped at Appendix VI(b). The Districts are:

District	Counties	
Central	Banff East Lothian Fife	Ross and Cromarty Orkney and Zetland
East	Angus Berwick Kinross Peebles	Perth Roxburgh Selkirk
Midlothian	Midlothian	
North	Aberdeen Caithness Kincardine	Moray Nairn Sutherland
West	Argyll Bute Dumfries	Inverness Kirkcudbright Wigtown

The Register of Sasines for the Counties of Renfrew, Dumbarton, Lanark, the Barony and Regality of Glasgow, Clackmannan, Stirling, West Lothian and Fife continues to operate for the recording of deeds which do not induce or follow registration in the Land Register of Scotland.

Appendix V

MAPS OF SCOTTISH LOCAL GOVERNMENT AREAS

(a) Scottish Counties before 1975

(b)   New Scottish administrative areas

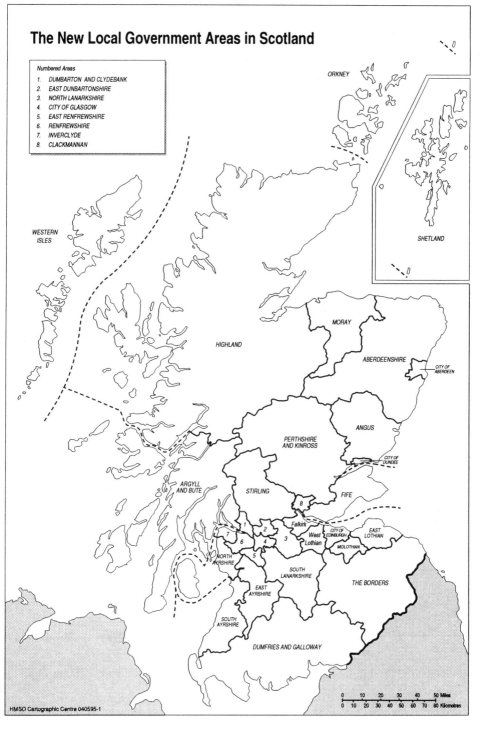

The New Local Government Areas in Scotland

Numbered Areas
1.   DUMBARTON AND CLYDEBANK
2.   EAST DUNBARTONSHIRE
3.   NORTH LANARKSHIRE
4.   CITY OF GLASGOW
5.   EAST RENFREWSHIRE
6.   RENFREWSHIRE
7.   INVERCLYDE
8.   CLACKMANNAN

ORKNEY

WESTERN
ISLES

SHETLAND

MORAY

HIGHLAND

ABERDEENSHIRE

CITY OF
ABERDEEN

ANGUS

PERTHSHIRE
AND KINROSS

CITY OF
DUNDEE

ARGYLL
AND BUTE

STIRLING

FIFE

Falkirk

West
Lothian

CITY OF
EDINBURGH

EAST
LOTHIAN

MIDLOTHIAN

NORTH
AYRSHIRE

SOUTH
LANARKSHIRE

THE BORDERS

EAST
AYRSHIRE

SOUTH
AYRSHIRE

DUMFRIES AND GALLOWAY

0   10   20   30   40   50 Miles
0 10 20 30 40 50 60 70 80 Kilometres

HMSO Cartographic Centre 040595-1

347

ENFORCEMENT OF
STANDARD SECURITIES

References are to the Conveyancing and Feudal Reform (Scotland) Act 1970.
SC – Standard condition of loan under Sch 3 to Act.

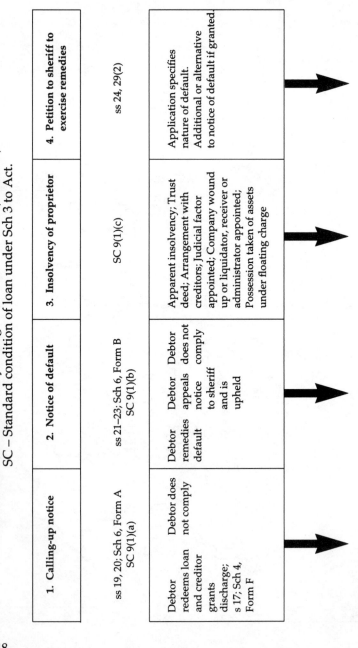

1. Calling-up notice	2. Notice of default		3. Insolvency of proprietor	4. Petition to sheriff to exercise remedies
ss 19, 20; Sch 6, Form A SC 9(1)(a)	ss 21–23; Sch 6, Form B SC 9(1)(b)		SC 9(1)(c)	ss 24, 29(2)
Debtor does not comply	Debtor remedies default	Debtor appeals notice to sheriff and is upheld / Debtor does not comply	Apparent insolvency; Trust deed; Arrangement with creditors; Judicial factor appointed; Company wound up or liquidator, receiver or administrator appointed; Possession taken of assets under floating charge	Application specifies nature of default. Additional or alternative to notice of default if granted.
Debtor redeems loan and creditor grants discharge; s 17; Sch 4, Form F				

DEBTOR IN DEFAULT – CREDITOR'S REMEDIES

Traditional remedies: 1. Personal action 2. Adjudication 3. Poinding of the ground	Any remedy outwith Act given by standard security: SC 10(1)	Sale of security subjects: SC 10(2). If sale is not possible then the remedy is **foreclosure**: SC 10(7) (sheriff court action)	Entering into possession and letting: SC 10(3)–(5) **Note**: this remedy may be accompanied by a court warrant for ejection in terms of the Act of Sederunt 1990 SC 1990(6) It is not strictly necessary on the expiry of a calling-up notice but may in practise be desirable. In most cases possession is sought first before exercising any other remedy.	Repair reconstruction and improvement: SC 10(6).

Appendix VII

PROFESSIONAL INDEMNITY INSURANCE

'Welcome to the world of professional claims – a world where your worst night-mares come true – a world full of snakes and very few ladders – a friendless world of reporters, notoriety – and financial ruin – and it could all be so different – friends, riches, acclaim.'
(Neil Douglas, indemnity solicitor, talk to diploma students)

Archie McPherson on Radio Clyde: 'Well, I don't know why the ref ruled out that goal. He didn't look offside to me. Possibly handball? What did you think, Davie Provan?'
Provan: 'Archie, the ball hit the side-netting. It's a bye kick to Hibs.'
(*The Herald*)

To err is human and most solicitors will have had at some time – whatever they may say – the horrible feeling that they may have done something, or not done something else, that may give rise to a claim in professional negligence.

At such times it is reassuring to know that you have your indemnity policy standing between you and a financial chasm. The minimum cover per solicitor is currently £1 million but this may not be enough. I believe that some larger firms insure for much larger sums per partner, but of course the bigger the firm, the bigger the business and volume of business, and thus the possibility of a bigger mistake. In any event it is really not a good idea to try to save expense by cutting down this cover. The premiums are obviously expensive, but thanks to careful management, have not reached the levels ruling in England, which in 1995 are 4% of the firm's turnover. In many cases this is a huge sum.

Examples of conveyancing mistakes that have occurred in the past and should not therefore recur, but probably will, are as follows.

1. The very worst mistake a solicitor can make is to forget the strict provisions of the Companies Act 1985, s 410 relating to the registration of charges created by a limited company. This covers not only floating charges, but also fixed charges, such as standard securities. Thus if a limited company grants a standard security over its land, the lender's agent must first record this document and obtain a date of recording from the Keeper. The recording date, in either the Register of Sasines or the Land Register, is the date of creation of the security, and within 21 days of that date the lender's agent must register particulars of the charge with the Register of Charges, kept at Companies

House, 37 Castle Terrace, Edinburgh EH1 2EB. Failure to do this will mean that the charge is void against a liquidator or creditor of the company, and the lender will rank only as an ordinary creditor instead of being secured. The loss due to the solicitor's error is potentially huge. Another danger is revealed in a letter from the Registrar of Companies in 1985 JLSS 11. The Registrar points out that details of such a charge should be intimated to him in Forms 410 (Scot), 413 and 413(a) (Scot) and 416 (Scot) in terms of the Companies (Forms) Regulations 1985. If one of these forms has to be returned to the solicitor for correction, it must be returned to the Registrar in correct form within 21 days, or again the registration is not complete as required.

2. Another point to watch is when you send your standard security to be recorded and you receive a recording date, and you then duly lodge your particulars of charge. Then disaster strikes, and the Keeper returns your standard security for correction. When you have made your corrections, you must then re-record the security, and *again* register details of the charge. The first notification is invalid.

3. You sell land for a client and allow the client to grant absolute warrandice, even though you know that ownership of part of the land is doubtful. The new owner is then interdicted from building on the area of doubtful ownership, and claims against your client under absolute warrandice. As a result your client has to buy the land in question at an extortionate price and looks to you for recompense.

4. Check all boundaries and areas carefully.

5. Ensure that building warrants and completion certificates are to hand at an early date, also agreement for replacement windows.

6. Don't undertake to deliver anything in a letter of obligation that you may not be able to deliver (eg a property inquiry report disclosing old adverse notices). See article by Professor Robert Rennie in November 1993 JLSS 431. See also *McGillivray v Davidson* 1993 SLT 693.

7. When acting for a lender, read the lender's instructions carefully and follow them. See Rennie 'Negligence, Securities and the Expanding Duty of Care' February 1995 JLSS 58.

For your own sake and for the sake of the profession, who have to pay sharply increased premiums each year, please try and avoid mistakes like these.

In a publication (September 1989) prepared by the Law Society and the Indemnity Insurance Brokers, entitled *Better Practice in Practice*, certain guidelines are laid down for solicitors. While, hopefully, all of these have been stressed throughout this book, these guidelines present a useful summary:

★ Take clear instructions from all your clients direct – that is to say, not solely through intermediaries.

★ Record properly all communications, all meetings, all telephone calls, in writing.

★ Enforce a good diary system – a double diary system, if necessary.

★ Read and check the file, and think before taking a decisive step.

★ Review all files regularly.

★ Always know what your assistants are doing.

★ Copy all important correspondence to clients immediately.

★ Only provide Letters of Obligation that you can personally meet. (**8.11**)

★ When going on holiday, leave adequate file notes.

★ Where reliance is placed on words, express them clearly, fully, and accurately and, wherever possible, in plain English.

★ Take expert advice in areas of uncertainty – legal or otherwise.

★ If you are using a lawyer in another town as a correspondent, bear in mind that your responsibility to your client is nevertheless not reduced.

★ Similarly, if you are acting as correspondent to another lawyer, keep the instructing solicitor constantly advised.

Every practising solicitor should be thoroughly familiar with the contents of this booklet.

To these guidelines, I would add another:

★ Never forget that you are responsible for all documents that you prepared. You should, therefore, check every document that you have prepared, *before* it leaves the office and is signed. It is not enough to leave the checking to staff, especially junior staff who may have just left school and who are set to comparing documents between making tea and doing the deliveries, and who cannot be expected to have any idea of legal terminology.

As an example of this, I saw a deed from a respected firm which stated 'I grant drainage rise' instead of 'I grant warrandice'. Such intelligent, but totally wrong, guesses of bad writing are always the hardest to spot, simply because they are so plausible to the untrained eye. (See also *Hunter v Fox* 1964 SC (HL) 95).

Written amendments on typed or word processed documents should also be carefully checked. One such mistake through a misreading of poor writing – I'm sorry to say it was my own – was to transform the term 'three miles' into 'three metres'. Had it not been caught in time, the result could have been hideous, as this was the area in which the seller of a business was not allowed to trade for a certain number of years!

When drafting deeds, approved styles should be used wherever possible. Conveyancing styles may be found in the excellent style book issued to diploma students, or in most conveyancing texts. Much useful information may also be gained from consulting English style (or 'precedent') books, most particularly Butterworth's *Encyclopaedia of Precedents*. *Care must however be used when following a style, and this must never be done uncritically, particularly in the case of English styles.* A cautionary tale unfolds in *Tarditi v Drummond* 1989 SLT 554 – a style from Halliday *Conveyancing Law and Practice* (II, 15–138) was followed, but the Court ruled that it was 'difficult to understand, and should not be followed slavishly in future.' This excellent advice applies to all style books.

In a speech reported briefly in the *Glasgow Herald* of 9 November 1985, Judge David Edward QC is reported as saying to newly admitted solicitors that they should not imagine that they could get through their professional lives without making mistakes, and it was important to admit when they had been made. He continued to say that 'clients and insurers are surprisingly sympathetic to the lawyer who admits to his mistakes.'

This is sound advice, for if an attempt is made to hide a mistake, it only gets worse. One would, I think however, have to be very careful about the exact admission made in case this prejudiced a valid insurance claim.

Please note carefully that any circumstances which might lead to a claim should be reported immediately to the indemnity insurers. Early notification can greatly ease matters.

Lastly, please use language carefully, and use language that can be understood by the average intelligence. Avoid horrors like the following definition of a bed:

'A device or arrangement that may be used to permit a patient to lie down when the need to do so is a consequence of the patient's condition rather than a need for active intervention such as examination, diagnostic intervention, manipulative treatment, obstetric delivery or transport.'
(NHS staff circular)

INDEX

Index

Charges
common, 10.8, 11.4, 18.5, 18.10–18.12
floating, 7.35
Register of, 8.2, 8.8, 8.9–8.12, 16.2
registered land, over, 16.2, 16.4, 16.6
unregistered land, over, 16.2
Charges Register
registered land, copy certificate, 16.2
search, 8.2, 8.8
   procedure, 8.9–8.12
Client
purchaser. *See* PURCHASER
seller. *See* SELLER
Commercial conveyancing
domestic conveyancing distinguished, 23.1-
   23.2
valuation surveyor, role of, 23.4
Commercial lease
assignation, 22.15
decoration, 22.17
expenses, 22.20
'fair and reasonable landlord', 22.2–22.3
fixtures, 22.19
form of, 22.5
guarantee from tenants, 22.18
insurance, 22.10
limited company, to 22.18
loan, protection of, 22.11
management charges, 22.14
meaning, 22.1–22.2
nature of, 22.1, 22.2
negotiation, 22.4-22.6
quiet enjoyment, 22.16
rent, 22.7
rent review, 22.8
repairs, 22.9
terms, 22.1, 22.2
title deeds, inspection of, 22.13
use of premises, 22.12
Company
floating charges, 7.35
Register of Charges, 8.2, 8.8, 8.9–8.12
sale by, 7.35
   insolvent, 7.23, 7.35
Conflict of interest, 1.13, 12.3
Conditions
fencing, 7.16, 7.17, 7.25
leases, assignation, 21.7, 21.8
missives, in. *See* OFFER
tenements, deed of, 18.3–18.5, 18.10
Contracts of ground annual, 7.39
Conveyancer
meaning, 1.1
Council tax, 10.6, 18.15
Creditor
sale by, 7.23

Date of entry
ancillary clause, 9.7
offer, in, 3.16, 4.1

Decree of irritancy
in absentia, 7.37
Deeds. *See* TITLE DEEDS
Development
See SITE ASSEMBLY
Discount
public sector tenant, purchase, 19.8, 19.11,
   19.12
Disposition
a non domino, 7.10
delivery, 11.2
draft. *See* DRAFT DISPOSITION
feu, 17.4
missives superseded on delivery of, 3.28, 7.4
per incuriam , 7.44
superiority, 17.5, 17.7
tenement building, flat in, 18.2, 18.3
Dispositive clause, 9.2, 9.5
example, 9.6
District council
responsibilities, 6.5
Dominium directum, 17.3
Dominium plenum, 17.3
sale, 17.4, 17.8
Dominium utile, 17.3
sale, 17.4
Draft disposition
ancillary clauses, 9.2, 9.7, 9.8
dispositive clause, 9.2, 9.5, 9.6
drafting generally, 9.1
narrative clause, 9.2, 9.3, 9.4
pacts of disposition, 9.2
purchaser's solicitor, duty, 9.13
testing clause, 9.2, 9.9, 9.10
warrant of registration, 9.2, 9.11, 9.12
Drainage, 3.23, 7.21
Dutch auction, 4.3

Electricity
wayleaves, 7.21
Estate agents
arrangements with solicitors, 2.3
commission on sale, 2.4
contract, terms of, 2.4
marketing by, 2.1, 2.3
solicitors and, 1.17, 2.1, 2.3
Executor
sale by, 7.23
   protection of purchaser, 7.12
Extensions
permission required, 3.24, 7.22
Extracts, 7.38

Factor
tenement building, 10.7, 10.8, 11.4, 18.4, 18.5,
   18.9, 18.11
Fees
builder's, 11.12
Inhibitions and Adjudications, Register of,
   11.18
Land Register report, 11.17

Index